The Elementary Structures
of Political Life

The Elementary Structures of Political Life

Rural Development in Pahlavi Iran

GRACE E. GOODELL

New York · Oxford
OXFORD UNIVERSITY PRESS
1986

Oxford University Press

Oxford   New York   Toronto
Delhi Bombay Calcutta Madras Karachi
Petaling Jaya Singapore Hong Kong Tokyo
Nairobi   Dar es Salaam   Cape Town
Melbourne   Auckland

and associated companies in
Beirut   Berlin   Ibadan   Nicosia

Library of Congress Cataloging-in-Publication Data
Goodell, Grace E.
The elementary structures of political life.
Bibliography: p.   Includes index.
     1. Social structure—Iran—Case studies.
2. Iran—Economic conditions—1945-   —Case studies.
3. Decentralization in government—Iran—Case studies.
4. Economic development—Case studies.
5. Iran—Politics and government—1941–1979—Case studies. I. Title.
HN670.2.A8G66   1986   307.1′4′0955   85-29690
ISBN 0-19-504031-7

10 9 8 7 6 5 4 3 2 1

Printed in the United States of America
on acid-free paper

Acknowledgments

The great Iranian poet Sa'di wrote that the sons and daughters of Adam "are limbs of the same body, all created from the self-same seed" (Israeli, 1972: 92). So, too, this book convenes many sons and daughters of Adam—peasants and workers, university professors, friends, family, "development" planners, and bankers—bringing them together in the Dez. Though it is impossible—in some cases, dangerous—to thank by name the diverse seeds that have brought this volume to flower, I should like to thank a few specifically, as proxies for all.

To the people of Rahmat Abad and Bizhan I owe a profound debt, for their warmth, intelligent participation in my work, and forbearance. They have written this story—and much more. *Allahu Akbar!* Local officials of the Khuzestan Water and Power Authority as well as many of the agency's employees including those in the Andimeshk guesthouse, tirelessly offered me assistance. To the former I am particularly grateful for our many discussions. Personnel in the Iran-America Agribusiness and Shell International spent many hours answering my questions. Mr. Lilienthal's Development and Resources Corporation, especially Mr. and Mrs. Ferrell Ensign, Dr. and Mrs. Richard Fine, and Mr. and Mrs. William Price were always ready to fill my needs—beyond a professional interest, as friends. The American Institute of Iranian Studies in Tehran constituted my Nelson's Pillar for intellectual life in the capital, as well as for resourceful solutions to practical problems that arose; I, like many other scholars, am indebted to those American individuals and institutions supporting the Institute over its many years and even now, in exile. Dr. and Mrs. Jerome Clinton, who directed the Institute during the period covered by my field work, helped me invaluably. Also in Tehran Mr. John Westberg and Dr. and Mrs. Bahman Amini helped me in ways no one else could, besides providing intellectual contributions to this study's development.

Different sowers planted other seeds in this soil, particularly my professors and academic colleagues. Collectively the faculty and students of the Anthropology Department at Columbia University brought forth among themselves an environment exceptional in its intense intellectual demands, the excitement of its challenge to anthropologists, and its diversity and persistence in theoretical pursuit. Above all, I can never adequately express the gratitude I hold for my mentor, Dr. Conrad Arensberg, an anthropologist whose renowned breadth admits no superficial inquiry, a scientist no less a profound humanist, a dedicated teacher, and exemplary friend. Many of his hours of instruction and patient criticism over the years lie behind whatever merit there may be in this study. The philosophical vision of Dr. Russell Kirk has constantly guided me. Dr. Abraham Rossman, who introduced me to the principles of social organization, gave penetrating direction and decisive encouragement. Dr. Morton Fried's provocative teaching and scholarly works laid the foundation for my interest in political structures, while Dr. Robert McCormick Adams, a bold and creative Mesopotamian guide, has inspired my research in Khuzestan from its inception and offered his support during these years. Similarly, Professors Harold Berman and Robert Nisbet have complemented their discerning theoretical and historical analyses, which underpin this study, with inspiration and advice. I wish to thank warmly Dr. Robert Jackall, of Williams College, for serving as the main reader for the manuscript and for offering very constructive suggestions as well as invaluable support.

Dr. James Bill offered me rich insights into Iranian urban society; Dr. and Mrs. Robert Dillon, Mr. Douglas Noll, Mr. Chris Paine, and Dr. Robert Schact provided stimulating discussions about central questions the study raised. To my friends and colleagues Dr. Philip Kohl and Dr. Rita Wright the book owes much especially in its final chapter. Dr. John Powelson and I debated many of these issues during the book's final draft. Dr. William Hanaway painstakingly taught me the basics of Farsi, and Dr. Bettina Warburg lent critical support during a turning point in the first draft. Drs. William Beeman, Mary Jo Good, Peter Kilby, and John Powelson kindly reviewed selected parts of the final draft for me, giving helpful assistance, as did Dr. Ahmad Ashraf. Dr. Ibrahim Pourhadi standardized the transliteration of Farsi words. Dr. Bahman Abadian threw light on the Dez Project's historical details. Ms. Joyce Monges frequently nourished with sunshine the seeds that were planted herein. Ms. Theresa Gross, Ms. Veronika Neudachin, Ms. Deborah O'Connor, and Ms. Virginia Quintero typed the manuscript, with cheerful persistence, into its final form. Ms. Susan Rabiner and Dr. Henry Krawitz of Oxford University Press shepherded it through to the end with enthusiasm and patience, for which I have been grateful, while Ms. Elizabeth Parry ably did the proofreading and Mr. Nicholas Humez the index.

I am moved to thank and once again lament the passing of my deeply admired friend and mentor, a pathbreaker in our discipline, the late Dr. Junius Bird of the American Museum of Natural History, whose certitude in the relevance of the present for knowing the distant past, whose sensitive appreciation of other cultures, and whose sheer delight in human society impelled me to study anthropology.

The field work for this study was funded by the National Institutes of Mental Health, as was the year I wrote my dissertation on which it is based. Thereby American taxpayers, too, are "limbs" of this same "body," as they are of many like it that could never be carried out without the public's generosity. While I did not accept a Fulbright grant to do this study, I could never have even begun or sustained it without the Fulbright Commission's insistence in Tehran that the Iranian government not interfere in it despite certain opposition. I am grateful to Mr. Jerome Cohen, previously of the East Asian Legal Studies Center at the Harvard Law School, for his characteristic interest in work such as mine, and for the lively environment of the Center where he welcomed me while I was writing the first draft. I thank Harvard Law School, Professor Harold Berman, and the Center for having accepted me back once again, after an interim of several years, as a Visiting Fellow during the book's final preparation. For enabling the long months of work required to transform my dissertation into this book I am beholden to the Scaife Family Charitable Trusts. Of course, none of these individuals or institutions bears responsibility for the weeds that have sprung up among the seeds that were planted.

Finally, I wish to thank various publishers and individuals for permission to quote from their publications for my chapter epigraphs. Chapter 1: Scholars' Facsimiles and Reprints; Chapter 5: George Allen and Unwin; Chapters 6, 9, 10, and 12: Cambridge University Press; Chapter 7: Routledge & Kegan Paul; Chapter 10, Little Brown; Chapter 11: Indian Council for Cultural Relations; Chapter 13: Professor Ehsan Yarshater; and for the concluding quotation of the Epilogue: John Murray Co. Parts of Chapter 13 first appeared in the *European Journal of Sociology (Archives Européennes de Sociologie)* 21 (1980): 285–325.

In conclusion, I recognize my profound dependence on my mother and late father, Grace and Joseph Goodell, who prepared the soil in which this study germinated, and were its first planters and gardeners. Individually and together they laid out for my brothers and me the basic issues of this study many years ago: autonomy; responsibility; authority; initiative; purposiveness; trust; the public life, especially locally and regionally; continuity and permanence; variety; integrity; and the transcending moral order. The single most formative influence on this book has been my mother's deep understanding of these concepts and their realization in society around us.

A wise old Lur, Mashal, from "behind the mountain," taught me this toast, which I offer now with him to those sons and daughters of Adam who have come together here in the Dez:

Here's to those who have upheld me without my knowing it, and to those I have thanked without ever telling them so.

In the Name of God,

The Beneficent, The Merciful!

Lord of all creation,

It is He who will judge us all on Judgment Day!

Contents

BLACK SEA

U.S.S.R.

CASPIAN SEA

TURKEY

●Tabriz

ELBURZ MTS.

SYRIA

Tigris R.

MESOPOTAMIA

Euphrates R.

●Kermanshah

ZAGROS MOUNTAINS

●Tehran

●Esfahan

●Baghdad

IRAQ

JORDAN

Area of detail

●Shiraz

PERSIAN GU

MAP SHOWING
LOCATION OF THE DEZ
IRRIGATION PROJECT IN IRAN

0   Miles   300

SAUDI ARABIA

The Elementary Structures
of Political Life

Introduction

Do not go out to the villages; going to the villages makes a dis-
believer of a man.   —Dezful Proverb

"You'd better not decide to live in our village," warned the seasoned old man, one eye squinting out from beneath a loosely wrapped brown turban. "I'm telling you now! If you come to live in Rahmat Abad . . . you'll never want to leave. Ours is the most wonderful village in the world, the Throne City of this region. You'll never leave." I took the risk. Two days later I went to live in Rahmat Abad. But Mash-hadi Muhammad was right. Although it would be unthinkable now for me to return, I have still not been able to leave Rahmat Abad.

In 1972 I went to Iran to study the Shah's most famous rural development scheme, the Dez Irrigation Project (DIP) in the southwestern province of Khuzestan, where the present war with Iraq is being fought. The Iranian planners considered the Dez Project their model for uplifting the vast Iranian peasantry (nearly 70 percent of the population at the time). Not only was the Dez Scheme the jewel of His Imperial Majesty's transformation of the "backward" countryside, but internationally it was renowned as the World Bank's showcase agricultural project, a development prototype brainstormed by no less an expert than David Lilienthal, architect of the Tennessee Valley Authority.

Unlike other social scientists, as an anthropologist I was required by my academic discipline to go beyond statistics, production figures, and ten-year projections to actually live at the grass-roots level, over a sustained period, within any society I proposed to understand. Since in this case I wanted to investigate "economic development," I would first have to live in an area representative of rural society prior to the Dez Project's transformational efforts (that is, in an area similar to but outside the project's domain), and then move into one of the scheme's new model towns (to which all peasants within its domain were being transferred). After surveying suitable areas outside the Dez Project, I had asked the villagers of Rahmat Abad if I could begin my study among them. Sixteen months later I would move across the river and into the new model workers' town of Bizhan, the heart of the project itself, one of the thirteen model towns in the DIP that would pioneer the future of rural Iran.

Ever since I had arrived in Iran, urban Iranians and foreigners alike (especially those in Khuzestan who were associated with the Dez Project) had assured me that the second part of my comparison would hardly differ from life in America—plenty of comforts in the new model towns. But everyone ruled out the very feasibility of doing the first part of my study: "Human beings" simply could not survive in the mud huts of Khuzestan. Well, in Rahmat Abad I would find out. After all, from Mashhadi Muhammad's point of view, I'd never be able to leave!

By the time I met Mash-hadi Muhammad beneath a splendorous portrait of the Shah in a ministry office in Dezful (the provincial town in the middle of the World Bank's and Lilienthal's project), I had already been in Iran three months, sitting daily for hours in Tehran bureaucracies waiting to meet officials, carrying daily what they said were their letters of introduction and requests from them to other incomprehensible bureaus, and having luncheons and dinners with suave technocrats to eke out further introductions and further permissions. All this finally paid off as I now made my way from the lower ranges and rambling corridors of old Persian officialdom toward—on the forty-third day—the shining Mecca of all bureaucracies, The Plan Organization.

Having secured the proper forms, permissions, letters, and verbal assurances from the Plan Technocracy, I then had to proceed to Ahwaz, capital of Khuzestan province; there a similar process was required: meeting with the Ministry of Agriculture, Ministry of War, Ministry of Cooperatives and Rural Affairs, Foreign Ministry, Ministry of Justice, Ministry of Water and Power, Ministry of Health, Ministry of Internal Security, Ministry of Education and the Ministry of Higher Education, Governor's Office, and, of course, SAVAK, the secret police. Letters, interviews, photographs, signatures, documents, outlines, permissions, certificates, and affidavits. From Ahwaz I finally reached Dezful town itself, where I needed the local approval of five ministries, various urban officials, and Lilienthal's American development firm—all this before I could visit a single village! (All villages in the country belonged to one ministry or another, but to different ones depending on which bureaucracy mainly took charge of transforming each one—malaria, irrigation, literacy, and so forth—and, hence, depending on which ministry had one bureaucrat who knew the road there.)

And so, at last, in my high heels and Parisian dress, I had wended my way through the "modernization" maze to find the Persian State's 250 peasants of tiny Rahmat Abad. My first night in Rahmat Abad, Madar-i-'Ali, an embracing woman who became one of my closest friends, briefed me on all the gossip she thought constituted the necessary sociopolitical foundation for a prospective Rahmat-Abadi. Summing it up, she admonished me sternly, "You'd better not stay in this village long, Khanom Grace. Your place will be empty if you leave."

The paradox this book explores is that Rahmat Abad, a remote little village in many respects hardly removed from the Neolithic Age, operated on the basis of extraordinary predictability and economic rationality, which derived from its free, public intercourse, individual and group initiatives, individual and corporate responsibility, unrestricted flow of information, and the intelligibility and reliability of past as well as future events. In effect, a well-defined, if unwritten, system of rules or law existed providing a framework within which all could act or speak with a sense of certainty and security. In contrast, the Iranian State with its wealth, Western technology, and highly formal, legalistic bureaucracy defied predictability or public intercourse.

The essence of law, without which sustained "development" is impossible, lies in the clear definition of memberships and boundaries, the predictability of rules of conduct to all those concerned, and the reasonable certainty of their enforcement. When social organization becomes more complex through an organic process, this clarity and predictability of law constitute the mortar between its bricks. In the Dez Project, the Iranian State and its numerous Western advocates proposed "development" without law—that is, without predictability and security (despite the State's numerous formal decrees). They set out to undermine the predictable, corporate integrity of village norms and structures and to replace them with the obscurantist although jet-age world of laboratories, factories, and multinational investments: a world that was obscurantist not, as is often said, because the new came too quickly for traditional Iranians to "absorb" it but because in social relations (the very mortar of society) the pervasive centralized State made Iran's modern sector secretive, personalistic, amorphous, and arbitrary. Life re-created by the State in Bizhan vividly dramatized this. Thus the paradox that this study elaborates: In mud-housed, illiterate, and poor Rahmat Abad, which the State set out to conquer, boundaries and relationships were clear and predictable; in contrast, within the modern sector that the State dominated, one moved about in murkiness and uncertainty. If the foundation for capitalist economic development rests upon the calculability of impersonal, purposeful actions, then that calculability was clearly found in Rahmat Abad, while development by the State destroyed these foundations and replaced them with the State's shadowy domain.

The significance of the contrast between Rahmat Abad and the State's model town within the Dez Project, Bizhan, does not lie primarily in the subsequent Iranian revolution (to which the Rahmat Abads of Iran apparently contributed little in an active way). Nor is the Shah this volume's focus or culprit. Rather, the study's main purpose is to examine the process of "economic development" under highly centralized direction that continues to be promoted today by economists, bankers, planners, and theoreticians as well as by Third World politicians, elites, and practitioners. Development economists continue today to subject people of totally foreign cultures we little understand to arcane society- or region-wide engineering, engulfing them in the centralized State as these experts carry to their logical extremes theoretical premises and mathematical formulas of "growth" developed for our highly industrial society during the depression fifty years ago but entirely exogenous to the societies of the Third World. In these deductive elaborations, those who remodel whole societies must necessarily insulate themselves from the primary underpinnings like law and accountability, predictability, social structure, and individual and group initiative, without which no society can sustain development.

Although events in Iran have shaken some economists' faith in their quantitative indicators of progress, current Western development theory and implementation continue virtually without hesitation to insist on the centralized State as the necessary director of "development," on highly deductive, academic "modeling" as its blueprint, and on speed and enormous scale for overnight transformation. The Shah is gone but the World Bank and its development paradigm remain. The World Bank's fundamental principles of "development" continue today as precisely the same ones that guided the elaboration of the Dez Scheme, which the Bank oversaw. This study elucidates them: the subjection of individuals as well as their local and middle-range structures to transformations directed by an ever more autocratic State, and the destruction of as many intermediate cultural, social, or political structures as possible—even economic structures and institutions that people have created between themselves and the State.

In understanding Rahmat Abad (and, presumably, tens of thousands of communities similar to it) and in examining what happened to villages like it when the Dez Project transformed them into new model towns like Bizhan, much of our analysis derives from studies of corporate groups: how they operate as society's elementary economic, social, and political structures; how they can combine into partnerships and confederations for larger undertakings; how the State can erode them; why it may try to; and what results when it does. Clearly defined corporate groups are indispensable for individuals to extend themselves substantively and in a sustained way into the wider society, especially to have an impact on its governance. By overlooking this, many political scientists err in insisting that "modernization" inevitably creates a greater desire for political participation, and that being able to cast a vote constitutes a significant form of participation. While anthropology offers a varied and probing corpus of ethnographic work on corporate structures, Professor M. G. Smith (1974) stands almost alone in the discipline for his theoretical analysis of the questions raised in this book, drawing on political theorists like Gierke and Althusius rather than on anthropologists.

Of course, the contributions of Professor Arensberg are essential in showing us how culture and social structures emerge out of actual behavior. When considering the effects of *political centralization* on such groups or on aggregates that may be forming along their lines, we will rely primarily on the analytical tradition of de Tocqueville, Burke, Durkheim, and Professor Nisbet. Finally, reading Professor David Riesman's *Lonely Crowd* several years ago confirmed many of my earlier field observations about the contrast between village individuals' character and the personality of their urban acquaintances, a contrast helpful in understanding the village social structures *above* the individual level.

These were the elementary structures of Rahmat Abad: individuals; families; permanent groups including those formed by contract (such as long-term partnerships); those emerging ad hoc out of repeated common action (such as the association of parents whose children attended the village school); and, finally, the village itself as a polity. While some of these could not be called *corporate* in Smith's terms (lacking, for instance, presumptive perpetuity), many could; all of them shared major strengths of corporate groups, functioning like them in important respects we will examine—above all, with respect to predictability. They were astonishingly corporate considering their history and environment of flux.

Each such elementary unit—and even the individual villagers themselves, although they call for special analysis—enjoyed its own clear-cut identity, which meant having limited boundaries and membership. Each articulated distinct affairs for which it accepted responsibility, acting autonomously in carrying out these affairs. Each one pursued its common affairs with organizational procedures (not necessarily formal ones) that enabled it to regulate its behavior, and with unitary relations vis-à-vis the outside. In short, each could be dealt with predictably, as a single unit. This would have been impossible if information about these elementary structures and their behavior had not been broadly accessible to most people interacting with and within the village.

These characteristics of Rahmat Abad's elementary structures and of the village itself as a corporate group were not prescribed by anyone: "This is what a community should be like, now go and make one." Instead, over time—though in some cases in generations long past—each unit had determined its distinct shape (and then continued to reshape itself) through the repeated, pooled initiatives of particular villagers toward specific ends they shared. It was *in that process* that these diverse initiatives, over and over again merging into a common purpose, crystallized in a common structure; it was in that process of congealing into a group through common and purposeful action, that those participating had established procedures and membership rules as well as corporate external relations. It was *the participants'* initiative and *their* interaction that incorporated them and that maintained each group's integrity. Form followed function (Arensberg, 1972).

Several aspects of these elementary structures of Rahmat Abad call for special attention here. The first is the emergence of a *public* as the essence of each primary unit above the level of the individual. Through the crisscrossing actions and counteractions by which the members of each of these elementary structures carried out their common affairs, they created miniature publics among themselves; these small arenas came together in the public of Rahmat Abad. In contrast to the "public" of parades or television viewers or even mass voting, these minipublics and their overarching polity were clearly structured, each autonomous component defined by its initiatives, patterned through time, for furthering specific affairs. Secondly, Smith emphasizes the *behavioral* basis of a corporate group's identity and governance. Rahmat Abad's elementary units were defined primarily by the common actions to which their members committed themselves, not merely by what they claimed, what they were called, or what was said about them. Otherwise, how could they establish predictability? As a consequence, the internal "government" of each structure corresponded closely to its members' actual behavior, and to the experience and norms—often precedents—upon which they based their behavior.

Thirdly, though each individual in Rahmat Abad was known to the others and enjoyed ample scope for initiative and responsibility on his or her own, it was only through *membership in groups* (including families) that most of them undertook large enterprises, made an impact on the village or regional society, and, in turn, found protection against the strong—even against the State, when it did attempt to penetrate village society. Edmund Burke called such a group an individual's "little platoon."

Since such groups are often the vehicles for individuals' initiatives in the wider society, since they teach participation and public accountability to individuals throughout society, since they offer locally based values and locally determined criteria for self-fulfillment, and since they buffer individuals from power—indeed, can sometimes bring arbitrary power to heel—for these and other reasons the centralized Iranian State naturally recognized them as obstacles to its own development thrust. In Bizhan, one of the Dez Project's most consistent and effective policies was to liquidate these middle-range groups and to stop patterned individual initiatives which, as Professor Arensberg has shown, eventually give rise to them. Correctly associating with traditional society such firmly structured units able to take initiative, the State incorrectly (but out of its own self-interest) accused them of *standing in the way of* "nation building," innovation, industrialization, hard work, and what it called "modernization." In committing this error, the Iranian planners could fortify themselves amply with Western development theory and with widely acclaimed examples of its "success"—successful development based on the liquidation or weakening of such intermediate-level groups: Tanzania on the left, for instance, and South Korea on the right, both levelers of associations and individuals who stand in the way of the State. Social scientists like Gunnar Myrdal (1968, I: 52–53, 60–64) have long argued that to liberate the factors of production for their most rational allocation—to disembed labor, integrate markets that are segmentary, remove "blockages," and so forth—and to weld together a "nation" obedient to the State's plan, first these stubborn structures of society must be atomized.

Within Bizhan, the new model town, the technocrats and planners opposed certain aspects of these elementary structures that villagers had brought with them from their traditional communities. The State especially opposed individual and group *initiative,* however trivial that might be; it determined to homogenize villagers' "animal-like" *heterogeneity,* their tendency toward variety and individuation (often a symptom of people's initiative or their deviation from the Plan); and it set out to reform their *"laziness."* By "laziness" the technocrats referred to the transposed villagers' reluctance to conform to the Plan's labor requirements in the model town; their mistrust of incentives promised for the distant future by the State, which had expropriated their lands; and their preference for job security over almost anything else.

Thus if predictability, initiative, and structure characterized relations in Rahmat Abad, then insecurity, impermanence, and fragmentation characterized those in Bizhan. Bizhan, a name and a place, had no public, not even at the neighborhood level. No individual or group in Bizhan could act autonomously, because all were there at the State's command, survived at the State's largesse. In Bizhan public information was discouraged. The State systematically pre-empted all efforts of the model townsmen to define common purposes around which some might rally. The boundaries and memberships of those groups left over from village life became blurred through disuse, petty factionalism, the impossibility of public life, or the State's deliberate manipulation of them. As village structures disintegrated, the leaders who had formerly articulated them became uncoupled from those villagers who had once made those structures. No one, least of all the State, held new townsmen or would-be groups systematically responsible for their behavior, not even "lazy" workers or those accused of breaking "the law." Social relations in Rahmat Abad, including those among kin, resembled contractual ties, whereas those in the Dez Irrigation Scheme (even among the Iranian millionaires and foreign capitalists) were founded on personal connection and pretentious display, intimidation, bribery, and secrecy, hardly legitimate or cohesive.

Above all, in the governance of Bizhan as in the governance of the Pahlavi State and in the Plan itself, society's rules and identifying symbols corresponded very little to Iranians' actual behavior (at any level of society). As Rahmat Abad's government and institutional arrangements had evolved organically out of its history and its members' initiatives and interactions, in just the opposite way the State's law was invented in Tehran offices or in the Imperial Palace itself, and imposed from there on distant rural Khuzestan. But fiat could not bring forth a new society. This failure of government within the State's domain to reflect behavioral reality or its underlying norms cast a dreamlike quality over urban Iranian society and gave the people of Bizhan their obsessive and singular definition of godlessness as *lying.*

In considering the State's relations both with Rahmat Abad and then, intensively, with the residents of Bizhan (for no one related to Bizhan as a polity), we must bear in mind that fundamentally we are observing *sys-*

temic processes, not an idiosyncratic or exceptional *Iranian* phenomenon. To be sure, Iran's ancient history of centralized, often despotic rule, its unique political culture, and some say its geography lend themselves to a highly centralized (or, alternatively, a chaotic) State. But the experience of the villagers who were transposed to Bizhan so closely resembles the empirical evidence from highly centralized systems in other cultures, that on one level at least it places the Dez Scheme squarely within the literature about such systems, enabling us to generalize further about their overall behavior. Weber, Wittfogel, Taine, Szasz, Laing, Besançon, and Solzhenitsyn, among others, have traced the connection between a system's extreme centralization, the center's opposition to all initiatives except its own, and its destruction of those intermediate structures that the particulars themselves put forth.

What may be unique about *this* study is that while the great theoretical and empirical works about extreme forms of centralization mainly describe and analyze them from the outside or from the elites' perspective, here we view one such system from within the very fabric of society. Given the power and paranoia of highly centralized States, the opportunity for a foreign social scientist to live at the grass roots in such a system, particularly among a population targeted for uplifting, is unusual. I was lucky to be able to conduct this study, and could not have done so without the help of key Iranians at several critical points when SAVAK tried to prevent its inception or end it prematurely. By taking advantage of the contrast between Bizhan and Rahmat Abad—both the grass roots of rural Iran, but the latter largely outside the State's domination—we are able to hold cultural factors constant and thus sharpen our awareness of how centralized power affects the elementary structures of social life.

Because the ethnographic materials of this study repeatedly confirm the *systemic* characteristics of the Pahlavi State's "modernization" efforts in the Dez Scheme, it should not seem too sharp a contradiction that the technocrats who planned and ran the scheme were on the whole well-meaning, genial, even kind men. I had numerous conversations with Mr. Lilienthal, spent many days with his company's Iran-based administrators (whose role in Dezful, at least, became increasingly limited to technical matters), and enjoyed two extended interviews with Minister Ebtehaj, head of The Plan Organization in the project's initial years. On a regular basis, I sought out discussions with technocrats in The Plan Organization and the Ministry of Water and Power (which during my stay there was responsible for implementing virtually all aspects of the Dez Scheme) in Tehran.

While in Khuzestan I became closely acquainted with those Iranians directly involved in the project's day-to-day operations. They were family men, religious, patriotic, intelligent, and thoughtful. One devoted part of his leisure time to charitable institutions in Dezful. Fully aware of their work's dramatic consequences on the lives of tens of thousands of nearby villagers and, by exemplary design, on Iranian peasants throughout the land, these men had at times questioned their actions; their having done so gave them confidence to be available to me whenever I wanted and to discuss willingly and openly all the issues I raised. Without these discussions I could not have understood the Persian State's limitless domain. These men justified the Dez Scheme in terms of the material improvement they saw as they drove down the new town's streets (almost all the mud homes had been replaced by cinder block); in terms of Muslim ideals of brotherhood and service; and in terms of Western, especially World Bank, theories of development.

In talking to these technocrats, to high officials in Tehran, to Mr. Lilienthal and many of his staff, as well as to the foreigners and Iranians who administered the agricultural enterprises where the new model townsmen were sent to work, I saw that few of those men striving to realize the great Iranian Plan considered the rural people to be fully human (even as individuals, and certainly not collectively). True heirs of the ancient Middle Eastern tradition that those living beyond the State's pale are uncivilized, they considered their work (when pushed in a religious sense) to be one of humanizing animals (*hayvan,* an expression they often used for villagers). "If we could only sell off the herd we could clean out the stalls," engineer Hasan used to lament to me, only half amused.

One would have thought that because the peasants were at least geographically more immediate to the *locally based* technocrats, it would have been the latter and not the planners in Tehran who would have had to provide the finishing touches to implementing the Plan, since they could see at closer range precisely what the State had to do in order to move Rahmat Abad's villagers into its central command. But I was frequently stunned by the extraordinary display of imagination (if not understanding) about the social, cultural, even psychological formation of the peasants and model townsmen which imbued dictates that came down from the planners in Tehran—almost a perverse *empathy.* At times their exacting attentiveness to domestic trivia recalled the most picturesque and penetrating Persian miniatures, another form of court art. Professionals in social engineering could never learn such details from books; it was as though, like the artists of the great miniatures or like Isfahan craftsmen, they had been doing this work for generations, their skills transmitted from father to son or master to apprentice beginning at an early age, and only to those with a flair.

To introduce the central questions of this book, I have cast Rahmat Abad and Bizhan in sharp contrast, a contrast that springs from what I observed there. No event during my two-and-a-half-years' acquaintance with Rahmat Abad suggested that the State ruled the village, even momentarily, either physically, psychologically, or culturally. But while Rahmat Abad remained firmly on the fringe of the State's functional boundaries (the State has probably rarely dominated the countryside in

Iran's long history), it would be a mistake to consider the village entirely outside the State's sphere of action, as a polar opposite of Bizhan. Though Rahmat Abad was not "scheduled to be taken" by Pahlavi modernization until some twelve years later, and the bureaucracies were far too busy elsewhere to notice the village (it was on the maps of only two government agencies in Dezful), peasants there indeed knew *dulat,* the State, from long contact, an all too familiar force against them. And now and again *dulat* did enter the village, if only to slosh its malaria poison over everything in sight.

One heard far more conscious deliberation about *dulat* in Rahmat Abad than in Bizhan, precisely because the former was intensely aware of the tension inherent in maintaining a position on the margin. (If the people of Bizhan analyzed the State much less, that may have in part been because, as they said, they were like Jonah inside the big fish that was itself at sea.) The Pahlavis had, after all, established a rudimentary order in the northern Khuzestan countryside, and then declared land reform; the State's domain encompassed the urban markets and social life that the village sometimes drew upon. Thus the contrast between Rahmat Abad and Bizhan describes the latter's submission to the State, not simply contact. When I knew Rahmat Abad, the village's corporate autonomy remained fully intact, even though it frequently dealt with the State. Like a silent trader, it did so with minimal communication, never looking *dulat* in the eye.

In addition to examining the effects of the centralized State's transformational efforts on a society's individuals and intermediate-range social structures, and analyzing how and why the centralized State carries out such operations, this book addresses several related but secondary problems: distinguishing between the almost contractual village culture and Iranian townsmen's obsessive personalism (for which I am indebted to Professor James Bill's work on the personalism of urban Iran); analyzing the challenges for continued political development that the corporate village faced, and why it had not met these; clarifying the determinative difference between Western and Japanese feudalism on the one hand and that in Persia on the other, from which I trace Iranian society's inability to hold its governors accountable; and, finally, indicating this study's implications for certain social science theories. These considerations we will develop intermittently throughout the book before bringing them together in its final theoretical discussion.

Before entering the village, let me introduce the reader briefly to the principal method of research I used in conducting this study, the anthropologist's standard one, participant observation. I went to Iran with an elementary knowledge of Farsi, the national language, though the villagers and new townsmen would entirely retool my speech to make it resemble theirs. In Rahmat Abad, I lived with a village family in a home where I had my own room whose door was always open—if for no one else, always for the children and black-turbanned swallows "on their way to Mecca." I ate with the family and shared their life fully, working in their fields and in others' fields, joining in family controversies and after-dinner storytelling, mourning as one of them, when Shahi died. In the village there was nothing to which I was denied normal access, not even the men's breast-beating sessions during Moharram.

In Bizhan I had a "house" of my own, one little cinder-block room on a vacant lot. Only the houses of several relatively affluent new townsmen could have allowed a family to squeeze my footlocker and me into the crowded space the State had given it. Furthermore, when I first went to Bizhan people there were far too suspicious of me to consider taking me in. By the time I left, though, I ate meals daily with my neighbors and friends. During this year in Bizhan, I also worked in the fields and around the house with people.

Except for the first six weeks in the model town, I was never lonely. In Rahmat Abad the villagers were so sincere, considerate, and good-hearted that I quickly found companionship among them, men and women, old and young—and the children! In Bizhan I was fortunate to discover a few distant relatives of friends in Rahmat Abad who provided a moral context for my first months there, if not a trusting welcome. But under the model townsmen's crust of suspicion and awe, they could in fact still respond to that minimal bond that villagers in Khuzestan feel for other villagers, even strangers or those of different ethnicity. Since by then many of my thoughts, preferences, customs, and even some details of clothing were those of villagers—not to mention my village vocabulary, prayers, jokes, swear words, and reminiscences—this common rural code helped many of them to recognize something familiar in me, connoisseurs as they are of the genuine and the fake. Had I gone to Bizhan without first becoming a Rahmat Abadi, I doubt that I could have gained anyone's trust in the new model town.

In recording what happened in Bizhan, I augmented what I saw and what the workers recounted with continuous discussions with the technocrats who ran the DIP, the model town, and the companies. Even enjoying very amiable relations with them, I rarely obtained a factual or consistent version of anything from them. Just the opposite of the villagers, the State abhorred public information or exchange. Thus if the State's version of certain events is poorly articulated, this is a consequence of its own designs.

Finally, to protect those who have so generously collaborated with my research, I have changed in this book all the names of villagers, model townsmen, and technocrats. The acronym Rahmat Abad is made up of the first initials of all my siblings in the beloved family that adopted me there. It means The Place of God's Blessings. Bizhan, after whom I have named the model town, is a hero in Ferdowsi's great Persian epic, the *Shahnameh*. The State gave all the model towns names of famous Iranian figures of power, but Bizhan, whom I have selected for our patron here, was a different sort of hero: Thrown into a pit of darkness to starve, he drew upon his courage and hope, and with the help of Manizheh, who loved him, he brought himself out of his dungeon.

Who is more unjust than he who devises against God a lie, or says His signs are lies?   **—Qur'an, Sura 7**

Chapter 1

The Dez and
the Rise and Fall of Dynasties

**Yon palace which used to rub its side against the vault of
heaven, and towards whose threshold kings turned their faces—
we saw a ringdove sitting on its battlements, and it was crying
"coo coo, coo coo!"   —Umar Khayyam, from *The Ruby'iyat***

Nothing

One morning in the late 1950s, the car in which the Dez Project's great
visionaries and planners were conducting a reconnaissance of the area got
stuck in the mud near the village of Rahmat Abad. Civilized men, they
panicked to find themselves in the utter desolation of "this bleak desert
... in the middle of absolute nowhere" (Lilienthal, 1971:75, 79). Their
appraisal of the northern Khuzestan countryside echoed that of virtually
all foreigners, urban Iranians, and indeed conquerors throughout the millennia: a dry, empty, treacherous land, sunbaked and uninhabited. Over
and over again we hear the same report from royal ministers conducting
periodic tours here, Arab travelers, Levantine caravan traders, Persian
tax surveyors, soldiers crisscrossing Asia in their numerous wars, British
explorers, French archaeologists, railway engineers, oil prospectors, military intelligence—and now, most recently, Mr. Lilienthal and Minister
Ebtehaj. Looking for a suitably destitute place to transform, where they
would have to create a new world, those who come to conquer need to
find a land "lying neglected and unappreciated for many years ... nothing, nothing but space" (p. 172). In this case they even assured us that
"no ordinary man" could have recognized the Dezful region as the
"potential Garden of Eden" that Lilienthal "promised" like God to bring
forth there (Friendly, 1969:31, Lilienthal, 1971:265). The following year
the Shah himself, venturing into the wasteland, marvelled at how quickly
villages could be destroyed to make way for the Dez Project's new State
plantation, the first step in the planners' grand design. "A year ago there
was nothing here!" he exulted at its inauguration.

Though the King of Kings and his courtiers could see "nothing" in the
traditional landscape of Khuzestan, throughout these millennia the fertile
soil and favorable climate have in fact sustained hundreds of villages for

15

miles and miles inland from the rivers, and even beyond in the *qanat*-fed drylands, each one nesting in its clump of orchard in the thin interval between earth and the burning sky. From the rooftops of any village, one can see at least one or two other communities in each direction, within a few hours' walking distance across the fields. The visionaries were in the midst of busy village life. "Where is Karbala?" I used to ask, wondering the distance to the Shi'ites' holy shrine near Baghdad. "Beyond the last village," said those peasants who used to journey there on foot, because settlements fill the landscape continuously as far as one would want to go. Here and there generations of farmers have left a Christ's thorn tree, gnarled by heat but indispensable for hanging a goatskin waterbag to cool while you sow your sesame nearby; here and there primordial water buffalo glisten in the sun, the herd boy's solitude belying those scores of villagers who will drink their milk tonight; here and there a stream runs through a well-kept channel that outsiders who call this land deserted mistake for a natural brook! Here and there the ruins of a worn-out village, of a mill, of a cemetery, or of bygone soldiers' huts now occupied by Nurshivan's owls. Howsoever minuscule, the anciently inhabited villages and the marks they imprint all around them rhythmically staccato this space between the horizons of northern Khuzestan.

What has seemed inhospitable and a technological imperative to the urban visitor may have been the endless sky and the endless history of this gateway between the Mediterranean world and all of Asia. "Who can measure the span of God's hand?" the villagers reflect upon the temporal and visual space of their homeland. But the ground is alive, and Lilienthal's judgment of its empty "neglect" bespeaks an untrained eye. It was here on these upland slopes of Mesopotamia that human society *invented* village life and agriculture, down through the subsequent generations and even now improving the native wheats, barleys, and other field grains of the region, and the gardens, orchards, and animal stock that ever since then have constituted the foundation of Indo-European mixed farming, not to mention the science of irrigation engineering. So thoroughly indigenous to northern Khuzestan are these mainsprings of agriculture that visitors in the winter or spring may assume cultivation to be effortless— perhaps even undeliberated; if these same outsiders would return during the intense heat of July and August, the rice lands lush in neon green would force upon them the pervasiveness of organized and long-sustained human diligence.

Rahmat Abad, Bizhan, and the Dez Project lie on the great Mesopotamian plain within the borders of present-day Iran, less than 100 miles from the banks of the Tigris River. To the north and east extends the Zagros range, the western wall of the Iranian plateau, within living memory impenetrable to anyone—above all the State—without a Kurd, Lur, or Bakhtiari tribal escort. (In olden times one could reach Tehran after months, the elders told me, by going via Shiraz or, more safely, up through Turkey and then by boat across the Caspian; but few could cross the mountains until Reza Shah decimated these tribes' leaders in the 1920s.)

The area comprises three major Iranian rivers, the Dez, the Karkheh, and the Karun: The Khuzestan basin as a whole, including parts of adjacent provinces, contains nearly one-third of Iran's annual surface water. Complementing these rich resources for irrigation are the region's broad alluvial fans of calcareous soils virtually free of salt accumulation or alkalinity. According to FAO soil classification, 70 percent of the Project area comprises good to excellent land. With its semiarid climate, northern Khuzestan has a long, hot summer, mild winters, but irregular annual rainfall. Possibly one year in three wheat may be sown and harvested on unirrigated land. The temperature soars well over 100 degrees Fahrenheit every day for three to four months in the summer, reaching 110 degrees for days on end during July, then falling as low as 40 degrees in January. Rainfall is inversely related: The area receives from 5.8 to 8 inches of rain in January, but rarely any at all between June and October. The annual mean is less than 12 inches. Frost is rare, so date palms and citrus trees can flourish.

In short, northern Khuzestan's abundant water available for controlled irrigation, its rich alluvial soil, natural drainage, and long, hot summers make it the most promising region in Iran for intensive food production under irrigation. This is the country's principal oil-producing province, too, though those resources lie far to the south of Dezful.

With good reason, then, many developers before Lilienthal have set their sights on the agricultural promise of the Dez region. Between periods of being described as a wasteland, it has served as the breadbasket for empires. Within the Dez Project area and only twelve miles to the south of Dezful town, at Susa, Cyrus the Great founded the world's first empire (in the sixth century B.C.) on the ingenuity and labors of this neighborhood's villages. Stretches of the fifty-mile-long "Darius canal" still serve the farmers here. Seven centuries later the Sassanian empire began to focus another long period of development efforts on northern Khuzestan. Shapur brought the vanquished Roman emperor Valerian and his troops as prisoners to supervise the construction of dams, barrages, bridges, aqueducts, and an extensive waterway—Roman engineering consultants!—while Shapur's dynasty complemented that infrastructure by introducing new plants and farming techniques to "modernize" agriculture. Khuzestan derived its name from the abundant sugar cane described by Arab geographers; and no wonder, for wasn't the caliph Harun-al-Rashid's fabulous Baghdad the capital then of this land? At that time fields of narcissus and verdant pasturelands made the area famous; medieval visitors praised its perfumed melons, exquisite brocades, and thriving markets (Adams, 1962:109; Lestrange, 1930:234–35). Lions and other wildlife delighted those who enjoyed the means to hunt—no doubt including wealthy chiefs with their falcons, for that courtly art persisted in the province as late as 1974.

Although the British were struck by the region's poverty, a century ago
trade prospered sufficiently to maintain two caravans a week between
Dezful—over its "Roman" bridge—and Baghdad (Curzon, 1890:524).
Boats navigated the Dez all the way to Shushtar, an agricultural and commercial center toward the east. During his visit in 1845, Layard reported
the area to be well-populated, mentioning by name some of Rahmat
Abad's neighboring villages that flourished during my field work
(1846:11). Throughout the second half of the nineteenth century, the British, establishing outstations here from India, continued to look for ways
to make the region more productive. When in 1903 a Dutch engineer
employed by the Shah proposed large-scale irrigation works here, Lord
Curzon, Viceroy of India, began keeping a closer watch on northern Khuzestan (Buchanan, 1938:184; Lorimer, 1915:1773). The British had
already begun to develop the oil fields to the south. By 1917 they had
established a Residency in Shushtar, and soon thereafter a military "con-
sul" in Dezful, where wheat and rice were exported to Iraq, and other
products including indigo and reed pens to as far away as India. Another
upswing was in the wind.

Land reform, an important impetus for the upswing we will watch in
the first half of this book, probably contributed to the region's agricultural
blossoming in *centuries past* as well. Nothing new to the Middle East, and
intrinsically congenial to imperial fiat's claim over all property in the
realm, land reform may well have been invented in ancient Persia. Over
and over again the ambitious monarch in the full momentum of a dynastic rise has redistributed the land to the peasantry to strengthen his own
power, undercut his enemies, and release productive energies from the
base of his "new" society. Ibn Khaldun described the process as early as
the eighth century (1958:105). Then little by little the land is consolidated
again in the hands of urban elites who cannot be held accountable, and
the dynasty takes a turn toward decay.

The peaks of rural prosperity in northern Khuzestan have been punc-
tuated by decline and devastation in equal measure, and centuries of
darkness. Since it lay so near to the heartland of civilization, it was rarely
in peace. The early agricultural settlements of the Mesopotamian uplands
were never secure from Elamite and Hittite raids; in the sixth century B.C.
the Persians descending from the east enslaved the region's capital of
Babylon, two centuries later abandoning their own palace at Susa and its
extensive agricultural lands as Alexander marched on to conquer them.
The villagers were then incorporated into Alexander's empire when he
established his capital at nearby Seleucia; but that then fell to the invad-
ing Parthians half a millennium later, whose administration the Sassanians crushed before they, in turn, embarked as we have seen upon elaborate agricultural reconstruction. Rural Khuzestan flourished under these
Sassanian projects and programs only until the Arabs took these lands
and villages in the seventh century A.D. Then came the Mongols, most
violent of all, burning crops to the ground and laying waste even to hovels

of mud. Finally, Rahmat Abad saw Tamerlane, too, devastate Baghdad during his second campaign.

Just as the great piecing together of Persia during its periodic upswings depends on radical centralization, during such periods of collapse or ruin the contrary dynamic plays itself out in the same extreme. The would-be coordinator at the center splits; the elites around the royal family turn against each other divisively; the nomadic and transhumant tribes wax strong in their independent domains; the towns and cities, now isolated from each other, assume virtual autonomy, while internal factions even within them fragment urban society further in chaos and drive neighborhoods behind separate walls. When society crumbles, the villages—largely self-governing except during the peaks of centralized command—withdraw farther and farther into themselves, virtually severing their urban links.

From the beginning of history the villages of the Dezful region have been a part of all the bitter campaigns and glorious new eras of Mesopotamia, and no doubt sent men to fight for them or rebuild the palace walls: Ur of the Chaldeans, Sumer, Babylon, Susa of Cyrus the Great and Darius, Alexander's Seleucia, Ctesiphon, which Trajan took for Rome, and Baghdad, all within ten to fifteen days' walk from Rahmat Abad. Because of the villages' proximity to these successive centers of power, the rise and fall of each empire has been the fate of these farming communities, their foundation. With accuracy perhaps beyond intention, the villagers of Rahmat Abad reiterate a common expression of theirs when *dulat* arrives once again to announce its latest uplifting plan: "We've sat through this show before."

Recent Antecedents to the Dez Irrigation Scheme

In the late nineteenth century, the Qajar dynasty's increasingly predatory taxation policies prevented northern Khuzestan from developing its rich agricultural resources on its own, although by then it enjoyed greater distance from the throne of the realm, which had been relocated in faraway Tehran. Najm ul-Mulk, an emissary of the Shah's who traveled here in 1881–82, lamented the ruin of all of Dezful's formerly prosperous families, the neglect of its orchards, the stark poverty of its citizenry (Lambton, 1953:170). Semiautonomous tribal khans and shaykhs governed the province, acknowledging tenuous relations with British India (if with anyone), not Tehran. The British played off one against the other, promoted rival secret freemason societies among the provincial elites, and succeeded in casting the blame for any serious problems on the Shah in Tehran.

When Reza Shah, father of the late Muhammad Reza Shah Pahlavi, ascended the Peacock Throne in 1925 after the Qajar dynasty had been overthrown, the new king resolved to destroy the tribal structures throughout Iran and forcibly settle the nomads and transhumants. Previous dynasties had contented themselves with governing the tribes through their leaders, but according to some estimates this would have limited Reza Shah to indirect rule over as much as a third of Iran's entire population.

In the Dezful region, three tribal or ethnic groups commingle: The Bakhtiari lands lie to the east of the river, the Lurs' generally to the west and north, and the Arabs' to the south and southwest. Many nomads took up farming during these decades, the remarkably porous peasant society here requiring but a few years, not even a generation, before calling a settled tribesman *mahalli* or *'ajam*—of basic local (sedentary) stock. Displaced or co-opted tribal leaders acquired large tracts of land and often established homes in town; the traditional wealthy families of Dezful and Shushtar consolidated their strengths as well. In the 1920s, many landlords planted new orchards, an investment that could be held safely behind the walls of each *ghalah,* or fortified village.

The centralized State's drive to power under Reza Shah brought mixed blessings to rural Khuzestan. At a moment's notice, farm boys and horses and donkeys were forced into the army for many years, often never seen again. When the Shah sent bureaucrats to register all people in his kingdom, these officials flew into a fit of rage to find that peasants had named their infant girls for the new queen: "Slime! Imperial law forbids you to name slime for Her Imperial Majesty the Empress!" Within a short time landlord cruelty increased; no longer unchecked by tribal organization, it knew no bounds. Some landlords—State officials—claimed the first night with any new bride. Relying now on his own corrupt authorities, the King failed to subdue the marauders and thieves who plagued the Dezful countryside, stealing flocks, robbing travelers (even peasants), and terrifying villagers, particularly at harvest time. Both landlords and government officials feared venturing into the countryside without military protection. The tension between urban factions, exacerbated by *dulat*'s officials and by the disintegration of traditional local governance, evolved into endemic warfare.

When Reza Shah abdicated in 1941 and tribal rule reemerged, perhaps the majority of peasants welcomed back the local khans to replace the predaceous State. Many of the indigenous and decentralized political forms, based as they were on ethnicity, kinship, and rural wealth, had retained their traditional checks against the misuse of authority which, of course, were absent from dealings with Tehran's officials. A few landlords who controlled single villages or areas began to move out from behind the *ghalah* walls to invest in irrigation improvements, new crops, fertilizer, and even new breeds of animals, responding to the region's increased access to wider markets during and after World War II. By 1957, the area counted over forty privately owned irrigation systems, including underground aqueducts (*qanat*s) and artificial open waterways.

One of the most popular folk stories of the area attributes the beginnings of agricultural investment in our period to the foresight and initiative of a firmly rooted local Dezfulli, and suggests that local initiative can be realized only when it catches the center of government off guard, stupid, or deceived:

A well-known and wealthy man of Dezful, grandfather of the present-day "old man Qutb," traveled the great distance to Tehran to present himself to Nasir al-Din Shah. He had come from Dezful, he said, to request the gift of a bit of land for an old mare he wanted to turn to pasture, to reward her in her old age. He asked His Majesty for nothing more than "a patch of weeds," just as the King would himself provide for any faithful servant (Persian history frequently confirming the value of a dutiful mount). The Sovereign, moved by such humble affirmation of his supremacy even in a region that he had never heard of, inquired,

"Where, then, is Agha Qutb's old mare and how much would she need for her last days' grazing?"

"O, My Father with the Crown," the obsequious Dezfulli bowed down and replied, "just the barren little strip of land that is useless for anything else, *az bala rud ta labe rud*—that is, along the river where she can quench her thirst in our hot summertime."

Consenting to this simple appeal, the imperial ruler chartered *"Az bala rud ta labe rud"* to the grandfather of old man Qutb ... a vast expanse of thousands of acres of the richest land in the area, from the present Dez dam and the fertile "Dez Bench" wheatlands across what is now one of the country's mightiest air bases and down through booming Andimeshk town into the luxurious compound built for foreign and Iranian engineers!

In telling and retelling this vignette of historical "fact," the peasants in northern Khuzestan could have been alluding to what was on many minds when the showcase Dez Scheme began to overshadow their lives: that kings in remote Tehran, naïve about the value of productive wealth and ignorant of the far-flung reaches of their kingdom, give away expanses of priceless land to the old horse of any stranger who can trick their vanity.

During the first half of this century, the government was so indifferent toward establishing even the most rudimentary administrative law in northern Khuzestan, and it was so weak, that even by the late 1950s, when the Dez Irrigation Scheme was in its early planning stages, there still existed no registry of agricultural holdings. Nor were most of Dezful's landed elites interested in bringing order to the countryside. The extraordinary fragmentation of their holdings and alliances testified to their basic independence from agricultural income, supported as they were mainly by bureaucratic and commercial revenues. By far the majority of the villages here were held by plural owners claiming varied and extremely complicated proportions of the crop (one-seventeenth, five thirty-seconds, and so forth), continually fighting among themselves, pitting leading villagers against each other, and thereby entirely precluding investment. Virtually all major Dezful landlords held piecemeal shares in far more villages than they could inform themselves about, while at the same time few villages were consolidated under single owners or partners able to agree to any unified management policies (see Goodell, 1980).

So harsh were many landlords that it was not uncommon for an agent to find his village empty upon periodic arrival there (landlords themselves being afraid to venture into the Dezful countryside). Villagers constantly scouted around for better landlords, moving their few belongings at a few hours' notice when they found one. Frequently new landlords recruited peasants away from their rivals, if they needed to give their own villages some ballast. Most villagers over forty whom I knew had moved at least several times in their lives. Brothers might be scattered among many distant settlements.

Muhammad's Typical Biography

The following case history of one village family illustrates the characteristic transience of these stalwart peasants' lives during the twentieth century, to which both the village community and the family itself adapted like accordions.

During my field work in northern Khuzestan, Muhammad was in his fifties. He was the eldest of Khudadad's six surviving sons; following him were 'Abdu, Esau, Nur, Rahim, and Sayyed, who was around forty. None of Khudadad's several daughters survived to adulthood, and two sons died as infants. The eldest four sons lived in the same compound together in Rahmat Abad, Rahim and Sayyed having emigrated out of the village. Khudadad, a widower probably around seventy-five years old, lived in Nur's house. His family always considered itself to be from Rahmat Abad; he himself had been born there. Some of his sons could name Khudadad's paternal grandfather, although none could trace what happened to other ramifications of the family.

Even before 'Abdu, his second son, was born, Khudadad had left Rahmat Abad and moved with his wife and the baby Muhammad to the nearby village of Da'iji because the landlord there offered him better terms. Several of his brothers and sisters remained with his parents in Rahmat Abad, although one brother had already taken the family's buffalo herd down the river near Ahwaz, in search of better grazing. Khudadad remained in Da'iji until all his children had been born, coming back to Rahmat Abad probably around 1935 because of a dispute he had with the Da'iji landlord. Back in Rahmat Abad, he married Muhammad to the daughter of an important "kinsman" whose relationship no one can explain. Muhammad was around seventeen; Shahi, his wife, perhaps twelve; as a mature woman she always felt that her mother-in-law had been her true mother.

Then came World War II. Esau and Nur, Khudadad's third and fourth sons, showed up for conscription under their older brothers' names. 'Abdu, who was needed to help Muhammad and their father on the land, had hidden out in an uncle's village until the military ceased scouring the countryside for draftees. Then he had returned and married, in part to bring in another adult woman to help with the housework. Times were difficult during the war, so even though Muhammad and 'Abdu wanted to form their own respective households, they had to stick with the family for everyone to get enough to eat. Esau escaped from the army and returned to live in Rahmat Abad; when the war was over, Nur settled in 'Ali Abul Hosein.

Then Rahmat Abad's landlords sold the village to a consortium of three men. The one assuming supervision proved so tyrannical that the peasants could soon take no more. Leaving the family with the flocks and their three units of sharecroppers' land, Muhammad, his young wife, and their two children emigrated to nearby Khanabad. One by one all of his brothers fled the cruel landlord and brought their families to join him; finally the old man Khudadad himself gave in. In Khanabad, Khudadad's wife died, leaving her small boys with Muhammad and Shahi.

After Mossadegh's fall in the early 1950s, Rahmat Abad changed hands once more. When its new purchaser went out to see what he had bought, he found his village abandoned. His nephew, appointed as his agent, recruited many of the best former peasants back to Rahmat Abad; most of the former core villagers returned. He bargained for Bakhtiari families belonging to landlords on the other side of Dezful, taking on their troublemakers, who it was hoped would settle down to work in their new milieu. Some of the villagers whom he "bought" he distributed to other villages he was managing for his uncle. This at least is the villagers' version of events; the nephew himself denied any hand in human reallocation.

Muhammad and his father and five brothers came back to their ancestral village. A few years later Rahim, one of the youngest brothers, took an agricultural job at the State sugar plantation and moved his family out. Sayyed went to live in his wife's family's village, which had several progressive landlords and plenty of land. Muhammad's wife, Shahi, made sure both of the young boys married into her side of the family, not Muhammad's. By 1965, Rahim had been promoted, arranging for Sayyed to take the position he himself had held; soon Muhammad's eldest son, Naser, joined them with his wife and children. In 1975 the three men were each earning between $2 and $3 a day, their combined families of fourteen people sharing a four-room dwelling in the town of Shush within the Dez Project to the southwest of Dezful.

After land reform in 1963, prosperity bloomed in Rahmat Abad. The four sons remaining there with Khudadad sold the old man's flock (without his consent), which had partly kept them together as a joint family. They formed separate nuclear households within the same compound and pooled resources with another villager to buy a tractor; but within a much looser overall patriclan, each family now encouraged the next generation's greater independence. They hoped the village had found stability at last, and with it better times. When the reform freed the peasants of northern Khuzestan from their landlords and made each a rightful owner of his farm, the villagers considered themselves reborn forever. Nothing under the sky would be able to stand in their way! "Like the Prophet Jesus who went up to heaven, he took us with him!" Mash-hadi 'Ali praised the Lord and the land reform.

In Rahmat Abad, the peasants determined that if they were to be lords of the land they would cast off their decrepit, pinched, and rat-infested "tomb" and build themselves a new community with wide, straight streets, huge houses, and the freedom of birds: a village unenclosed by any traditional high wall. What now could they fear? And so, like many other Iranian villages after land reform, collectively, with argued deliberation, the villagers laid out a new settlement not far from the old *ghalah,* established fresh rules to ensure from the outset that it would never deteriorate, become polluted, or overcrowded, and then constructed an entirely new village they nicknamed "Throne City," where indeed no defensive village wall blocked their view of the far horizons. In time they would replace these spacious mud houses with ones of brick, the latrines with bathrooms, the sheds with garages, perfecting each detail one by one.

Professor Lambton found this same burst of village construction in many parts of Iran after land reform (1969:137–91), reflecting the villagers' sense of transitoriness under the landlords, which they often explicitly stated. When neither the landlord nor the peasants had specific, permanent claims on the land (as they did not under the traditional system, deriving as it had from imperial tax farming), nothing could endure. In the old village the villagers' houses had sat upon the landscape as little more than tents, constructed with minimal investment—even the roof beams belonging to the landlord!—empty of anything that could not have been moved in a flash.

Land Reform and the Dez Irrigation Project

The State implemented land reform in northern Khuzestan swiftly and relatively thoroughly. Thirty-five percent of the peasants with land rights benefited in the first phase (which affected all landlords owning more than one village), and virtually all others in the second phase, launched in 1965 and completed in 1967. For the peasants, even the thirty-year lease they received spelled unimaginable permanence. There was no longer any reason to be on the move. The government made agricultural credit available through its cooperative program, and encouraged them to use fertilizer. In the Dez area, only in the late 1950s had progressive landlords

and the government begun to experiment systematically with new cropping patterns, seed varieties, and cultural practices, so peasants now managing their own farms found few well-tested and economically profitable
innovations at hand. But never mind—in Rahmat Abad as in villages
throughout the region peasant farmers tried their own experiments with
new crops and farming techniques; they immediately sought to imitate
large mechanized farms by investing in tractors, pesticide sprayers, and a
village truck. They built a mosque and a village school, purchased sewing
machines, shoes, and Western clothes; they began learning to read. Their
cooperative claimed the high credit repayment rate typical of most villages in the area, the peasants no longer having to sell the crop before
harvest.

Unlike Rahmat Abad, the 58 villages embraced by the Dez Irrigation
Pilot Project (established in 1963 and intended eventually to extend to
all 145 villages in the DIP) received special technical assistance and uninterrupted water delivery from the new irrigation system. The 13,000 peasants in this pilot program quickly proved what could be achieved when
the villagers' tremendous energy released by land reform was harnessed
to good irrigation and technical advice: In the first three years after land
reform, they more than doubled their crop yields and greatly increased
their livestock production, raising their per capita income from 9,000
rials in 1960 ($130) to 30,000 ($430) in 1966 (Salmanzadeh, 1980:43,
quoting the Head of the Agricultural Division of the DIP). In their
response to mechanized harvesting, they supported a demand for over
thirty combines, while their need for employing more landless labor had
already begun to attract villagers from marginal lands into the DIP. Thus
within the Dez Pilot Project, as well as outside of it in communities like
Rahmat Abad, the villagers of northern Khuzestan, now yeoman-farmers, lost no time in compressing centuries of agricultural change into several years. Their achievements in such a short time serve as a baseline for
what they might have gone on to accomplish economically if the land had
been left in their hands; they indicate that rapid change need not be
destabilizing if initiated by local people themselves.

Despite this ready response, northern Khuzestan's land reform, like
decrees delivered by footrunners in the ancient empires, was obsolete in
Tehran before even announced out in the province. Already in 1956, six
years before land reform, Lilienthal and his TVA partner Gordon Clapp
had proposed to The Plan Organization that *they* and not local people
determine the future of northern Khuzestan through the centrally commanded Dez Project: 14 dams including the great "high" dam on the Dez
with its 16,000-acre reservoir; 6,600 megawatts of electric power to be
produced annually; the integration of Khuzestan's petroleum resources
in a region-wide manufacturing complex; and the radical modernization
of large-scale, capital-intensive agriculture over two and a half million
acres of land. Already in 1957, five years before land reform, the State
had expropriated 30,000 acres of prime farmland and dozens of peasant

villages but fifteen miles south of Dezful to begin the scheme with its own sugar cane plantation at Haftepeh as a model for other consolidated agribusinesses to come. (Indicatively, and indeed setting a "model," the plantation grew voraciously year after year, expropriating more and more land as it did and paying owners barely 20 percent of the land's value.) Already in 1960, two years before land reform, the semiautonomous Khuzestan Water and Power Authority had been created to direct the agroindustrial transformation of all resources within the Dez Project, and the government along with the World Bank had drawn up plans for the Dez Scheme's $100 million irrigation system, costing approximately $700 per acre to construct (long before OPEC affluence). Already foreign scientists were at work at the Safiabad Experimental Station conducting research for large-scale, capital-intensive farming in the Dez Irrigation Project.

Thus when land reform came, where could its yeoman-farmers with their new Throne Cities of mud fit into such a showcase world? Would the State leave in *their hands* these ambitious investments and the unlimited potentials promised by Lilienthal's corps of planners? Hardly.

By 1966—but three years after the record-breaking production increases following land reform in the pilot extension program—the DIP Plan demanded that large-scale farming replace all smallholders. That decision had been anticipated for fully five years. Having ridden in on TVA's "grass-roots" reputation, Lilienthal's Development and Resources Corporation persuaded His Imperial Majesty that foreign agribusinesses could best realize the potentials of the Dez Irrigation Scheme. Having demurred momentarily—Ladejinsky weeping for the small farmers of the Dez (in a visit even some of them recall, although they did not know its purpose at the time)—the World Bank agreed to finance the Empire's yearnings to uplift Khuzestan once again, according to centralized Plan.

And so, in a surrealistic script all too plausible in this land, even as the Dez peasants, like those in Rahmat Abad, embraced their new managerial challenges, even at that moment their exit from the stage had already been written. Their newly acquired land would be taken away from them ("repurchased") and leased to foreign agribusinesses, which would hire those of them who were needed on a day-wage basis, subject to seasonal demands. The new villages they built would be demolished to force them into one of the thirteen *shahrak*s (new model towns that the technocrats called "labor centers") that would "service" the agribusinesses. The Ministry of Water and Power would build and manage these new model towns for the companies and assign each family to one. A hundred villages were to be liquidated within the DIP, and thus rehoused to make way for the four agribusinesses, each of which undertook to farm an average of 42,500 acres. British, New Mexican, Australian, French, New Zealand, Californian, Dutch, Japanese, Canadian, Israeli, Hawaiian, Scottish, Roumanian, and Danish companies and their experts came to the Dez Project to bid for its land, to import cattle and spray planes, to mechanize the cotton and sugar beet harvests, and to establish feed lots and complementary processing factories; the World Bank appointed a special "Agricultural Task Force" for Iran; other international agencies, Tehran millionaires, and the royal family all converged on northern Khuzestan once again to help bring forth the King's showcase. The land foreigners did not seek would be handed over to State farms, also for consolidated management. Hooglund (1982:85) estimates that 75,0000 people were actually displaced in the project's first stage, only one-seventh of whom received alternative housing.

The *Shahrak*s, Agribusinesses, State Farms, and the Plan

Each model workers' *shahrak* in the DIP consisted of approximately 500 brick housing units (many but not all with electricity), which according to government statistics accommodated an average of four people each; but as rural families in the Dezful area averaged six in 1974, and as most *shahrak* families included other relatives, too, whom resettlement had left homeless, the number of people crowding into each *shahrak* house exceeded six. Each family received two small rooms, one 12 by 18 feet and the other 6 by 9 feet, plus 600 square yards of land for a garden. Because in the second half of this book we will move into Bizhan, one of the most favored *shahrak*s shown frequently to foreign visitors, this introduction suffices to outline the town that was meant to serve as a model for the entire rural sector of Iran.

The Plan called for those peasants within the Project who were not transferred or scheduled to be transferred to *shahrak*s (because foreign investors found their land unsuitable) to "request" that the State take their lands back from them, too, and form them into "farm corporations" where they also would seek day-wage employment. These consolidated farms, ostensibly shareholding companies run for and by them, were simply *State* agribusinesses (although less complex technologically than the private ones): The Minister of Cooperatives and Farm Corporations was an army general. Each of these State farms would eventually comprise a rural resettlement center constructed as a second-class *shahrak* on the basic model—although the labor centers for the private agribusinesses were to take the lead in elaborating the details of a *shahrak*. Thirty-two thousand acres within the DIP had been set aside for four such State farms.

The State referred to the *shahrak*s as "model" towns not only because it considered their conditions ideal, but also because it planned to redesign Iran's *entire countryside* on their pattern, with the agribusinesses and State farms as integral parts of the paradigm. Large-scale private agribusinesses and State "farm corporations" constituted the Fourth Plan's (1968) two nation-wide pillars for agricultural development (although it made ample provision for other types of parastatal plantations, such as, for example, in the greater Dez Project area, special vegetable farms run by the Ministry of War, and a Forestry Service cattle ranch on expropriated nomad lands). Having paid no attention at all to agriculture until the mid-1960s, the State in the Fourth Plan ordered that *one-quarter* of all the irrigable land in the country had to be completely mechanized and managed by foreign agribusinesses within the following *decade,* each agribusiness exceeding 12,000 acres and each with its labor centers built according to *shahrak* design. Muhandis Safid, supervisor of the model town program, told me that 2,000 *shahrak*s would eventually be built on this pattern.

In a country that is predominantly desert, by 1978 thirty-six agribusinesses had taken over some 500,000 acres of the country's most productive irrigated land. In addition, the Fourth Plan mandated that by 1978, 150 State farms should flourish throughout the nation, merging 1,200 villages and bringing over a million acres under the State's direct control. On these State farms, second-class *shahrak*s were to be formed at the rate of thirty a year, consolidating the State's control over some 350,000 laborers and their families. In short, the agribusinesses and the State farms of the Dez Irrigation Project, with their *shahrak*s, were to serve as blueprints for the rural advancement of all Iran. Elsewhere in the country, the State immediately began elaborating others on the Dez design.

The Shah and his technocrats abhorred being the rulers of peasants and donkeys. Quite likely this disturbed them more than statistics about per capita consumption. Entire villages were sometimes leveled so His Imperial Majesty would be saved from the sight of them during a one- or two-hour visit to an area. Ministry officials cited several such examples to me during my years of field work in Khuzestan, and cases around Shiraz were notorious (especially in preparation for the Twenty-Five-Hundred-Year Dynastic Anniversary). The Dez Irrigation Scheme spared nothing in order to mechanize and rehouse the Empire—to mechanize first of all. Even orchards, sacred to Muslim law and particularly to the traditional Iranian, were bought by the Ministry of Water and Power only to be uprooted for machines' freer movement across the landscape. So that the Plan could transform the millennia-old villages throughout Iran overnight into agribusinesses and State farms, fiat created special laws, incentives, prerogatives, and explicit schedules and quotas for agribusinesses and State farms in each of the more favorable agricultural regions. A pan-Iranian crop map completed by the Ministry of Agriculture in 1976 dictated what should be planted in every field throughout the nation.

These two models covered only the nation's prime and secondary agricultural resources: What about the rest of the villages in the country? The Plan could not leave them untouched. A third design existed for these 50,000 or more villages that were not targeted to be subsumed either by private agribusinesses or by State farms because their land was poor, unirrigated, or remote. These villages were to be grouped in "rural development poles" to which millions of people would also be moved. Each "pole" would focus on a modern resettlement center or third-class *shahrak* of 5,000–6,000 people, with a handful of satellite villages around it. Like the agribusiness *shahrak*s and State farms' rural centers, these resettlement centers were meant to be relatively distant from town and offer only the most minimal urban services, so as distinctly to preserve their rural character. The Plan anticipated needing some 5,000 of them in order to embrace into a rural development pole or satellite village every single settlement in Iran that had not been taken over by a *shahrak* or State farm center. Following close on the heels of the Fourth Plan, the Fifth Plan targeted 25 percent of the nation's rural communities—over 13,000 villages—to be merged into 1,180 such poles within the first five years!

Before twenty years had passed, the State would obliterate well over half the nation's villages—those The Plan deemed "unviable." The 5,000 central "poles" or third-class *shahrak*s would absorb their people, each of these settlements experiencing a thirteen-fold increase in population in two decades' time! While these resettlement poles would not enjoy funding of the same magnitude as the *shahrak*s, from their description in the Plan it is clear that they, like the State farm centers, looked to the new model *shahrak*s—to Bizhan—as their model.

The Dez Irrigation Project played a central role in the planners' comprehensive design for transforming the nation's countryside. Not only would the DIP fix the pattern for how the entire rural sector would live— socially, politically, and demographically—but, in additon, as The Imperial Plan Organization's major regional project, it would establish the *economic* paradigm for raising Iran's annual growth rate in agriculture (4 percent during the period preceding this study) to one more closely approximating that being achieved in industry (7 percent targeted for the period covered here). Comprising the largest agroindustrial area in the country, the Dez would show how capital-intensive agriculture under direct or indirect State control would completely replace traditional peasant farming by 1990.

The Dez Project's Denouement

By the mid-1970s, the ability of the private agribusinesses and State farms in the Dez Irrigation Project to provide a livelihood for the thousands of peasants whose land they taken away was already in serious question. In 1974, five years after the first two agribusinesses were incorporated and three years after the first State farms began to operate, the best wage that former peasants could hope to earn working as unskilled laborers on either type of farm, in the heart of the Dez Project (indeed, on land that *had been given to them* less than a decade earlier), was $2.50 per day. Of the thousands of peasant households that had already been displaced by the agribusinesses, only 1,028 laborers had found full-time jobs in the companies, which included a large number of single, unmarried men, drastically qualifying the number of households actually supported. The Ministry of Water and Power guaranteed each former landholding family one job, but not those who had been landless in the traditional villages and who had also lost their livelihood. Most of the men whom the companies could not absorb were put to work as the technocrats' personal domestics and gardeners, or as watchmen; sometimes three or four middle-aged men would be paid to guard a *shahrak* schoolhouse! The State farms, less heavily capitalized but well subsidized by the government, offered somewhat more employment opportunities, but never succeeded in paying more than $10 in annual dividends to their "shareholders" whose lands they had taken.

If we compare the annual per capita income that Lilienthal's company reported many of the peasants to be enjoying in 1966, when they farmed these very same fields under the DIP pilot extension program (as *owners*)—if we compare this income with their wages in either the agribusinesses or State farms in 1974, we find that under mechanized, large-scale farming each *family* was living on approximately the income they had proven themselves capable of generating per capita under the pilot program eight years earlier.

Admittedly, nation-wide figures show a similarly dramatic decline in rural income during the decade in which the Dez Irrigation Scheme reached its apogee. In 1966, four years after land reform, peasants and farm workers claimed a 26 percent share in the GDP, and their average earned income was 50 percent of the average national wage; ten years later when agribusinesses and State farms were in full swing in the most productive areas throughout the country, the rural population's share had fallen to 9 percent, comprising but 30 percent of the average national wage (Salmanzadeh, 1980:267). Some of this decline could be explained by the migration of approximately half a million people out of agriculture during that period. But the principal cause was the failure of the State's sweeping agricultural transformations: namely, the State farms, centrally managed production cooperatives, and large-scale private agribusinesses owned not by provincial landed elites who in many cases were experienced in local agriculture, but by foreign entrepreneurs unfamiliar with Iran. (Many of these last-mentioned firms had agreed to operate an agribusiness only under government pressure, in exchange for access to other sectors of the economy.) The State farms and agribusinesses had chosen the most productive farm land in the country, precluding the gains in production that the pilot extension project for small holders had begun to witness in the Dez Scheme's initial years.

We have glanced only at a preview. The State's domination of rural society at virtually every level bred "a corrosive degree of uncertainty which militated against long-term private investment" in the production base (Salmanzadeh, 1980:267–68). Between 1969 and 1972 the country was importing an average of $200 million in agricultural produce; this figure rose to *$2,550* million five years later. Locally, two decades after the inception of the Dez Irrigation Project, when the large-scale firms were in full flower, experts estimated agricultural output in the areas they had "reclaimed" to be *less* than it had been under traditional agriculture before the project had begun (Salmanzadeh, 1980:270)!

Bankruptcy followed decline. Already by 1975 the first two agribusinesses to invest in the DIP sold the greater part of their assets to the Iranian Agricultural Development Bank, owing several million rials for rent, irrigation charges, and other dues. According to the Agricultural Development Bank, the four agribusinesses' cumulative losses by 1979 exceeded 2,057 million rials ($29.4 million), their debts to the Bank itself reaching 2,256 million ($32.2 million), and their debts to others, 1,347 million ($19.2 million). By 1976 all four companies were declared bankrupt. Explanations for their failure centered around their lack of expertise in the environment of northern Khuzestan—the agronomic, the socioeconomic, and the institutional. They were too large in size; in almost every case the technology they imported proved unsuitable for Khuzestan and their own managerial resources there. The companies blamed government bureaucratic inefficiency, deliberate obstruction, and corruption; both the companies and the State cited labor problems as unresolved obstacles to effective management. The State farms suffered the same difficulties, although since they were well protected from public scrutiny it was harder to document their mistakes. A higher proportion of "shareholders" migrated to the cities from the State farms than even from the agribusinesses, in search of basic subsistence. In 1975 the average "shareholder" in northern Khuzestan received a $1 dividend for the fields he had "requested" the State technocrats to take from him after land reform.

By 1978 (well *before* the revolution) the State began asking the peasants who had tenanted and farmed this land of the Dez for generations, for millennia, to buy it back. The Project was not two decades old. Tens of thousands of villagers, who had become owners of the land at last, had then been uprooted and betrayed for Lilienthal's promise that "the Dez area will be watched throughout the world" (p. 265). Hundreds of millions of dollars of debt had been incurred. The Dez dam's original life expectancy of eighty years had been revised to thirty. Despite the World Bank's generous loans and guidance, despite the economists' projections, when completed the vast new system of canals had added *less than 30 percent* to the original irrigation capacity that the peasants and landlords on their own had financed, constructed, and maintained since time immemorial (even with the low incentives of traditional agriculture). Large stretches of farmland within the Project area, after $1,700 had been invested per acre (Peterson, personal communication), lay abandoned. The State could find few bidders among those very peasants who sixteen years earlier had readily taken on the difficult challenge of modernizing agriculture.

Had Lilienthal and Ebtehaj returned to northern Khuzestan for a second reconnaissance twenty years after their first visit, they would have found a wasteland that had not been there when they had described a wasteland before. And on its surface they could have seen the "real things" which they and those who controlled the Plan had set down in their confidence that power can bring forth everlasting improvement:

> How wonderful it is to be able to see one's ideas and words take root and become real things, as real as miles of sugar cane, a factory shining and eager to go, a great dam rising where before was emptiness like a crater on the moon. This is the deep satisfaction I crave . . . a sense of the everlasting, and of the majesty of man who undertakes to master this behemoth (Lilienthal, 1971:177–78).

When the Dez dam—the highest dam in Western Asia—silts up, it will blend into the landscape with the ziggurat at Choga Zambil, the palatial Achaemenian complex of Susa, the Sassanian barrages and diversion canals, the foundations of the "Roman bridge" across the Dez. Here in the Iranian homeland the Shah and MacNamara, Ebtehaj and Lilienthal built within an ancient tradition. Not to be outdone by Darius and Alexander, they had vowed to transform moonscape into 4,000 square miles of lush farmland overnight (Clapp, 1957:3). To do so, they built the behemoth State. The drama Rahmat Abad has watched in this compressed span of twenty years comprehends two extremes: the absence of the State and then its all-commanding fullness. When I lived there, the peasants kept trying to construct a new village between the two.

Unlike Lilienthal and Ebtehaj, the villagers of Rahmat Abad have never stood at the foot of a ziggurat, nor did they know there was a Plan. But their norms, skills, expectations, and institutions for building corporate interaction and accountability are rarer and more vital to the future than the planners', bankers', and engineers' skills, or those of the prognosticators and visionaries. One question this book must ask is why the Rahmat Abads that are left each time have never mastered the behemoth.

Say, O God, Lord of the kingdom! Thou givest the kingdom to whomsoever Thou pleasest, and strippest the kingdom from whomsoever Thou pleasest; Thou honourest whom Thou pleasest, and abasest whom Thou pleasest; . . . Verily, Thou art mighty over all!   —Qur'an, Sura 3

PART ONE

RAHMAT ABAD

Chapter 2

Socioeconomic Structures
in Rahmat Abad

The wolf that has come through the rain is wise.
—Lur proverb

Rahmat Abad's two wide, straight "avenues" crossed each other at right angles in the center of the village as they transversed the length and width of the community and at each end opened onto the surrounding countryside. The villagers had deliberately founded the new Rahmat Abad on this primary expression of space and order, to rectify the old *ghalah*'s narrow, twisting, overly accumulated alleyways that symbolized the past they were leaving behind. The new arteries had to be wide enough not just for several donkeys laden with hay to pass each other with ample room, but for a new tractor with its discs! And through the centuries ahead no building would be allowed to encroach into these two thoroughfares. Onto them and the village's one smaller lane some twenty house compounds opened their large wooden doors, never closed in daytime. A chanar tree marked this center of the community, where the villagers gathered for informal business and relaxation. The cow herd assembled here, the village truck departed from here, women on their way to the canal crossed paths here, the barber, peddlers, and darvesh preachers attracted the villagers to this meeting place, and the headman's busy compound at the corner confirmed the intersection's centrality.

Inside each house compound (of varied design and character) a few trees lent color and shade to the great work area crowned by a beehive-shaped oven that filled the air with the smell of bread. Here in the compound each separate family spread out its rich assemblage of animals and tools, possessions, and daily luxuries that embodied its material existence: duck pens; an old tire; the donkey's hay; a plow; puppies; the ubiquitous plastic water pitcher for washing hands and face; a discreetly walled latrine; goatskin water coolers and a cradle in the shade; grain bags; turbans, shirts, skirts, and sparkling pots and pans drying in the sun; the outdoor hearth; and perhaps a bicycle. Almost every compound brought together more than one household—indeed, one was shared by five nuclear families and one extended family. Many compounds adjoined one another without separating walls; by means of stairs and ladders the compounds continued up onto the flat roofs where grain and beans were dried, where we slept at night in summertime, and where one could keep an eye on other people's business in their compounds, or look out to the fields, the threshing floor, and the road. From the roof a young girl could smile at a lad passing—well timed—along the street below. Living space, like Mahmut's prayer call at sunset, flowed over the house roofs and down into other work areas nearby.

In 1974, Rahmat Abad's 250 people comprised forty nuclear, joint (two or more brothers in partnership, often with one or both parents), or extended families (a man and wife sometimes with unmarried children, sharing the store room with one or more married sons), plus one polygamous family of two wives. The land reform had given twenty-five families rights to village lands, based on their having the means to plow, while fifteen remained landless. Several families in the village spoke Arabic in the home but the regional Dezful dialect as well; several others referred to their Bakhtiari or Lur tribal background. But almost every family in Rahmat Abad had been settled agriculturalists for at least three generations, and considered that they had always been of local peasant stock. The average village household had six members. Only two adult villagers could read and write. Self-sufficient in food, the village raised everything fundamental to its diet except cooking oil, tea, and sugar. Characteristic of Iranian peasant villages, virtually no craftsmen lived here, no one had a store, and no Muslim clergyman regularly served the community.

Besides the anthropologist, at the time of my study Rahmat Abad hosted its first literacy corpsman and later its first justice corpsman as well, both city boy draftees owing twenty-four months of service after high school. Cut off from the mainstream, the village still depended upon and received its share of traditional rural visitors mingling with these emissaries of *dulat:* peddlers, a snake charmer, and a preaching darvesh with a bull horn; the occasional sideshow troupe with a strong man whose jeep would drive over him when the frightened corpsmen were not in the village to prevent the stunt; small-time produce buyers from town, numerous beggars, government officials, and a traveling knife sharpener; census takers and mosquito sprayers, an itinerant barber, mullahs reading the Qur'an, a wandering healer, snappy contraceptive dispensers from the State in their short white miniskirts, red-lipped gypsy dancers, the ex-landlord and his family calling upon the headman, and friends and relatives from far and near.

In 1972 the first road arrived in Rahmat Abad, and ended there. Several villagers formed a partnership to buy a pickup truck that made one trip a day to Dezful eight miles away. The road passed near five other villages before reaching Rahmat Abad. Although no road connected Rahmat Abad to many settlements near it, ancient and frequent links on foot had formed some twenty core villages into a regional community with another fifteen to twenty peripheral settlements more loosely integrated into the network. Members of each of these villages could reach those in the nearest neighboring villages within two hours on foot.

Appearing on no map or government administrative chart as such, this cluster of villages constituted a distinct sociological area, although I never had any evidence that it had been governed by one tribal khan or related landlords. Through the centuries and still in 1974, almost all young people drew their marriage partners from among these villages, which also served as one another's primary source for shepherds, housebuilders, specialized healers, animals, and any other transactions that depended on a socially certified reputation (as does the selection of a marriage partner). Traditional intervillage fights took place between villages in this area far more than between any of them and outsiders. Each core village always sent a delegation to the mourning ceremony of any household within the area, and most peripheral villages did as well. Someone with special assets could be prevailed upon to give priority for their use to others within the area before going outside it—hiring out his tractor, for instance.

The many life histories villagers related to me revealed that the endemic disruptions of village life until the mid-1960s had added to the cohesiveness of this regional community; almost invariably the villages where men and women mentioned having taken refuge against thieves, cruel landlords, the military draft, or other predators were other villages in this core area—even when they had no relatives there. Sometimes one particular village would have "taken in" almost everyone who had fled from a nearby settlement. Given the frequency and intensity of these disruptions in the traditional countryside, and given their life-and-death importance to such extremely poor people, it is no wonder that through the years the intervillage dependencies that rural violence caused evolved into such an identifiable region.

Toward the end of my study, I learned from officials in Tehran that on paper the Plan had already assigned each of these villages to one of the three basic models for all rural settlements in Iran, which we have already reviewed—although it would be another twelve years before the State would get around to enforcing its design for them. Rather than building on these villages' regional self-consciousness, interpersonal trust, and extremely effective information network by endorsing the region as one unit, the technocrats had assigned them (with no consultation, of course) to five entirely separate administrative centers!

Rahmat Abad's Calendar of the Year

Two systems of dividing time impressed themselves upon the lives of Rahmat Abad villagers, neither of them the Western or official State calendar. The agricultural seasons marked the most important cycle of time; the religious calendar, a secondary one.

During the years of my field work in northern Khuzestan, Rahmat Abad planted wheat, rice, green beans, mung beans, sesame, cucumbers, and eggplant, in addition to barley and clover for cattle, and enough onions for domestic consumption. As the villagers were constantly experimenting with new crops, others might be added from year to year. The first rain in October or November, the only distinct meteorological event of the year, set the agricultural year into motion. The men sowed the wheat in early December; in mid-January they started building the paddies for cucumbers and eggplant, and began cutting the clover by the end of February. In April and May, everyone picked the cucumbers and eggplants. The men harvested the wheat in May, then sowed the mung beans and sesame. By early July they were planting the green beans and preparing for the great task of transplanting rice. The headman contracted for the hired labor the entire village would need, while the community built the visitors' temporary shacks, bracing itself for the most arduous month of the year.

Virtually everyone toiled in the fields, transplanting rice throughout the four weeks of August, ten hours a day, jabbing millions of rice seedlings with a forefinger into the thorny, rocky mud, one by one. As the weeks went by, the wavy line of brightly colored workers, our village, slowly filled the seemingly endless fields with the tiny plants. In a good year, right after rice transplanting everyone headed out to pick the green beans, a heaping trayful steaming and sprinkled with salt crystals set before the hungry workers while they sorted each day's harvest: the yellow for home, the green for sale. Rahmat Abad held high hopes for a good year of green beans, which like the rice and the cucumbers had a totemic personality of their own, almost as members of the community (probably because all three were considered wage earners!). Then, while the men harvested the mung beans and sesame in early October, the women and young people threshed and cleaned them with graded sieves, a very long process. That finished, several weeks later the men harvested the rice. If the rains delayed until late December, the villagers would reap little wheat on the unirrigated land.

No villager knew the acreage of Rahmat Abad's fields, nor were Ministry statistics consistent; but I estimate that traditionally the community cultivated between 600 and 800 acres, some 75–100 of which were from time to time sown in dryland wheat. When they could count on abundant irrigation, the villagers always extended their rice lands, which they converted back into dryland wheat when something endangered their canals.

As of old, Rahmat Abad drew its water directly from the Dez River a couple of miles away. Rahmat Abad had no *qanat*s or wells. A small government canal reached the village in 1973, an improvement that *decreased* the acreage that the villagers could irrigate. Cutting across Rahmat Abad's main canal, it blocked access entirely to many of the village's lands that lay to its east. Once the engineers had departed, though, and despite considerable conflict with the bureaucracy, Rahmat Abad had refashioned parts of its original irrigation system and had installed supplementary conduits to overcome the drought caused by the State's innovations, recovering almost 90 percent of the community's irrigation capacity and former lands.

Like the crops, the animals of this mixed farming village had their cycles, too. Following the harvests, the cows and sheep grazed on many village crops. After the 700 ewes that constituted the 4 village sheep herds dropped lambs, the women milked them for about six months. The 250 cows and the 20 water buffalo also gave milk during the same period. Even the women's 800–1,000 hens were subject to seasonal changes, their numbers reduced by two-thirds during the colder winter months.

Not correlated with the coming and passing of the seasons, but rotating through the year as a moveable feast was the celebration of Moharram, the only annually recurrent event beside those of the agricultural cycle (and anniversaries of recent deaths) to measure the passing of time for Rahmat Abad. When I was living in Rahmat Abad, Moharram, a ten-day memorial for the Shi'ites' great saint Imam Hosein, who died in a bitter religious battle near Baghdad, came in the spring. The villagers celebrated Moharram intensively that year. During a peak of agricultural activity, it would have been impossible for the villagers to dedicate much time to this religious celebration. The fact that Moharram's date moves around the calendar indicates Islam's indifference to the agricultural cycle (quite in contrast to Judaism and Christianity).

The calendar used in daily business affairs in Iran traditionally has been the Persian calendar with New Year's falling on the first day of spring. The villagers were only remotely aware of this calendar. Finally, as the Iranian State grew in power and insecurity, it invented its own calendar—or, more accurately, one egocentric to the Shah—which it imposed on the urban Iranian society, its domain: particularly on the bureaucracy and all who dealt with it. This official Iranian calendar derived its first two digits from the length of time since the coronation of Darius (2,500 years), and its last two from the beginning of the late Shah's rule. Thus not only was the villagers' ritual cycle out of synchrony with the agricultural seasons they lived by, but the Shah's imperial calendar was out of synchrony with both the traditional secular and religious calendars—and (for those trying to modernize the country) entirely incongruent with the calendar used by the commercial sector of virtually all other countries in the Western world.

The Village's Economic Organization

We will better understand the village's corporate character, and compare its potentials with those of the Dez Project's agribusinesses and State farms, after we consider the village economy more closely. Even in 1973–74, when I conducted field work in northern Khuzestan, the villagers of

Rahmat Abad were starkly poor. Only in the schoolhouse and the rooms of the teacher and justice corpsmen was there any furniture (other than cradles, a few storage chests, and gas stoves some families had recently purchased but never used). The villagers' spacious rooms, cool in summer, were practically empty from wall to wall. Each family kept the few household and personal possessions it had in a couple of boxes or a trunk; in cubbyholes in the mud walls (the house lantern, matches, and so forth); hanging on nails on the walls (a picture of the Prophet, or clothes); and around the main hearth (pots and pans). All life was carried out on the dirt ground where we prayed, cooked, ate, conversed, and slept. As soon as a family could, it bought a carpet used only for visitors—factory made, of synthetic fiber, but nevertheless a Persian carpet! Poorer families sat on felt or coarse cloth.

Nor did the village count a single eating implement or plate; we ate with our hands from the one family tray, family members sharing the one tin cup. Wealthy families owned cheap tea sets brought out only for special guests. On such an occasion almost any family could afford to kill a chicken, which would feed the visitor and as many as ten other people. The more prosperous villagers always ate rice daily and often several times a day; the poorer ones, several times a week. Most families survived on unleavened whole wheat bread, yoghurt, and milk (every household had at least one cow), various types of beans, tea, vegetables in season, the occasional egg, and now and then a treat from town such as potatoes, chick peas, or a watermelon.

A handful of more affluent men owned four or five shirts and three or four pairs of pants; most villagers had one change of clothes. During Reza Shah's rule, an edict had gone forth that Western dress had to be worn in towns, as though clothes would modernize society. So the headman of Rahmat Abad had taken up a collection and the village had bought a pair of Western trousers along with one pair of men's shoes. As late as 1970, when a peasant had business to do with bureaucrats in Dezful he would carry these collectively owned trousers and shoes with him until he reached the old bridge, where he would slip them on for his brief entry into the Shah's world. Upon exiting he would change back immediately and return home barefoot, so that the one otherwise superfluous costume would not be worn out by use.

As for savings, villagers set aside what they could in the form of sheep and women's gold bracelets, although fewer than half owned any sheep, and jewelry was in fact scarce. As early as 1960, the former headman had purchased a small plot of land in town, but many men and women over forty had visited Dezful only a few times in their lives, if ever. Despite their proximity to the hydroelectric plant at the Dez dam twenty-five miles away, and despite the villagers' frequent petitions to the Ministry of Water and Power, the community did not have electricity, which after land reform would have given them an incentive to invest in appliances.

The heart of village entertainment comprised the wonderful stories the women and young people told around the hearth in the evening as they savored village personalities. Their art of mimicking soared to new heights with me as a subject—even dressing me up in an old bridal costume sometimes! Every villager longed to make a pilgrimage to Mash-had, where several families managed to go during my year in Rahmat Abad. They traveled in the train almost like cattle but experienced a visit they would recount throughout their lives. Like those who had gone in previous years, they spent as little time as possible—if any at all!—in holy places and most of their time at the zoo, the animals quite naturally interesting them far more than mosques and shrines! Then Rahmat Abad's pilgrims would befriend an urban baker to get a good look at how he baked the thick bread which city people ate, in a commercial oven. These matters comprehended, they would return to Rahmat Abad, educated but scarcely impressed.

The annual cash income of the eight representative landholding families whom I studied in the village varied from approximately $550 to $4,500, with an average of $1,500 (per family, in current prices). This included nonagricultural income (Goodell, 1975). Although a few landholding families in Rahmat Abad diversified their investments, they derived almost all their income from agriculture. In virtually every family the women insisted on knowing the details of family finances, and they kept the keys to the money boxes.

Like the landed families, the landless did not depend on the cash economy for their staples of wheat and rice, which they received as payment for their work in the village. During the busy seasons, the landless found abundant employment near at hand; farmers had to reserve the most industrious of them months in advance. Many landless families earned a higher income than some of the landholders who managed their farms inefficiently, because through hard work (for instance, gathering and selling brushwood), specialized skills (sheep herding, cooking for large gatherings, and so forth), and thrift the landless enjoyed striking mobility. The poorest families in the village, whom I know well—poor mainly because of a shortage of able-bodied adults, a situation remedied in time—ate a very monotonous diet but were never in danger of starving.

Land reform released enormous pent-up energy in Rahmat Abad; the villagers' constructing "Throne City" was only a beginning. The landholding villagers invested heavily in agriculture once they began farming for themselves. All began applying chemical fertilizers and pesticides, which they had not used previously. Quite in contrast to Dr. Lambton's appraisal that the Iranian peasant "resists tenaciously any efforts to change his age-long habits, whether as regards his living conditions or traditional agricultural methods" (Lambton, 1953:263), they experimented avidly. In the five years preceding my study, they had already tried to cultivate grapes, strawberries, limes, cotton, pomegranates, and

Mexican wheat, and they raced out to plant the popcorn I introduced for a winter night's diversion. In that brief period of time, between land reform and my field study, two village partnerships had bought Roumanian tractors and their necessary complementary equipment for plowing and hauling ($12,000); another partnership had bought the pickup, mainly for taking produce to market ($4,500); five farmers had purchased insecticide sprayers ($170 total); and many had increased the size of their flocks and herds, and had planted small orchards. We have seen how they maintained and improved the village irrigation system. They paid the State regularly for their land certificates ($20,000 all combined). In addition, villagers invested in a secondhand minibus for urban transport ($1,000), ten motorcycles for commuting to work in town ($5,000), twenty bicycles, including those for the first boys to attend junior high school in Dezful ($1,000), two sewing machines ($130), and status items that served as rewards and incentives for work, such as radios and watches (for further details, see Goodell, 1975:277). When the resident schoolteacher offered evening literacy classes, thirty farmers enrolled; they would sometimes be at his door at dawn the next morning (long before *he* arose!) to find out the solutions to the preceding night's homework problems before heading to the fields!

Land reform did not achieve one of its aims in Rahmat Abad: to break up the ancient *joft* system of communal land holding. Prior to land reform the landlord owned the land or held it from the King and granted peasant plow teams (*bonku*s) access to it in return for a percentage of the yield. Peasants gained membership in a *bonku* by contributing the labor of one adult male and either the plow or a draft animal. They organized most of their field work by plow teams, directed by the *bonku* head who made many decisions. After land reform, they dissolved this organizational unit for all purposes except the purely administrative procedures of land measurement at the beginning of each season and the assignment of irrigation turns; abolishing the *bonku*s freed those with land to make their own farming decisions and to arrange for shared or hired labor individually.

In traditional agriculture the landlord often financed a hard-working peasant's initial capital outlay. Men who did not know how to manage a farm were taught by other villagers. Owning a draft animal or plow qualified one for a share in farming the land. This share, called a *joft,* could not be considered a right because the landlord could withdraw it (although he rarely did). Rather, *joft*s constituted villagers' *claims* to the opportunity to cultivate the landlord's land. Since all *joft*s were equal, the acreage to which each *joft* gave access was inversely related to the total number of *joft*s in the village at any given time, a number that could and often did change from year to year according to the village's qualified work force. The extent of each village's land also affected the acreage attached to each *joft*. For example, if the village had 300 acres and twenty villagers with draft animals (twenty *joft*s), each *joft*holder would farm 15 acres. Given the frequent variation in these factors, in the early twentieth century around Dezful a *joft* ranged from 20 to 45 acres.

If a peasant commanded twice the resources others did, he could hold two *joft*s. Under relatively stable conditions the distribution of *joft*s could become quite skewed, as some peasants accumulated greater wealth (and, no doubt, influence) while perhaps others fragmented theirs through inheritance. On the other hand, until land reform fixed the number of *joft*s in each village permanently, the flexibility of the system (which ensured everyone with the basic means of plowing one share in the land) enabled considerable upward mobility as well as efficient adjustment to the decline of families' productive resources, outmigration, and so forth. It reflected the continuous flux in the countryside, and indeed promoted the mobility of labor and productive capital, since villages where *joft*s had become large would attract farmers from those where they were small.

A *joft* did not refer to any specific parcel of land. Following a complex regime of crop rotation and fallow, the villagers would sow a different crop in each field each year. At the beginning of each planting season the *joft*holders paced off each field to be sown into as many equal parcels as there were *joft*s; they marked the parcels clearly and then drew lots to assign each parcel to a *joft*. If the village had fifteen *joft*s during one season, they would divide each field into fifteen parcels; if there were twenty *joft*s next year, each parcel in that field would be smaller to accommodate twenty equal shares. Thus every *joft* received one parcel *in every field,* but only by coincidence did a *joft*holder get the same parcel that he had cultivated previously, or even a parcel the same size as last year's. If rice were to be sown in eight fields and beans in three, then a farmer would have eight separate plots of rice and three of beans, each located in a different place within each field than where he had cultivated the previous season. (For production data, see Goodell, 1975; for further description of the *joft* system, see Hooglund, 1982:23ff., 103ff.; also Salmanzadeh, 1980:173–178.)

At the time of land reform, there were twenty-four and a half *joft*s in Rahmat Abad distributed among twenty-five households. The headman held four *joft*s; one household held three; and one, one and a half. Ten farmers had a single *joft* and twelve, half a *joft*. The reform expressly outlawed the *joft* system's annual rotation of plots among shareholders as I have described, claiming to put a higher priority on private property (but probably in fact more concerned about mechanization). While the villagers consented to fixing permanently the number of *joft*s and which households held them, they adamantly refused to accept the permanent designation of shares to specific plots of land, even under threat of being disqualified from the reform. Although, as Professor Ashraf has pointed out (personal communication), the *joft* system had probably originally been imposed on the peasantry for tax purposes, in Rahmat Abad the villagers were aware of some of its advantages to them even after land reform.

The *joft* system welded together the core landholders of the community through the shared responsibility, trust, and frequent interaction that it required. Because it scrambled farmers in dozens of combinations throughout the village holdings, each shareholder always had to be ready to collaborate with anyone else whom the lottery would make his field neighbor (for irrigation, pesticide application, the timing of harvest, and so forth). By distributing risk and attenuating the economies to land consolidation, it slowed the widening differential between large and small shareholders in the community. Finally, it ensured all *joft*holders' identification with the *entirety* of Rahmat Abad's productive base rather than with only certain canals or fields, bridges, pathways, or boundaries. Anything that affected one part of the village's lands was of concern to everyone. What could replace this mechanism for harnessing to the common weal the clever, the wealthy, and those more powerful politically?

Despite the benefits of land reform, the villagers sensed that it had abolished one of their two defenses against *dulat:* the landlord. *"Dulat* took its shirt off (to show its muscles)!" Gholam explained. They could not allow the State at the same time to undermine their only other buffer, the community itself. They understood the advantages of fixed, individually "owned" fields—namely, the ability to mechanize harvest (they had already mechanized land preparation) and the greater incentive to invest in the land. But given their grasp of urban and bureaucratic Iran, the villagers never confused that "ownership" granted by the State with permanence or with genuine opportunities for them, as did many Westerners—or men like Arsanjani.

Although when the planners considered the consequences of land reform they worried about who would offer the economic inputs the landlords had provided, the villagers perceived that the landlord—even at his worst—had made a much more valuable contribution by symbolizing and focusing their social cohesion. How could the State's agricultural credit replace this? They valued individual mobility, accumulation, property, new freedom, just as the modernizers claimed to. But what good were these if the community fell apart? All the more reason, then, that at the time the State was removing the landlord from the village context, its cornerstone, the villagers sensed land reform's profound implications for their communal security. They discussed eventually phasing out the *joft* system—later on, perhaps. But not at this critical time. "It will take time to digest what we have eaten," said Akbar.

The peasants of northern Khuzestan were connoisseurs of safety, not only of physical safety, but, deeply interconnected with this, social safety. Hardly "conservative" economically or technologically, certainly not in religion, they relished individuality more deeply than many Westerners. But to them expansion, risk, individuality, self expression—perhaps even freedom—were inconceivable apart from a firm corporate structure of family and community. Without the social and economic foundations of Fortress Rahmat Abad, they could not safely come out from behind the centuries-old *ghalah* walls in which they had traditionally enclosed themselves.

A second vital economic institution in Rahmat Abad, the *bildar* (which means shoveling), tapped the same communal bonds as the *joft* system and integrated into it. Through the *bildar* the landed households carried out communal projects to which every *joft* had to contribute one worker (half-*joft* holders being paired). During my year there, nonattendance averaged less than 10 percent—usually no more than two absentees, and rarely the same ones. Approximately fifteen half-day *bildar* projects were called during that year; they could serve any purpose, although they almost always related to maintaining the irrigation system, constructing bridges, improving animal access to fields, facilitating tractor routes, or developing new canals and related structures.

Besides operating the *joft* system and supporting *bildar*s, the landholders united as a group for many other endeavors whenever a need arose. They maintained the threshing floor as communal property. They jointly hired irrigators for mung beans and rice, the rice guard with rifle and dogs to keep out wild boar, sometimes bird boys, and an irrigator for the wheat. Economic enterprises were launched on the basis of voluntary contributions of labor or money, a resource fund used imaginatively but with restraint. In this manner they bought materials for repairing canals, aided families having to finance funeral services or a wedding, and paid for the mullah visiting during Moharram.

Many peasant communities rely on labor exchanges in which one partner might not repay the other for months, even a year—an arrangement common in Rahmat Abad. But lest anyone take advantage of the familiarity these links fostered (hence, restricting their partners' future flexibility), friends, brothers, even children exchanging labor kept a careful count of half days owed. Villagers frequently paid one another in cash or kind for services rendered. In their insistence on individual freedom, landless households were free to work for whomever they wanted. Finally, many *joft*holders farming the land alone created semiformal partnerships to pool labor or other resources—the use of a donkey cart, the labor of extra women for threshing—always keeping their respective harvests separate. Often nonkinsmen joined together in these partnerships, and when they terminated no one was obliged to renew them the following season.

The villagers used their cohesive skills and expectations not just to form links among themselves but in combining with outsiders to gain greater economic and political power. During periods of price fluctuation, they bargained collectively with urban vegetable buyers for favorable sales. They dealt as one body with knotty problems of a townsman's proposal to use marginal village lands, and with the former landlord's retention of one piece of land not affected by land reform.

While it frequently was subgroups within the community that organized themselves, the community as a whole also sustained many corporate economic activities, some enduring through the years. We have seen the relative ease with which it organized construction of the new Rahmat Abad, but other examples abound. The villagers taxed themselves to pay the headman a small "salary" for his trips to town, his organizational services, and some entertainment expenses. Everyone in the community dropped what he or she was doing to help extinguish house fires, even when these did not endanger him or her directly. They negotiated with a cowherd collectively. They hired a minibus from a total stranger (who offered a better price than the minibus owners they knew personally) to take them on a local pilgrimage.

Characteristically, the entire village built a mosque to serve one particular darvesh from Dezful and his twenty-five to thirty followers in Rahmat Abad. Although most households had nothing to do with the sect, many slightly disapproved of it, no one went to the mosque to pray, and communal religious rituals never were held in it (a matter of principle), the villagers looked on the mosque with civic pride and prepared food for the followers' annual celebration. In Rahmat Abad corporate unity embraced pluralism.

The villagers defined communally the policies governing Rahmat Abad's two tractors and pickup truck, and they agreed on the prices for these services through corporate bargaining with the vehicles' owners. From the owners' point of view these prices compared favorably with those outside the village. The tractors and truck were considered scarce resources that must be shared by all. Any villager investing in such an asset knew he would be subject to negotiation with the community about certain regulations. For example, the tractors had to plow Rahmat Abad's fields before going outside the village (an agreement farmers from other villages often tested unsuccessfully by making urgent requests and offering bribes to the owners and drivers). The truck had to carry market produce free if accompanied by a passenger, except on special hauls of vegetables and grain. It had to stop at the mill when requested, had to transport a sick person to town at any hour, and had to serve wedding and mourning parties (for a reasonable fee). In exchange, the owners of these vehicles were protected against competition from the outside, villagers assisted them in collecting delinquents' debts, and social pressure assured them that no one demanded exemption from the negotiated prices or from the working rule of first-come, first-served within the village.

The villagers' readiness not only to adopt mechanization, but to plunge right into buying and managing the vehicles themselves—radically new responsibilities for such poor people—illustrates the compatibility of Rahmat Abad's overall corporate cohesion with many other forms of organization that it embraced. Their rapid adoption of machinery also shows the primacy of social organization—far more important than education or government assistance—as a foundation for spontaneous "modernization." When the challenge of new technology called for more capital than any one household could afford, or when it called for greater bargaining power than individuals could mount on their own, these yeo-man-farmers had at their disposal an extraordinarily plastic set of insti-tutions, norms, and skills for linking reliably with others to meet new needs. And nothing stopped them. The range of lasting, publicly visible, and jointly accountable arrangements that were possible in their tradi-tional tool kit of ways to combine effectively with others knew no bound-aries of kinship, ethnicity, residential locality, or even nascent "class." With the flexibility these arrangements afforded, with the optimism and self-confidence they fostered, and with the underlying trust among villag-ers throughout the immediate region (or when dealing with others outside whom someone could certify), the villagers drew on a large pool of poten-tial partners for enterprise or negotiation. Their open public arena did not encumber them with the costs of secrecy or public justification.

The tractor stockholders—not all kinsmen—held business meetings at appropriate intervals to decide whether to invest in new equipment or simply divide the earnings, to determine the operators' wages, and to set-tle other questions about their investment. The written accounts that one tractor owner kept helped him and the other tractors' shareholders to argue jointly for hikes in their service charges. In the case of each of these partnerships, the original set of shareholders remained unchanged throughout the first five years of the venture, and I have no reason to think that they have not continued until now. This stability gave pre-dictability to everyone's dealings with them.

While the communal demands upon the tractors and the truck pre-vented these village entrepreneurs from accepting the most profitable jobs they could find until after they had served the village's needs, all three vehicles made considerable profit. Their owners were able to replace worn-out parts regularly; within five years the tractor partnerships fully repaid their loans; and in 1974 one shareholder entered into a part-nership to buy a second pickup. After all, servicing the village's needs—profitable in itself—was limited to particular times, leaving the vehicles free at least 60 percent of the year.

Although no one in Rahmat Abad could drive when the first tractor was bought, the fact that the tractors were firmly "tethered" in Rahmat Abad meant that many young men and boys in the village had to acquire valuable mechanical expertise, and the pressure on them to serve Rahmat Abad's needs (during peak periods, operating day and night) made them improvise repairs. Once a season they dismantled as much of each tractor as they possibly could, from spark plugs to axles, spreading scores of its parts in neat rows all over the compound, inspecting and cleaning them one by one with the girls' help, and then "rebuilding" it.

The communal advantages that Rahmat Abad gained from the *joft* sys-tem's tempering individual enterprise and from the regulations placed upon the vehicles (as the primary symbols of their new-found entrepre-neurial vigor) included local stability, predictability, and self-direction, essential foundations for sustained productivity. At such a precarious time, just as Rahmat Abad was immersing itself in the cash economy after land reform, these constraints protected village unity—necessary for the entrepreneurs themselves—from divisive intrusions that would seek to control its resources. Achieving a careful balance between entrepreneurial freedom and corporate social structure, these constraints did not discourage enterprise but at the same time did modulate the pace of opening up to the outside, so that villagers could absorb the political implications of "modernization" and adjust to its corrosive effects gradually, never losing a sense of control over their own communal destiny. The community had to train its elites, only recently released from the landlord's domination, in a new type of civic responsibility, which required strong self-restraint. (After all, the landlords certainly offered no models the villagers wanted their elites to emulate.) From family, village, and intervillage region, Rahmat Abad would gradually expand the world in which it felt able to operate predictably; but it never allowed its affirmation of change and a new economic order to threaten its fundamental social integrity, never submitted to the random forces of anarchy it thought lurked beyond the intervillage boundaries it knew.

Indicatively, in dealing with Rahmat Abad financially *dulat* denied the village's corporate responsibility upon which some landlords had insisted (when not deliberately encouraging factions). The State taxed each household individually. Consistent with this policy it also required *joft*holders to render their payments to the land reform commission individually, whereas the farmers themselves proposed to pay their annual dues as a group. In certain matters, like meeting attendance and group pressure for uniform repayment of agricultural loans, the State sought cohesion but at the same time did whatever possible to discourage it.

The Family

The range of kinship-based organizational forms in Rahmat Abad during my field work and the decades preceding it manifested a breadth similar to that which we have seen in the non-kin forms of association. Villagers recognized a very limited patriclan of three generations' depth. Its authority rarely remained uncontested, and its bonds sometimes were very weak. Of the village's forty households, thirty-four comprised nuclear households. Six of these included a widowed parent of the husband, and two consisted of widows with no married children. This left only six other households: two extended, three joint, and one polygynous. In our review of the biography of Muhammad, son of Khudadad, we have already seen how this typical peasant and his father, brothers, and sons with their wives and children moved in out of Rahmat Abad several times in their lives, and in and out of shared households.

Scholars studying rural Iran in this period have concluded that the relatively high number of nuclear families brought to completion (probably permanently) the disintegration of the joint or extended household; they attribute this to "modern" forces such as the cash economy. Although not confirming the explanation, since it was hardly in the cash economy, Rahmat Abad appears quite consistent with that trend. (See Salmanzadeh, 1980:107; Goodell, 1977:199.) When we examine from the inside and over time the dynamics of family and household consolidation in Rahmat Abad, we have no substantial reason to believe that "traditional" rural society favored one type of organization or another through the generations; we certainly find no conclusive evidence that Iran's "modern" sector fostered nuclear families or households. To consider this further we need to look behind standard demographic categories like "extended household" or "joint family" and appreciate how they hide crucial economic, political, and social relations.

Consider, for example, a married son living outside the village, who contributed money to his father's household and, in turn, claimed his share of the family's harvests and herds. Their common pool of primary economic resources but entirely separate households calls attention to the distinction between households and families as organizational units. As a rule of thumb, in Rahmat Abad women had somewhat more control over the former, men over the latter. In this case the two units functioned as an extended family but lived in nuclear households. Beneath the statistical predominance of nuclear families and/or households recorded for rural Iran during this period, many types of kin-based partnerships proliferated, often representing quite distinct loci and objects of political control.

Let us look more closely at the sequence of stages in Muhammad's biography, which we reviewed earlier. After Muhammad farmed his father's land with his father and three brothers for several years when they returned to Rahmat Abad, his first step toward self-reliance was to establish his own cooking pot. But, not laying claim to his separate inheritance, he continued working essentially as his father's subordinate in the field. Establishing a separate cooking pot meant that Muhammad's wife gained control over her own labor, a more expensive and inelastic resource than *joft*s of land. After some years Muhammad moved his home. In doing so he separated from his partnership with his father at a yet earlier stage in the production process, when they stored the grain. No longer withdrawing daily needs for daily use, but rather claiming his total annual share at harvest, meant for the first time disembedding the value of his labor from the collective enterprise. Now he negotiated with his father over payment for his labor, which, however, he still pooled with his brothers' work on Khudadad's land. Next each son wanted control over his separate *joft* of land, his inheritance, which suddenly left their father with nothing. From being master, Khudadad became the dependent of his fourth son.

Some time later still, the sons insisted on dividing the family flock of sheep. Unlike the establishment of separate grain stores or *joft*s, this step indicated the brothers' interest in individual control over accumulation of wealth, since sheep constituted the principal form of savings. They still plowed their separately identified *joft*s and irrigated and transplanted rice jointly, rather than entering into partnerships with others or hiring labor. In this they preserved the traditional plow team's form. Later still the four men agreed to carry out all postharvest operations separately, showing the women's influence again as threshing is under their command. (In shared threshing, which is very labor-intensive, women with more household chores or fewer working children pose a free rider problem.) Appropriately, at this stage of separation each wife built her own oven.

Land reform prompted the final breakup of the joint preharvest work force into four farms managed completely independently. When the brothers worked together in the fields, it was through explicitly arranged partnership. But immediately after land reform the brothers constructed one grand compound for the patriclan in the new Rahmat Abad, comprising what were by then six households and specifically leaving room for more in the next generation. At the same time, too, they entered into an expensive joint venture together, buying and managing a tractor (although not with equal shares). Having achieved independence in food production and household management, they moved straight into other forms of partnership more amenable to contract, which offered greater specificity in obligation than kin-based arrangements. Around the same time, Muhammad's two youngest brothers plus one of his sons, workers on a nearby plantation, pooled resources to form a classical joint family and joint household—one grain storage and one cooking pot! Under stringent economic conditions, the form that the family had embodied a generation earlier reappeared. So did the classical extended household, when one of Muhammad's sons remained in his father's house upon marriage, working for him in his fields. In 1974, each of the nine newly married couples in Rahmat Abad had joined the husband's father's household.

The villagers' family organization closed in and expanded as it responded to many different conditions. Usually the process of changing from one form to another was gradual, as Muhammad's case illustrates, allowing everyone to assume new risks incrementally. Conditions pervasive throughout the region may have fostered a wide distribution of one household form, but each family's own economy, its stage in a marriage cycle of many decades, its relationship to other family members' resources and lives, and its expectations for the future also affected a couple's desire and ability to become independent. The adjustments we have reviewed express renegotiations of a primary relationship, renegotiations based on pragmatic issues mainly about agricultural and "household" production.

The fact that villagers were too poor to accumulate many material possessions and that family was not rooted in immovable property as it is in many societies (where the anticipation of inheritance holds married sons within or close to the family); the fact that no actual land and not even a house plot (which was the landlord's) embodied and symbolized the patrimony; and the fact that in some situations landlords financed a young man's purchase of a plow or bullock, his first major step toward independence—these factors gave the family an exceptionally pliant economic base, broadening its organizational criteria. Many peasant families of this region derived from nomad stock, although perhaps long ago. Among the nomads of Khuzestan, each nuclear family had to fend for itself economically; brothers rarely even camped together. When nomad families did become settled agriculturalists, they often found a turbulent countryside where one had to secure a wide network of family and friends in different villages.

If the trend that prevailed in the generation preceding my field study has continued, many of the nine couples forming extended families with the husband's father's household in 1974 may have created their own nuclear families by now, just as the young men of Muhammad's generation did thirty years earlier. On the other hand, by ending the *joft* system's reallocation of shares to anyone able to farm, land reform may in time require many nuclear families to incorporate in joint or extended households. The rural instability caused by the State's efforts to control agriculture in the 1970s—and more recently the revolution and war with Iraq—may have had the same effect.

Thus it is likely that temporary and *relative* economic or social conditions account for the predominance of nuclear *households* in rural surveys of the 1960s and 1970s, not an overall historical trend or a final consequence of "modernization." Many of these conditions could apply to rural life in other times. The contemporary period is hardly the first in history when young married couples have enjoyed the relative luxury of being able to assert such independence. It is true that tribal leaders who played a role in the governance of peasant villages earlier in the century no longer did so in 1974, nor did lineage-based neighborhoods in Dezful and Shushtar articulate their solidarity by warring against each other, as they had in the 1920s. But these forms could quite conceivably reappear, and may have during the revolution.

Because villagers enjoyed such freedom and skill in objectifying family relations, the "household" constituted a much more definite unit for surveys to investigate empirically than did the "family," which could hardly be confined to a single set of parameters. In such a contractual culture, reliance on a shared storeroom must vary considerably in response to year by year alternatives available to would-be dependents. If we turn to the villagers' religion for clues to their anciently cherished values, we see no religious celebration extolling the family or clan at weddings, births, or circumcisions, nor did the villagers' other rituals exalt models of the corporate patriarchal family. By ordering an equal inheritance for all sons (which, however, is by no means obeyed in Rahmat Abad), Islam encourages segmentation over consolidation, parity over intergenerational unity. Kinship strength rarely even appeared in the villagers' religious legends or doctrines, in their descriptions of afterlife, or in their genealogies, reminiscences, or folk stories. Far from venerating ancestors, most Rahmat Abad families could not name a great-grandfather, and the great religious epic of Moharram dwells relentlessly on the fragmentation of family. In Rahmat Abad, at least, "modernizers" cannot blame traditional kinship forms for obstructing individualism or the rational allocation of resources.

Contractual Links Within an Overarching Corporate Community

The villagers' confidence and burst of energy at the time of land reform might seem to have required the intensification of kinship, with its roots in secure personal ties. Other than stronger family bonds, what could take the place of the authority and resources of the ousted landlord and the traditional mores he embodied, as a guarantee of continuity? Indeed, other than family what could underwrite the villagers' aggressive expansion, morally, legally, politically, as well as economically? With the State only marginally present in Rahmat Abad, no new urban patrons on hand, the landlord's able late headman deceased, and the darvesh preacher playing no significant role in village affairs, how could a new order be launched on nothing but the vacuum left by the old order's dismissal? On nothing but a collection of nuclear families?

Taking what they found suitable in their kinship repertoire, the villagers imbued their family links with an almost contractual agreement, holding in check the constraining personalism of kinship, which by its nature can make sweeping claims on people who are eager to be on their own. Then to these relatively flexible links they added the freer and more numerous non-kin options available throughout the region. Thus they remained within the nuclear family and even the loose patriclan but went beyond both; they remained within the village but went beyond it, too. We see the abundant empirical evidence that this happened, but upon what invisible foundation?

The relatively corporate village of Rahmat Abad provided the foundation that enabled the villagers to bend family structures or to separate from them when need be. This foundation gave them partners throughout the intervillage region. To grant *dulat* its due, the minimal State that Rahmat Abad knew did establish a context—a distant authority few considered lawful—for the community's resilience. But primarily the villagers' ability to move beyond the personal ties of kinship derived from their village's corporate character. This corporate foundation had not suddenly been laid at land reform, but through the generations and centuries before it. Rahmat Abad had adjusted socially and politically to the landlord's removal with little need of innovation, because while he had provided an overarching symbol of its identification, his living in town and his general indifference to village affairs had made him superfluous to the community's social and political base. In short, the family persisted as each individual's terra firma, but all forms of family and household drew their strength and suppleness from Rahmat Abad itself, which we will examine more closely in Chapter 5.

The advantage of kinship as a basis for the often more ambitious new arrangements that a dynamic and expanding economy needs is that it fosters a high degree of predictability. A person has deeper and broader knowledge about family members than about most non-kinsmen: Information normally flows more readily and accurately along kin lines. One usually can count on his or her family to make members reliable; the family is more likely than non-kin associations to have ready at hand mutually recognized authorities and channels to ensure agreement and its enforcement. A family is frequently willing to run interference for its members and to defend them. For undertaking initiatives larger than one person can mount or sustain, these advantages of the kin group make it a natural basis for consolidating or exchanging resources. In Rahmat Abad, villagers used these advantages fully, members of the nuclear family combining with kinsmen outside it in work teams, in marketing partnerships, in joint ventures that sowed rented lands, in common sheep herds, and in village-based enterprises.

These strengths of kin ties would seem unsurpassable for organizing social, economic, and political activities. But if a community is sufficiently cohesive and permanent, it may offer its members a basis for non-kin links as well, which have advantages that kin ties do not. Rahmat Abad, for instance, assured the accessibility of a pool of potential and reliable economic or social partners beyond one's family or close friends; it provided predictability about their behavior, open access to information, and communal pressure guaranteeing that conflicts be resolved ("everyone must greet everyone else on the path"). The community's cohesion recognized authorities and effective methods for enforcing agreements and rules. The village went beyond the traditional family in offering individuals and groups the option of *impersonal* or *contractual* links, which are difficult for kinsmen to forge. For example, such links would include arrangements firmly binding but only for the limited period agreed upon, which need not evolve into interminable personal relationships as kin arrangements do; arrangements that lay claim to one specialized aspect of each partner but do not implicate the whole person as kin links do; and arrangements between partners of different statuses, in which neither exerts a personal claim to superior authority (hence, arrangements subject to mutual accountability regardless of status). These advantages of contract distinguish non-kin relationships crucially from linkages based on personalistic relations; they are invaluable when the complexity of society requires one to form partnerships selectively or for a limited duration, or to deal with strangers.

Because Rahmat Abad, as a genuine community, offered an arena for reliable, accountable non-kin association similar to the practical aspects

of trust possible within families, thereby enabling contractual relationships that could have more specific focus or more limited duration than
family links allowed, the village could complement kinship (or even substitute for it if need be) as a basis for predictable organizational forms.
On this foundation individuals and nuclear families could expand into
the public arena beyond the kin group. The advantages of contractual
links within the village (in contrast to the all-encompassing personalism
of family relationships) gave villagers positive incentives to form partnerships and exchanges in this wider social field instead of within the
domain of kinship. Thus when village entrepreneurs sacrificed a certain
degree of freedom for the sake of local corporate cohesion, in exchange
they gained much greater flexibility and a far larger pool of potential
clients or partners: In short, they gained the underpinnings of the law.

If couples forming their own households risked the inevitable anger
and even retaliation of the husband's parents, Rahmat Abad offered a
protective milieu independent of the family: The community made certain that no one starved; it rallied to defend any household against
thieves; it collectively consoled the bereft; and upon occasion its members proved ready to endanger themselves to save fellow villagers. Poor
families, the two widows, and sons who had left their fathers' compounds
did not need family ties to find refuge and companionship in larger compounds within the village. Nor did one need kin as a buffer against the
world outside of Rahmat Abad. Someone in Rahmat Abad could always
be found to mobilize urban contacts when it was necessary for a villager
to deal with *dulat* or powerful townsmen. Because the community
required everyone to remain at least on speaking terms, it pressured relatives not to perpetuate their bitterness against sons who left the paternal
household. The cohesion and effective strength of *the corporate village*
enabled the nuclear family's independence, enabled its *integrity*.

Rahmat Abad, in turn, belonged to a regional, *intervillage* arena with
similar predictability and accountability, because the region bound
together many communities like Rahmat Abad. For generations villagers
here had been knitting together links in one another's communities. The
discrete corporate villages at the base underwrote villagers' contractual
arrangements with non-kin outside the village throughout this region. But
this intervillage region's microworld of rural predictability was clearly
demarcated. The accountability it offered most villagers never extended
into dealings with townsmen or the vast realm of *dulat,* because in neither of those did villagers have access to good information or to protective political leverage.

A striking feature of kinship relations in Rahmat Abad was that with
this firm communal foundation which one could always fall back upon,
and with contractual arrangements pervading the village culture even
between nuclear families in the same patriclan, those who held subordinate positions within their families often bargained with relatives above
them as though they were dealing on an eye-to-eye basis with non-kinsmen. This assertive independence even within close family bonds—

expressed quite explicitly and consciously—bore little resemblance to the submission to kin authority generally attributed to Middle Eastern and Mediterranean family relations. The common sign of deference in the urban Middle East, a young man's not smoking in front of his father, would have been entirely foreign to the villagers' culture.

From the time a son reached maturity, he was quick to establish a quid pro quo relationship with his father based on the considerable value of his labor. Even children often refused to run errands if made unhappy, or they placed conditions on their assent. Rahman, a lad of fourteen, would not irrigate or pick the summer vegetables for four days (jobs entirely relegated to him) until his father let him buy a pair of corduroy pants. Young village girls successfully denied the family their cooperation until allowed to attend school. Women frequently went on strike because of overwork, lending a rugged give-and-take to family relationships. The five cases of divorce were all caused by women seeking better marital conditions even under the difficulty of finding second husbands. Faridun, a man in his forties, negotiated stubbornly with his elderly father, 'Abbas, for improved terms of employment on the land they worked together. When Ma'sume's husband despaired of her laziness and wanted to send her home, her father negotiated with his father, and Ma'sume with her husband, in terms of a complex business deal. In a similar vein, to strike an agreement about remaining in his father's household, Gholam attached specific limitations to the work required of his young wife: namely, that she would wash all the clothes but do nothing more. In each case what one might expect to turn into heated argument between family members tied by a close personal bond became tough bargaining instead.

While not entirely successful, junior members of a family could expect objectivity from those in authority, and could demand reasons and negotiable terms. They knew that they could walk out; a relative somewhere or a sympathetic friend would take them in. Except in the case of children, the community itself could be an individual's last resort, even after the kin group. The villagers' concept of other authorities resembled and was shaped by this primary experience with authority in the family. The landlord never held ultimate authority over Rahmat Abad, because the villagers could walk out. Pervasive throughout the villagers' culture was the assumption that one negotiated the willingness to be governed. This is partly why villagers claimed the prerogative of picking and choosing what programs and services to accept from *dulat*.

This negotiation within close family relations increased the flexibility of kinship arrangements possible within Rahmat Abad, and by offering the alternative authority of village society itself, it held family patriarchs to a more predictable course. After negotiating separation from them, sons could recombine with family units for specific purposes, thus keeping alive the patriclan as an institution for future need.

By no means was the nuclear or joint/extended family or household in Rahmat Abad reduced to a matter of contract. The family continued to hold emotional sway over its members. When urgent, many patriclans could act quickly in concord. Sympathetic, playful, warm, and self-consciously autonomous, these family units nurtured their members, awarded them deep respect, demanded their contributions, and defended them. But the family head could claim undisputed authority only through wisdom.

Central to the thesis of this study is the organizational strength of the corporate village. Based on *functional* and *objectively defined* ties like communally held land and communal defense—Durkheim's territorial principle—the integrity of this local unit enabled the rural culture to evolve beyond the kin-based principle of social, economic, and political linkage to *impersonal* organizational principles. As the overarching environment of *the region* became more secure, the nuclear family disembedded itself from the larger kin matrix. Kin relationships remained and could be mobilized, but when individuals and nuclear families wanted to create new organizational forms, they were no longer restricted to linking with kinsmen, a bonding which inevitably brings with it personalistic demands.

Social and Economic Mobility

The flexibility of clearly bounded, pragmatic organizational forms, both kin and non-kin, as well as the open, contractual environment in Rahmat Abad's intervillage region offered many opportunities for economic and social mobility, and had done so for decades. While Rahmat Abad embraced no class stratification, families were ranked along a spectrum of considerable differences in wealth. It is impossible to speculate to what extent this was due to the relative prosperity of the postwar period, or even to land reform. Within Rahmat Abad, according to my estimates, annual family income in cash ranged from $550 to $4,500, excluding households of one person (widows). On the other hand, the village strongly suppressed evidence of such a gap, channeling to the city many of the manifestations of wealth. The primary indicators of real prosperity that were visible to the public in Rahmat Abad comprised the three vehicles (each owned, of course, by a number of partners), sheep, and the size of one's compound (not its contents). The first two indicators were in themselves productive and as symbols of prosperity encouraged productivity. The community allowed little ostentation in clothes or the frequency and style of entertainment. Without electricity no one could show off an appliance. Families of medium incomes invested more in education than did the most affluent.

Admittedly, those who had settled in Rahmat Abad more recently, poorer families, and several who still claimed tribal associations lived on the fringes of the village while some of the more prominent families had secured house plots toward the center. But the former experienced no segregation whatsoever in village functions, not even in decision making that affected the community as a whole; two boys in a poor household had landed the best urban jobs among those few who now and then commuted from the village. Four of the six families retaining ethnic identification—Arabic, Bakhtiari, and Lur—held land. The poorest family in Rahmat Abad took pride in an urban relative who visited regularly on the most expensive motorcycle anyone had ever seen, parking it, of course, in a conspicuous place. Such a man of means could be called on.

Because it was so easy to enter into reliable partnerships with others of complementary resources, throughout its recent history Rahmat Abad had witnessed very dynamic movement among families (given, of course, its own standards of wealth). Of the six wealthiest men in the village in 1973, as young boys two had earned their livelihood as shepherds, not for the family's sheep but for those of others; another prosperous villager, orphaned when a young man, had been left with but a *joft* of land to support a large family of brothers and sisters as well as the wife and several children of a deceased uncle. The headman inherited his wealth from his late father, but the latter had been born in a forlorn settlement of wattle huts in a river wash to the south, where even in 1974 his family recognized a host of miserable relatives.

Villagers let their accomplishments be known, but these showed the continual process of moving upward. Reza, who with the help of a teenage sister supported a family of six, had worked with extraordinary perseverance since his father's blindness three years prior to the study; they had sent a younger brother and sister through primary school, moved the family into a new three-room home with a separate stall for the cow, built a house for Reza next door, and before finding a wife to complete it endowed it with a cement floor, tin door, windows, gas stove, and a metal clothes cabinet. Through this family's industry, they made almost the same profit on a half share of village land as many farmers did on a full share. Success in Rahmat Abad depended not on birth and connections but on one's hard work and acquired skills.

Not everyone moved up. Families incurring debts due to poor harvests, expensive celebrations, or prolonged illness stood on the brink of a downward spiral. A serious cause of economic decline was the failure to give birth to a son, or even the delay in doing so, as labor was relatively expensive during peak periods. Still, families suffering such hardships remained independent. People made jobs for them and their children. A wealthier housewife might send grain after harvest, but Rahmat Abad knew neither indentured labor nor charity. The worst fate anyone could imagine was to be poor in Dezful. Knowing that, two poor families of villages being expropriated by the State applied for permission to move to Rahmat Abad, and were welcomed there.

Most successful men attributed their rise to more than simply hard work; they had snatched the opportunity to make a *sharik,* a partnership of reciprocal benefit. Shepherding, the most arduous job in the village because of its high risks and the shepherd's exposure to the weather, was a typical example of such a partnership. Most shepherds were landless, but the job promised high rewards since the shepherd was often paid in lambs. The most prosperous families in the village had become wealthy from herds, so it is no wonder the villagers believe that at the Last Judgment the Chosen Ones will ride over the bridge into Paradise on the backs of sheep!

After land reform and despite its prohibitions, subrenting began to flourish, as poorer families formed *sharik*s with those who, like the headman, had more land than they could manage well. In other *sharik*s some of the landless and those with small holdings proposed joint schemes with landlords who retained parcels of land in the surrounding countryside; sons of poorer families quickly spotted the tractor-driving jobs. Murad, for example, vigorously sought out *sharik*s, and his hard work never cost him the villagers' respect as it would have in town: In the literacy class he persuaded the justice corpsman to teach him to chant the Qur'an for religious occasions, which gave him prominence and an aura of learning. When *dulat* built its road, he worked overtime for free in exchange for a culvert blueprint the foreman gave him along with instructions for supervising parts of its construction. As a tractor driver, he volunteered for the unpopular jobs far from home, where he could look for other employment opportunities—and the best wife he could find in the region. We will return to the *sharik* form of economic organization in Chapter 4. The schoolchildren reflected this spirit of hustling in keen competition over their schoolwork, older siblings challenging those who followed them to match or surpass the grades they had made. Many children cried for days when told they could not continue on to junior high school.

Primarily through these *sharik* linkings the poorer villagers moved upward, hitch by hitch, turning to their advantage the great variety of different households' resources and complementary needs. At the same time, village culture assumed that, except in the case of unavoidable bad fortune, poor kinsmen would be ashamed to expect those moving upward to support them: And the latter felt no obligation to do so over any extended period of time. The very process we have been observing enabled individual nuclear families to "declare" their terms of independence quite specifically, independence both from relying on the patriclan for support and from having to share gains with it.

Rahmat Abad and Dezful Families Contrasted

Thus the most elementary structure of social life in the village was the nuclear family and household, which could join into extended or joint families or households when need be but also assured individuals freedom from the encumbrance of kinship and access to a wide scope for linking with non-kinsmen. Village culture encouraged these links because they allowed greater mobility and autonomy. Above all, while the nuclear family nurtured its members with love, respect, protection, and sustenance, its hallmark was its objectivity, which combined sparseness with an explicitness of relational terms. In this economy and clarity, the village family contrasted sharply with its urban counterpart. A consideration of this contrast helps throw the distinctive characteristics of the former in relief.

The Dezful families I came to know and discuss with the villagers typically sprawled as unbounded archipelagoes of networks and personalistic claims reckoned to distant degrees of real and fictive kinship. Facing the opportunities the villagers saw about them in the 1970s, most village families *trimmed* the scope of their personalistic ties to gain greater independence. In an opposite dynamic the urban family *burgeoned:* The key to success within *dulat*'s domain was not self-reliance but the personal power that bonded others to oneself or the other way around. People villagers visited in Dezful spent a large part of their time personalizing subtle forms of dependence; they liked to imagine being able to activate for assistance relatives they claimed to have in the United Nations "office" in America, the "university of Germany," Mecca, Tehran, and, of course, the nearby provincial cities, like a vast extended family. "We get ahead by plowing the field with care," explained Reza; "they get ahead by plowing and planting family." After all, didn't the Shah at the apex of urban society spend millions of dollars trying to establish his royal pedigree of 2,500 years since the founding of the empire of Darius? What townsman could reject as his ideal such a vast entourage of kin?

Prosperity in urban Iran enhanced the cast of personalism—whom one knew and whom one could call kinsman—while the same relative prosperity of the 1960s and 1970s led Rahmat Abad's villagers to free themselves of all-encompassing relations and to forge more impersonal or non-kin links.

At the same time, within the extended family and its affinal links, Rahmat Abad farmers created many clearly specified, often short-term partnerships; indeed, they frequently subjected even the nuclear family to bargaining over specific terms for particular arrangements. To protect their independence, whenever possible they made interdependence explicit. In contrast, since urban families sought vague, generalized obligations of kinship even when these increased the individual's own involvement, they avoided *explicit conditions* for commitment, and certainly the suggestion of *self-reliance,* just the values village families emphasized. As we have seen, the villagers frequently negotiated with authority figures in the family; each step in Muhammad's separation from his father was an effort, although painful, openly to clarify the locus of authority on specific matters. In contrast, their urban counterparts *diffused family power* among many "uncles," "Tehranis," and illusive authorities one never met.

The urban family in its *undefinable spread* and *shifting authority* precluded the public articulation of its form and members. A local Peace

Corps volunteer who made a family tree of one lower-middle-class Dezful family could never get agreement as to who was "in" or "out," but he still ended up with a more definite picture of the outline and contents of what they called their "family" than anyone on the chart had in mind. Those few village men who were employed in Dezful only reluctantly took on informal odd jobs, and they avoided performing favors or services for townsmen for which they expected recompense, because when they wanted to settle an account it often seemed impossible to ascertain who was the functioning head of a family! Madar-i-Karim contrasted the tangible and visible village family with the amorphous family in Dezful, which she considered deliberately clouded in secrecy: "The gates of our compounds are open for everyone to look in and come in; everyone, even peddlers, knows who we are and what we are up to. In Dezful the family, whoever it comprises, gathers and does its business behind closed doors." We will return to this contrast in Chapter 5, where an elaboration of this contrast will shed further light on Rahmat Abad's corporate social character.

The family and household units of Rahmat Abad, the *sharik* partnerships and joint ventures, the communal undertakings, and the village as a polity each defined itself as a social unit with a clear, pragmatic purpose; this purpose gave each its integrity and allowed others within the public arena to hold it accountable. In providing an underlying predictable order, the corporate village both enabled and required the integrity of its constituent social structures. Either through individual action or by organizing with others, villagers had the ability, in their own hands, to control the social conditions which affected their achieving their purposes; without that control they would have given them up as illusions. It was the predictability and substantive, autonomous direction in Rahmat Abad and in the surrounding region that made it possible for villagers to turn outward from subjective personalistic bonds toward contractual links in mutually complementary enterprises, even to see family itself in these terms. The villagers' friends in Dezful lacked this corporate foundation with its predictability and local control.

Amongst the faithful are men who have been true to their covenant with God, and there are some who have fulfilled their vow, and some who wait and have not changed with fickleness.
—Qur'an, Sura 33

Chapter 3

Political Structures
in Rahmat Abad

**The sheep are not for the shepherd, 'tis the shepherd who is for
the sake of the sheep.**   **—Sa'di, from *The Gulistan***

When the cry "Thieves!" shattered the still of the night, Rahmat Abad
would spring against the invader as a single force. The great compound
gates were thrown open, the vanguard of dogs plunged forth, donkeys
brayed, cocks flew to the trees, the men and boys raced into the fields and
wasteland beyond in pursuit of any figure they could spy through the
darkness. The women, infants in arms, took to the rooftops for surveillance; older children slipped through the sesame on reconnaissance.
Shaken from deep slumber, every living being strained in concert not just
to protect Rahmat Abad but to capture and punish its enemies once and
for all. "Allahu Akbar—God is Great!"

Defense of Rahmat Abad was extremely risky: Thieves fell upon the
village heavily armed, while the peasants had only one rifle among them.
One villager I met had been blinded in both eyes defending his village
from thieves. Especially in summer when the day's work was exhausting,
alarms might rouse the settlement four or five nights in a row. The
thieves' main target was the wealthier families' sheep, but the village men
risked their lives because they considered an attack on anyone an attack
on all.

Collective defense was the villagers' definition of social integrity. They
taught each new generation of Rahmat Abad, as they taught me, that
moral decay began, geographically, precisely where a few miles before
reaching town after passing Bonvar, the last community with corporate
security, we came to the first villages in which each household had to
protect itself on its own. From that point on was the Town, *dulat,* moral
dissolution, and above all society that had no knowledge of collective
defense.

What compelled people to defend Rahmat Abad's society (but not Dezful's dormitory villages); to define and preserve Rahmat Abad's discrete
family boundaries (but not those of urban families; and to keep intact
Rahmat Abad's ancient *joft* system (although not, presumably, arrange-

ments that bureaucrats had inherited) was the community's moral order. That, in turn, derived from its autonomy.

The substance of Rahmat Abad's social life grew out of daily interaction—picking cucumbers with Avdah, borrowing yogurt starter from Shiri, buying green thread in town for Maryam, teaming with Rajab season after season to use his old brown mare, admiring Fatimah and marrying her. In their individual as well as communal undertakings, the villagers worked alongside each other without avoiding or discriminating against particular families. The women doing their washing congregated along the canal mainly according to what they were washing and who needed to borrow soap from someone else, not in permanent cliques. In communal feasts and meetings, I compiled over thirty-five seating charts throughout the year, which show the men sitting next to many different friends and neighbors, almost randomly. Villagers gathered spontaneously around a visiting darvesh preacher with his colorful canvas illustrating the events of early Islam, or around the dramatic productions at a wedding: Age and gender determined their clusters, but otherwise those who arrived at the same time stood side by side (which is how groups were formed in village dancing). These unconscious configurations for relaxation reflected the matter-of-fact character and the integration of Rahmat Abad's social life.

Rahmat Abad was not a village rent into factions, although quite predictably certain recurring controversies elicited the same camps on each side, time and time again. If a fight in the village escalated to violence, that meant fisticuffs, nothing more, never involving more than several individuals. Members of the antagonists' immediate families remained aloof, entering only to drag home the combatants. The region's recent history recorded no salient rural feuds. To the contrary, relatives and friends of a troublemaker publicized their embarrassment. Between certain villagers animosity did persist for many years; a few violated the community's rule that, at the minimum, individuals and families should remain on speaking terms. But villagers regarded warily those known as chronic troublemakers; especially the neighbors and age-mates of troublemakers did. To run to the gendarmerie was a public act of betrayal, both a breach of communal faith and stupidity. ("Robbers at night, gendarmes in the day—don't let them in to look the place over.") The villagers asserted proudly—although somewhat inaccurately—that no police had ever set foot in the new Rahmat Abad.

Thus through the decades, the generations, the villagers' initiatives and purposes shuttled their daily interaction back and forth, back and forth across one another's strands. Following patterns their own traditions had given them, and instructed by Rahmat Abad's custom, the villagers had woven the community fabric—and kept weaving it—by going about getting their daily projects done. A variety of such large and small enterprises, ends in themselves, brought forth Rahmat Abad's public arena;

nothing external to the village brought it into existence or gave it its constitution, not even the landlord.

Community would not have taken the shape of commonwealth without political life: those seasons of debate whether to plant clover or barley, those decades of trying to rein in corrupt headmen, those years—those generations—of struggling to transcend factionalism, the landlords' divide-and-rule, those evenings spent weighing small policy alternatives that constantly arose in village governance.

One would not find the village polity by calling a meeting as *dulat* was wont to do; such a well-knit community conducted most of its business informally. Fortunately, no villager, not even the most prominent ones, had an opinion on every issue; most people preferred to leave governance to the few, unless especially aroused by a question. In that case the men and women concerned would lobby for their position informally for a few days, testing public opinion and forming it. In the bean field, a farmer or his wife might bring up the matter with others nearby; when a woman saw a discussion underway at the cross street, she would pass by on an impromptu trip to the canal and speak out vigorously. If a disquieting tension filled the air, someone from each family—usually a man—went to Musa the headman's teapot circle after dinner in the evening, where decisions often crystallized. (Some villagers nicknamed such an evening session Rahmat Abad's "Little Parliament"—*majlis*—as though the village could learn parliamentary democracy from the model Tehran offered!) At the *majlis* a spokesman would informally represent each family that wanted a say; if family members did not agree on an issue, each spoke on his own behalf.

Villagers found many ways to participate in political life. Women often pressured their brothers or sons or husbands; they had gossip and ridicule at their disposal, too. In the vegetable fields or on the threshing floor, they brought up public discussions. Fawziyah talked loudly over her fence; Madar-i-'Ali would seek out Musa directly or any other man involved in the affair. The landless voiced their views when a question affected them. Nothing held back one widow skilled in synthesizing opinions and sharp in oratory. Even the children had something to say in the streets.

The political life of Rahmat Abad saw few *arguments* in the public forum. Rather, through the process of confirming the facts and reviewing the pros and cons, villagers with a stake in an issue sorted out its details and began to form a consensus around those who assumed leadership. By no means the same people in each issue, such figures were never limited to the wealthy or elders. Good politicians might push a question into the public arena in one year so that the following year it might gain acceptance. Time and repetition could deepen consideration. Villagers guarded their independence. A single strong veto removed any matter from the community's agenda. Rahmat Abad appreciated with caution the nuances of participation, being extremely sensitive to power. Because the village—close to the margin of subsistence, in its eyes—had work to get done, and a pragmatic understanding of what that was, politics retained an impersonal detachment: No matter that Abul's silence raised suspicions, he got the canal opened on time so he was the man to take charge.

Direct feedback into the public arena usually assured more accurate information and a wider range of considerations than had existed at the outset of a discussion. Haydar could remember what the community did the last time someone blocked its canal; four of Sakineh's children attended school so she knew accurately how often the teacher had been absent; Amir had a cousin in Da'iji who had discovered a new pesticide effective against worms; Murtaza warned the village against a town merchant he knew who was offering a marketing bargain. Usually people with a special interest in an undertaking provided the leadership for organizing it, and often even the necessary materials: Hosein arranged for the minibus to go on the pilgrimage to Shah 'Abbas; Mahmut bought the wooden supports for the bridge over *dulat*'s canal; Madar-i-Haji told the birth control ladies never to come back, when everyone else was afraid to confront them; Mullah, a religious man, maintained a beautifully kept room for Moharram events at his own expense. Rahmat Abad received these initiatives openly—indeed, what was the village but their cumulative effect?

A sample of policy issues that the community had to settle in 1973 included internal economic, religious, demographic, and technical questions; routine undertakings such as scheduling, arranging, even financing communal events; and matters of foreign policy toward outsiders or *dulat*. In the space of a single year Rahmat Abad had to determine whether to tax each household to purchase a bullhorn loudspeaker; whether to build a bridge over one canal; whether to share irrigation water with a neighboring village and, if so, how much and when; whether to allow gypsy dancers to perform for the King's birthday celebration that the State required, even though it fell during village mourning; how to handle the village cowherd's inflationary prices; what amount of rice to plant and which transplanters to employ communally; whether to let darvesh beggars from town drive their new pickup truck right onto the threshing floor for collection on the spot!; how much of a monthly bribe to pay *dulat*'s irrigation engineer through the summer; whom to hire as a "dog-foot" to keep wild pigs out of the rice; how to allocate tractor time; how to wangle out of exploitation by the State justice corpsman without being offensive; what to do about thieves; whether to hire a more expensive mullah for Moharram; whether to permit a new family to immigrate; and how to make peace between the village truck's driver and an insulting but important man in a nearby village, so that the truck could resume servicing that village.

When the villagers had constructed the new Rahmat Abad, they had established zoning laws (no orchards or even canals for domestic water within the village); noise pollution rules (no loud radios after dark); a village plan (no extension of buildings into the wide streets); and an educational program (coeducation covering five grades, the school open to children of all families regardless of their ability to help pay the teacher, who before 1971 was recruited and paid by the villagers). These policies had to be maintained. Community welfare assured that no one went hungry and that victims of house fires could start life afresh. *Joft*holders had to carry out their *bildar*s. Through Rahmat Abad's political arena flowed a thousand visible, concrete events that had to be performed, watched, and evaluated: not just matters for gossip, but the day-to-day running of this autonomous settlement. What was at stake, whether trivial or crucial, fell entirely in the hands of the community; neither in 1973 nor even before land reform was there anyone else trustworthy to fall back on.

The Headman

Tentative political structures were beginning to appear in Rahmat Abad—spokesmen for the larger families, commissions for particular purposes, minor village officials. While the public arena needed no formal appointments for it to function in good order, Rahmat Abad did strongly support its headman, Musa. Villagers traced the office of headman to the landlord, but millennia ago on these same Mesopotamian slopes a Neolithic settlement would probably have brought forth a similar office on its own, since the headman served many necessary functions. Indeed, just as *dulat* had abolished the *joft* system at land reform, so had it proclaimed the village headman displaced by the President of its new State farm cooperative (or so Rahmat Abad understood).* And just as Rahmat Abad had retained the *joft* system anyway, so, too, had it retained its headman. Each *joft* paid him 900 pounds of rice and wheat annually for his services. The village and its headman had made an important transition: Whereas earlier the headman accounted upward to the landlord, he now accounted to his constituents, the villagers themselves.

While Musa performed his services informally, and various men could have done most of them just as well, yet an *office* of headman was indispensable as a focal point for organizing community affairs and articulating community decisions, both internally and to the outside. A young man in his twenties, Musa had few specialized resources and skills, only those that pertained to Rahmat Abad's external affairs—his ability to read, his expertise in dealing with townsmen and *dulat*, and the valuable

---

*Elsewhere in Iran the State appears to have retained the headman as well as inventing the new office of President, trying to co-opt both, although reports based on empirical evidence rather than official rules are scarce. It is possible that, expecting rural unrest in the DIP and mindful of Dezful's elites' notorious opposition to the Shah, the State went to special lengths to destroy the traditional village leaders' institutional legitimacy as well as any lingering ties with urban landlords.

contacts he inherited from his father. Several other families could have approximated these, if not matched them. Since Musa owned the largest block of shares in the village land, self-interest frequently motivated his performance, which the pragmatic villagers considered all to their gain because they did not fear his unchecked power. Musa rarely reached a community decision alone, and even as he carried out his tasks he tapped other villagers to accompany or help him. Others often took initiative in questions to which Musa had not responded. Certain older men bore the responsibility of authority in disputes or matters requiring decisive leadership, for Musa lacked forcefulness. Consistent with Rahmat Abad's pragmatism, Musa was a leader among equals.

The headman had not always been that, of course. Before the land reform, the headman had held an office of controversy and prestige as the landlord's henchman-in-residence, and therefore as representative of the State. Yet no headman ever knew security. Often the landlord or several of them would appoint opposing headmen simultaneously, to play local powers off against one another. In 1973 the residue of these generations of political enmity among Rahmat Abad's leaders remained (although some of the major figures had died). Villagers could vividly re-create their former struggles when asked. But despite such a long history, the speed with which these former rivals and their families welded together a united vilage leadership (once the outside left them alone) testified to these men's intelligence, civic imagination, and self-discipline, and to Rahmat Abad's practical grasp of its post-land-reform challenge.

At the time of land reform, Musa's father had held the headman's office by himself for several years. Since landlords had resided off in distant Dezful—indeed, had frequently feared entering the countryside—and since most issues in the village had not directly affected the landlord's interests anyway, it is impossible to know to what extent Mash-hadi 'Abdul (Musa's father) had owed his former authority to the landlord, to the local order embodied in his office, or even to the villagers' acceptance of him, personally, as a leader. Their subsequent confirmation of the office's necessity and benefits suggests that scholars who attribute the authority of village headmen before the land reform entirely to the landlord may be mistaken. Still, the day could arrive when villagers would demand a change of hands. This community suffered no lack of skilled leaders.

Mash-hadi 'Abdul had been a man of the time for Rahmat Abad, perhaps a man of subtle charisma. He had played a major role in inspiring the community to build the new village, and in developing workable plans for it, although many villages in Iran did likewise at that time. Not without detractors, however, Mash-hadi 'Abdul soon after the move had become involved in a dispute in Rahmat Abad, accused of complicity with thieves. Under great pressure from his accusers, Mash-hadi 'Abdul had agreed to swear an oath of innocence at one of the peasants' favorite shrines in Dezful, the only time in village memory that recourse had been taken to such a drastic measure. How else could Rahmat Abad try its own governor when need be, then or in the future? Rahmat Abad's new "constitution" was tested almost at birth. By vowing before God and adversaries, Mash-hadi 'Abdul had acquitted himself. Two weeks later death inexplicably laid hand on him in his cucumber field, apparently from a stroke. He had been ill; doctors had warned him to avoid overwork; but to a few villagers his death had confirmed his guilt and punished a false oath.

Whatever the truth of the matter, the weight of the office had made the incumbent highly vulnerable to the community's new standard of official morality and accountability. Perhaps Mash-hadi 'Abdul had accomplished too much, sparking a minirevolt against him to usher in the new order. Perhaps once he had steered the village to new ground, it had had to retire him so that its new democracy and self-direction could start on a fresh basis. In Musa it found an ideal transitional figure and compromise, keeping Mash-hadi 'Abdul's name—not betraying their loyalty to him—and practical assets, but retaining these in a hesitant young man upon whom the elders repeatedly impressed the fact that he was "no one," and that, after all, according to *dulat* there was no headman.

In the villagers' eyes the headman answered to no one on the outside, because now there *was* no one to answer to on the outside. (Admittedly, Musa should deal with *dulat* when *dulat* demanded—somewhat as a foreign power!) Because the headman was now subject to local control, at the time of land reform the position acquired greater legitimacy; it now fully belonged to the village. Since the headman had a large stake in the community's welfare and had always essentially been of the community himself, this legitimacy followed quite naturally once the landlord was removed, especially since Musa's family did not perpetuate any substantive private ties with the landlord. Previously the headman had funneled outside demands downward onto the village; now he would coordinate the village's needs and demands, if necessary, upward.

That was precisely what *dulat* feared. Because the office of headman was so intermeshed with the ancient, organic forms of grass-roots rural society; and because almost automatically the villagers turned it into a vehicle and symbol of their autonomy, the Shah's "White Revolution" that proclaimed land reform had at the very same time to destroy the authority of any representative the self-incorporated free farmers might appoint for themselves. If the village kept the headman accountable, it could focus its identity and initiative all too effectively through him (as Rahmat Abad did when it constructed Throne City). Should this go on very long, out in the impenetrable *biyaban*, the rural wasteland, "like mushrooms or frogs after a rain, villages with their own ideas might spring up everywhere!" one technocrat panicked. Then how would *dulat* establish *its* rule over Rahmat Abad when it decided it wanted to?

Thus at the time of the land reform, the Shah's White Revolution of rural programs officially obliterated the very name by which local history had identified this settlement from time immemorial, "Rahmat Abad," and imposed on it a name in the State's own image, King Darius the Great Rural Cooperative. Then with a flourish of antilandlord propaganda, *dulat* replaced the village's office of headman, a political embodiment of ancient "Rahmat Abad," with a populous Village Council plus an equally large Directorate of the King Darius the Great Rural Cooperative—intending to disperse village power as the landlord had often done, but going beyond that to trivialize it. These creations of the White Revolution do not concern us any further here in our examination of the community's political organization, because in 1973 *dulat* was not serious about running Rahmat Abad; it had its hands full elsewhere in northern Khuzestan. So when the bureaucrats' jeeps had departed, Rahmat Abad had resumed normal life as time-honored Rahmat Abad, reinstating the office of headman as an institution vital to Rahmat Abad's survival. Periodically, Musa gathered everyone together for some reelection or other that the New Order was coming to the village to sponsor; a few minutes before the bureaucrats arrived, on each occasion he would dash around with notes he had taken at the previous election, reminding each villager which title he currently held in which staff of the White Revolution's exalted governments! At Rahmat Abad's cross street by the chanar tree, this ritual to the White Revolution, stage managed by Musa whose authority the White Revolution had made extinct, dramatized the vast gap between village realities and *dulat's* gestures to establish claim over them.

As for carrying out the office of headman, what had happened to Musa's father must have left an imprint on the young man's interpretation of the office. Intelligent, earnest, and respectful, he listened to correction or suggestion. Like many of the middle-aged men in Rahmat Abad, Musa frequently kept his thoughts to himself, but with the assurance he derived from his family's assets and a five-year schooling, he was easily accessible. Villagers—including the women—approached him on countless matters with opinions, requests, and complaints. He accepted his elders' counsel even when he had not asked for it, but more frequently he actively sought advice and tried to form a consensus.

Musa lacked that ripeness characteristic of the older villagers and even of some men his age who had assumed responsibility earlier than he had. His quick smile suggested wistfulness, although tinged with uncertainty or even slight cynicism, which must have partly accounted for people associating him with the Iranian Arabs of his father's ancestry. Slightly built but hardly frail, Musa alone among the young men of the village unabashedly acknowledged physical weakness; and so (haunted by his father's death?), he usually watched from the sidelines the others' sportive tests of endurance. In village terms, that fittingly underlined his relationship to the community's strength.

Though Musa never shirked responsibility, I noticed him slip away on his own as though in need of finding himself, the only villager I knew who deliberately—yet unobtrusively—put himself apart from companionship for recreational moments. In a culture that feared solitude, he would ride to town by himself on his motorcycle without waiting to find a companion, irrigate the beans alone late in the evening, draw out his prayers twice as long as need be when company had come, sneak away to hunt birds beyond the village fields, not asking a friend to come along.

As was the case with Musa's father, villagers distinguished between Musa the man and the headman's office, undefined as the position was, outlined by unexpected needs that arose and by Musa's own ad hoc initiatives. Some villagers recognized that he had a hard job to learn and would make mistakes. As it was, there was little the headman could do unnoticed to use the office for personal benefit at the community's expense (*that* had not been the charge against his father). Musa had to have leeway—but not too much.

Musa's mother, whose compound Musa inherited upon his father's death, the compound where so much of Rahmat Abad's political interaction took place, lent decorum to the young man and his office. Wielding influence over him, old Ashraf complemented Musa in age, gender, and disposition; the villagers respected her as a ballast and firm rudder to the ship. Sensible—indeed, shrewd—formal, and polite although capable of deviousness, quietly compassionate, thoughtful, and fair about matters outside her family, Ashraf could appear the retiring matron serving her eldest son, or a vigilant lady of iron.

Fulfilling a central part of the headman's job, Ashraf kept open house day and night in their large home right at the village cross corners, reassuring each visitor with hospitality measured according to the changing nuances of presence and occasion. When an outsider arrived with a few well-dressed cronies, the best carpet would be laid out under the portico, the silver-plated sugar bowl would be scrubbed sparkling clean with sand, Musa would be summoned from the fields, and a chicken would be killed for lunch. Then the same acquaintance might come again by himself, clearly no business at hand, to be greeted on gunny sacks in the open yard, the children allowed to urge him into rough-house, Ashraf not interrupting her work of cleaning grain or sorting beans. He would be offered a water pipe. Cordial but offhandedly domestic, Ashraf would learn more from him in a casual setting. Thus under Ashraf's invitation—and direction—the gate of her compound issued into Rahmat Abad's public arena. Expertly, she gauged each innuendo of official protocol.

Mourning for Mash-hadi 'Abdul had reached every corner of this intervillage region; Rahmat Abad honored him by a two-year moratorium on public celebration; even a year after his death people came from miles and miles around for memorial feasts. Rising to fulfill his legacy may have brought out latent qualitites that Ashraf had not developed before. Now a prominent widow, she carried herself ceremoniously in her mourning clothes, which to the unfamiliar disguised her activism. But in the morning you could find her poking around the truck that was loading for town; during the day, on the threshing floor supervising the family and hired hands there, at the canal doing the dishes, or on the roof drying out rice (and keeping check on the universe); in the evening, following alertly the discussions around her teapot, which drew every male villager to it at some time or another. A public guardian, Ashraf would have denied being called a public figure.

For, in the hot mid-afternoon, in the lull between chores and politics, Ashraf's prerogative as an old widow was to nourish her brooding upon her late husband's "empty place" and upon the events of life that flowed into it. With her water pipe, it was hers to ruminate, commingling pity and pride. His witness—no one could share this with her. In this way she completed their relationship. In this way, too, she gave solemnity to Musa's office, the office of headman of Rahmat Abad. As Musa and others solved its problems, its disputes, met its new challenges, paid its debts, and repaired its canals, Ashraf presided over the forms of the office, attentive to dress and seating arrangements and well-trained attendants. She kept its ritual.

Rahmat Abad delicately poised the office of headman against Musa's dispensability. Had the villagers dismissed him, perhaps with old resentments surfacing again, the Little Parliament would have moved to another evening teapot, visitors and bureaucrats to another silver-plated sugar bowl. The White Revolution's New Order could not comprehend this organic dimension of the position, which gave Rahmat Abad a formal overarching unity.

As headman, Musa held responsibilities to three levels of the social order: to individual constituents and their families (who mainly needed his urban resources); to the village as a whole in internal affairs (in which it tapped his coordinating and leadership abilities); and to the village and the State when they dealt with one another. Sometimes Musa was called upon to mediate between the village as a whole and other villages or townsmen.

First, the favors he performed for individuals and families. When a villager's affairs required going to other villages in the region, he or she rarely needed the headman, because the rural region comprised a coherent social fabric for peasants within it. But villagers constantly needed the headman to mediate between them and the *urban* world. As the village modernized, Musa's cumulative contacts in town increased in substance and diversity, and in their importance to Rahmat Abad; this was especially true since Iran's urban culture depended so heavily on subjective, personalistic bonds rather than on those related to market values, job achievement, a bureaucracy's written regulations or procedures, personal attributes, or other objective criteria. For instance, when a village widow's house burned, Musa secured a reduction in the $60 bribe the statistics official demanded for replacing her and her children's identification papers (which were necessary for admission to everything of *dulat*'s, from schools to cemeteries). When the army drafted a young man supporting his family of six, Musa helped him claim exemption by getting

his blind old father admitted to a clinic every Wednesday for eight consecutive weeks until a ponderous consortium of doctors agreed to certify
that the old man was, in fact, blind. When a villager required an emergency operation and was told all hospital beds in Dezful were occupied,
Musa found a vacant one permanently reserved in case a certain army
doctor would need it for his private practice. In Rahmat Abad's predilec-
tion for playing with language, the villagers had named Dezful *daste
pul*—a hand grasping for money. Musa could soften the grip.

In addition to Musa's contacts with those who could affect the control
of such resources, and his ability to mobilize them, the villagers also
required his support, advice, and encouragement, even his geographical
guidance into the labyrinth of Dezful and *dulat*. Since the villagers operated in such an open-book world of direct relationships and accessible
public information, where most people agreed on basic values and one
could count on help in remedying injustice, Musa had to explain the quite
opposite world of Dezful to them; he often had to prompt them before a
bureaucratic encounter—and after it reassure them of their dignity. Other
villagers, of course, could tap similar resources in town. Several families
in Rahmat Abad frequently assisted villagers as Musa did.

Still, Musa had the widest repertoire of urban associations because he
had inherited so many of them from his father. Contrary to Rahmat
Abad's politics and social relations, the crucial acquaintances and skills
for dealing in town were cumulative ones. Mistrust was so pervasive in
urban affairs, and competition so keen, that not even villagers' own personal networks of shopkeepers, street neighbors of their urban cousins,
assistants they knew in doctors' offices—not even these would offer
advice or protection in the most routine business with *dulat* or in any
unusual bazaar transaction.

The villagers' inability to count on their own urban connections for
dealing in Iran's personalistic urban world was not a result of these
friends' *status*, since the system of interpersonal confidence in Iran is
well-known for spanning class differences. (One of Nasir al-Din Shah's
favorite wives became so through being the attendant of his favorite cat;
one of the most important figures in the Qajar dynasty served the Shah
as a water carrier and at a crucial time assisted his horse on a trail, which
began his career; the great Amir Kabir was the son of the prime minister's
cook. Examples of personal proximity determining who fills positions of
great political power are innumerable, a fact peasants counted on in
mobilizing their connections. See Bill, 1973:784.) At the villagers' level
and for their needs in dealing with Dezful or *dulat*, it was not status that
determined which connections would be useful, but whether personal
claims on one's connections had been seasoned over time—preferably
over *generations*. Thus, far more decisive than money were the relationships Musa's family had built up as part of the family line, their obligations passing from father to sons, even uncle to nephews. Furthermore,
one had to have mastered the skills for using these contacts, skills trans-

mitted only through apprenticeship but guiding adults for years in townsmen's social maze.

The second area of Musa's responsibilities as headman comprised his duties toward the village as a whole, serving as its organizational focus. For these communal services the landholding families paid Musa at harvest time. We have reviewed many of the village undertakings that he led, such as coordinating the division of the village fields into *joft*s, the *bildar*s, and Moharram ceremonies, and arranging employment agreements with those agricultural workers shared by all *joft*holders or all village families (such as the rice transplanters and cowherd). Musa visited everyone who was critically ill and attended all funerals in Rahmat Abad, where he had to sit in a prominent place. Either he or Ashraf headed every party from Rahmat Abad to mourning sessions or memorials in other villages. Musa usually accompanied other villagers from Rahmat Abad when the community had business with neighboring communities, but as with all village affairs such a delegation eventually had to consult widely at home.

Finally, although in judicial matters the authority of certain older men in the community carried more weight than his view, Musa arranged mediation and attempted to ensure that any agreement held. The community's de facto judiciary (as distinct from the White Revolution's "Village Judge") rarely appeared because there were few occasions when it thought it should intervene. Consisting of a handful of respected men most readily available when trouble broke out, the judiciary strictly respected family autonomy and the autonomy of constituent units in managing their internal affairs, only intervening when violence spreading between families made the matter a communal one: twice in my year and a half in Rahmat Abad.

Thirdly, in his capacity as headman Musa performed official functions vis-à-vis *dulat* (notwithstanding the principal Ministries' insistence that on paper they create their new microbureaucracy within Rahmat Abad). Musa supervised the villagers' purchase of fertilizer through the semidormant "cooperative"; he entertained visiting bureaucrats; he helped accommodate the White Revolution corpsmen sent to Rahmat Abad; and he tried to persuade villagers to comply with their often outlandish requests. Musa cajoled the canals commissioner to obtain favorable irrigation and maintenance services once *dulat*'s new canal disrupted the traditional system. He rounded up men to provide urine specimens for the schistosomiasis team, children to receive vaccinations, and women to hear lectures in family planning. Finally, Musa reported to the secret police on anything of interest to them in Rahmat Abad: me (whom he regularly consulted in the matter).

Dulat's dealing with Musa as headman even of a peripheral village revealed some of its interests. When I tallied up the time Musa spent for *dulat* during some seasons, I asked several technocrats why their minis-

tries did not pay him as the landlord had done and as the village continued to do. "If we paid village officials, then even the poor might volunteer
to serve!" they objected. "The wealthy should rule." Although all other
agencies made a pretense of appointing New Order officials in Rahmat
Abad, this was not true of the secret police. They found their own, and
in Rahmat Abad the traditional headman was their man. Like the villagers themselves, SAVAK had little time for White Revolution
propaganda.

We have reviewed the village political arena and the office of headman
that focused its initiatives and controversies. The community knew no
"power" within its own boundaries or within those of the region of villages of which it was a part. Charismatic power was unheard of in the
countryside; even the Arab *shaykh* whom large crowds buried in Dezful
in 1974 was famed for his down-to-earth pragmatism. The villagers suspected anything that might tip a political balance; when we listened to
Ayatollah Khomeini's broadcasts from Iraq, they shook their heads: "He
will fill the streets, Khanom Grace," they worried.

The decades preceding my study in northern Khuzestan offered no evidence that through the preceding years or decades long-lasting factions
had formed within the political arena of Rahmat Abad. Animosities,
yes—but not factions. Karim's family had presented the most sustained,
organized check on Musa's father as headman under the last landlord,
frequently siding with Musa's principal adversary, Ashraf's brother
Hamda, a notorious busybody. But Karim vigorously helped Musa
launch some of the village's major work projects. Before the end of the
second year of my field work, he asked for the headman's oldest sister's
hand in marriage for Karim's dapper brother Hasan. So much for factions. Rivalries and even antagonisms provided checks and balances in
village affairs; they embodied alternatives, and stimulated political
expression. But with the landlord gone, Rahmat Abad's thoughts were no
longer caught up in the quest for power.

On the other hand, whereas the village's ability to steer clear of factions
boded well for its cohesion, a tendency toward the office of headman
becoming hereditary did not. During my acquaintance with Rahmat
Abad, circumstances did not call for testing this possibility, but its danger
remained near the surface. This may explain why villagers warned Musa
now and then that he was no one, and why the story of Mash-hadi 'Abdul
had become a part of their folklore. As we have seen, traditionally the
villagers possessed little wealth that they would pass on to their children;
their poverty contributed to the absence of hereditary political offices in
Rahmat Abad. But villagers knew that within *dulat*'s world personalistic
connections counted far more than individual skills, and therefore the
headman's scarce social resources would increase in value as *dulat* drew
the village into its orbit. In short, those resources that spelled power in
dealing with *dulat* were political resources requiring a long period of

accumulation and attainable only by inheritance, not by hard work or
personal attributes. The more the community opened itself up to the
urban, "modern" sector, the more strongly it would depend on those
assets the headman offered which increased and appreciated (admittedly,
for everyone's benefit) by passing the office from father to son. This did
not reflect the village's own value, but was a necessary concomitant of
integrating into the modern State.

Furthermore, as a community would have to deal more frequently with
dulat, the office of headman would demand more time, no longer an avo-
cation for a yeoman-farmer but only for the wealthy. That was particularly true given the bureaucrats' disdain of peasants in general. Rather
than viewing the marriage of Karim's brother and Musa's sister as the
resolution of a latent friction within the village, a few villagers saw it as
removing one further check against political concentration.

Cases That Clarify Rahmat Abad's Political Structure

To understand more deeply Rahmat Abad's political arena and corporate
integrity, let us glance at three salient cases that arose during my year
there: characteristically, extremely simple cases—almost parables—
because the village's shared tradition enabled directness, and its pragmatic values sought dispatch.

Gholam

Although social pressure within the village generally elicited members'
adherence to communal policies, the free rider problem lurked in the
background. Gholam, an older man with only a half share of land, regularly failed to show up for *bildar*s when work projects were numerous
during the spring of 1973. His two teenage sons left for work in town each
morning. Gholam enjoyed sufficiently good health to go to the fields, and
in consideration for his age would have been allowed to stand by and
watch the work most of the time; but one had to attend. He just stopped
appearing at all. Not a very sociable man, an Arab living on the village
periphery, he would have suffered little inconvenience having to avoid
other villagers for several days after missing a *bildar*. Musa's uncle
Hamda, a neighbor of Gholam's, began to catch the habit of staying
home, too. However, because his house was right at the crossroads where
*bildar*s gathered before setting out, he could be more easily moved by
criticism. Still, the fact that Hamda often tried to follow his neighbor's
pattern worried the *joft*holders. What if others followed?

One day after Gholam had declined to join seven or eight *bildar*s in a
row, Musa, pressured by a disgruntled group on its way to yet another
work project, went to Gholam's house and urged him to come. Gholam
refused to budge. Finally, Musa burst into an insult, guardedly not using

a religious curse but certainly strong language. We left on that day's *bildar* without Gholam. The villagers agreed that Musa had taken the utmost possible measures. A fine or punishment was unthinkable. In fact, Musa later confessed to me that he regretted having even taken the drastic steps that he did. He would never do that again. "Nothing is worth not being able to speak to a fellow villager when you meet him," he explained. He later apologized to Gholam—who, for his part, never changed his mind that year, nor did he ever send a substitute.

The case illustrates the limitations and liabilities of Rahmat Abad's self-governance as long as it remained reluctant to let authority emerge clearly. History and circumstances had led the villagers to intensify and fine-tune horizontal relations among themselves, even prompting them to preserve mechanisms like the *joft* system by which they locked themselves (as it were) into the obligations that the community's horizontal ties carried with them. Most of the time the resulting bonds were sufficiently strong to maintain order in the community, as Hamda illustrated when he gave in. But when they had failed to move Gholam, Musa, sensing an urgency on the spot, had resorted to a solution not normally within the village's political code—indeed, which the village continually rejected in its political affairs: overt personal pressure. Musa insulted Gholam, not so much revealing his inexperience as his lack of any other tools for carrying out the mission the *joft*holders had sent him on. Gholam's case laid bare the fact that when the village's horizontal relations failed, the community had no strong but impersonal vertical bond upon which it could fall back. The authority of the most respected men appeared only on an ad hoc basis to safeguard civil peace; otherwise Rahmat Abad lacked someone who could act decisively and impersonally in its name.

The *joft*holders recognized and worried about the free rider problem. Pragmatically, no one referred to Gholam's laziness, which seemed perfectly natural. No analysis focused on Gholam's personality, age, ethnicity, or personal circumstances, nor did anyone propose making Gholam feel more a part of the community. Not self-pitying about themselves, villagers wasted little sentimentality on others. Certainly they never cited Qur'anic injunctions to perform one's share of the community's work. Rather, many saw clearly on this and other occasions that the village simply needed a stronger authority, someone who could make Gholam turn up for work when he didn't make himself. Once when I asked Karim and his elder brother what would happen if Iran were governed like Rahmat Abad without an autocratic ruler, they replied, "We Iranians can't rule ourselves, Khanom Grace; don't you remember Gholam?" The challenge, then, was how to evolve that authority which some villagers consciously knew they needed, without re-creating a regime like the landlord's or *dulat*'s, which they also determined to avoid.

Throne City's compact was still emerging. The village had evolved institutions for impersonal collaboration, had evolved the norms necessary to support impersonal partnership and responsibility. A community transcending familiar bonds had clearly emerged out of the villagers' sustained interaction with each other; this interaction had already given them a concept of their unity and autonomous polity: Rahmat Abad. Further, their corporate identity had evolved its symbols, its self-conscious history; had indigenized its office of headman. But this emerging incorporation had yet to crystallize at a political level *above* the links that held the villagers together as individuals: in a vertical bond of impersonal authority—a semiformal law—of Rahmat Abad.

But that a mere six years after its independence the village had not reached the political maturity required for its challenge hardly warranted the State taking it over, as most analysts urged immediately after land reform—calling on *dulat,* for instance, to co-opt the village's emergent leaders to make them "decisive" agents of Tehran's designs (Salmanzadeh, 1980; 127–28).

As we have seen in the villagers' monitoring of their headman, they had come to their hard-earned self-governance after land reform deeply wary of any political power, especially power in their midst. To put it positively, they now vigilantly guarded their political equality. The explanation does not lie in their being ideological, which they were not, but rather in their awareness that the village did not yet have the means to check egregious abuses of power. They feared that authority would open the door to political and economic inequality. Better not to raise the possibility at all.

It would take time to evolve the authority that the community needed for cases similar to Gholam's, while at the same time ensuring the mechanisms for holding such authority responsive to the polity. The community would have to face repeated crises, each of which required such a full-fledged office, before Rahmat Abad would begin to consent to its establishment. Even then, only through trial and error, revisions and changes of leadership, would Rahmat Abad be able to bring forth a responsive new organizational level, incorporating hierarchy into its corporate integrity. The village was admirably equipped to meet this challenge—far better equipped than the urban population, whose social organization and political culture had involuted away from an impersonal public order with its expectations of predictability and free information—away, too, from clearly structured social units that could hold others accountable and, in turn, be held accountable themselves. But despite its favorable endowments, Rahmat Abad would not bring forth an accountable governor overnight.

If anything, the Shah's notion of creating the Directorate of King Darius the Great Rural Cooperative or of the State putting its seal on a Village Council set back the community's political development, because the increasing threat of *dulat*'s domination made the emergence of a village hierarchy seem *all the more dangerous,* lest it come under the sway of Tehran's arbitrariness (precisely what those technocrats had in mind who advocated co-opting the village leaders). Only the villagers themselves could combine authority with mechanisms to hold it accountable.

The Aqueduct

Our second case takes us further into Rahmat Abad's political development. In mid-summer of 1973 a major aqueduct that fed a third of the land which the village that year had planted to rice collapsed about six weeks before harvest. To produce a yield, the field had to remain flooded. *Joft*holders had foreseen its possible collapse but had not taken the relatively costly measures needed to prevent this because only when planting rice, with its intensive irrigation requirements, did they need such an expensive structure in that particular field. According to their crop rotation system, it would be some years before they would again sow rice there. So they had hoped the structure would hold, and they had decided to take the risk. When the aqueduct fell in, the *joft*holders estimated they could lose over half the crop in the affected area, despite some relief from a subsidiary canal.

The only feasible solution proposed within the village's available resources was to weld together some fifteen large oil drums opened at both ends, and extend them across a broad drainage gully, propped up by wooden braces thrust into the muddy sand below. Villagers discussed the project for several days and concluded that it looked promising. However, after five long afternoons of *bildar* work, the aqueduct that they had engineered, constructed, and laboriously set in place—breathlessly suspended on the best supports the men could fashion—began to buckle under the weight of the water flowing through it. The villagers invested several more *bildar*s in attempting repairs and firming up the base, but by the middle of the following week the two halves of Rahmat Abad's pipeline lay at the bottom of the gully.

The *joft*holders' strenuous collaboration and their persistence in this project had exemplified one justification of the *joft* system, that by allotting all farmers a plot in every field, the system gave them all a stake in maintaining each field's capital infrastructure. The creativity and drama of the project had also stimulated wide participation. The usual repetition of *bildar* announcements and urging had been unnecessary. Although not every *joft*holder had put in the same amount of time, the project never lacked manpower and brains. Even old men who could not work had turned out day after day in the hot sun to add what they could, holding ropes, offering advice and encouragement, pacing off distances, handing tools. People had contributed in other ways, too—the truck owner had not charged for bringing the welder back and forth to town, old Muhammad had given two gasoline drums he had been hoarding, several villagers had offered beams they had been keeping in reserve for housebuilding. Each shareholder had invested some five to ten dollars in the project and six or eight afternoons of labor. Still, the project had failed.

Musa and Karim, the largest *joft*holders (although not necessarily the ones who would suffer the most from the harvest losses), tried to organize a very credible alternative scheme. They widely advertised and explained their suggested plan, offering to shoulder most of its costs. But they stirred little interest. The farmers probably based their resignation on an estimate of the likely marginal returns to further effort, which justified a more expensive attempt for Musa and Karim who held considerable land, but not for those with smaller shares. But I wondered why the latter two did not simply go ahead on their own? No one would have objected to their carrying out their plan; indeed, everyone would gain! Karim told me he and Musa did not have the "face" to do so. Resolving the problem had to take place in a communal context, even if not on a strictly equal cost-sharing basis, or not be accomplished at all.

Although eager to try their solution, Musa and Karim never bargained with the rest of the *joft*holders over it; only Karim could even articulate what held the two of them back from taking an independent initiative. A delicate balance lay between on the one hand, the wealthy paying more than their share in a village undertaking (quite acceptable), and on the other, their voluntarily assuming major village production costs. They knew and the villagers knew that somehow Rahmat Abad could not authorize the latter (not, at least, in circumstances short of desperation).

Replacing the aqueduct had presented a corporate challenge to the *joft*holders, the classical challenge of irrigating commonly held land. Therefore, no one was to blame for the project's failure. Those who had foreseen the existing irrigation structure's collapse said so without bearing special responsibility; those who had most forcefully put forward the proposal that had been tried had no need to apologize for its failure. Villagers' matter-of-fact values left no room for such subjectivity. What was done was done; everyone assumed responsibility. Next year rice would be in a different field. In the same vein, it would not have occurred to the *joft*holders to ask *dulat* for technical advice or assistance, although the structure that had collapsed had been built by the Ministry of Water and Power. Rahmat Abad took seriously the independence that it had gained at land reform.

Although losing so much rice in the face of a conceivable remedy dispirited everyone, never during my stay in Rahmat Abad did villagers lose their ability to laugh at themselves and others. One night over our family hearth the fiasco inspired Rasoul to tell us how *dulat* commissioned Throne City's engineers to build a great dam (suggestive of the Dez dam that many knew about) under which an unlucky royal prince lay down for a nap on the fifth day after its completion! Echoing the technocrats' claims to indispensability, villagers exclaimed that the kingdom would disappear if left in the hands of engineers like us. *Ya* Allah!—we'd better go back to our donkeys!

To planners and development economists, this incident may substantiate their accusation that peasants' demand for conformity jeopardizes a nation's staple crop production, the improvement of its agricultural infrastructure, and the emergence of its potential entrepreneurs. Like Rahmat Abad's refusal to accept the State's enlightened proscription of the *joft* system, doesn't the aqueduct case suggest the villagers' insistence on communal cohesiveness over economic progress? But attributing mawkish conservatism to the villagers and pitting it against economic considerations deny the political foundation that in the long run economic development requires if it is to be sustained.

The aqueduct case extends the understanding that we had begun to elaborate when we considered Gholam's challenge to the community's lack of hierarchy. When I lived in Rahmat Abad, it had already become apparent to many villagers that social pressure—their strong horizontal bonds—would not suffice for Rahmat Abad's self-governance. The village needed to let its communal endeavors coalesce in a vertical coordinational focus, subject to the community yet embodying and able to assert its authority. Now in this our second case we see such leadership, a latent new level of organizational initiative, trying to emerge. Fearing the implications of letting hierarchy evolve—albeit, its own hierarchy—Rahmat Abad held back.

This is not to suggest that the village was *consciously* afraid of authorizing this emerging differential. Most of the village was aware that leaders like Musa and Karim were vital to the community's prosperity, even to its survival—both cautious men, civic minded, highly responsive to community opinion. In proposing their scheme, neither of these two had threatened the *joft*holders by an overbearing manner. However, even with Rahmat Abad's need for an authority figure entrusted with wider scope than those who settled the occasional dispute, even with its need to encourage good leaders and to grant people with resources and ideas freedom, the village was going to let hierarchy emerge only very gradually, lest its members lose ultimate control over their new-found corporate autonomy. Without a foundation of experience, precedent, "constitutional" norms, institutional changes, and widely disseminated political skills for dealing with a village-authorized authority—that is, without a firm foundation that would prevent domination—the village community was loath to hurry back into the dangers it knew so well, of hierarchy, power, and dependence.

Had Musa and Karim, in solving the village's problem, borne the overwhelming share of the cost, that would imply the *joft*holders' dependence on them. To pragmatic peasants, especially those who have recently won title to their land, what you pay for is yours—or so they hoped. The farmers had been subservient to the landlord for too long now to become subservient to fellow villagers who offered to foot the bill for agricultural infrastructure.

Because the only form of governance villagers had evolved within the new Rahmat Abad was governance by persuasion, one could gain influence over their little commonwealth through symbols of prestige but not through outright power. Signs of effective leadership and of productive wealth constituted symbols that the village awarded with prestige, but again with a hawk eye for proportions lest the balance be tipped. For example, Karim's older brother who had a permanent job as a gardener for *dulat* left his best city clothes in Dezful when he visited Rahmat Abad. Several of his brothers sported digital watches, but the family had to wait for a few others in the village to catch up before bringing out their next display, Rahmat Abad's first brand-new motorcycle. Remember Musa standing on the sidelines when the young men would compete in physical skills?

Rahmat Abad had begun to transform itself economically since land reform; its embracing mechanized agriculture and the cash economy comprised only the most obvious evidence. But its pace required firming up the *political* basis upon which each step was taken, before moving on: keeping prestige and, hence, its symbols in proportion, despite their economic benefits to all. Mullah's assuming virtually all the costs for the comunity's religious meeting room never made the villagers feel uneasy, because religious honor rendered no political or economic claims in Rahmat Abad. On the other hand, while Musa's and Karim's main purpose was not to show superior wealth, nevertheless that *would* have been an inevitable consequence of their saving the rice field on their own—too boldly approximating the symbols of affluence that spelled power in the urban world and the State.

For their part, Musa and Karim did not push their proposal insistently. Perhaps they, too, sensed the community's fear of being dominated by certain individuals before the checks and balances were in place. Certainly they recognized their own dependence on Rahmat Abad; at least Musa was well aware that no family, howsoever wealthy or entrepreneurial, could deal squarely with townsmen and *dulat* unless it could count on the support of the community. Although they would have liked to have carried out their scheme, both concurred with the *joft*holders' restraint.

In as much as the integrity of the community came out of and flowed from *joint* initiatives and joint responsibility, in as much as *common enterprise* gave Rahmat Abad structure, progressive members had to move the others along with them. They need not always wait for total agreement, but a major undertaking should affirm the combined initiative of the village, and it could not do so if most families gave only passive consent to it. The polity of Rahmat Abad had to mature at its own speed, through discussion, failures, learning certain broad lessons together. The precocious economic advance of certain individual members could jeopardize that political development.

It was not the evidence of an *economic* differential between Musa and Karim on the one hand, and many of the *joft*holders on the other, which made the community restrain the former. The burst of prosperity after land reform testified to the fact that they could all raise their standard of living together, that one family's gain did not require another's loss. Rahmat Abad's conservatism was political, not economic: Surely their investing in two tractors, the pickup, ten secondhand motorcycles, twenty bicycles, five insecticide spray tanks, thirty radios, thirty gas cooking units, ten new watches, and two sewing machines in the few years since land reform attested to their economic openness, as did their quick adoption of fertilizer, and their experiments in planting grapes, cotton, strawberries, Mexican wheat, limes, pomegranates, and my popcorn! Rather, it was this very economic openness and aggressiveness of theirs which sharpened the haunting question: how to uncouple Rahmat Abad's hard-won new political equality from these economic resources and symbols of prestige that were beginning to flood in . . . and to which the urban world attached power.

In the aqueduct case, we see Rahmat Abad's understandable worry that what it had gained in land reform it could all too easily give away. How could the community allow the higher level of governance it needed to emerge without reverting back to the old order of landlord power, the power and claims of the rich? Even though progresssive and civic-minded fellow villagers might constitute the emerging hierarchy, how could the village give them leadership without giving them *command?* The episode echoes the village's refusal to give first priority to economic values, which it manifested when it retained the *joft* system. But we have no reason to believe that its twin mistrust of a higher level of authority and of greater leeway for the wealthy would have persisted indefinitely. In their realism the villagers knew they needed both. Hadn't they faithfully kept a two-year-long mourning for their late headman, for his and his family's prestige? Hadn't they accepted Mash-hadi 'Abdul's son as headman? Didn't they pay him a salary out of each harvest? Weren't they proud, in Dezful, of "their" tractors and truck? Didn't they protect their entrepreneurs from external competition? Didn't they celebrate warmly the marriage between Musa's family and Karim's?

To summarize, then, to one degree or another most adult villagers were aware of the community's economic and political limitations that we have reviewed here. Many of them consciously appraised Rahmat Abad's political assets as pluses (especially in contrast to Dezful's)—its impersonal norms for conducting affairs, its unity, its public accountability, its moral order. But despite this awareness each stage of Rahmat Abad's development required experience, gradually changing precedents that tested the community and individuals. First establish itself on more secure ground politically; that would diminish the risks inherent in giving the wealthy free rein.

The Townsman's Bid for Land

Our third case considers how Rahmat Abad was affected by the uncertain political order the village had to rely upon when dealing beyond the boundaries of local accountability.

In constructing its new road to Rahmat Abad in 1972 and the canal that extended on beyond, the State cut some 90 acres of village land off from the traditional irrigation system that served the villagers; this land, ideal for cucumbers and watermelons, could also support a crop of winter wheat. (In good years, with supplementary irrigation, each *joft* had harvested enough wheat there to bring it well over $100 in extra cash.) To reclaim this field would have required a relatively expensive waterway entering from a completely new direction, and that, in turn, would have necessitated settling conflicting claims to property through which it would pass—property claimed by Rahmat Abad, a neighboring village, and a landlord who still held some land in the area. The village postponed any solution the first year. The second spring, Agha Kayhan, a townsman, offered to rent the land from Rahmat Abad, secure the proper permissions from the other two claimants, and install the necessary irrigation structures, if in exchange the village would let him farm the land for three subsequent years. At the end of the contract the land and its improvements would return to the community.

After discussing the matter for several days, the villagers called a meeting to reach a conclusion. Whether to trust a city man or any bidder for rights to the soil, whether to develop the land themselves, or whether to entertain other proposals about its use were not questions that could be settled through informal consensus, but rather demanded an assembly of all the *joft*holders (as though the formality of land rights required a formal deliberation). This was the only meeting I ever saw the village itself call.

Discussion at the meeting was lively, bringing out many different aspects for consideration. Musa guaranteed the prospective client's integrity, although many already knew and trusted him. Reza offered to develop the irrigation canal himself the following year, thereby keeping the land within the village; but who could tell what would happen a year later? If Rahmat Abad accepted Agha Kayhan's proposal, he would probably form a partnership with Muhammad to supervise the operations, and Muhammad's tractor would benefit from additional work. Many villagers, including women and children, could find day-wage labor cultivating the summer vegetables Agha Kayhan would plant, and in the long term Rahmat Abad might get a canal. Then it could resume using the land itself. But in the end the meeting rejected Agha Kayhan's proposal and heard no concrete suggestions that would move the land closer to resumed cultivation.

This case, on the surface a simple one, was fraught with the uncertainties Rahmat Abad encountered once *dulat* had begun to penetrate the intervillage region around Rahmat Abad that previously had enjoyed a relatively predictable social order on its own. Admittedly, from time immemorial the region had suffered chronic insecurity from the hands of landlords and brigands; but this had not destroyed the channels of information, the reliability of acquaintanceship and social pressure, the basic trust many villagers had built up among themselves and were now extending as a network throughout the intervillage region. Like Rahmat Abad's internal politics, this self-contained and internally accountable region had begun to face the limitations of the traditional order for the new requirements of economic development, if economic development meant integration into the centralized State. What the network of villages needed (in an evolutionary step parallel to Rahmat Abad's need for stronger authority in the headman's office) was some sort of intervillage council of its own making, for reaching agreement on just such matters as this one, the ownership of a disputed piece of land.

These villages had many of the requirements for such a council. They had long been resolving conflicts among themselves informally, sometimes with the mediation of landlords but far more often without. They already had in place the mechanisms, recognized leaders (familiar to one another), and even the suitable occasions for routine discussions at the intervillage level. They were already coordinating some resources on their own—certain canals two or more communities shared, truck schedules so as to avoid redundancy, the Moharram ceremonies at Dubendar, and so forth. But none of the mechanisms for coordination above the village level had been institutionalized, nor did the villages invest any explicit, formal authority in what was emerging as a system of intervillage policy making and conflict resolution. Rahmat Abad hinted at the next stage of such a development by joking about being the region's Throne City.

Even though the core villages around Rahmat Abad had been spared incorporation into one of the Dez Irrigation Project's transformational schemes, some of those on the edges of the region we are discussing had not been spared, and others knew the State's aggression by its recent road and canal. They had suddenly become aware of *dulat*'s proximity. In the villagers' deliberations about how to develop the tract of land under question, they emphasized that with this new player in the game, the State, their former assumptions and methods of resolving such matters at the intervillage level could no longer be relied upon; but neither could anything *dulat* offered instead. Thus, for instance, how would they now deal with the other village and the landlord who claimed parts of the land through which the new irrigation canal would have to pass?

Formerly, in such a situation the two villages along with the independent landlord, the third party, would have entered negotiations as clearly bounded and publicly identified corporate entities whose reputations one could ascertain and who (in the case of the villages) would secure their various members' acceptance of any agreement reached in their name, giving all parties relative assurance of an enforceable agreement. Traditionally the issue might have been worked out at the landlord level, but not necessarily, since most landlords took little interest in the villages' productivity. (Throughout the generations the resolutions reached in land disputes would never have been upheld if they had depended only on the landlords for enforcement and not on the agreement between villages as relatively autonomous actors. Rahmat Abad had dealt directly with other villages over innumerable land and water claims even before land reform, and during the first couple of years after the reform it had negotiated as a corporate entity both with other villages and with landlords farming independent of any village.) In those days, everyone's awareness that having to resort to the State would only make things worse had lent pressure to reach viable compromises.

On the other hand, when landlords *had been* traditionally involved and had authorized agreements among themselves at their level regarding intervillage matters, even then enforcement had been fairly reliable—although not without inequities. Like the villages in this region, the landlords of traditional Dezful had constituted a community small enough to enjoy much more effective mechanisms for accountability than the modernizing State provided once it subjected all local law to the Tehran-controlled Plan. Nor did the modernizing State, in compensation for its arbitrariness, assure greater equity than had the landlord regime.

With *dulat* in the region no longer as a backdrop but now entering as an aggressive and highly unpredictable actor, Rahmat Abad could trust neither of the two other parties with which it would have to deal in building a new canal, and with which traditionally it could have dealt confidently. (The village expected that reaching an agreement would pose far less of a problem than ensuring its permanence.) With *dulat* now an actor, the village no longer had any clear sense of who in fact the parties would turn out to be, or how to reach trustworthy common terms of negotiation. Nor could it any longer trust any social system that might back up a possible resolution, holding those who agreed to it accountable. *Dulat's* "law" was lawless. The Ministry of Water and Power was certain to leap into the affair, although it knew nothing of the history of the case and no one could predict what solution it would favor. It would necessarily fight the Land Reform Commission, both sides with vested interests—although no one could predict what they would be! When appraising the risks in generations gone by, the villagers would have sized up the landlord with whom they had to deal in terms of the landlord community in Dezful, whose intricacies at least a few of them could unravel. But now they would have to size him up in terms of the unfathomable world of the State. He was reputed to have special connections in the Ministry of Justice, hitherto unheard of in the region and, again, far more likely to take an active role than *dulat* ever had taken before. In addition, it was said that one *joft*holder in the other village, who opposed any solution, could if need be mobilize a kinsman who was tea boy for one of the generals at the nearby military base. Finally, if *dulat* did sponsor an "agreement," what in the world did *that* mean, since the State itself was so subject to persuasion at all times?

With all these unpredictable factors and the range of influences and power expanding beyond its ken, Rahmat Abad concluded that the outcome of any possible dispute would hardly depend on the merits of its case. When I suggested that there must be a board of land registration that would back up an agreement, or even a court system, the villagers laughed and told enough stories to fill Dezful's own *Thousand and One Nights.*

Agha Kayhan and Reza had been right to suggest that an individual could much more easily move about in the State-dominated environment of power (since it required obscurity), and could arrange more viable short-term canal rights with the other two actors, than could Rahmat Abad as a village. Once *dulat* cast its shadow in the regional arena, Rahmat Abad had virtually become obsolete as a vehicle for collective endeavor, bound as the village would be to the traditional rural culture's mode of corporate and therefore public accountability. An individual could contact the other two claimants on a private, temporary basis, and quite secretly; he could avoid raising the whole issue of claims on the land by acknowledging with duplicity and bribes that *each one* was the rightful owner. Then, too, the other claimants would have less hesitation about committing themselves to an agreement with an individual, since an individual could hardly protect his investment should the other party change its mind. In contrast, Rahmat Abad acting as a village might defend its investment with a group of angry farmers, so the public agreement would have to hold!

Rahmat Abad was far too pragmatic and its mode of operation too objective for the obscurantism and personalism now required to resolve this problem. If Rahmat Abad were to try to deal with both parties as a corporate entity, the land claims would quite simply have to be settled, permanently and publicly. That meant that the agreement and the investment it would enable would take on a stability only tolerable in a predictable and relatively balanced political context, that is, in an environment founded upon law. This in the long run would be more economical and reliable, whereas having individuals patch together a solution was costly and risky; but only the latter mode of operation was feasible within *dulat*'s domain.

These considerations clearly favored letting an individual build the new canal, rather like a front man; once the canal had been installed for a few years and the unresolved claims were no longer the focus of attention, Rahmat Abad could slip in and recover from him the use of its own land. Still the question remained, how could the village trust Agha Kayhan to return the land at the end of the contract? What if he planted alfalfa or even a few fruit trees, deep-root crops that gave customary rights to the land forever? The village could monitor that, of course, but again, how could it enforce an agreement once so many outsiders and bureaucrats, including the gendarmerie, entered the political equation?

The following year Reza did not develop the canal; to do so was expensive. The land continued in fallow. The head of the Ministry of Water and Power in Dezful blamed that on the villagers' "typical" laziness.

In discussing the earlier cases, we saw Rahmat Abad's need for a firmer figure of authority within the village itself. An analogous focal point or institution was needed at the regional level for the villages among themselves to articulate intervillage coordination when that was called for. At the time that *dulat's* presence had begun to discourage further political development in this regional arena, Rahmat Abad had evolved a more effective governor at its level than the region had at the *intervillage* level. This was to be expected, partly because frequency and intensity of interaction, which call forth new levels of coordination, were much greater between individuals in the village than between villages in the region (Arensberg, 1972). Furthermore, the development of more mature institutions at the regional level had to wait for the emergence of more clearly articulated offices of village authority. Still, both arenas were evolving rapidly as internally consistent systems, probably toward formal articulation in time.

The State, centralized in personal power in Tehran completely beyond accountability, could not have supplied a responsive, reliable, stable governance for the regional level as it purportedly aspired to do. *Dulat* knew no law in the sense of predictability. What *dulat* accomplished by its increasing presence was to put into question the traditional rural order that *did* provide prospects for an increasingly higher degree of predictability. *Dulat's* presence in Dezful town had the same effect; indeed, so did its presence among even the wealthiest families of Tehran. The centralized State was arbitrary. Zonis describes the ultimate aim of urban entrepreneurs at the national level, who realized that to remain self-directed in their projects they had to minimize contact with the State (1971:29).

While the little intervillage region around Rahmat Abad where this case should have been resolved still had no *formal* mechanisms for whatever coordination might be needed, an embryonic informal system was already functioning. Confirming the evolution of a cohesive field of interaction above the village level, the communities around Rahmat Abad ceremonialized the region's social reality every year at Dubendar, where they came together, each under its banner, in their ancient ritual that we review in Chapter 5. We cannot even speculate how this emerging *regional* polity might have shaped itself had it been allowed to do so. In 1975 the Shah asked Mr. Lilienthal to design a pilot program for participation in local self-government. Lilienthal advised against it: The population was not yet ready for such a radical idea, he said (Lilienthal to me, 1975.)

Interdependence Between the Community's and the Region's Political Development

Although the emergence of a responsive governor had progressed farther in Rahmat Abad than in the intervillage region as a whole, these cases illustrate the extent to which Rahmat Abad's continued political development depended on there being a reliable and participatory forum for coordination at the *regional* level above it. In our third case we see village ingenuity, initiative, and its ability to rebound from a frustrating setback thwarted by the unpredictability that had come to characterize wherever *dulat* dominated the world *outside* the village boundaries. For local groups to evolve politically they had to be able to take initiatives outward, which, in turn, challenged their internal organization to greater efficiency and complexity (as happened in building Throne City). But if the villagers had waited until after the new road revealed *dulat*'s interest in the area, Rahmat Abad would not have enjoyed enough sense of permanence and self-reliance to have constructed Throne City. Consider the political development that might thus have been lost for the gain of *dulat*'s road. In building itself a new village, the community had strengthened its corporate autonomy, had confirmed the power of *its* initiatives just at the time when land reform threw it on its own, and had begun to retailor the office of headman thoroughly within its own domain. In short, *Rahmat Abad's* continual political development depended on being able to take corporate initiatives, and this in turn depended on a predictable environment *beyond* the village.

The two levels of political development depended to some degree on each other, just as the nuclear family's integrity and that of impersonal *sharik* partnerships depended on the stability of the corporate village and vice versa. Seeing the *region* relatively stable politically gave a green light to further *local* endeavor, which in time would have forced to the forefront the need for firmer *village* authority. That, in turn—and the community initiatives themselves—would have enabled the region to move closer toward a coordinational focus on its level.

Even if *dulat* had left Rahmat Abad alone, the State's increasing domination of *the region* would have prevented the emergence of a responsive but firm headman *in the village*—not only because Rahmat Abad's internal development depended on continued and more ambitious community undertakings that were discouraged by seeing *dulat* on the horizon, but also because concentrating community authority in one office became all the more risky with *dulat*'s aggressive presence nearby. The villagers had long experience in powerful outsiders co-opting their leaders; they could evolve the next step only when they perceived that their political environment was one they—at the base of society—could control.

Eventually, whether at the level of the intervillage region or in the town of Dezful, Rahmat Abad would have come to loggerheads with *dulat*'s bureaucrats. That was already occasionally happening in connection with the State's new canal. As we have seen, the village's development as a corporate entity remained contingent upon its ability to deal systematically with those authorities above it in its social system. Therefore, Rahmat Abad's emergence as an articulate, self-directed building block of rural society—initiating its own projects and fostering the integrity of its constituent units because it could defend its own interests and theirs— ultimately required its being able to hold the State itself accountable. The social levels between the village and the State—the region, townsmen's interventions, even landlords and their Dezful community in former days—could provide buffers from *dulat's* predatory arbitrariness, although these buffers protected one less and less as one moved up the hierarchy. During the period of my field work, the community, just emerging on its own, was relying on these buffers. But already it was apparent that *dulat* in its coordinational function at the top was not politically analogous to the emerging office of headman at the top of *the village* polity, nor to the *intervillage* region emerging out of the communities at society's grass roots. The village and intervillage region crystallized *out of* the initiatives and interactions of their constituent members, focusing them, whereas *dulat* invaded from the *outside and above.* Since the villagers were the mainspring of the office of headman and the intervillage regional arena, they could enforce accountability; but *dulat* descended unseen from beyond the mountain range. It had no organic connection whatsoever with Rahmat Abad or with local people. The headman and regional arena reflected and responded to villagers' actual norms and behavior. However, in contrast to these elementary structures *dulat* considered the norms and behavior in society at best irrelevant and mainly threatening to its own welfare.

In Rahmat Abad's drive to build its political foundations cautiously and slowly as it developed economically, the village and its sister communities working together could conceivably, in time, have demanded a predictable environment from *Dezful* town. They were beginning to work themselves into the fabric of Dezful through trade, part-time employment, even kin. Their achieving predictability at that level would have strengthened their own structures, in turn. But the gap in power between their political tools and *the State's* left them, as they knew, helpless— hence, whenever they touched the edge of that gap, passive. This lack of control outside the region, and now even penetrating within it, stymied the village's own plans and actions. The more *dulat* tried to convert the countryside, the more certainly it retarded local and intermediate-level political—hence, economic—development.

> **It is not for a believing man or for a believing woman, when God and his Prophet have decided an affair, to have any choice in that affair.   —Qur'an, Sura 33**

Chapter 4

The Individual and Rahmat Abad

Therefore should I not persevere in following the path to my own land? ... No longer able to bear the grief of estrangement and care, I will return to mine own city and become mine own King. —Hafiz, from *The Divan*

By six-thirty in the morning, seven-year-old Shiri, carrying the family eating tray on her head piled high with pots and pans, cooking utensils, and dirty clothes, was headed out to the canal to wash them, her younger brother Amir trailing along. Her mother had instructed her not to let her mind wander as she worked, lest someone borrow the soap without returning it; and not to lose sight of Amir, lest he fall in the canal and drown; and not to dawdle, lest the rice burn on the hearth back home, which she was also tending. By the age of fifteen, Mansur, Shiri's cousin, had primary charge of the eggplant and cucumber plots, which if he did a good job would bring his family over a third of their cash income for the year. He had graduated to that job from several years of herding the family's large flock of sheep, virtually its entire savings! Many a family simply could not spare boys like him for even five hours a day at school.

When Madar-i-Nur, the chief woman of an extended household, died, six neighbor women had to begin sharing the tasks she had performed each day, until her family shifted the residential location of two other households to carry on her labor and services, central to their complex network of operations. Mullah's illness during the several peak periods of farmwork cast his family in debt for hired labor that it would take them years to repay, because despite their owning a full *joft* of land, Mullah was the only adult able to do field work. Little Naser, left at home to rock the cradle so the baby would sleep, keep the chickens away from the cooling bread, and await a cousin expected to arrive from another village while his mother took a few minutes to fetch water, burned down the storage room and cattle stall playing with matches she had forgotten to put away.

In Rahmat Abad, villagers from the age of three assumed their share of responsibility for the family's job of feeding and sheltering itself. If you failed, few alternatives existed; life was precarious. No one I knew held pleasure as a value, but rather producing food, and, after that, beginning to accumulate some durable, productive wealth that might last. Although the young people's thoughts about marriage tempted them to dream for a moment about physical beauty or laughter, they soon returned to the primary requirements of industry and character. If Rahmat Abad demanded accountability in its polity and social organization, that was because life itself demanded accountability, beginning at the earliest age; if Rahmat Abad figured those accounts in impersonal measures, that was because its bottom line was the returns to work, not sociability.

Even primary bonds hinged upon extreme risk. The man a girl married would take her from her compound and often from her village; what happened to him determined her destiny: If he was lazy, clever, demanding, or ill, she would have to compensate singlehandedly; others had their own problems, and her family might live far away. Rahim's brother was shot dead one night, leaving Rahim and his wife with six additional children to rear on the wheat and rice for a family of four. One could count on no replacements, no standbys; the village knows no interchangeable roles. Out of the very simplicity—the *sheer*ness—of the village economy, such events reoriented others' lives down a long chain.

Each villager's ever-changing configurations and challenges created an evolving and sharply etched individual. Indeed, fellow villagers were the only *facts* of life. Adults began evaluating children's tolerations, liabilities, and tendencies of character almost as infants, to size up early on what one could count on Chanar to do, how far one could push Esmet, what would be Murad's typical reactions. Because of the compression of society in Rahmat Abad, people savored the distinctions between one another's life paths more philosophically than anything else they considered. In the biographies and autobiographies they related, they emphasized the extraordinary uniqueness of each life experience. All village fields bore names referring to events perhaps lost to memory but still immortalizing an individual who had lived in this community: "Mirza's Watermelon" or "Safar's Dead Horse." Around the hearth at night, their stories about a few hours in town, events of the past, a conversation in the field relished particularistic details about individuals familiar to us all—the way old Haji in the bazaar squinted as he stingily counted out eight small cookies, how 'Alieh raised her expressive eyebrows when the darvesh beggar began to pray.

The villagers' work was very hard. Although farming and housework forced a certain amount of leisure upon the villagers (since they had no other remunerative projects they could do at home), no one could become inured to the drudgery of scrubbing heavy work clothes between one's knuckles with only local soap to cleanse them; covering oneself in sweat and dust even to one's skull, nostrils, and underclothes while threshing grain; or following the herd of cows to make patties for fuel out of their freshly dropped dung. Khuzestan's months of searing heat coincided with the heaviest demand for field labor; during winter and spring, the deep mud everywhere during the rains, and the bitter cold (for people never were warmly clothed) made even getting around outside arduous. By the age of fifty, men and women were old.

Villagers rarely begrudged lending possessions of capital value—an insecticide sprayer, breakable cups and saucers for special guests, a large pot for cooking quantities of rice, even a bike or motorcycle; and, if anything loaned were broken, the borrower had no obligation to repair it. Yet they never requested or gave free labor outside the family and not always even within it. Frequently we would see old Yusuf struggling to lift a heavy load off the mare while his boys would sit by watching; the child Nabi would refuse to interrupt his play to bring his tired mother a cup of water or a fan as she stopped to rest. Labor, the key to Rahmat Abad's survival and upward mobility, each villager jealously meted out; this single precious thing, one's definition of self, one saved tightfistedly as though one could count all that one had left.

Expert judges of effort, villagers often conversed about work. They drew refined distinctions about others' diligence, comparing the exertion of different types of work, pitying the *zahmat,* or trouble, that had burdened someone. No one would ever pass near a person who was working, not even a stranger, without shouting out to renew him, "God give you strength!"—the same greeting we offered one another as we sat down to eat right from work.

Finally, much of the villagers' work was solitary. Although the men's *bildar*s and the women's hours of washing at the canal brought villagers together, as did men's work partnerships (especially during harvest), villagers carried out most of their work alone: planting, inspecting the crop, irrigating and picking the vegetables, bringing the harvest home or preparing it for sale in town; feeding the animals and milking them; cleaning and storing the grain; cooking, cleaning the house, and tending the children; even relaxing in the sun in late afternoon. During a good part of the day, members of forty separate family units would be going about their work on their own self-determined schedules, getting done what tasks were theirs and had to be finished that day, before the individual workers gathered to sit down on the earth together, as darkness fell, around a steaming tray of beans and bread and onions at forty separate hearth fires: forty families.

These intrinsic characteristics of what each villager did day in and day out gave one a keen realization of self-worth within one's social world, Rahmat Abad, although this self-awareness was not always *consciously* derived. Central to almost every individual's sense of identity was the fact that the contributions he or she made to the family economy directly affected its survival, or, beyond that, determined its material improvement in concrete steps that were easily appraised. A profound recognition of one's own worth dwelt in this knowledge that you made a significant difference to such an important enterprise. For adults, of course, this difference was life-giving, and it was so every day. But even children knew that, for instance, if they spilled the yoghurt they had been asked to carry, the hungry field workers would eat only bread and onions for the noon meal, or that if they were not attentive, a baby sister might wander too close to the hearth and catch fire as a cousin had done.

Second, because the work each person was given was strenuous, frequently painful, accomplishing it gave him or her a palpable sense of mastery. Even if only by persistence or endurance, each difficult challenge tested one's competence; in pulling through it, you time and time again had a tangible measure of your inherent strength. "*Ya,* Allah!" villagers would exclaim upon reflecting on the completion of a difficult job: a relief that simultaneously expressed self-discipline and conquest, the discovery of God's power in oneself. Then the solitude and independence of each villager's responsibility within the family—that no one else could do your work (if only, as in the case of children, because the adults were all occupied elsewhere)—focused the importance and accomplishment of your responsibilities once again on self-reliance. When Masalu refused to help with the household work unless her father allowed her at the same time to finish third grade, she saw that he had to give in because with her mother often ill it was up to her whether those jobs got done or not; there simply was no one else to do them. Villagers frequently witnessed this indispensability of a single person when family or neighbors died, when a young man was drafted into the army, or when a daughter was taken from the household in marriage.

Rahmat Abad could count on no specialists in its midst except one for healing sheep. If the crop looked bad or the house roof collapsed in a storm, you had to figure out the best solution on your own and act on it alone. Advice abounded but not the advice of professionals. Indeed, professionals in Dezful only made one's burden of responsibility heavier, as they would assume no responsibility. When someone died of illness, relatives blamed themselves bitterly for not having tried to insist on a change of doctors. Years later mothers would still not have forgiven themselves for having entrusted a deceased infant's health to the wrong doctor.

Thus, when all by yourself you bore the responsibility for decisions and work which determined a whole family's welfare, and when that work was itself so physically and mentally demanding, what you did every day by its very nature confirmed your singular identity and indispensability, confirmed the resources you had within you. Villagers' conservatism in clothes and fashions, in status symbols, in social rules, in economic arrangements like the *joft* system—even in attending Little Parliaments and in dancing at village weddings, where the individual was allowed little leeway for showing off—seemed evidence to outsiders that Rahmat Abad suppressed the development of individuality. But the individual's much more profoundly secure identity had no need for the panoply of props and adornments the villagers found so odd in townsmen: a family's celebration of its members' birthdays; parents' search for a name for their newborn child that had some kind of intrinsic meaning; teachers' rewards and enticements for children's good grades.

The villagers had a close-up look at the strange culture of middle-class urban Iran when Mehrabani, a high-school graduate from Tehran drafted into the Rural Development Corps and stationed in Rahmat Abad, came to live among us. It was Mehrabani's urban culture in which a person needed to keep diaries and scrapbooks about himself that he perused meditatively, needed to cover his entire living space and surround himself with photographs of himself, needed to listen to music for hours in which a stranger assured him she loved him, and then had to mount a sign by the road stating that *he* lived in this little village which otherwise a traveler passing by would hardly have noticed. It was the townsman, not the villager, who felt enhanced by uniforms, whose work one person could pick up and perform as easily as he himself could. It was the townsman who needed such smiling comrades and who displayed on his wall official government certificates saying he had done a good job. In contrast, the fundamental solitude of much of the villager's work and day-to-day responsibility integrated his or her personality on a level incomparable to that which our representative of the New Order sought.

Beside the importance, the difficulty, and often the solitude of each villager's work, other aspects of it heightened the individual's responsibility, which in turn gave him and the village ample, concrete proof of his ability. For instance, even at this fundamental level of responsibility the demands of change constantly challenged and tested each person. Crop raising and family rearing essentially required the intelligence and alertness for managing continual flux: No two crops, no two years or months, no two children, not even two fields were the same. One was always being tested in new ways. Then, too, each family member, so critical to the enterprise, had a life of his or her own whose year by year changes reverberated throughout the family system. 'Ali will be needing a wife and then might leave the household entirely; Mansur will not put up with his shepherding job any longer but Rasoul is too young to perform it in his place; Sakineh will be too pregnant to do all the bean picking herself but Rajab is going blind and can no longer help with the work; relations between Tuba and her daughter-in-law worsen every day . . . by spring the family and its undertakings will constitute an entirely new puzzle to piece together! If the specialized but standardized jobs in town were designed to reduce surprises and to avoid the dependence of any part of the system upon one individual, just the opposite was true of the village economy, which villagers were never allowed to forget.

Another factor that heightened each individual's responsibility was that he or she had to draw upon a wide spectrum of innate skills, especially ingenuity. The unpredictable challenges in farmwork and family management, the absence or unreliability of professionals, and the necessity for each villager to handle many different tasks demanded broad competence. One could not learn any villager's work by rote, from a man-

ual, or from a two-week training course in Dezful. Culture provided overarching guidelines, but in such a time of flux people who could lose so
much by one mistake continuously had to question and test even these
guidelines. When the boy Ahmad lay dying, having drunk pesticide, what
could his grandmother and the neighbors do miles from the town, the
truck gone for the day and the tractors in the field? They could hardly
look to precedents from childhood to tell them. When a house caught fire,
how could the four women alone in the compound extinguish it, the community having determined for health reasons that no running water
should pass through the village? When Narquez encountered complica-
tions giving birth to her fifth child, who knew a remedy? Saving the
mother and child depended entirely on those women present right then
with her in Rahmat Abad. In many instances we have seen the villagers'
ingenuity, which sprang from this self-reliance: their improvising a new
aqueduct on their own, constructing and running their own school, chas-
ing thieves although they themselves were unarmed, devising their own
town plan with its zoning and pollution laws.

Tradition and custom had not eliminated from community life scandal
and crime, bankruptcies, deaths that could have been averted, the loss of
almost an entire crop in a field next to a flourishing one. The household
time-use charts I compiled (Goodell, 1975) show a multiplicity of immi-
nent risks that the two or three adults in some families had to face by
themselves even in a single year, the corresponding diversity of solutions
different families attempted for similar problems, and wide variation in
work habits and economic strategies employed even within one family: a
range of choice open to villagers, which increased the weight of making
each one. Rahmat Abad offered no architects, lawyers, psychiatrists, agricultural experts, or veterinarians to help simplify one's choices or lighten
one's responsibility in making them; no bank accounts to fall back on,
insurance policies, newspapers describing how others deal with similar
problems.

Finally, intrinsic to each villager's experience of his or her responsibilities was the fact that in the long run one could hide nothing fundamental
from the Rahmat Abad community. The village had a deep respect for
privacy to a degree rare in urban society. In a small community others
see through fakes and efforts to fudge; sooner or later the concrete results
of one's actions become evident to everyone. How could Naser's mother
explain away to the village that the child had burned down the storage
room and cattle stall because of her negligence? How could Guhar, after
four children died in infancy due to what everyone recognized as her
neglect, blame her husband for taking a second wife? When Reza built
himself a one-room house next to his father's, plastered and whitewashed
it, cemented its floor, furnished it with a metal cupboard, and got himself
a wife, he knew that the village had seen him the last to leave the fields
at night for several years, working double shift on the tractor, renting a
half*joft* of Musa's land to plant more vegetables, and spending nothing

on clothes. Like others' failures, his accomplishment spoke for itself to everyone, and it spoke of him.

Despite this minute scrutiny of its members' public actions virtually throughout their lifetime, the village of Rahmat Abad retained its fundamental rules of respect—one had to greet whomever one passed on the path—and of assistance in the hour of dire need. The ongoing evaluation that each member had to accept, devoid of sham or counterfeit, relieved him or her of the burdens of wearing a mask. With your limitations and idiosyncracies known, you belonged to this community. That was what the teenagers becoming full-fledged members of Rahmat Abad were exploring, rehearsing, testing so often at night as they entertained us with their warm Jane Austen characterizations. In the end the village accepted Gholam, even when he refused to contribute his share to its work. One of the questions villagers asked me most persistently was whether, when someone falls down in America, people help him get up. Each individual was held responsible, and ultimately each passed the test.

The Individual Villager and Townsman Contrasted

Juxtaposing the villager beside Mehrabani or the villagers' urban acquaintances will bring out more sharply the foundation of the individual villager's character and prepare the way for our better understanding of the village's relations with the domain of the State.

As we have seen, because pragmatic values so profoundly determined villagers' identities and how they measured themselves, even within the family each individual's relationships with others rested on a highly objective foundation. Villagers understood responsibility as a job that had to get done. As evidence of responsibility fulfilled, they had the product of their work. While relationships amounted to far more than material benefits, they were firmly rooted in concrete, visible contributions and in sharing the burdens of subsistence itself. This contrasted radically with the villagers' urban relatives and acquaintances in the middle class whose values were essentially personalistic, stressing the private rather than public arena, attractiveness rather than hard work, communicative rather than productive skills, social rather than material achievement, and psychological rather than behavioral evaluation. Mehrabani embodied these urban values of personalism, as did many townsmen the villagers knew; they prized getting along with and impressing people, for which the villagers who watched them closely had a derogatory term, *fis*.

Unlike village boys his age, who measured themselves mainly by each harvest and the household improvements it enabled, Mehrabani found his self-worth in his ability to multiply social relations by being "smooth" and by acquiring new things to win others—a Japanese cassette tape recorder, a calendar of sexy pictures, "Beatle" bell-bottom trousers. Connections won in this way constituted the key to success in his world. For instance, after Mehrabani finished in Rahmat Abad, he planned either to attend university where his uncle was lobbying for his admission, or work in a Ministry where his father would secure him a job. So, whereas the village young men's prosperity depended largely on their own individual skills, Mehrabani's depended on what he could get other people to do for him. Whereas the young men of Rahmat Abad looked for companionship from their friends, Mehrabani looked for utility from his. It was urgent for him, at his age in life, to expand his popularity in wider circles.

Because his investment in people would, Mehrabani hoped, assure him long-term gain, and because it essentially required spending money with people, he placed a high premium on "having a good time." The walls of his little room in Rahmat Abad told the villagers how to do this, as his many photographs depicted Mehrabani surrounded by his handsome crowd, strolling in parks, smelling a rose with a friend. In his pictures Mehrabani always smiled; he was always at ease. (In the pictures villagers had taken of themselves on pilgrimage, they stood almost at attention, which is how they wanted their image recorded.) The villagers who thought Mehrabani's life seemed purposeless could not grasp how building networks of happy friends might pay off as much as, for instance, enlarging one's flock of sheep would, or (as in Reza's case) memorizing a culvert blueprint. But more was going on in those lolling photographs than met 'Abdu's and 'Ali's eyes: Mehrabani was learning how to manipulate people, his resources; he was building the foundations of his future in the Shah's Tehran.

Just as Mehrabani's obsession with sociability confounded many villagers, so their pragmatism shocked him. On occasion he found them hypocritical, when they could form work partnerships with people they disliked or even marry a woman for her industriousness. To Mehrabani that revealed insincerity.

The religious ideals Mehrabani tried to inculcate in the "materialistic" villagers epitomized his conviction that the essence of a true human relationship was feelings. Every Muslim must commit his heart to a relationship with others in "acceptance" and "love." When he extolled his religious devotion to me in many long discussons, over and over again the young man described religion as a framework for being with others whom he could "love," a framework for being assured by them. Islam was "fellowship." God realized Himself in giving Mehrabani Muslim brothers and sisters—if all over the world, all the wider Mehrabani's circle of support.

To preach that religion was fellowship was incomprehensible to the villagers, whose life and community placed individuals in a radically different relationship with one another than did the social relations of middle-class Tehran. Rahmat Abad had built a mosque for the Dezful darvesh but never gathered there; on the contrary, each villager prayed the *Namaz* prayer in utter solitude, whether at home or in the field. During Moharram and funerals, villagers celebrated their corporate solidarity (hardly

Mehrabani's "fellowship") in ritual, but on a day-to-day basis, prayer amounted to a thoroughly concrete *sharik* arrangement with the Lord, having little to do with other people: a relationship strictly between the individual and God. Every day at five specific times, a Muslim should render to God his prayer in its specific, predetermined form, with its specific content. This prayer ruled out *personal involvement,* since most villagers understood nothing of what it said. Never mind, rendering this prayer in the correct manner constituted each individual's part of the contract, a demonstration of his or her compliance to duty. (To be sure, a male head of household frequently prayed the *Namaz* in a place withdrawn from but within view of everyone, and in a tone that might have seemed slightly conspicuous to a Westerner. But rather than expressing sociability or the desire for recognition, this ritual separation from the gathering emphasized his individuality as representative of the household, his responsibility—his loneliness.)

Similarly, the villagers found Mehrabani's talk of "Islamic brotherhood" gobbledegook. How could anyone see whether brotherhood had been performed? It sounded to them that in "Islamic brotherhood" one's obligations would wed one to everyone else in the world, a bit risky as far as any villager could imagine it at all. Once when Mehrabani was praising Islamic nationalism, old Eber, looking for its objective purpose, said it sounded to him like an enormous *bildar,* which removed the very mystique Mehrabani cherished. The intrinsic independence of the villagers' relationships with one another and their carefully measured accountability shaped the concept of a religious duty to God. That constituted formal Islam to them, just as Mehrabani's yearning for social support determined what Islam meant to him.

Everyone in Rahmat Abad must have sensed some spiritual tie that bound the village as a whole when each evening Muhammad Hosein or young Abul would call out the evening prayer at sundown, closing the day communally. Unlike the urban call to prayer, ours elicited no collective action from the male villagers because anyone who did pray would have done so according to his own convenience, upon returning home from work. But to the extent that this simple ritual affirmed community beyond the individual, its modest, intimate reassurance joined people familiar with each other through thick and thin, our little Throne City, hardly merging us with the universal Muslim masses.

Rahmat Abad's *Sharik* Partnerships Contrasted with Townsmen's Personalism

Mehrabani's personalism, the personalism which the villagers so often observed among townsmen, was founded upon social links that necessarily carried with them personal attachments. Such links were ill-suited for Rahmat Abad because they would have required committing one's whole person for life to everyone with whom you enjoyed a substantive relationship (the essential basis of personalism). While it is true that Rahmat Abad as a community guaranteed an ultimate support for its members, in everyday interaction even within the family the villagers often defined the duration and content of their obligations with each other so as to avoid open-ended and interminable claims. A *sharik* partnership united partners only for a particular undertaking or as shareholders managing a specific productive resource; it never implied generalized mutual bonding. For instance, in agricultural work such a partnership, even between brothers, was renegotiable seasonally. Villagers kept track of labor units offered and received. Even children's negotiation over favors they rendered emphasized the discreteness of interpersonal exchanges. In contrast, townsmen's personalistic bonds worked against giving someone only a part of oneself in this way—one's physical labor in harvest, for instance, or one's specific masonry skills for building a house. The all-encompassing personalism of townsmen's relationships required each side to put his total person at the other's disposal, neither person limiting the currency of exchange that bound the relationship nor specifying a time frame for making return claims. In their personal bonds even non-kin townsmen assumed they could make claims on each other as individuals throughout life. Because this was in fact impracticable, it constantly led to elaborate lies and subterfuge, as each individual wanted to expand the scope of this fiction but not to be held to it himself. As a result, the impossible implications of personalism had to lead townsmen to adopt an entire ethic of interpersonal compromise, with no expectation of firm accountability.

Given Rahmat Abad's turbulent history, villagers needed the flexibility of their far more practical, concrete *sharik* agreements, each with its highly specific purpose and duration (usually short-term). Unlike Mehrabani's experience in Tehran, for years villagers had seen many of the poorest families move upward entirely on their own or, when they needed others, through relying on objectively circumscribed *sharik* arrangements, not owing their success to personalistic bonds. In discussing the village economy, we saw examples of these partnerships, one of Rahmat Abad's most common organizational forms, but here they interest us as they throw light on the individual villager's character.

The labor partnerships that abounded in the village, as well as the labor exchanges of a few days' work when two men had separate projects to accomplish and each would help the other on his, offered ample institutional scope for pooling complementary resources. Quite the opposite of all-encompassing personalistic relations, *sharik* partnerships enabled each party to quantify the work he expended and attach to it a specific exchange, often a cash wage (even between kinsmen!). The villagers of Rahmat Abad engaged in few generalized exchanges at all outside the family, which anthropologists find common in other peasant societies, and they never entered into unbounded exchanges of labor. Since their contractual terms allowed them to take a particular work relationship out of the context of friendship, the *sharik* terminated when the partners completed the task to be shared or when each paid the time he owed to the other. Then both would be "even," avoiding later claims one had not intended to take on at the start. The men and women of Rahmat Abad felt a profound commitment to each other beneath the level of everyday cordiality, but their circumstances advised against entanglement. Townsmen *sought* entanglement. Of course, rejecting others' personal dependence on one in turn prevented a person's being able to call on others readily, even on family. That reinforced your self-reliance. As small children, boys and girls learned such independence even in close relationships. When little Nabi refused to bring his mother a cup of water as she rested, his pride hardly allowed him to come crying to her when Mansur hit him later that day.

In the village many occasions presented themselves in which people could easily have pooled their labor, but instead each ruggedly carried out the same job independently. For example, I often wondered why two women in the same compound, house neighbors, wouldn't take turns, one doing her housework so as to enable her to watch the children, while the other went to the canal to do her wash. That would have solved the difficult problems of children accompanying their mothers to the canal, where they often fell in. But in all such cases I found villagers avoiding arrangements that lacked clear-cut boundaries. For instance, once started, the women's baby-care pool could have continued for years; it was too involving: How would one be able to leave it? Thus just as personalism made urban people hold very loose standards of individual responsibility and accountability, the contractual culture of the village reinforced these standards, even at the cost of convenience or short-term economic gain.

The villagers employed the institution of *sharik* creatively, sometimes engaging in several at once. But living in a small and poor community made each individual more vulnerable to becoming personally indebted to others and involved in their lives, since in certain crucial respects (like the *joft* system, irrigation, or defense) the villagers *were* so interdependent. Townsmen, too, were interdependent, but they could and vigorously *did* avoid meeting those to whom they owed favors. In contrast, Rahmat Abad's requirement that everyone at least remain on speaking terms with everyone else could all too easily be exploited. Above all, interpersonal obligations threatened the villagers because they vigilantly defended their political equality. Thus while the village *economy* demanded the self-reliance and integrity of each separate member, so, too, the *size and social cohesiveness* of Rahmat Abad called for what sometimes seemed to be stark personal independence. With that independence a villager could then be available for contractual partnerships in which each member remained in full control.

Just the opposite of Mehrabani's culture and that of Iranian movies, Rahmat Abad's stern individuality barred the individual from showing sentiment that touched too closely upon emotional involvement. Men and women wept only under the strict controls of ritual. Children loved to mock affectionate relationships. The first thing old Muhammad said to me when we met in the technocrat's office in Dezful was essentially a warning to me and to the villagers that my living in Rahmat Abad might lead to attachment. That evening, my first in Rahmat Abad, Madar-i-'Ali had warned herself and me once again. I hope in the end that for their sake they followed their own warnings better than I did.

The Individual and the State

There was one relationship that villagers especially feared as totally engulfing them: their relationship with *dulat*. We have seen that traditionally the villagers could walk out of their arrangement with the landlord, their one implicit right (see Lambton, 1969:176 and Goodell, 1980:308). But unlike the landlord's terminable claim on them, *dulat* was perceived by the villagers as trying to make their relationship to it a bond of immeasurable obligation and unlimited duration, which violated their fundamental social principles. They detested military service not just for their loss of indispensable labor and for the degradation a man suffered, but more deeply for the State's being able to demand it at all, an individual disappearing for years on end into the votrex of *dulat*'s command. Not based on a reciprocal claim (which was the only service they knew), thus not eliciting a man's *duty,* the draft derived from nothing more than the State's power. Unlike feudal "service" in Europe, which constituted the basis of law in the West during its agrarian period, this vertical bond—the one binding vertical bond the villagers knew outside the family—was devoid of any moral claim on the individual whatsoever, because while the State demanded total "service" as it saw fit, the individual could claim nothing from the State in return. How could the villagers forge for Rahmat Abad a tie of mutual accountability between the individual and the polity out of this, their only model?

According to many of *dulat*'s officials—from Mehrabani himself to economists and planners in Tehran—in exchange for *whatever* service the State might expect from its villagers, the latter were benefiting in return, by being "modernized." Echoing Western theorists, these urban Iranians thought that only in the diversity and complexity of urban life, only in the amenities that the State provided, could individuals find the freedom and scope to develop their personalities. If it is partly by making choices that individuals define themselves, then to what kinds of choices did the modernizers attribute individuals' personal growth within *dulat*'s realm, which they could not realize in the likes of Throne City?

When Mehrabani glorified Tehran's opportunities for the self-realization that the villagers were missing, he located development of the individual in Tehran's diversity of movies, styles, girlfriends, foreigners on the street, radio programs, tall buildings, things to do on weekends, places to go, things to buy: the city's infinite choices. One day when he was lamenting the lack of individual challenge in Rahmat Abad, I pointed out that just that day Maham had decided to buy a new gold bracelet for Goltela, his wife, who had been psychologically depressed for some time; the cost of this difficult choice was that Maham had had to sell two of his four ewes, which would have dropped lambs in a few months' time. Wasn't this a choice that defined and strengthened Maham's individuality and asserted his autonomy? It was not a decision between disco clubs to take her to, but surely it constituted a self-actualizing decision unimaginable in the television romances Mehrabani missed so much. To Mehrabani I had failed to catch the point. All Maham and Goltela could get in Dezful were gold *bangles:* That confined their individuality. Had I ever been in the jewelry bazaar in Tehran?—streets and streets of shops with lockets and bracelets and necklaces and pins and rings and earrings and brooches and pendants, not to mention more kinds of watches than one could find in all the stores in Dezful combined! To him, such were the choices that developed the individual's personality.

Another day I pointed out that after a long consideration Ebrahim's family had decided to invest earnings from their eggplant crop to enroll their six-year-old in school, the first family member ever to learn to read. Although they had no idea whether the little girl had any aptitude at all for learning, or what she would do if she did, yet they took the risk— leaving the family penniless for emergencies. Wouldn't following the course of that decision deepen the personality of each member of the family? Mehrabani could see no personal growth in such choices because the risks were too high. To him, by definition choices that carried responsibility *restricted* rather than expanded the individual.

Villagers readily admitted Throne City's limited scope in matters in which Mehrabani prized choice. Indeed, at the same time that urban life even in Dezful broadened beyond Rahmat Abad's comprehension the range of *things* from which one could choose, townsmen's specialized jobs freed them further by diminishing the number of difficult decisions they had to make in earning their daily livelihood, and reduced, too, the costs anyone had to pay for error. Townsmen enjoyed more safety nets. In short, rarely did they have to make a choice that was crucial and that no one else could have made in their stead. Furthermore, *dulat* gave town life so many things and required them to subscribe to so many others— schools and health programs, for instance—that whole areas of choice which comprised fundamental responsibilities to villagers disappeared entirely from the decision making of their Dezful cousins. All of these advantages within *dulat*'s urban domain reduced the hard choices people had to make, but did that *strengthen* individuality? (If villagers wanted a school or a vaccination, they had to bear the cost themselves; and in any event, since such benefits were still *optional* to them, they had to deliberate upon their value, not just submit and receive.)

Most significant of all, the very size and fragmentation of urban society, its obsessive personalism, and its political vacuum precluded accountability in countless difficult choices or commitments that one had to stand by in Rahmat Abad. When villagers and I talked about the townsman's range of choices, which Mehrabani and others cherished, it was difficult to find any examples of employers or family and friends ever holding townsmen accountable for choices rooted in actual behavior and important enough to involve risk. Certainly bureaucrats like Mehrabani never lost their livelihood because of decisions they made, as villagers might ruin a crop. Mullah (who had worked in town for several years) said townsmen gained thousands of easy choices, "like stars above our heads!" while at the same time being relieved of the most painful ones, "like the ground under our feet."

Presumably, exchanging the choices Maham and Ebrahim had the freedom to make for those Mehrabani liked constituted urban Iran's greater opportunities for self-expression and personal growth. During my second year in Iran, a popular Tehran television serial we watched in the new model town featured two young men courting beautiful, coy, identical twin damsels, whom neither they nor others—nor the audience!—could always distinguish from each other. Still, each hero would happily wind up with one or the other mutually replaceable doll by the end of every evening's tale: a profound "folk" expression of the sameness, the arbitrariness, the assured but empty success of choices in which the urban producers and audience recognized themselves. (In contrast, the only program the villagers liked when they had a chance to watch the urban relative's television was Charlie Chaplin, thoroughly based on objective behavior and hilariously insistent upon suffering the consequences of one's misdeeds.)

It was just the kind of scope and freedom that Mehrabani and so many other bureaucrats found conducive to personal development, *against which* village adults warned the three boys from Rahmat Abad attending junior high in Dezful. The boys themselves feared this range of "opportunities." In the camaraderie of junior high, the three of them stuck together defensively; they steeled themselves against movies, alcohol, urban distractions, even urban friends and eating places that might "contaminate" them with the townsmen's seemingly obsessive search for "self-expression." Like skilled social scientists, they had composed a telling litany of what to avoid: window-shopping along Pahlavi Avenue, reading movie star magazines, standing around the carrot juice parlor, buying tight-fitting pants or shirts. Villagers like these boys experiencing the shock of two conflicting moral orders constantly struggled within themselves to penetrate the urban guise but not to give into it. One village boy said such choice brought only "thirst," and how long could one say no?

Only a handful of villagers considered themselves devotees of Agha Nurshani, the darvesh holy man who often came to Rahmat Abad, where he would stay for several days at a time. A prosperous merchant in Dezful and a spiritual man, Agha Nurshani was the one townsman who came to the village at least in part out of a certain appreciation of its life and its values, as though his own Sufi quest for peace and truth brought him there. The darveshes worshiped at night, because their spiritual medium was darkness. Accompanying the holy man into the village mosque in pitch dark, his handful of followers prayed together for love to bind them one to the other, for clarity of purpose, for simplicity in their commitment, and for a glimpse of concentrated brightness, a focused light in the long night. Through ascetic simplicity they sought personal integration and spiritual wholeness. The darvesh dwelt at length on the terror of being conscious of being alone in the grave after death.

While most villagers did not comprehend what he spoke about and so preferred to gossip and tell stories around their family hearths instead of becoming a darvesh, the handful of men who followed Agha Nurshani faithfully were all villagers who had returned to Rahmat Abad to farm after some years of semiskilled work in town. And each of the several village boys who worked in town in the day aspired to be a darvesh as well. They themselves pointed out to me who was likely to become a darvesh in Rahmat Abad, and why. Only these men—villagers still, but with a taste of the "individual growth" Iran's urban world offered—understood what the darvesh townsman longed to see, a singular, sharply-defined light in the dark; how he perceived one might recover wholeness by rejecting luxury and multiplicity; and what he feared, being alone in his grave after he died. The villagers who had not been immersed in *dulat*'s world for long did not have these spiritual needs, although as a kind of public service they were prepared to help those in their midst who did.

Commitment to Others

Thus it was in Rahmat Abad that Iranians realized individuality and self-fulfillment through responsibility rather than through the choices of Tehran's bazaar. But if accountability so heavily underpinned their relations with one another, where among adults was the bond of love the darveshes who were "contaminated" by town longed to find? Having experienced no substantive human bond in the personalism of Iran's urban society, did Rahmat Abad reject the personal challenge altogether? Where was *community?*

Perhaps the village most poignantly gave its answer to this the night that the boy Ahmad drank insecticide. Not a well-liked boy and, in any case, not originally from Rahmat Abad, at seventeen Ahmad seemed lazy and supercilious by village standards. A fight with his uncle caused him to try to kill himself, an intent the villagers considered sinful. Despite his unpopularity and despite the fact that it happened in late afternoon just as we were returning tired from the fields, almost every adult male in the community responded immediately to the news, rushing to minister to the young man and his family, going out to locate a vehicle in a neighboring village, and when that was finally found, heading to the public hospital in Dezful with the unconscious lad, several on each bike and motorcycle following behind the truck.

In Dezful the doctor announced that if Ahmad were to survive he would have to have an immediate infusion of twelve pints of blood. Who would give it? He pointed to the pallet and the awful blood-letting apparatus hanging above it. Without explanation or assurances he demanded, "Give it now or I can't save him."

The village men blanched at the physical details of puncturing the vein and hooking up rubbery tubes, watching the blood-sucking machine with its glistening glass jar fill up with great draughts of blood right from one's heart, stretching out solitary on a white cot as though also dead, everyone looking on—the sight of Ahmad there already pale. The men's families depended on their physical strength, their blood. The doctor never bothered to explain that their bodies would regenerate new blood. All of them distrusted doctors, especially doctors who worked for the State. Ahmad seemed dead already. Nevertheless, without drama or even discussion each villager volunteered to give his blood. Neither then nor later at home in the community—as those who gave blood lay around weak and dizzy for several days—at no time did one hear a word about personal sacrifice, not a mention of "brotherhood." The villagers' almost appalling matter-of-factness about the ordeal implied that they had performed nothing more than an everyday gesture. Their code knew neither sentiment nor self-advertisement. But commitment, it did.

As soon as the last villager arose from the cot with the doctor's twelfth jar now full of red blood, and the doctor stashed away the blood of Ahmad's friends in a refrigerator like gold bars in a vault, he pronounced the boy dead. The villagers' judgment of his perfidy and of Ahmad's lifelessness had both been accurate. Blood was sold dearly in urban Iran, jar by jar. I was told villagers' blood brought a premium, having strength and being free from "contamination."

We wept for Ahmad and the community's loss of him. He had tested its bonds beyond "accountability."

The Level of Individual Development

Not all urban Iranians under *dulat*'s shadow resembled Mehrabani. Those townsmen who shared his subjective rather than objective values were frequently ones who had been uprooted involuntarily or through their own ambitions from the structures of social accountability that the State sought to displace. For instance, personality differences and political and social contexts (although not social class) affected the degree to which the self provided an individual with ever-sliding standards of behavior, and thus the degree to which an individual craved the constant affirmation of others. Having no experience of a social core outside of himself, a bounded social core based on responsibility, Mehrabani could hardly be governed by such expressions of social cohesion as the requirements of dignity, service, duty, or even the fear of God, standards that in the villager's case transcended an individual's feelings.

It has often been argued that peasants, "embedded" in the social life of small, traditional, and sometimes poor communities, have less evolved personalities or individual character than do people who enjoy the benefits of cities or industrial society. This ethnocentric theory associates the development of individuality with technological advance and factors such as a high per capita income or gross national product. But the contrast between mature individuality in Rahmat Abad on the one hand, and the personalistic culture of the most "modern" sector of Iranian society on the other, inimical to individuality, contradicts this theory. To the extent that individuality is rooted in society's insistence that each person is a responsible moral agent, the exigencies of village life *required* individuality. *Dulat*'s "modernity" did not. The distinction between Mehrabani and the villagers dramatized the difference between individualism and individuality. In the urban world the State's arbitrary power combined with its paternalism to foster subjectivity, dependence, hence individualism, while often undermining individuality.

In the traditional village, many factors favored and, in turn, were favored by the articulation of individual integrity. These included the rural population's considerable geographic, economic, and social mobility based on pragmatic criteria; the extraordinary flexibility of kinship as well as residential forms, along with a tendency toward nuclear families when conditions allowed; the absence of ties between the peasant family and the land it tilled; and the objective, contractual basis of resource allocation even among kinsmen. Giving scope for individuals to develop their potential were the villagers' impersonal but trustworthy institution of *sharik* partnership, whereby individuals could bind themselves in specific short-term arrangements without generalized obligations; the free flow of information in rural society; the village culture's recognition of a range of individual rights vis-à-vis social groups; the polity's internal political balance and accountability; and all villagers' access to the community's support, its political arena, its judiciary, and its government. Finally, the villagers' unabashed response to economic opportunity through domestic and civic investment, agricultural experimentation, and entrepreneurial verve enabled an individual's creativity to contribute substantively to his immediate society.

These and other aspects of village culture that promoted individuality cannot be explained by the growth of towns or the penetration of the market economy, population increase, the spread of Protestantism or of Renaissance individualism, to which Weber and others have attributed the development of the individual in the West. Rather, the individual's clear articulation in Rahmat Abad sprang from the rule of customary law in village society and the rural region with which it interacted, a law accessible and predictable to all the villagers, shaped by their day-to-day behavior, a law kept steady and if need be enforced through corporate action. As we have seen, the individual depended for his or her development on family autonomy and the cohesive community, which in turn depended upon an accountable regional environment responsive to initiatives from groups that constituted it. To be sure, the State had contributed in an important way toward establishing this predictability by reducing the brigandage in the Khuzestan countryside. But as far as Rahmat Abad was concerned, almost every other measure the State had begun to take to foster "development" on the village's horizon simply enhanced the arbitrariness of power in Tehran, making the individual more dependent on personal ties, because the State itself was not founded on the social accountability of law. Individual development derives not from economic or demographic factors primarily, but from political and moral ones.

Thus three of the primary structures of political life in Rahmat Abad— the individual, the family, and the *sharik* partnership—were endebted to the village's corporate character for their own strength and freedom. It is then to this corporate polity of Rahmat Abad that we must next turn.

God never fails to keep the tryst . . . [but] He will not task a soul beyond its scope.   **—Qur'an, Sura 3**

Chapter 5

Rahmat Abad,
the Corporate Polity

**Everyone who is sundered far from his origin longs to recapture
the tune of reunion.** —Rumi, from *The Masnawi*

Before we move beyond Rahmat Abad to examine the community's relations with the State, and ultimately the relations between villages like it
and the Shah's Imperial Plan for Development in Bizhan, let us establish
the corporate character of the village along with its limitations. In this
chapter we will first review central characteristics of the village's structure, which we have already observed in the ethnographic material, clarifying these when necessary through contrasts with the social organization of *dulat*'s domain. Then we will review how Rahmat Abad and its
sister villages crystallized this corporate structuration of the rural region
in their religious rituals, always a key to people's daily experience of
social organization. Thirdly, we will discuss the relevance of Rahmat
Abad's corporate structure to certain aspects of current economic development theory and practice. Finally, we will examine the crucial limitations in Rahmat Abad's corporate structure, and the possibility that the
village might have resolved them in time.

Central Characteristics of the Village's Corporate Structure

Its Observable Unity

The very physical layout of Rahmat Abad spelled out in concrete form
its corporate structure, as the villagers had consciously shaped the settlement to embody the geographical and political order in which they lived.
What could be plainer? You could walk around Rahmat Abad's territory
in less than an hour by following its irrigation system, its lifeline. You
could locate its social, economic, and political center by going to its geographical center, the cross street where most of its initiatives began and
where the major village families had built their houses. Thus the community's positive action as a corporate entity reflected its open-book
physical form. The village's constituent building blocks, its families, outlined themselves so distinctly that everyone in the polity over ten years

old could describe the boundary of each family according to which it would likely take common action. Major changes in these boundaries (new families formed, old ones splitting or consolidating) were events of general public knowledge within twenty-four hours of the change. When a family no longer could act or be dealt with corporately, it redefined itself in public. Other constituent building blocks of the polity shared this same clarity: the short- and long-term partnerships, the *joft* units, the village officers and informal commissions with the specific tasks each performed. To become a member of Rahmat Abad one had to apply and be accepted.

Except for guilds and brotherhoods (and certain minority sects and foreign associations), few urban groups in Iranian society maintained definite boundaries, least of all the urban family. Given the fact that personal connections provided the best protection against the political instability of life within *dulat*'s regime, as well as the fact that all power beginning with the King himself and the royal family was based on personal status and not legitimately obtained through public office, townsmen's highest priority lay in being able to make as many all-encompassing kin claims as possible on as wide a network as possible—that is, to blur boundaries rather than draw them. Claims should be as loosely defined as possible so that one could make claims but not be overburdened by excessive commitments. Urban social organization was governed by just the opposite dynamic we have seen in the rural area, where villagers pared away kin involvements in response to the challenges of economic development, and where frequently and repeatedly even over generations the same individuals, calling themselves Rahmat Abad, publicly and behaviorially established their unity through collective projects.

Its Institutional Permanence

Besides the clarity of organizational expression, endurance marked the village's corporate character. Although Rahmat Abad had suffered an extraordinary history of instability, the community confirmed its institutional permanence by recomposing itself after each diaspora fate periodically imposed on it, most of its principal families returning over and over to this spot, this village, this community that was theirs. Certainly it was not peasant "rights" to the land that rooted them so deeply in Rahmat Abad or brought them back here; the villagers were free to go wherever they wished. But here were the people each villager knew, his or her font of memories and associations; here were the decrepit cattle stalls and little alleyways, the fields and canals one knew, one's childhood places, one's routines for interaction. The community reassembled. Through a constantly changing formal authority, its landlord, the community persisted; through the authorities' divisive formation of rival factions within the village, it persisted, too. When the State changed the village's name, its offices, and all its officials, the community restored them.

Tajeh, a nearby village, was said to have been punished collectively by Reza Shah the Great earlier in the century; he dispersed its population to many other parts of Iran, some as distant as Mash-had. Under the more lenient conditions of the 1960s, these villagers and their descendants began returning to Tajeh, one by one recomposing the community, meeting grown kinsmen or former neighbors they had been too young to remember or perhaps had never known themselves. They found that Tajeh the village had persisted, right there in the same place, with its same canals and roads, its neighboring villages, its same functional purposes. Like Rahmat Abad after periods of rural insecurity, Tajeh had continued as an actual, ongoing, and clearly identified social entity in its own right, even though temporarily it saw a change of its personnel.

In contrast to urban Iranian society where dynasties were invented and as soon disappeared, ministries, agencies, firms, organizations, friendships and partnerships, even families came and went more fleetingly than the individuals who lived within them—institutions being but toys for rearranging power—the institution of Rahmat Abad endured beyond the lives of all those who constituted it and it refused to be destroyed by power. Rahmat Abad's mourning rituals affirmed this. Such permanence derived from the community's reliance on custom, tradition, precedent, and community-held norms for its law, all of which resisted the whims of any single strongman.

As for *dulat,* its administrative authority over the Khuzestan Development Scheme gave good example of the State's ever-changing nature. Whenever a rising new figure in Tehran wrested Iran's grand experiment from someone whose star was in decline, the major responsibilities for the Khuzestan Scheme shifted from one year to the next, between the Ministry of Water and Power, the Ministry of Agriculture, the Ministry of Rural Affairs, The Plan Organization, and even parts of the royal family. Recall how *dulat* abolished the landlords and officially declared the villages free, then abolished the free villages' names to make them State cooperatives, then abolished these to put them into model towns and agribusinesses, then sought to abolish these. That was normal operation, "progress," for the State. Similarly, townsmen's families called themselves by different names in different years to emphasize this or that important ancestor whose connections and reputation would be more in favor. We have seen how the King concocted an entirely new calendar based on himself, and with this whim mandated a transformation in how the entire realm reckoned the passing of time. To avoid such flux, Rahmat Abad had to remain outside of Iran's "national" life.

The principal reason for such institutional instability in urban Iran was that personal power enabled men as individuals to change basic institutions under their control by their own enlightened fiat (like trying on different costumes or uniforms), according to shifting nuances around the court that caused local tremors in the provinces, or according to new resources, new social configurations, even according to brilliant new insights. Since there was no accountability to a public arena and certainly no positive value placed on precedent, what appeared to be institutions in Dezful were nothing more than the tools of central power manipulating the local setting—social arrangements to be split, combined, rearranged, renamed, given new charters at will. Institutions in Dezful did not comprise organic social entities with a life and legitimacy of their own in society—much less, autonomous corporate identities. This made it difficult to define the institutions that were players in *dulat*'s arena at any given time, and to know what background to take into consideration when dealing with any one of them. The technocrats could not distingush between Rahmat Abad and King Darius the Great Rural Cooperative as "institutions."

Corporate Representation

The villagers of Rahmat Abad did not always interact with the outside through the village as a corporate entity. But when they did, as we have seen, they could tap many mechanisms for collective representation and corporate action to deal with produce buyers, neighboring villages, villagers the community hired year after year for services, and others in the intervillage region. Only because its leaders and spokesmen formed an integral part of the community both politically and culturally could Rahmat Abad become a reliable unitary actor in the wider rural arena.

An analysis of district-level political representation in Iran's Parliament illustrates how hollow was townsmen's concept of institutional representation in the public arena. Shaykh 'Ali Khan Dashti, whom Professor Bill calls a "typical" case, represented the district of Savah in the fifth, seventh, and eighth Parliaments, Bushir (at the opposite end of the country) in the sixth and ninth, Damavand (again in another direction) in the thirteenth, and Tehran in the fourteenth Parliament (Bill, 1973:793). Imagine Musa serving as headman of Rahmat Abad one year, then headman of another village the next, then crossing the river to some unknown village where he would serve there before returning to the second village, meanwhile Bonvar's headman and Tajeh's representing Rahmat Abad to others. If there were so little functional relationship between the office of headman and its village, how could villagers ever have held him accountable, and if he had so little relationship to those he represented, how could others have dealt with any village through him?

Widely Shared Information

The predictability that enabled Rahmat Abad's corporate structure and the articulation of a similar structure throughout its intervillage region depended upon the open exchange of public knowledge among all interested players in this rural arena. Although mainly illiterate, the villagers insisted upon a "free press" within its boundaries, a free flow of information based not just on the words and claimed intentions of all actors but on their behavior and on judgments of their character, liabilities, strategies, and aspirations from long familiarity. Every adult in Rahmat Abad understood the community's political language, the nuances, symbols, and precedents that underpinned the issues being discussed. In such a small polity, with its emphatic pragmatism and objective criteria for most interpersonal relations, "back room" politics were conducted in the public arena itself. Although hundreds of thousands of Iranians in the urban sector had attended a university, many in America, the environment in which they lived offered little exchange of accurate and crucial economic or political information in a public arena.

What kept Rahmat Abad's public arena stable despite its flexibility, its acceptance of new initiatives, and its experimentation and discussion was its members' commitment to their very important (often life-and-death) common purposes, not just sentiment, and the community's autonomy against arbitrary outside determinations. On this basis of a genuinely *functional* or purposive community, the open exchange of information did not seriously threaten the polity; on the contrary, it strengthened it by increasing public interaction and rational allocation of resources.

Because the corporate community valued behavioral evidence more than personalistic arrangements, it could foster everyone's access to public information, whereas within *dulat*'s realm of personal power many of the crucial actors could obscure themselves, sending all decisive information through private channels to avoid exposure to the public. In contrast to Rahmat Abad, on the national political level individuals who were "the most effective carriers of demands and information" had to remain unknown so as not to compete with the Shah. Without public exposure, they could always change their positions or the information they packaged and handed on. The names of these key intermediaries and Imperial confidants were seldom printed in the press and never found in the rolls of political parties or other listings; these intermediaries never became prime ministers or senators, and conscientiously avoided public positions (Bill, 1973:781). Such secrecy was part and parcel of *dulat*'s world: Urban Persians notoriously presented a different "face" to the public than to intimates; their poetry returns again and again to the discrepancy between public "truth" and reality. The singular driving theme of the Qur'an, a townsman's epic outpouring, is *deceit* to others.

A Genuinely Public Arena

Rahmat Abad's corporate public not only provided an arena of institutional continuity and open information, but on this foundation enabled the villagers themselves to determine all of the community's major policy decisions. The village comprised a genuine "public," which can only be brought forth and maintained through participation and community. The villagers expected a public hearing about all land transactions and many labor contracts associated with them, any business arrangements affecting the village and involving considerable sums of money, and the utilization of any public facilities, properties, or funds. Whenever relevant, the villagers assumed that the public should know the ownership and management of "firms" working in the area, with their transactional links; all partnerships in town that exploited land adjacent to the village or regional resources which might be useful; the coming and going of strangers. Villagers inspected new property any among them acquired in town. They knew the relative wealth of those enjoying greatest prosperity, which constituted the basis for certain forms of taxation (expecting these villagers to finance many rituals, a larger proportion of communal investment in the canals, and so forth). Through *public* mediation, Rahmat Abad settled quarrels that might affect the community as a whole.

We have reviewed the village's economic undertakings that it elaborated either corporately as an entire unit (automatically assuming responsibility for the landlord's irrigation management, the *joft* system, corporate dealings with urban wholesalers, and so forth) or in partnerships and families. So lucidly did Rahmat Abad organize its production that even the locations it assigned to families on the threshing floor out beyond the village directly corresponded to their relative house locations in the village itself, making the great workshop of these grain farmers a micromap that exactly replicated the geographical order of their homes.

Finally, the community placed demands on its public servants such as Musa, whom it expected to put at its disposal certain resources and the information he gathered (a central part of his job was to gather and then broadcast important information). Because Musa embodied public morality, Rahmat Abad reviewed his conduct and that of his family more critically than that of an ordinary villager. When a public servant did not perform his job, he was fired. The villagers had dismissed schoolteachers it had hired who were absent too often from school, although they were not allowed even to complain against *dulat*'s teachers, sometimes absent for an entire week. They had fired community irrigators and rice guards not on the job, although they were not allowed even to complain against the unreliable service they received from *dulat*'s irrigation canal, and certainly never against the gendarmerie.

Contrary to Rahmat Abad's rule, public figures and those who succeeded within *dulat*'s domain would have considered it an insult to have to report to the public or to be held accountable ethically or morally. Of course, *dulat*'s urban world did have to operate with some degree of accountability, and personalistic societies have certain private mechanisms (accessible mainly to the powerful) for embarrassing individuals who take too much advantage of their position—at least those individuals relatively low in the social scale. Still, the lack of coherence between function and form permeated Iran's entire urban culture. In national basketball, for instance, it was "not the best athletic administrators who administer, nor the best coaches who coach, nor the best players who play, nor even the best shooters who shoot. It is those who have the right personal contacts who see the action. The most famous Iranian basketball player is an individual of mediocre basketball ability who also is a police captain with the right connections. The Iranian Sports Federation is actually a federation of individuals and cliques whose primary goal is to grasp and maintain political power. More emphasis is placed upon personal sociopolitical advancement than upon team success" (Bill, 1973:787).

In short, none of Rahmat Abad's political prerogatives, expectations, skills, or undertakings essential to a self-governing polity and to an open economy did Iran's *urban* world even perceive dimly, least of all the corporate initiative and accountability within the public arena that constitute the foundations of autonomy.

Individual Autonomy

Because of the urban world's insecurity and the State's domination of the urban world, the personalistic networks through which virtually everyone could tap someone in government (if only through a janitor or a tea boy serving the great) precluded among townsmen the individual autonomy that was so pronounced in Rahmat Abad. Despite the vigor and authority of the village's public domain, which exceeded that of its urban counterpart in openness, participation, predictability, and clarity, Rahmat Abad protected its members' privacy far more effectively than did *dulat*. The community never interfered in strictly family affairs unless these escalated to an interfamily level, and then only when they threatened civic life. Except for the senior women of the community, villagers rarely approached others' homes without invitation or specific business (the headman's compound was, of course, a different matter). The fact that public authorities could search one's house, a fact taken for granted and upon occasion experienced in Dezful, would have been unthinkable in Rahmat Abad. Contrary to the prevailing political science theories about building the "nation State" (Myrdal, 1968, I:52–64), the village polity's corporateness rested on the integrity and relative autonomy of its constituent units, not on compromising, co-opting, or destroying them. Even when something was thought to be missing, having been carried away by a child or borrowed some time ago, a neighbor or kinsman could not look for it freely in another's yard, not even within the same compound.

We have already contrasted individual personal growth in Rahmat Abad, which corresponded to this safeguarded privacy, with the personality development urban Iranians sought. Not surprisingly, mature villagers reflected in their personal autonomy structural aspects of other organizational forms they experienced socially, especially that accountability and responsibility which endowed them with a determinative role in their society. Townsmen, lacking the chance to make such vital contributions within *dulat*'s paternalistic realm, and lacking an environment in which they could create their future by objective achievement alone, often turned toward expanding their family tree to as vast an empire as possible, sometimes largely fictitious, as though to overcompensate for their having so little individual autonomy. In this search for identity and security through personal connections lay the bitter irony that these all-encompassing networks were by their very nature more ambiguous and unstable, and less accountable hence less certain than the impersonal ones in Rahmat Abad, and inevitably *corrosive* of one's individual integrity.

A Charter of Clearly Delimited Purpose

The balance that Rahmat Abad maintained between its active public domain and the privacy and self-reliance of its constituent members derived from its definite—although unwritten—charter. Rahmat Abad's charter specified many responsibilities that the village assumed, but with equal resoluteness it excluded innumerable functions and issues as being outside the community's affairs. While primary education *was* the corporate community's business, supplying marketing facilities, a public bath, or a religious shrine was not. Nor did Rahmat Abad take upon itself such responsibilities as making education compulsory, urging Bakhtiari and Arab children to speak the community's language in public places, or requiring members to worship in a certain manner (or at all!). Just as Rahmat Abad's territorial boundaries delimited the area of agricultural domain, so the village charter was able to delimit which of the infinite initiatives and regulations *possible* in governance it would assume any responsibility for. Basically, it kept its Little Parliament's agenda as brief as possible.

In this restraint of its authority and responsibility, Rahmat Abad sharply differed from the most common forms of social, economic, and political association in urban Iran, where groups and firms of all sorts, clubs, even Ministries, and certainly the King knew no limits to their expertise or attempted command. In Khuzestan the Ministry of War ran a profit-making truck farm; the Ministry of Water and Power an agricultural research station, its own separate telephone system, a hospital, and a preparatory school. Mehrabani considered it an affront when the villagers doubted his authority in repairing Roumanian tractors that he did not even know how to drive. Clergymen from Dezful never hesitated to instruct women in midwifery, while shopkeepers in town often scolded them about village child care. In town, personal status often defined a person's qualifications, as much as his or her objective achievements did. When I asked Mehrabani what gave The Plan Organization the right to require peasants to use a certain type of fertilizer, he said the King wanted it—that was reason enough. (In contrast, when I asked the peasants, they presumed The Plan Organization had experimented with many and found this fertilizer the most effective.)

Without any models of behaviorally evaluated limitations or objective qualifications or purposes, townsmen the villagers knew experienced little structure in any aspect of their lives, even the primary structures of commitment and rejection, inclusion and exclusion, affirmation and negation. The only thing that determined the limits to a man's power was his personal network. Consistent with the villagers' observations in Dezful, but played out on the national level, Professor Bill mentions six prominent Iranians during this period who among them accounted for forty ministerships; the scope and the transience of the offices they held reflected the disjunction between functional expertise and accountability on the one hand, and personal power on the other. "Iqbal, for example, has been Prime Minister, a Deputy Minister, and Minister of Health (5 times), Post and Telegraph, Education (2 times), Roads (2 times), and Interior. He has been Minister of Court, governor-general, university chancellor, Senator, and Majlis [Parliament] representative. In 1968 an Iranian newspaper listed 36 jobs that Iqbal was then holding. The daily *Ayandigan* carried a subsequent article indicating that the 36 positions were not a complete list since Iqbal's major position as Chairman and Managing Director of the National Iranian Oil Company, for example, had been omitted" (Bill, 1973:793).

Incremental Expansion of Predictability Grounded in Local Political Capacity

Because the landlords had neglected the day-to-day regulation of affairs in Rahmat Abad, the villagers at the time of land reform enjoyed a head start in developing the expectations, norms, skills, and institutions for regulating their affairs themselves in ways that remained responsive to local control, hence predictable to local actors. For many years they had been coordinating and regulating village activities largely on their own. Then at the time of land reform, since they were loath to invite in *dulat* to take the landlord's place, they had begun to face the more difficult challenges of self-governance as local affairs became more complex. By the time of my stay there, the primary attitudes and skills for participating in a polity and economy on a *scale* that was locally manageable had become widely dispersed throughout the village population. Even landless laborers, villagers from ethnic minorities, newcomers, and women could hold one another accountable and could join in keeping the community on a steady course, or in directing its changes gradually so that everyone could keep abreast of them. This predictability of one another's behavior within Rahmat Abad's public arena was backed up, to be sure, by access to social pressure and other mechanisms, not just resting on sentiment. It was this sense of stability and local control that underpinned the villagers' ambitious, energetic investments, and their impersonal partnerships after land reform. But even before then it contributed to the phenomenal leap in village production in response to agricultural extension within the DIP trial program discussed in Chapter 1.

Having achieved relative predictability and local control in Rahmat Abad itself, the villagers had begun to move beyond its boundaries into the intervillage region they already knew so well, expanding their economic sphere of interaction at a *pace* that their sphere of predictibility kept up with. We see partnerships of various sorts, investments, and the rudiments of intervillage coordinational efforts expanding into this social field outside Rahmat Abad, but still within familiar territory of frequent interaction. For example, several villages began scheduling the trips of their pickup trucks in coordination with one another to avoid redundancy, and joined in regulating water from a canal they sometimes shared. This wider region still lacked even informal regulatory mechanisms, but the Dubendar ceremony on the tenth day of Moharram confirmed that beneath these regional-level partnerships and nascent coordinational endeavors a fundamental social field had already coalesced, with a specific membership, of clearly identifiable units, explicit boundaries, history, and a shared trust. The villagers were beginning to structure this predictability for particular intervillage needs.

Because of the differential in power between the centralized State and the village, and because of the centralized State's arbitrariness, the villagers would have found it impossible to begin evolving these norms, skills, and institutions for accountability and predictability had the protective boundaries of the corporate community and the intervillage region been removed. That would have left individuals and families with only the elementary political skills and institutions they had developed, exposed helplessly to the predatory, all-transforming State (which rarely responded to even the villagers' most innocuous initiatives, much less would have allowed them to hold it accountable). If these firm, locally accountable structures had been destroyed as the Shah and his advisors wanted and then replaced by the centralized State, how would people at the grass-roots level have retained even a model of accountability, impersonal law, or self-governance? How would they have kept alive the experience and expectations, the skills and institutions basic for social predictability?—not through the institutions and expectations that Iranians experienced within *dulat*'s domain.

What was at stake in the evolution of local and then wider predictability was—among other things—necessarily a matter of the *pace* of development. Building up a field of predictability and trust from the pre– and then the post–land reform village's small arena to a larger one step by step, and from the larger to yet a slightly larger one when ready, necessarily took time to experiment with new agreements and ventures; invent alternatives; test, back off, learn about others' miscalculations, and start again; convince one another, watch certain linkages fail or correct themselves; and, finally, through repeated efforts evolve the skills and institutions that local accountability required. Then participants had to disseminate and solidify these expectations and skills throughout the population, and expand them gradually to a wider environment (see

Arensberg, 1972). Trust and law evolve but gradually, on the basis of repeated empirical tests. Rahmat Abad's pace of change, although in some respects rapid since land reform, still held back those in the fore-front, still guarded the community's corporate integrity at their expense. By doing so Rahmat Abad determined to retain the incremental process through which the polity itself and its moral underpinnings could keep on top of change, *its* change and no one else's, preserving accountability and participation in governance. In contrast, urban Iran within the State construed the need to modernize as a crisis requiring speed, a classic ploy for those who wish to exercise power unaccountably.

To establish the corporate or institutional strength of the local social units at each stage was indispensable for local trust—the family units as they defined themselves (whether nuclear, extended or joint), the part-nerships, the villages, and so forth—as these primary forms then expanded outward by linking with others. Only first in such primary units could individuals learn and develop the political skills that accountability and predictability require. Once these units clarified themselves as relia-ble actors in the public arena, which anyone could recognize, appraise, and make responsive, then *through mobilizing them* (often only implic-itly) the villagers could extend their sphere of predictability beyond the individual or family.

Within *dulat*'s realm, in contrast, intermediate-level social groupings and institutions—neighborhood efforts, political parties, interest groups, ethnic and religious associations, lobbies, confederations of organizations with shared concerns—never achieved this permanence, public exposure, or accountability, leaving individuals with no long-enduring and reliable organizational vehicles larger than family for extending into a wider arena of interaction. Hence, investments and development initiatives within the State's domain as well as policy decisions and "law" sprang largely from the State itself, and when they did not, people attempted to secure what initiatives they took themselves, by personalistic ties to those in power, not through public measures.

In these ways, then, the local associations and groups incrementally and gradually expanding between the individual and family on the one hand and the State on the other, provided the essential foundation for Rahmat Abad's and other villages' remarkable release of energy. The more responsive to local control these intermediate-range social forms were, the more effectively they could check anything that jeopardized an environment predictable to its members.

Moral Cohesion

The final tribute of Rahmat Abad's corporate structure that requires con-sideration is its moral cohesion as a community. The village derived its moral fiber from fulfilling its members' primary needs of life, sustenance and social order, plus a third one: protection or help (see Nisbet, 1969:

54–57). Despite the villagers' strict quid pro quo calculations, in emergencies they set these aside: While the village men made themselves overcome their anxiety about giving blood to save Ahmad, it was the urban, professional helper—*dulat*'s doctor—who calculated the value of their blood in rials he would receive. On another occasion, when Gholam went to the hospital, neighbor children were sent to help his wife pick beans; when Hasan Quli's horse fell dead the first day of harvest, someone offered to loan him a donkey free; when Sultan 'Ali married, villagers contributed generously to his wedding, knowing the debts he had incurred with family illness; when Hamda's cowshed burned down, Hamda suffered no shortage of help to rebuild it, although he was hardly a popular man. We have seen the villagers' contempt for human settlements that knew no collective defense of every member's home.

Although in its campaigns for rural pacification *dulat* had diminished the brigandage rampant in the countryside before the 1950s, villagers feared *dulat*'s help and protection. (Townsmen, without mutual aid, needed it.) Of *dulat*'s protection, villagers asked who would protect them if they then were encompassed by their protector? *Dulat* did not comprise a moral order. It did offer free medicine for simple ailments, and sometimes during emergencies, free food rations; but everything from *dulat* and from elites in *dulat*'s world—above all, their *protection*—had to be won through subservience, bribery, and interpersonal connivance, and thus had a bitter moral price. Everything charitable or protective *dulat* extended smacked of self-advertisement, hence manipulation, and trumpeted its professional superiority, hence the inadequacy and dependence of those it helped. In contrast, as we saw in the hospital when Ahmad needed blood, Rahmat Abad extended protection and help in such a matter-of-fact manner that it was difficult to recognize assistance as such, or where it was being given. No one "helped" a family put on a funeral or wedding; no one "helped" put out a fire or console the seriously ill; these were things that had to get done. No one "donated" to visiting darvesh beggars; villagers simply scooped out rice when one who seemed genuine came to the house. Beneath the community's public and charter, its boundaries and structure, and its incorporation of individual initiatives, beneath these was a moral experience in which we all found ourselves in life together—vulnerable human beings.

Understandably, townsmen with no equivalent social form were fatalistic: I found the villagers not even fatalistic when confronting death, but only when off against *dulat,* an amoral force against which the community knew it had no chance worth rallying the collective strength. When the Justice Corpsman preached nationalism, the villagers could not grasp what "Iran" meant; and when they asked me about my country America, my *mamlakat,* they wanted to know how many streets and tractors it had: Rahmat Abad was their nation, their fatherland.

It was the congruence between this objective, functional, pragmatic village Rahmat Abad, and Rahmat Abad the villagers' moral community, that gave Rahmat Abad and, in turn, its members their strength. Although their mosque belonged to the village, not to the darvesh, the villagers could not bring themselves to pray or hold religious rituals in it even when the Justice Corpsman insisted they should: The mosque was located out beyond the edge of Rahmat Abad and had been built later, added on. The villagers wanted their religious rituals housed within the community, nested in its very comings and goings—a profound expression of its moral integrity. And so the villagers prayed on the rooftops or by each hearth; they rotated their Moharram ceremonial meals from home to home; the young men conducted their Moharram breast-beating rituals in one villager's special room with its fertilizer sacks and grain stored on the side, the children and chickens coming in and out. Within the heart of Rahmat Abad, the village would celebrate the transcendent. For Mehrabani religion belonged inside a holy building, not a secular one, even if the former happened to be outside the village; for the villagers, too, religion belonged inside a holy building, and Rahmat Abad itself was that building.

In summary, because the polity emerged out of the villagers' interaction and was not created by force from on high, it constituted a solid basis for predictability, the sine qua non of sustained economic "development." It preserved this predictability so essential for "development" by acting responsibly with clearly defined but limited corporate purpose, expecting similar accountability of others (including its officials); by assuming without question that all important economic and political information be broadly disseminated; and by achieving a close congruence between the actual behavior of day-to-day life and local governance. As a microarena for mobility, free interaction, and institutional integrity based not on status but on objective achievement and publicly scrutinized, functional behavior, the village much more closely approximated the optimal conditions for Weber's rational choice than did Iran's urban culture, including that of the Western-trained technocrats. But ultimately the community of Rahmat Abad embodied moral values, and as its response in Ahmad's suicide epitomizes, it was prepared to act upon these. The villagers observed this moral foundation in their religious rituals.

Ritual: A Summation of the Villager's Corporate Structure

Rahmat Abad celebrated its corporate structure and crystallized this structure in visible, dramatic form in its religious rituals, which anthropologists read as a shorthand code to a community's social organization and moral texture. Primordial among these rituals in rural Khuzestan was the *ruzah khanah* for mourning, which followed a death and which the villagers repeated sometimes four or five times a day for weeks thereafter, an extended funeral. Some years before I went to Rahmat Abad, the

State, probably in kahoots with the clergy who had much to gain, had outlawed village cemeteries, so the washing and immediate burial of a corpse took place in *dulat*'s cemetery in Dezful, an extraordinarily perfunctory event—disorganized, stiff, without ritual unity, and certainly without a spiritual setting. In *dulat*'s cemetery the bereaved found themselves thoroughly exposed to the idle, the destitute, and the deranged of Dezful who wandered among the tombstones begging, stealing, drumming up jobs of chanting and wailing. One wanted to get out of there as fast as possible. Total strangers unconnectedly were burying their kinsmen and friends in adjacent graves with no room even for each group to gather round what it was doing, townsmen no one knew gaping distractedly: a burial hardly to be called a ceremony, severed from its ancient moorings when transposed to this alien place. *Dulat* had forced a powerfully symbolic change upon Rahmat Abad when, as practically its first encroachment into the rural landscape, it had required the villagers to bury their dead in the State's soil, no longer in their own out in the *biyaban*.

After the Dezful burial, the villagers would return home to the countryside, where the real mourning rituals would begin, a veritable funeral. When Madar-i-Tulaki died and had been buried in *dulat*'s cemetery—a woman of stout character in her fifties—all Rahmat Abad prepared for the mourning in her home within her community within the region of familiar villages, a region she had crisscrossed so often fleeing landlords with her family, taking the children to visit kinsmen, attending others' funerals. The ceremonies would last for weeks with every attention to detail and respect. The men of Rahmat Abad constructed a canopy of branches and leaves under which they would often repeat their part of the ritual; they had black clothing made quickly for the family and everyone close to it, slaughtered the sheep to be cooked in a special funeral delicacy, bought the potatoes and chickpeas, sugar, tea, and cigarettes in town and even began helping to cook. Meanwhile the village women set themselves to cleaning grain; borrowing huge cauldrons for the rice, extra trays and bowls for the stew, and additional cooking utensils; and sweeping the house and courtyard Madar-i-Tulaki had left behind, where the funeral feast and then the individual mourning sessions with each visiting delegation would be held.

As news traveled throughout the region, delegations of from twenty-five to fifty adults from each village in the surrounding area set out for Rahmat Abad, arriving at different times and on different days depending upon when they received word. From the rooftop one could see each delegation as it came in a small, resolute body across the fields. "Bonvar is about to arrive," one of the young people on watch would announce; "it looks like Dubendar has finally heard, as I see them coming at last." Occasionally a distant village arrived by minibus (to be parked outside the village). The nearest sent delegations on several consecutive days. As each delegation approached, the men and women in it walked together proudly as a formal union, into Rahmat Abad, down the street, into the compound where villagers who awaited them stood aside for the solemn little band to pass in silence, straight to Madar-i-Tulaki's house. There the men and women separated—the men to their gathering with the men of Rahmat Abad under the canopy, the women into the empty house with the women of Rahmat Abad. The women broke into wailing and cried together, sobbing disconsolately, blurting out poignant memories of Madar-i-Tulaki or expressions of her admirable attributes. After a quarter of an hour or so, a leading woman of Rahmat Abad would indicate an end to the lamentation, everyone stopped, and she and her friends would serve tea and cigarettes. The women would exchange news and gossip. Meanwhile the men sat beneath the canopy where a villager or visiting mullah intoned the Qur'an or chanted an event from Imam Hosein's religious battle at Karbala, the central event of the villagers' Shi'ite Islam; this prompted the men, too, to cry together, heads bowed, under their own careful control. They, too, would drink tea, smoke, and exchange news before summarily departing with the women as a single body, cleansed, having honored Madar-i-Tulaki and the village of Rahmat Abad.

In Madar-i-Tulaki's case, over thirty delegations arrived to mourn with Rahmat Abad. The duration, the expense, the collective effort mounted, and above all the intensity of these days were far out of proportion to her inconspicuous life or her family's importance in the region. Except for delegations from the nearby villages and those where she had lived, rarely did a mourning party include more than several people who had actually known Madar-i-Tulaki. Rather, the villagers came in compact little bands representing community by community in the region, to share the sorrow of a sister community. They wept communally for a communal loss, affirming in the way they arrived, wept together, and left, the moral solidarity of each village's corporate boundedness and the moral fabric of one community's link with the other, the enduring social structure that would remain behind when they themselves died.

Besides the funerals, it was the religious feast of Moharram that gave Rahmat Abad its most intense occasion for celebrating its corporate identity, cohesion, and the dignity of its measured emotional restraint, a ten-day memorial for Imam Hosein's tragic martyrdom with his family and followers in the Karbala battle near Baghdad. During these ten days almost every household in Rahmat Abad prepared a banquet (or, in the case of the poor, afternoon tea) to which all heads of house in the community came, the landless as well, often one being held at noon and another at night. Family and neighbors served the men as they sat in a single circle and conversed. After the meal or after drinking tea, the visiting mullah—a simple man of rural origins himself, not an urban cleric—narrated an event of the famous battle: how the Prophet's steadfast followers were one by one betrayed, often by their closest kin, and heinously slain. Moving his narration gradually into a chant, the mullah would accelerate its tension of love, violence, and agony with increasingly more vivid details, he himself now in a low wail as he led the men into the depth of the holy martyrs' sufferings, and into their own group of sorrow that finally welled up in trance-like but tautly restrained communal weeping for the excruciating pain these early Islamic saints endured, and for our share in it. The simple ceremony would conclude right after that with a brief prayer, tea, cigarettes, and conversation.

Each evening during the ten-day period of Moharram, in a special room that one villager called Mullah maintained (he was not a mullah but only nicknamed that), the younger men of Rahmat Abad united themselves in a heated athletic breast-beating ritual chanting to Imam Hosein as they recalled the Karbala battle again: lifting their arms high in unison, thumping their fists down on their bare chests together as one body, momentarily relaxing only to lift high again over the head, thump down, the heavy thud-thud-thud contrapuntal to their young chanter's flute-like voice in the night air. If the young men of a neighboring village arrived to share this ritual, they entered the village as the mourning bands would, in a compact group, Rahmat Abad's young men going out to greet them in the street in a similar close knot. Each group, facing the other, would acknowledge its own and the other's corporate separateness in rhythmed statement and reply—one chanting and striking their breasts in unison while the other waited, then the other responding similarly, before they joined together in the ritual inside. Whenever this took place, the Justice Corpsman did his best to force the two groups to shake hands all around when they met, which would have dissolved the ritual's very tension and synchrony in his culture's personalistic cliché, would have melted those very boundaries the ritual confirmed, and would have denied its symbolic function of preparedness. (Some scholars trace this breast-beating ritual back to a period when Shi'ites had to maintain martial vigilance to protect their faith.)

As Rahmat Abad's men celebrated in unison their combined agricultural and martial strength, the village women kept their unique Moharram ritual, too, corporately observed. The women after all knit together Rahmat Abad in their visits to one another's houses, in their gossip and work together at the canal, in serving almost as gifts in marriage linking one family and village to another. On the eve of the Tenth Day, late at night, the women and some older men made the round of each house compound in the community, going straight to each beehive-shaped oven. There, while the group encircled the oven and chanted, someone would extend a small lantern into its depths as though to bless it for renewal, Rahmat Abad's universal sign of womanhood. This ritual, perhaps Zoroastrian in origin, commemorated holy Zaynab, who in the aftermath of the Karbala massacre found Imam Hosein's head among the slain on the battlefield and hid it in her oven from desecration by the enemy, richly merging many symbols of woman's preservational role.

On the Tenth Day of Moharram, the entire village carried Rahmat Abad's great looming banner bedecked with black drapery and pennants and streamers, to the regional folk shrine at Dubendar, a couple of hours' walk from the village. Along the way the young men would regroup us now and then to chant and beat their breasts as though to infuse fresh morale into our procession. Approaching Dubendar through the fields of wildflowers and scampering field mice (Moharram fell in early springtime in 1973), we began to see many other tall banners waving and jutting forward across the horizon as the communities of the region came together from all directions at their ceremonial center, in this thrilling triumphal march across the landscape. Beginning ten days earlier, the constituent families of each community had feasted in each home together over and over in religious testimony to each village's corporate constitution; each community's young men and then its women had also dramatized their respective unions and purposes. Now, with that primary order of the village fortified, religious celebration would go on to confirm the same structural integrity and convergence at the next organizational level, the intervillage region around Dubendar.

At the gate to Dubendar, in some years antagonistic groups of youths were said traditionally to have fought each other as their bands approached to enter the shrine's compound. If such fights had taken place formerly, they were unlikely in 1974, because the Shah's bayoneted gendarmes interlaced the shrine crowd, their sharp daggers and the clergymen's black robes marking the urban figures in this rural convocation. Since there had been no talk of impending quarrels that might break loose, and since the older men did not remember any for many years past, everyone knew *dulat*'s armed presence there had other intent. Could the State leave the clergy to preside alone over this remote gathering so deeply indigenous in its initiatives and organization—the only assembly of peasant society in this area throughout the year—after *dulat* had expropriated the holdings of many clerical landlords, had begun handing over to foreigners villages now owning their lands, had damaged most local irrigation systems for its modernization plans, and had limited the acreage it would allow many communities to plant in rice? Throughout the Pahlavi rule, devout clergymen had hated the regime, notably in Dezful, Mossadegh's stronghold and a reactionary bastion of Shi'a Islam. (Since the late 1960s neither the King and his family nor any high official had visited the city; according to rumor, attempts had been made on his life each time he had come in years past.) Recalling as it did how at the very birth of Islam saints had attained glory resisting Yazid, the despotic usurper, Moharram lent itself easily to political suggestion. The unsheathed bayonets formed no honor guard.

Nor was it convincing, though, that the peasants had come to hear the Dezful mullahs. As the men in black preached and prayed into their microphone, the villagers found friends and relatives, exchanged invitations, news, marriage speculations, prospects for closing a deal or switching to a better one; young people met; everyone entered the shrine to kiss the saint's tomb. With characteristic pragmatism the occasion hardly lasted two hours. When the processions began to leave, village by village assembling by their banners to head off across the plain in different directions, the gendarmes' jeep covered with palms put itself in the front to lead out of the shrine. But beneath the clergy's and *dulat*'s competition to use the villagers for townsmen's ends, this ancient folk meeting had once again articulated the region's strictly rural organizational structure.

When I asked old Rajab later about the bayoneted gendarmes, he called *dulat* "a dear guest," *mahman-i aziz:* a colloquial village term for a guest whom you must treat dearly only because he has invited himself to be your guest—indeed a guest who would make you *his* guest.

The Corporate Village and Economic Development Theory

Many economists, planners, most Third World rulers and their advisors such as the Shah and his, and many development theorists (notably Myrdal, 1968, I:52–63; Hyden, 1980: 31–34, 225–32) promote the destruction or at least the weakening of all social and political groups, especially indigenously rooted and corporate ones like the village, intermediate between the State and the individual or family. They consider these to obstruct "development": "enclaves," "segmented markets," villages and tribes, strong provinces and subregions under local control, religious institutions that affect their members' important decisions, minority groups that preserve their own languages, and so on. The more effectively organized these are by their members, the more antithetical to "development." These modernizers argue that in its drive toward "development," the State must liberate individuals from their traditional social context so that, *economically,* they can seek out and make more productive links with complementary resources throughout the economy—for example, pairing their labor with others' land, their land with others' capital, even their own capital or savings with others' technological or managerial expertise; and so that *personally* they can realize more fully self-determined individualities.

According to these theories, cohesive social structures between the State and the individual will not release their members' resources to the wider society for availability (their individuals, their land, their savings, and so forth), thereby depriving society of these reserves. At the same time, these conservative structures resist others' penetration by requiring a tight personalistic tie, unavailable to outsiders, for any coupling with local resources that does take place. On both scores, then, intermediate-level structures prevent economic rationality, which Weber and others have shown to be necessary for economic development. Furthermore, such groups often guardedly retain their own norms, rules, institutional mechanisms for establishing internal predictability, their own means for settling disputes—in short, their own informal systems of law, hardly homogeneous with officialdom's formal legal apparatus that to planners provides the only basis for "development." Standardization, "integration," universality are said to be prerequisites for all growth, all progress. (In this assumption planners and theorists in general overlook the fact that Western development was firmly founded on locally responsive, *plural* legal systems—see Berman, 1983:528–37, 555.) Finally, those who would undermine these grass-roots associations and institutions find, as we have seen, that in their closeness they prevent the individual from personal growth.

Despite the theories of economists, planners, and rulers about the inhibiting forces of cohesive structures between the State and the individual, we observe Rahmat Abad's villagers within Throne City's corporate structure, and within its structured regional enclave, acting in just the opposite manner from these predictions. They eagerly moved beyond the family, patriclan, *bonku* plow team, and even the village to link with others within their range of predictability. They ruggedly insisted on individual independence even within these traditional structures. Indeed, the sharp articulation of these middle-range organizations, and their corporate *strength,* were what ensured the freedom of individuals and of economic resource allocation. Quite the opposite of "modernization" theory's argument, it was in the technologically advanced, urban society Professor Bill so accurately described—*dulat*'s modern sector with virtually no corporate structures between the family and the State—that people obsessively sought and clung to personalistic forms of social organization, resisting economic rationality.

Thus the evidence from this study suggests that three of economists' requirements for "development"—the mobility of resources; their allocation according to impersonal, economically "rational" criteria; and the ability of resources to join contractually, not bound by status—all depend, first and foremost, upon a predictable local environment: predictable to the *local actors.* These requirements found wider realization in Rahmat Abad than in Iran's "modern" sector. Such predictability—in the *local actors'* minds—is contingent upon clearly articulated local corporate structures that as autonomous units regulate their local affairs internally and conduct their own external relations. That is, their members themselves coordinate and regulate their affairs, which are not directed by outsiders. These corporate structures derive their locally based predictability from their local direction. Only such locally accountable structures can again and again check external arbitrariness. This internal and increasingly external predictability that economists' mobility and rationality of resource allocation require depends then on *structured, locally governed* organization. The security it provides enables social units to link with one another on impersonal grounds, which, in turn, favors the growth of the relatively autonomous and not psychologically dependent personality.

Conversely, in direct contrast to contemporary development theory and endeavors, the personalism of villagers' relatives and acquaintances within the transforming realm of *dulat* indicates that the highly centralized State—because of its arbitrary power—destroys local predictability. That loss of objective stability and the experience of being overpowered, in turn, keep individuals from seeking a more self-determined personal growth.

By retaining the *joft* system Rahmat Abad did, of course, prevent the release of local resources from their corporate environment, a qualification that we must consider. Furthermore, not all peasants everywhere or people with such intermediate buffers act like the villagers in Rahmat Abad: There is some empirical justification for the economists' generalization, which we must try to explain. In the following pages let us first spell out how the underpinning of local predictability and control that emerged out of Rahmat Abad's corporate structure enabled rich and poor villagers alike, those with capital and land and those with only their labor, young risk takers acting alone and older established families, to join in corporate local improvements (like the construction of Throne City and the repair of irrigation canals the new State system had damaged). It was this underpinning that also enabled the burst of large and small partnerships and individual investments which we have seen. Once we have understood this dynamic, we can then place the villagers' retention of the *joft* system within our theoretical argument, throwing light on many similar cases that at least in part justify some scholars' and planners' concern about the conservatism of local social structures.

To illustrate the connection between local corporate predictability and the release of individual resources from their traditional bonds, let us return briefly to the history of Muhammad and his brothers, Khudadad's sons. As we saw, once the family resettled in Rahmat Abad under the new landlord (who they had hoped brought a new stability), the villagers moved almost right away to loosen their associations based on personal status and form new ones based on functional objectives. They formed their own nuclear households and in a few years went so far as to separate out their respective herds of sheep from the family flock; Muhammad even entrusted his flocks to an Arab shepherd—a man not a kinsman and in fact of a traditionally antagonistic ethnic group. That, in turn, freed Muhammad's son for expansion of the cash-crop vegetables, and it soon enabled the Arab to invest as a shareholder with other villagers (neither Arabs nor kinsmen of *his*) in the village truck. Family bonds remained essential, but because Rahmat Abad seemed so stable and because its effective common law could ensure fairness, individuals and nuclear families could extricate themselves from the all-encompassing demands of traditional personalistic ties for greater mobility and a much wider choice of potential *sharik* partnerships. Then, too, given Rahmat Abad's predictable environment, the extended family and tight community associations did not need to cling parasitically to individuals who became successful on their own, because the prosperity of those remaining behind within the traditional social unit did not simply depend upon personal favors from people who were getting ahead: Rather, the former could advance themselves on their own strengths and partnerships as they saw others doing.

This same centrifugal force *out of* traditional bonds had accelerated as soon as land reform signaled to the villagers a long period of stability and local control. Now they even began to reach beyond Rahmat Abad. Investors in one of the tractors—and in 1974, a second pickup truck—undertakings for which villagers needed to draw on a *broad* pool of resources, included non-kin shareholders *from other villages*. Having experimented with and routinized reliable impersonal linkages *within the village itself*—the communal cowherd, village partnerships for the tractors and truck, village-level regulation of their operations, village work partnerships among non-kinsmen, and so forth, not to mention the firm evidence of village solidarity in constructing Throne City—having experimented with and established reliable impersonal forms of resource combination and organization *within Rahmat Abad,* now people were venturing farther afield.

For instance, the *joft*holders of Rahmat Abad had no difficulty whatsoever contracting informally with a stranger from a village to the south for something as complicated and relatively long-term as the labor of scores of rice transplanters. The "partnership" was risky on both sides. The village needed these outsiders, with whom it had no previous ties at all, to work intensely for over a month, labor not being available at the last minute if they failed to come or if they proved lazy; on the transplanters' part, they would receive their full payment only months later, at harvest. The two sides made such arrangements with ease, no landlord or urban authority there to ensure them. (For many years the villagers had relied mainly on their own and relatives' help, hiring some workers through the landlord.) The villagers and those who contracted with them informed themselves about one another's reputation before entering into the agreement, and they knew that they could rely on intervillage mechanisms to hold their partners accountable if need be.

Through such expansion the villagers' organizational skills, their expectations and nascent institutions for local regulation, and their confidence developed. Launching new projects, in turn, strengthened further their existing partnerships, corporate villages, and the intervillage environment of trust. As local coordination and regulation expanded the arena of locally based governance, and integrated the miniarenas of separate villages into the predictable intervillage environment, the predictability of the corporate structures at the base and new ones being tested encouraged greater mobility of resources seeking complementary linkages, free to establish them with strangers. We see a reciprocal dynamic between the cautiously expanding environment of trust that enabled greater resource mobility, and the corporate accountability of intermediate-range structures that ensured the reliability of each linkage. In only a few years the rural society here had moved to a far richer and more complex organizational stage than existed when the countryside had comprised few social arrangements besides families, plow teams, villages, and ephemeral landlord-tenant relationships. The village and region provided an umbrella of security under which innumerable new, functionally based, and increasingly more extensive organizational forms had begun to emerge (the vehicles, for instance, which would take from five to ten years to amortize).

It is necessary to distinguish between villagers' willingness to invest in education (perhaps in order to *leave* the village)—and even their willingness to make individual investments such as in fertilizer or a pesticide sprayer—and their investment in Throne City, its tractors, bridges, and new waterways, which sprang from their commitment to their agricultural and rural future, hence from their trust in the reliability of a political organization they themselves could control. None of them left for the cities where there were few jobs, as they saw opportunities at home instead.

The sky seemed the limit for decoupling from the extended family, plow team, or even the village module to form ambitious new links. Or rather, the edge of the intervillage region was the limit, beyond which lay the arbitrariness of *dulat.* Only a few years after land reform, the villagers already began pressing up against the existing boundaries of reliability, wanting to go beyond them. Their difficulty in developing the land cut off from its former irrigation canal illustrates their dilemma when approaching this outer edge, as did the offers they received but had to turn down from produce buyers based in the provincial capital. They and their arena of mutual accountability had expanded so rapidly that the most entrepreneurial among them (who were not the wealthiest) had begun to exceed the threshold of their regional security. They needed to roll it back further to give themselves more room. In the slack season, for instance, one tractor *sharik* had the idea of sending the tractor to work on a distant agribusiness, where they were offered a job. But although they could link with strangers in the intervillage region around Rahmat Abad, they had no way of guaranteeing a contract overarched only by *dulat.* Someone would trick them. Two wealthier villagers invested in land in town as a form of savings, but they would not engage in any form of *productive* enterprise on that land as they did so vigorously in the village, because they had no control over its outcome.

If it is true that local predictability established by locally emergent corporate structures enabled the villagers to move beyond their traditional bonds and make their resources available to the wider society through impersonal partnerships or other arrangements, then what is our evidence that within the State's domain the opposite dynamic took place?

After all, most modernizers would argue that this release of local resources and energies was the result of the State's penetration of Rahmat Abad.

Again if we refer to Muhammad and his brothers and sons, whose biographies are representative of what many other village families experienced, we recall that just as those men who settled in Rahmat Abad were relying less and less on tight family links under greater local security, *at the same time* Muhammad's younger brothers who had crossed over into the urban world of the town of Shush not far away were reverting back to kinship as the only trustworthy principle for alliance. They could find jobs only through kinsmen, and then, having done so, the two brothers plus Muhammad's eldest son formed a traditional joint household, managing their affairs together as the most effective form of security in the urban environment. This pattern was found among all the villagers' urban acquaintances and relatives. Of the hundreds we visited together or who were described to me during my stay in northern Khuzestan, there were no nuclear families and relatively few nuclear households, nor did anyone secure a job from a stranger on purely functional criteria (not even a coolie job). In the agribusinesses themselves, the Shah's peak of agricultural modernization, all jobs, promotions, contracts, and subcontracts, even at the highest levels of administration, were governed first and foremost by personalistic bonds, preferably kinship. The notorious personalism of Iran's urban world and the State's power pervaded all economic and legal relations, even—we are told by social scientists studying Tehran elites—within the wealthiest and most modern sectors (Bill, Lilienthal, Westberg: personal communications).

Indeed, it was Mehrabani, and not the villagers, who spent his savings to shore up his personal ties; it was Mehrabani and not the villagers who clung to personal status and his tight knot of family in looking for how to get on in the world; it was Mehrabani and not the villagers who sought emotional security in inwardly intense little cells of Muslim brotherhood. These social forms were of a completely different order than the *sharik*s and corporate community in which the villagers "invested." Mehrabani retrenched into personalism because of the arbitrariness and purposelessness of his urban environment, finding in his obsessive sociability and his idealization of fellowship a false protection that could hardly match the stability and moral cohesion of Rahmat Abad, where villagers were moving away from dependence on personal bases of trust.

The evidence from this study suggests that when local predictability guaranteed by the *strength* of village and regional corporate structures expanded, the villagers' operative kin networks contracted, increasing resource mobility, since the corporate structures made possible their members' far more flexible impersonal linkages. Conversely, whenever the predictability of voluntary, impersonal structures between the individual and the State was threatened, or whenever villagers found themselves within *dulat*'s domain, which systematically fragmented all such structures, then individuals took refuge in stronger kin ties, expanding them to many forms of personalistic claims and becoming increasingly dependent on them. Such retreat was most marked in the "modern" sector. Next to kinship, villagers in town sought to bolster family relations with other bonds of close personal familiarity—personal ties forged within the mosque's mass congregations, the personal trust between members of the same ethnic group or people from the same village, close attachment to charismatic father figures, and so forth. Thus emerges one of the ironies of this study, that contrary to current theory the uncertainty of the environment governed by the State *strengthened* personalistic status links between individuals, while the predictability of a corporately structured rural environment, still relatively autonomous from the State, provided the most favorable conditions for the mobility of economic resources allocated on the basis of impersonal economic "rationality."

Law

Why could the Iranian State not have provided this impersonal predictability as some other nation States do, and which presumably economists and planners thought it could—and still think other States like *dulat* can? Law within the Iranian State's domain (and, hence, all coordination and regulation upon which predictability within *dulat*'s realm depended) was formed in *just the opposite dynamic* from Rahmat Abad's, where general norms, rules, and policies derived from the particulars. Similar to the emergence of law in the village, norms and rules at an even higher level of generality—in the rural region beyond the village—also derived from their arena's constituent institutions and actors. As a mirror opposite, the State considered all constituent groupings to derive from it, downward, and thus to exist in order to articulate *its* purposes. The Shah determined to rule everything from the center because he and his specialists were enlightened and because he thought the country first needed to be pulled together into one nation beneath his rule. Centralizing thousands of spontaneous little regions like Rahmat Abad's, the Shah and his planners perhaps regulated society in a manner predictable to themselves, but certainly not predictable to the social base in northern Khuzestan.

The Shah's overnight decrees and his ministries' willful, sometimes suddenly brilliant, and usually—to the public—inexplicable changes of mind (tied to no anchor of consistency, precedent, or even viability in the day-to-day world) reverberated throughout every level of society, permeating it with uncertainty about what would be thought up and decreed tomorrow. As even villagers in Rahmat Abad saw, and certainly the model townsmen in Bizhan did, over time those in power all down the line had established miniregimes on the same principle. Many of these arbitrary edicts, programs ordered, or regulations enforced on the spot when an official visited an area, many of thse radical improvements—

especially some the technocrats dreamed up—were in themselves bene-
ficial technically and economically. The computers constantly improved
their calculations, and thus called for alterations in the Plan. Many such
overnight edicts were founded on altruistic social intentions. Many made
good sense at the economists' level of sectoral "integration" or international exchanges. But what affected society far more profoundly than
these decrees' macrolevel logic or their specific short-term efficiencies was
their *endemic political arbitrariness,* their incomprehensibility, their
manifestation of absolute power and its deep root in personal power.

We have an illustration at hand in what happened to the villages within
the Dez Irrigation Project. It is not difficult to imagine that each stage of
their odyssey was intended by the planners and carefully calculated by
the economists to improve upon the preceding one, as experts learned
more about a situation, refined their models, and sought to establish with
each stage the possibility of carrying its strengths to the next logical one—
from oppressed peasants to yeoman-farmers liberated by land reform and
from land reform to California agribusinesses, from mud huts to the
shahrak's brick houses and electricity, from the fragmenting and backward *joft* system to highly productive mechanized agriculture in State-
funded farm cooperatives, and then from cooperatives to the mastery of
all modern agricultural technology in farms the State ran directly. But
even if these economic judgments were correct, did any economist or
planner ever ask whether honoring precedent—*whatever* "backward"
precedent might exist—or whether submitting to local control had *in
itself* an intrinsic value for sustained economic development, a value that
might be more important than these short-term economic gains, given
the way they were achieved? And, indeed, did they ask whether Iran
might not find it harder to recover the rule of honoring precedent and
local control, once lost, than it was to construct behemoth dams?

The development of law in medieval England, "law" in its primordial
sense of "order," took a decisive step forward when the King was forced
to agree that although he made the law and in doing so could make any
law he pleased, once made, even he had to adhere to it. Society had to
establish continuity per se, predictability, even before justice (Berman,
1983:145, 292).

Within *dulat*'s domain in northern Khuzestan—in the towns and cities, as well as in the Dez Irrigation Project—the extraordinary unpredictability anyone who ventured beyond the links of family and intimate
friends felt lay not in the Shah's secret police, SAVAK, but quite the
opposite, in his *law,* whose universal arbitrariness ran riot wherever the
State reigned. Popular urban culture came to project this arbitrariness
onto SAVAK, one of the few concrete local symbols—which townsmen
could physically locate—of society's inability to hold power accountable
or on course. But the villagers who could see more clearly from the outside simply called this destabilizing and fragmenting phenomenon "this
fog," *dulat.*

Whereas Rahmat Abad's corporately structured predictability rested on precedent, *dulat*'s law was often shaped by its technocrats' professionalism, which may have reached more "accurate" or "correct" policies in some absolute sense but policies incomprehensible, hence, unpredictable locally. Thus, in the rural region around Rahmat Abad, farmers, tractor drivers, and the tractor shareholders knew that what the tractors charged in one year, plus the increase in the cost of fuel and maintenance, determined quite plainly what they would count on charging the following year. They would bargain, of course, but most farmers easily estimated the range of possibilities and the outcome. In contrast, sometimes tractor drivers in the agribusinesses hardly knew from month to month their actual take-home pay: According to one informant in the technocracy, the annually revised national minimum wage was fixed and then readjusted by *dulat* in distant Tehran by amalgamating national labor surveys from five different ministries, current international standards of basic necessities, nutrition technocrats' calculations of caloric intake, and Keynesian formulas for stimulating the economy through a healthy level of national employment; then this minimum wage was subject to company alterations contingent on international sales and in time on the importation of large numbers of Korean workers to the area. No doubt all of these factors were crucial for some aspect of the national economy as well as for national demographics and even local welfare—but at the same time their importance destroyed one more small area of local predictability and local control: the ability of a tractor driver to predict his wage.

Another aspect of centralized governance that made it impossible for *dulat* to provide the local predictability needed to loosen traditional bonds was the State's personalistic power. As we have seen, Rahmat Abad was founded on the impersonal grounds of tradition, precedent, consensus, and the objective evaluation of observed behavior—all bases of governance that transcended individual judgment or personal whim, and were thoroughly subject to public information. Within *dulat,* however, policy making inescapably terminated in some network or other of the State's personalistic rule. This by its nature divided individuals rather than joining them, and relegated to the private realm their actual norms and behavior rather than articulating these publicly for general access. Personalism drove the State to command rather than coordinate social interaction, and it precluded mechanisms whereby those in socially lower positions could hold their "superiors" accountable. Such law became a *threat* to stability.

For example, when the State installed its new irrigation canal, it had not understood local village water use, and so the canal created continual conflict among villages that formerly had divided water peacefully according to ancient agreements and local bargaining, and that continued to collaborate peacefully with respect to their traditionally shared canals. The State's irrigation engineer played the villages off against each other for personal favors, which during peak seasons sometimes escalated between morning and afternoon of the same day. Surely the project's expensive irrigation technology could reduce water distribution to an impartial, objective standard of allocation, but not when such a resource is in the hands of unchecked personal power. When the villagers of Rahmat Abad finally found a contact to the key engineer's superior through that man's wife's French poodle's groom, they seemed ahead for a few days. However, finally they learned the engineer's superior would take no action because the superior's cousin was married to the engineer's brother. A week later a rival village found a more direct and stronger personal claim on the superior through its network. Calculating each actor's odds of turning up the most powerful personal connection through the infinite number of possible routes society offered to every man in power, and then being sure that once his decision had been made on that basis another contact would not be found by a different party to supersede the first one—such infinite possible determinants, none of which could be weighted in advance, removed allocating resources on a personal basis from any chance of prediction, even when such a contest was carried on by the most powerful ministers in the realm.

The integrity of social structures intermediate between the individual and the State is closely linked to society's long-term, sustainable economic development. This link rests upon the preservation of customary law, as we have seen in Rahmat Abad and its emerging intervillage region, within each subfield of economic or political interaction, arena by arena, at all levels of society. These subfields, the constituent parts of society built up by people interacting with one another frequently, in patterns, need not all be territorially based. In contrast to fiat, customary law (formalized, if need be) expresses what is predictable and reasonable to those who by their initiatives and their comings and goings create a field of interaction into a public arena. Making law continually reflect people's actual norms and behavior is nothing easy; neither lawyers nor legal scholars can do it on their own. It entails a never-ending political struggle that in a large society requires people's own groups constantly feeding back into law—if necessary, through *insistence*—continuities or changes taking place "on the ground," the continuities or changes the real actors ratify. They must also ensure that law remain in the public arena, not secretive.

In addition, the link between the integrity and freedom of local social structures such as Rahmat Abad and long-term, sustainable economic development derives from the fact that intermediate forms enable individuals to extend their initiatives beyond themselves into society at large on a weighty, more lasting, hence, predictable basis. If these intermediate groups are corporate, they make it easier, cheaper, and more likely for people to keep a strong check on arbitrary power, the most serious threat to sustained development.

In sum, the challenge for sustained development is to establish the underpinnings of law, if by law we mean predictability within the given public arenas in which an individual operates (for elaboration, see Goodell, 1985). Law within each subfield of interaction requires the accurate reflection of participants' norms of behavior (*not* economists' or rulers' norms), so that those who constitute the field can make and act on reliable predictions. Law also requires constant watchdogging against arbitrary governance. In Iran *dulat* could provide neither aspect of law. Indeed, *dulat* considered its essential lawlessness the key to rapid development.

Accountability

Rahmat Abad demonstrated another error in the development theorists' analysis, which is that strongly cohesive social forms between the State and the individual jeopardize the processes of "modernization." These theorists argue that because they are isolated, corporate groups such as Rahmat Abad or well-structured rural regions such as that around Dubendar retard the development of *individual* accountability, when independent-minded decision making is so necessary in a highly developed society. According to "modernization" theory, the *urban* individual under the State's direct tutelage is a far more independent, responsible, and broad-minded person—thus freer to allocate his or her resources accountably. But to the contrary, we see that Rahmat Abad's open political arena and predictable environment could only have been brought forth and sustained by individuals who expected to be held accountable themselves for objectively defined responsibilities, and therefore by individuals who knew how to hold others similarly accountable. An individual who depends, as Mehrabani and many in the "modern" sector did, on the psychological, even therapeutic, value of others to define and support his self-respect, personalizes the functional purpose and the clear boundaries of any endeavor in order to establish the groundwork of subjective trust that he needs. In doing that, he makes any organization of which he is a member more vulnerable to private, often shifting assurances or to interactions that might at any time be taken personally, disrupting organization itself. He narrows the scope of his potential linkages, reducing predictability especially from the perspective of those outside any arrangement. Since he depends so keenly on the subjective affirmation of others, he can hardly hold them accountable.

When Mehrabani lectured the villagers for several nights on improved agricultural techniques, they offered him a good plot of land where they would help him try out his recommendations himself. If they saw that his ideas worked, next year they would adopt them. The villagers' response was a classical one for their culture, holding the Tehrani "expert" empirically responsible for his advice. Frustrated, he insisted they should adopt his suggestions for the sake of the White Revolution, to which they should be grateful after land reform; for Iran, as good nationalists (to feed their urban brothers); and for the sake of their friendship with him. He would get a promotion in the Justice Corps if his supervisors saw that he "modernized" the villagers' agriculture. "Don't you trust me, after seeing that I've given up two years of my life to come help you?" The following week Mehrabani put up his large metal sign on the road proclaiming what an important official lived in Rahmat Abad (a non sequitur in what the villagers considered an agricultural discussion)—presumably to recover his self-respect and perhaps to intimidate them into implementing his suggestions. His response represented a classical one for an individual in *his* culture, too: to reduce the issue to a personal matter, obfuscating its objective content, and then to assert his personal status so as to win on the basis of it.

It was the "modern" townsman who had no experience of objective accountability in a functional and purposive group like Rahmat Abad, and who could not fall back on the concomitant support that such groups provide. It was the townsman like Mehrabani who was ill-suited for complex society's greater demands on individual integrity, independence, empiricism, and the internal conviction of one's worth. The more townsmen had at stake, even those who dealt with vast sums of money and highly complex technology or in fields, like banking, that were firmly institutionalized, the less they seemed able to stand independently on empirical merit. Professor Bill introduces us to one prominent urban Iranian who poignantly dramatized this retrenching into subjective values and power. From a daily scrutiny of obituary columns he filled an enormous chart depicting the intricate family ties that related political and business leaders throughout the country. "When he needs a favor from anyone on the chart, he locates the various connections, and approaches the individual through the relative he is already acquainted with or through the one easiest for him to contact" (1973:784). Reza and many Rahmat Abad villagers enjoyed greater self-assurance, independence of mind, and individual confirmation than townsmen whose success was similarly based.

Rahmat Abad's acceptance of the individual and his spare nuclear family, even if his patriclan rejected him when he separated himself from it, and Rahmat Abad's opportunities for clearly measured accomplishment with the ultimate certainty of the community's moral bonds, underpinned a radically different culture. Empiricism and public accountability are far more conducive to the economic "rationality" of sustained development than the environment that places such a high value on personal status, which the nation's technocrats and millionaires so frequently did.

The Mobility of Economic Factors Versus the *Joft* System

We are now in a much better position to examine why Rahmat Abad held on to its final control over wealth derived from land, the *joft* system, despite the community's remarkable opening up to give individuals and their resources mobility beyond the community's traditional social forms as soon as villagers perceived their environment to have become more predictable.

To begin with, the economic incentives for replacing the *joft* system with consolidated individual holdings in the form of specific plots of land might not have been as great as the State technocrats thought. The main benefit to be derived from consolidation would have been mechanization. But the villagers had mechanized all operations available to them except harvesting and winnowing, while the low cost of local labor relative to combines for harvesting wheat did not make further mechanization much more profitable. The main benefit to be derived from the *joft*-holders' holding property rather than claims allocated seasonally to different plots would have derived from their ability to invest in the land. But with *dulat* moving to control all irrigation, the State limited the further gains possible from private investment. Given the villagers' available technology for their agricultural base—field grains, legumes, and unimproved rice varieties—and given the economic advantages the *joft* system offered especially in collective maintenance, even the economic arguments for disbanding it seemed inconclusive.

But the villagers may also have been reluctant to free their land from its traditional bond for political reasons. Despite their eager embrace of impersonal *sharik* arrangements and their readiness to disengage many productive factors from the community's social context, the peasants loosened their traditional bonds gradually, not overnight. Since the *joft* system constituted the bedrock of their livelihood, the land that it governed constituted the last resource pried loose from the social matrix. By the time of my field work, but a few years after land reform, virtually no other traditional social form seriously restricted the mobility of productive resources within the intervillage region. What held the community back from releasing its last, its fundamental resource was its need to develop a more effective internal political order appropriate to its increasing social complexity, so that releasing its land would not indirectly cause political havoc. As we have seen, Rahmat Abad had yet to resolve the twin challenge it had come to face, how to allow an articulated economic elite to emerge within the community (via the land) while still holding that elite accountable politically. In the following section, the last in this chapter, we examine that challenge the village faced, which certainly held back its release of members' land from communal holdings.

The *joft* system's economic limitations, to the extent they existed, had to be weighed against the substantial social and political advantages the system gave Rahmat Abad. Nor should the villagers' conservatism in this area obscure their rapid move toward independence and mobility in most other areas of production. For instance, the villagers had completely dissolved the *bonku*, or plowing team, which had dominated their economic organization at the time of land reform, thus freeing its members from group decision making and group labor as well as from the *bonku* leader's authority (see Hooglund, 1982:23, 103). The joint and extended household had practically disappeared, replaced by nuclear households entering into a sweeping variety of impersonal *sharik* partnerships. The community itself, retaining its corporate political strength, had begun to integrate itself into the intervillage region around it, encouraging members to move beyond its corporate bonds. Despite its history of insecurity, its extremely low technological level, its poverty and lack of education, the village had radically streamlined its social organization to provide a solid foundation for gradual economic modernization—while its urban counterpart (possibly even the bazaar), *economically* centuries ahead of Rahmat Abad, was reverting more and more to traditional bonds of kinship, personal status and connection, and social rather than functional ties.

Rahmat Abad's Corporate Structure Qualified: The Twin Problems of Hierarchy and Authority

Having reviewed the corporate integrity and economic "rationality" of Rahmat Abad's society, and having considered the vital role such a social form may play in economic development, we need to return to the issue that Rahmat Abad's political structure raises—why by 1973 the community had not yet developed mechanisms for internal regulation that would allow a greater economic differential to emerge as well as a more focused and decisive communal authority. Any member could veto collective action with one dissent; the community had no way of requiring cooperation from a member not moved by social pressure or a sense of individual responsibility; although the villagers were able to form far more secure, impersonal links with others in the area than townsmen could with potential partners who were strangers, they had not completely disembedded political influence within the village polity from its social and economic matrix. They seemed to fear that those who might push ahead economically would dominate everyone else politically.

In evolving a more decisive office of headman and allowing economic elites to emerge at the same time assuring that neither threatened the polity's prized self-governance, essentially the villagers of Rahmat Abad faced the challenge of moving their community to a more complex level of social organization: from a relatively egalitarian corporate community to one with an articulated second level—in short, economic and political hierarchy (which, contrary to some theorists, need not preclude accountability). To retain their corporate structure and autonomy required readjustment of the community's internal mechanisms for regulating its affairs, so that the members would keep its political organization abreast of the social, economic, and technological diversity it was eagerly embracing.

As we have said, many villagers knew the next step Rahmat Abad had to take in its political development, although they would not have discussed it in these terms. They were consciously proud of the village's organizational integrity: that when attacked by thieves it acted together, that it built Throne City, that it undertook ritual responsibilities communally when any villager died. Some were aware, too, that on such occasions leaders came forth whom others recognized and followed. The villagers appreciated the value of strong leadership, a topic they frequently discussed, comparing their needs and terms of leadership with those of townsmen, citing examples and the assets of outstanding men and women leaders within the community. (However, not even the most politically reflective villagers would have suggested that it was Rahmat Abad's increasingly complex economic, technological, and political environment that required a more decisive headman. Speaking comparatively, they associated the need for such strength far more with the political intrigues and the multifarious tasks imposed by the landlord regime at its worst. not with modernization.) Thus while this tiny community included no Thomas Jeffersons or Edmund Burkes in its midst, relative to its population it could count on a degree and distribution of political understanding about its needs probably comparable to those in more "advanced" societies, including urban Iran. The villagers' failure to devise a more sophisticated political system did not come from a lack of general awareness.

Nor was the fundamental challenge that confronted the villagers in 1973 new. They had faced it for many years: how to allow a higher economic stratum to emerge right in their midst and give one or several of its members a decisive position of leadership, at the same time holding both him and the economic elites politically accountable. If anything, this challenge had been more critical under the landlords, when on the one hand, the economic gap between the most comfortable villagers and the poorest had been more extreme, and on the other, the community's political urgency for someone to focus its initiatives in firm action had at times approached desperation. So on that score the villagers had needed a firm hierarchy accountable to them even more acutely in previous years. The failure to allow a political authority to emerge out of the wealthier stratum cannot simply be explained in terms of the time required for evolving new institutions.

The principal reason the village had not resolved the twin problem of internal hierarchy and accountable authority is that it had not been forced by necessity to do so. Coming to grips with this two-pronged problem would have raised the village to a new level of social organization, permitting much greater social aggregation and complexity and a tighter internal structure. Because society is conservative and because pushing through to a firmer, more systematic and more complex constitution is difficult and costly, a social entity usually requires an extraordinary pressure to force it to move itself to a new organizational level. And when this does happen, it takes place over time, not immediately. In short, an urgent and sustained challenge is usually necessary. Rahmat Abad had not yet faced such a critical challenge.

The challenge of *opportunity* (in contrast to *desperation*) had induced organizational endeavor in Rahmat Abad and its surrounding region: villagers forming intervillage *sharik* partnerships to buy the tractors, for instance, or launching a parents' group when the community controlled its own school. Indicatively, where *dulat* undertook those and similar responsibilities—such as in State farms, which the State provided with tractors and schools—local organization became flaccid. Not perceiving that substantive purposes are indispensable for collective integrity, Mehrabani, who came from *dulat*'s paternalistic world, considered the villagers "stupid" for rejecting his and other officials' offers to help Rahmat Abad do things the community thought it could do on its own. Still, such challenges of village autonomy had not forced Rahmat Abad to resolve its problem of internal authority.

It may shock us at first glance to say that through the generations, probably through the centuries, Rahmat Abad had lacked the sufficiently intense pressure to make it move beyond egalitarian consensus to a more articulated and complex sociopolitical form. Surely if anything might challenge a community's political organization, the oppression of Persian landlords would! However, within that oppression the peasant always retained the right to flee the village with his family when the landlord's treatment became intolerable. And that is what he did. We have seen Rahmat Abad's villagers exercising this right; many studies and official documents during the past century confirm the pattern elsewhere in Iran, historically (for example, Arasteh, 1970:18–19; de Morgan, 1914:587; Lambton, 1953:23, 55, 61, 74, 83, 153, 163, 171, 297; Layard, 1887:270; Wilson, 1895:131, 273). When the landlord's demands became too harsh, rather than banding together under a leader to fight him, the community would disperse. Other villagers in the region, under different landlords, awaited the fleeing peasants and would take them in, even give them land; indeed, rival landlords frequently offered peasants refuge in their villages. Fleeing peasants could settle in the rainfed wastelands on their own, or even join nomadic kinsmen in the tribes. When a new landlord or even new administrative officials replaced the old, inducing villagers back with more favorable terms, they would return.

The option which the villagers often exercised, of *fleeing* the landlord's cruelty, relieved the pressure that just at that point of most bitter challenge might have brought them to a firmer internal structure, to the acceptance of and control over an emerging internal hierarchy. The peasants' ancient right to flee the land had kept them from taking into hand collectively their need for greater yet still accountable internal hierarchy and authority, in the same way that, according to Alcoholics Anonymous, helping an alcoholic before he or she "hits bottom" will prevent him or her from reaching a new level of internal discipline, pushing through to a new structural articulation. Of course, the landlords' playing off villagers and headmen against each other did not facilitate Rahmat Abad's political development, but had they been desperate enough villagers could have overcome this, too: They were quite aware of its effects. Thus the *severity* of the Persian landlord's oppression, which most observers and scholars have stressed, in fact had a less determinative impact on the village than did the *structure* of their oppression—that is, the landlords' leniency in letting the peasants flee when they could tolerate no more. We will return to this issue in Chapter 13.

The organizational challenge that Rahmat had to confront was, specifically, a political one—one of internal, vertical authority. None of the many other challenges to the village's corporate integrity that we have reviewed—the thieves, building Throne City, the communal fire brigade, and so forth—posed the political problem of stratification and authority. None of these challenges required Rahmat Abad as a social entity to accept and at the same time to control a socially "superior" (wealthier, more prestigious, more powerful) rank in its midst, or a permanent political authority. (Its judiciary was occasional and ad hoc.) Although these frequent demands that the villagers act in concert for the commonweal of Rahmat Abad did solidify the community's integrity, they were by their nature military (thieves), economic (the *joft* system), or social and moral (Ahmad's suicide), calling upon villagers to deal with each other as *political equals*. Only the landlord as a political authority of a clearly distinct economic stratum—the landlord with his henchmen in the village—could have forced them to hammer out, collectively and consciously, indeed institutionally (vis-à-vis him and those fellow villagers who were his officials but their elites) the law of political accountability, reconciling different economic strata within the same corporate unit. Only such a crisis of authority could have pushed the village to disembed its law from its social matrix.

Recall that Musa, in trying to require Gholam to attend the *bildar,* had reverted to a personal insult as his only means of pressure, and Gholam on his part took advantage of the village's interpersonal congeniality. The problem of authority Rahmat Abad faced was to forge norms and the institutional means for conducting that dispute about responsibility, in *impersonal* terms. But the landlord had never forced the challenge, had never provided the external necessity the community required to push itself to an internally controlled formal authority while remaining corporate. He let the villagers periodically abandon the village instead of "hitting bottom" (see also Hirschman, 1977).

Perhaps a *desperate* challenge was no longer needed to move the village to a more complex form of organization. Land reform had made the resolution of these twin problems easier by removing the landlord's intimidation. Furthermore, the *joft*holders had greater incentive to resolve the problem now, as they could no longer walk away from the village as easily as they had done under the landlord; land reform gave them permanent rights in Rahmat Abad's land while virtually precluding their access to similar rights in other villages.

Holding a designated political authority accountable even though it enjoyed greater wealth should have been easier after land reform than before, since the gap between the prosperous and the poor no longer began at the very margin of subsistence, and since land reform had removed the special advantages through which the village elites had profited from the landlord's favoritism at the expense of the poor. Whether Rahmat Abad, apparently on the brink of resolving this challenge in 1973 under the many pressures of economic, political, and social change around it—whether it would have allowed an articulated stratum of economic elites to emerge, entrusting the headman with more decisive authority while retaining its insistence on participatory control, is, of course, impossible to know. In six years the village had accomplished a great deal, politically. But certainly once the State was in the picture, Rahmat Abad could no longer trust its ability to hold any governance on course.

In the absence of the landlord, *dulat* itself could have provided the village with a similarly severe external political challenge. Could *that* have called forth within it the requisite organizational response? It could not and did not, as we will see in Bizhan. By 1974, 10,000 villagers or more had succumbed passively to the State's expropriation of the village lands for agribusinesses and State farms in the DIP. The challenge *dulat* presented these villagers did not elicit a new organizational level within their communities because that challenge was too overwhelming: Since the communities could not possibly win it, such a disproportionately overpowering challenge only enervated local organization, rather than tightening it. For deep organizational change a serious challenge is often needed—but precisely one that a more concentrated organization might successfully meet. As *dulat*'s power increasingly pervaded the society of northern Khuzestan, the corporate structures of village life along with their norms and institutions of functional, objective purpose, of self-governance and mutual accountability, of individual responsibility and the open flow of information—these fundamental characteristics of Rahmat Abad, so conducive to sustainable economic development—could not negotiate with and transform the wider social environment *dulat* made its own. Instead, village culture with its "modern" organizational norms, institutions, and skills, would have to succumb to *dulat*'s personalistic, absolute power.

Had development been more piecemeal and granted the rural sector a stronger—at least balanced—position (as it had in feudal Europe and Japan), these norms and institutions taking firm hold at the intervillage regional level and then within the area of the provincial town might have slowly expanded the community's scope of self-governance and accountability (as, again, happened in feudal Europe and Japan). Then perhaps Rahmat Abad would have forged the level of organizational accountability it needed, allowing economic elites to flourish, and the village would have imposed its "rational" norms, expectations, and institutions on a wider and wider area as it extended its interactions further afield. Iran was, after all, predominantly rural.

Suppose what we have been describing had also been taking place in other villages and microregions. The characteristics we have discussed here, which are vital to democratic sociopolitical development and to an environment of predictability, necessary for sustained economic development, largely derive from the fact that Rahmat Abad was a small, relatively isolated agricultural community. Anthropologists frequently find such a public arena and corporate structuration flourishing in small communities like Rahmat Abad. It is relevant that during the 1970s most Iranian villagers were located as far from *dulat*'s rule as Rahmat Abad, or farther; and that the median size of rural settlement in Iran was almost exactly the same as Rahmat Abad's—265 inhabitants (Abrahamian, 1973:12. Eighty-five percent of Iran's villages had fewer than 500 people—Hooglund, 1982:29). Indicatively, too, this was the average size of the English medieval village out of which the modern British parliamentary system eventually emerged by the very process I have outlined (Beresford, 1976; see Goodell, 1980). We cannot speculate how Rahmat Abad would have resolved its internal political challenge had it been able to evolve at its own pace, but in many of its cultural and structural characteristics that we have reviewed here it resembled the European and Japanese medieval foundations of those cultures' subsequent "development" achievements (see Goodell, 1977).

The vast majority of Iranians today derive directly from the village culture we have described. Even those who migrated to town took with them these individual and institutional expectations, these political and social skills: Iran's inestimable wealth. But in the face of the disproportionate power that lay beyond the community's intervillage region, how could these villagers re-create Rahmat Abad's structures and values within *dulat*'s realm? In Part Two we shall follow Rahmat Abad further as its sister villages ventured into *dulat*'s world.

> **Do not attack the army in its breast but in its heart.**
> **—Ayatollah Khomeini, 1978**

> **They will not fight as one body. . . . Thou dost think of them as**
> **a whole but their hearts are separate; that is because they are a**
> **people who have no mind.**   **—Qur'an, Sura 59**

Chapter 6

Rahmat Abad and the State

O tired nation, plan thy salvation independently of the King!
—Bahar, from *Khurasan*

The Holes

One afternoon an immense truck roared up *dulat*'s new road and, having confirmed that it was at Rahmat Abad, turned in beside the village. Knowing precisely where he wanted to go, the driver drove to a strip of untilled ground on the east side of the village where he and a second man spent the rest of the day unloading huge long pipes and mechanical paraphernalia. Nothing more was said to anyone, as though there were no people at all in the place.

That night at supper no one even mentioned the great truck to those who had been working in the fields, although usually the villagers were ready to share any excitement at all, even to magnify a small one. We talked instead about the peddler who arrived with fresh grapes. I was bursting with speculation—what was this enormous vehicle doing, parked across the east entrance to our inconspicuous little community of 250 souls, miles from town at the end of the road?

"But it's not just a flock of sheep!" I exclaimed.

"No, it must be a truck from *dulat*."

"Musa, *you're* the headman; aren't you going to find out?" Wasn't the very essence of Throne City, controlling the destiny of this little plot of land?

"Khanom Grace, it's a truck and two men from *dulat*."

It was as though by refusing to acknowledge the truck's presence in speech or even in the slightest glance at it the villagers might somehow shield their lives from whatever *dulat* would do. In time some village children asked the two men with the truck what they were doing and were told "drilling." No one asked more—who sent them, from where, or why, although we all knew that Iran's oil came from Khuzestan province, and several villagers did know what "drilling" meant. We were just glad the men's instructions had not directed them to the middle of our compound!

The men drilled for weeks—bang-banging with a racket that bored into my nerves, although the agricultural quiet of our countryside absorbed their banging like a mattress. They camped by their hole. A few villagers living nearby offered them the occasional fresh bread or cigarettes. Several weeks later when they had bored two small holes side by side, they plugged them up level with the ground and packed to leave. Seeing this, Hamda, in a unique manifestation of curiosity, invited them to tea to try to find out something. Solemnly declaring that he, too, was *"dulat,"* the highly respected village judge of Rahmat Abad's White Revolution, sworn in by the State at a ceremony in Dezful, Hamda ventured inquiry as to which Ministry had sent them. "Tehran," they said. This was the only place in the province they had come to drill, and now they were going back to Tehran to get a new assignment.

"You mean in Tehran they know about our little Throne City and sent you all the way over the mountains for days with all those things to put two little holes in the ground here?" stammered Hamda's little son, astounded.

"Let the man drink his tea, son," Hamda admonished, after allowing a hopeful pause. "Tehran sent them and they don't know why. God is Merciful!"

Fifteen months later we had still not received any indication what the two little stoppers in the ground were all about. When Musa once inquired at the Ministry of Agriculture in Dezful, he was told that a well had been drilled alongside King Darius the Great Rural Cooperative. "But why should you ask?" demanded the State agent, affronted by Musa's brazen question.

Dulat's Modernization Program

As far as the State was concerned, Rahmat Abad was a patient etherized upon a table, unconscious, awaiting operation by the master surgeon. While on their part the villagers did not entirely accept these terms, they did imply that conversation with *dulat* might lead to peril from which there would be no escape.

When the villagers financed and managed their own fledgling school and even later when *dulat* sent its first teacher, a lively parents' group blossomed, brought together by the challenges the school presented to pupils' parents. The first State-appointed teacher, himself a villager from Shiraz, lived in Rahmat Abad. For this reason and because he was rarely supervised (having an assignment that the State considered so peripheral), this young man made himself accountable to the villagers, often seeking parental participation in running the school. As a special interest group, parents built the school toilets, helped him and the children plant a school garden, organized informal religious classes for themselves as part of the school activities, and undertook a rotation system to invite the teacher to dinner every night.

Then when Dezful teachers took over the school, they lived in town and came out daily when they came at all. The first women teachers the villagers had seen, they wore immodest miniskirts. By their rudeness and condescension, they thoroughly insulated themselves from parental accountability. Officials appeared on the scene more often in order to emphasize *dulat*'s authority over the school. They changed many of its policies radically without even acknowledging that the children had parents. The teachers announced openly that the children belonged to the State, which is why they never so much as entered the streets of Rahmat Abad or conversed with fathers and mothers. Even hostility would have required more contact that they had with the village. "If we speak to parents, they will hold us in less respect," one teacher explained to me, indicating the purpose of *dulat*'s distance. Amir contrasted feeling a horse's will through the halter when you ride it, or even the response of a fish at the end of a line, with a parent's inability to know anything about the school or teachers through the children's conversation. Mothers no longer ever went to the school to discuss their children, communicating through older children instead (who, indicatively, complained of the teachers playing them off against the parents). The association of interested parents dissolved because their organizational purpose had been taken from them and they could no longer initiate any school projects. *Dulat*'s school, located on the edge of the village, became an army camp on occupied territory. As for the children, they were being socialized into their world of the future.

Still, the parents continued to want some policy direction over the school. Courses were being taught that some questioned, such as making paper dolls and streamers for Pahlavi holidays or telling the children they had to sleep in pajamas. The women's dress offended the village. The costs of sending the children to learn in school escalated. Besides free farm produce, the teachers demanded payment for class photographs and for the children's transportation to town to have them taken; for a school garden right before summer vacation (actually, for the inspector's half-hour visit!); and for all fifth-graders to buy bell-bottom trousers so they could take an examination in Dezful without looking "like peasants." Finally, when the teachers demanded donations for the hungry people of Africa, the villagers reached the end of their tolerance.

The parents began sending down cold soup and withered cucumbers for the daily lunches they provided the teachers; someone deliberately oversalted the rice one day, and another family laughed about sprinkling tiny stones in the rice they cooked for them. A neighbor woman near the school began piling her cow-dung patties all around the school every day to dry. This was one of the few positive protests I ever saw the villagers initiate against *dulat*—like the well drilling, conducted in utter silence from both sides. *Dulat* endured. The following year the villagers capitulated, seeking a route through the kin networks of the teachers' supervisors in Dezful.

Although the villagers' children were at risk in the school issues, both in that case and in the drilling the standoff between *dulat* and Rahmat Abad took place—symbolically—on the edge of the village. But when the malaria spray team periodically visited Rahmat Abad, *dulat* invaded the heart of the community, again with no consent and hardly even an exchange of words. Within minutes of the sprayers' unannounced arrival, they plunged into every room in the community: fast, marching, efficient, their pungent white film sprayed on everything, indiscriminately. Pity a woman alone at home with small babies, pregnant, sick, or weak—worse yet, if no one was home at all. The village men were in the fields, and the spray team was not paid to move anything in its way. Leave a cup in the niche, a photograph of the Prophet on the wall—God forbid, a baby in the cradle!—swish, swish, finished. Next room. An open can of cooking oil on the shelf, the baby's pacifier that fell down as he was being evacuated, Gohar's brand new dress hanging behind the door, Amir Hosein's school books: DDT. When I asked the spray team how they would like someone to act that way in their homes, they were surprised by the suggestion of any comparison: "The place belongs to *dulat* and it is infested," they pronounced, "only the poison will kill the disease." One could not help but wonder which vermin *dulat* hoped to exterminate.

The Shah's White Revolution comprised the backbone of the State's program for Rahmat Abad, implemented by its various rural ministries. *Dulat* told the *joft*holders they had received the land in land reform, and certainly they did prosper by no longer having to pay the landlord. But since they had not gained land reform through any initiative of their own and since they considered all townsmen dishonest, they looked upon *dulat*'s announcement as a gimmick of the King's. "If the Shah is powerful enough to wrest the land from the rich and give it to us," 'Abbas accurately reflected, "how much easier it will be when he wants to take it back from us at his pleasure."

To supplement land reform, *dulat* tried to modernize agriculture. The *joft*holders could belong to the village cooperative (which *dulat* insisted was obligatory, but in practice was not), which extended production loans for fertilizer and pesticide and which helped arrange finance for the tractors, but in no way comprised a "cooperative." The villagers' loan repayment rate remained high. But no agricultural extension accompanied these loans, leaving the farmers to experiment freely with the chemicals until they concluded on their own that the traditional grains they sowed benefited little from them. (Nor did the vegetables, which were afflicted by pests at times. The villagers never found the correct insecticide for them and lost a large part of the cucumber crop one year as a result). *Dulat*'s cooperative meetings and "seminars" consisted of engineers lecturing the farmers on parliamentary rules such as how to handle a runoff for electing three Sergeants at Arms, and how many terms an Assistant Secretary can serve in British cooperatives, the world's ideal. Admittedly, *dulat* did occasionally convene the farmers to urge them to grow more wheat, repeatedly proposing a complicated financial incentive (*dulat* laying claim to the harvest in advance) that the *joft*holders angrily rejected as fraud. Even with their minimal comprehension of mathematics, they saw through *dulat's* "bonus" program, spending the rest of one afternoon explaining its implications to the engineers sent out to enlist them into it!

Once, when an epidemic threatened the village's cow herd, the White Revolution did attempt to assist the villagers with veterinary service. Apparently the problem had reached province-wide proportions. The Ministry of Agriculture's technicians arrived late one night after everyone was asleep. Observing that their only interest was to clip the ear of every cow, Sardar, a shepherd, suggested politely that it was the syringe that mattered to an animal's health, not clipping its ear; the technicians insulted his "rustic" science. (In truth, if an inspector followed them, he would check the ears as evidence of coverage. No one would ever check to see how many cows survived the epidemic.) In any event, having only brought one syringe full of vaccine, the technicians soon asked if they could finish the job by just clipping all animals' ears, which they assured the villagers would suffice. The villagers replied that by the greatest coincidence they, too, had just run out of cows. Again, the two sides avoided meeting.

As part of its agricultural uplift, *dulat* had installed a new canal network, which we have seen removed a section of Rahmat Abad's formerly irrigated land from access to any irrigation at all. By replacing the village's canal, which directly drew off the river, with one that now first passed through several communities upstream, *dulat* also brought garbage and waste and body dirt into Rahmat Abad's drinking water. As the new cement canals were much deeper, with stronger flow than those the villagers had through the century constructed, several people in the region drowned in them during the first year of my study. But the villagers' principal objection to the new canal sprang from the monopoly control it gave *dulat* over their most crucial variable resource, water. Controversial as ancient water accords had been between villages and with the landlord (concerning construction and maintenance costs), at least the villagers had been able to count on them once everyone reached agreement each spring, whereas dealing with *dulat* placed water on—literally—a day-to-day contingency, sometimes (as during rice transplanting) requiring hour-by-hour haggling. The traditional system had never entailed the constant uncontrollable costs of bribes, costs borne entirely by the peasants.

Learning Governance and Law from *Dulat*

In addition to land reform and agricultural modernization, the White Revolution set out to restructure village government, as we have already seen. We observed what a farce the Village Council elections were. Still, in requiring formal elections periodically for White Revolution apparatuses in the villages, *dulat* recognized the cultural gap between townsmen and peasants. Only once in their lives had the State let *townsmen* vote for their municipal government, and then with only one party from which to choose.

At the same time that it established the King Darius the Great Rural Cooperative and the Village Council, *dulat* had villagers elect a judge, presumably because down through the millennia Iranian villages had never devised a system of communal justice, and needed the help of an autocrat to do so. They chose Hamda because he was a central trouble-maker and at least somewhat literate. When *dulat* installed him in Dez-ful, it armed Hamda with *The White Revolution Imperial Law Book for Village Justice,* surely the most remarkable document produced by the White Revolution.

One night by the flickering flame of Hamda's little oil wick, Mehrabani made our Judge dig his Imperial Canon out from the bottom of a dusty trunk so that the Justice Corpsman could instruct him in its use. Hamda had never opened it. As the young man read out each "law" with its three degrees of punishment, even he choked in dismay at the code's detail and comprehensive scope, which he lauded for reflecting The Plan Organi-zation's jurisprudential genius and its fatherly love of the peasantry. How omniscient the New Order technocrats in faraway Tehran must be to understand the people so intimately, as they codified everything the vil-lagers might do to harm themselves: Peasants must not disobey a Justice Corpsman, must not light cigarettes on the threshing floor, must repair their house walls after a storm, must send their daughters to school, must sweep up all manure, must not leave tools lying around the house, must bring all their animals out for vaccination when *dulat*'s veterinary con-tingent appears, must use toilets eight feet deep and three feet wide with cement bases according to the Swedish Plan of Hygiene for the Middle East, must obey all orders of all State officials, must not eat three-day-old bread, and so forth. The legal code was organized by topics. A couple of hours after Mehrabani had begun this session, he reached the imperial proclamations on rats: a $1.50 fine for the peasant who fails to stop up a rat hole in his section of the threshing floor, $3.25 for the second offense. . . . Another serious fine for the mother who allows her child to pick up a dead rat by the tail, double the fine for his playing with it, $4.50 for the second offense. . . .

The mention of rats awoke Hamda, who rose to the occasion. "Sir," he asked Mehrabani, "do you have any rat poison to hand out? We've been getting a few around here." For Mehrabani, such a response to this important training session once again testified to the villagers' backwardness.

Mehrabani saw nothing backward about himself. He had come to Rah-mat Abad to light the flame of progress, whose essence was purity. When villagers asked him why he had come, he sometimes replied that he had come to clean up the filth here (by which he referred to virtually every-thing about Throne City). For a starter, once he had taken over the only plastered room in the community from a newlywed couple, he put the children to work arranging and then painting little whitewashed stones around its entrance, in imitation of the royal palace north of Tehran. Next he ordered all homes to do the same. Then he announced that the village would finance a road grader to level the main street of Rahmat Abad, which sloped down in the center forming a drain. Since he left the village when it rained, he thought the drain simply ruined the symmetry of the street. One village family living on that street protested, their opposition increasingly more trenchant as he became more dictatorial. In a maneuver uncharacteristic of Rahmat Abad's politics but forced on them by Mehrabani's fiat, they confronted him. "No one rules in this community; we discuss things and then decide." As the woman of the household grabbed hold of him to slap him, he slapped her first, losing all credentials as a lawmaker and arbitrator, which he saw as his major role.

Mehrabani's official title, Extension and Development Corpsman, belied his principal purpose, to bring Rahmat Abad's law and order finally and completely under the Shah's central rule. He himself claimed to be employed by the "Justice Corps," but also purported to serve Iran's agricultural interests. Straight from a middle-class family in Tehran, he knew nothing about agriculture. This did not reveal the inefficiency of the White Revolution as it might on the surface appear to. When an international expert hoping to incorporate Extension Corpsmen into an agricultural extension program elsewhere in Iran complained to the Assistant Minister of Agriculture that the corpsmen were concerned only with law and order, not agriculture, and thus would not collaborate with his program, the Assistant Minister informed him that agriculture was in fact "quite outside of their (the corpsmen's) responsibility." They had actually been sent to "assure the King's command in every community in the land" (Goodell, 1977:349). To this end the State planned continual upgrading of their instruction in "justice," each year making the outstanding urban high school graduates into an elite corps of paralegal authorities representing *dulat* in permanent offices in every village. Since in reality Mehrabani served as a Justice Corpsman, I use this title for him rather than the State's camouflage title, Agricultural Development Corpsman.

After an area is overtaken by force, it must *first* surrender its law. The early medieval kings of Europe claimed a judicial role long before they began to legislate. Local norms and customs are the greatest single threat to State domination. Calling these young idealists Agricultural Corpsmen offered a legitimate guise to their real purpose, at the same time adding technological shine to the White Revolution, as thousands of young "technicians" penetrated the countryside to produce the soaring statistics on Ministry charts of agricultural production.

Although Mehrabani hated the Shah, adoring whatever Mao Tse-Tung did and placing Islamic nationalism almost in the same shrine, he took seriously the power he thought a deputy of His Imperial Majesty must command in such a barbarian outpost. "L'Etat c'est moi!" he would often exclaim in Farsi. *Dulat* had given him some training in its concept of improved "justice," and he reported weekly on the matter. Whenever he could, Mehrabani leaped into the center of a village dispute or a discussion of village policy. Because he listened to the radio in his house all day and because villagers painstakingly kept every issue or controversy they could from his ears, he did not often hear the crackle of a village quarrel; but when he did he was prompt to spring to the call of Righteousness. "In the name of Muhammad the Prophet you must love one another! In the name of the King of Kings Muhammad Reza Shah Pahlavi, His Imperial Majesty, SI———LENCE! ENOUGH!" Mehrabani made no inquiry into local custom or law; he was there because peasants were lawless. In his sagacity he almost invariably differed from the villagers' appraisals. Since he never even learned most of their names, he could hardly find out or keep straight the factual evidence behind any question, much less grasp the character of each disputant (which he usually misjudged, being vulnerable to flattery and resenting any villager's independent mind). When he embroiled himself in a physical fight with the village woman, his arrogance and ignorance cost him and the White Revolution the villagers' respect.

Nor did Mehrabani contribute a single thing to the community's welfare. To prompt hard work among its thousands of corpsmen, the State sponsored a competition for them; the ones who improved their villages the most in justice or material aspect won automatic admission to college and full scholarships. (Whereas in other countries like Peru or South Korea it is villages that receive recognition for self-improvement, in the White Revolution a community that was progressive secured a snug place in the technocracy for *the corpsman whose orders it followed*.) *Dulat*'s first schoolteacher in the village, who had fit in so well and whose students consistently distinguished themselves on national examinations as the villagers with the highest grades in the province, left without any commendation because his supervisor found cobwebs in the ceiling corners of the schoolroom. But Mehrabani received high official accolades when he installed a conspicuous yellow mailbox outside the village where it could be seen from the road. His supervisor came to Rahmat Abad, photographs were taken, and Mehrabani was proclaimed a patriot. The fact that few in this largely illiterate village had ever seen a postage stamp or envelope, the fact that no rural postal service existed, and the fact that Mehrabani installed the mailbox without the slightest collaboration on the part of the villagers hardly constrained *dulat*'s self-congratulatory esteem of his duty and Rahmat Abad's progress. The following evening he preached to a men's group on the need to respect him as boss, being grateful to him for his selfless service to their mud community, working hard according to his example of hard work, and on the importance of realizing that he knew every villager's mistakes before they were even made. According to Dezful authorities I knew, *dulat* was very pleased with Mehrabani's ability to assume authority. He won a high place in the corpsmen's competition.

As the winters were too cold and the summers too hot for Mehrabani, as he was in love with the schoolteacher in the spring and fall and between seasons he had to "visit his mother," village justice remained largely in the villagers' hands. However, Mehrabani was present in the village during the long funeral for Madar-i-Tulaki, when men who could chant the Qur'an had to take turns doing so for hours each day. Through the holy book's flowing poetry the soul of each chanter shone clearly: in Mehrabani's chant, the soul of the State, whose uniform he wore throughout.

The mullah whom villagers hired from town for the funeral urged the sacred book upon us in plain song—outside the community yet with us as a teacher, he preached the holy words with a tinge of the townsman's ubiquitous self-consciousness, a sermon showing off the Qur'an's beauty and calling us to the devotion that he obviously thought he himself exemplified. One of the villagers, 'Aidi, a man who had worked in Dezful for a few years before taking up farming again, also frequently chanted in these funeral ceremonies. His was such a muted, mellow expression that one could not understand any of his words: He offered no message, but the listener sensed a deep return as he poured out sorrow and faith over the bent heads. Sometimes he seemed not to stop for breath, inhaling and exhaling as the scripture flowed through him. Completely unselfconscious of his role, in his inarticulate communion he disregarded the text except to give utterance some vague shape, disregarded, too, where he himself stopped and the community around him began.

Then Mehrabani volunteered to chant, attending every session in order to do so, polishing his brass the night before. When the Justice Corpsman of the Imperial King of Kings took the holy book in hand and clasped it resolutely, he grasped the preeminence of the loudspeaker and podium as well—a vast piazza lay before him, like Red Square, filled with the masses awaiting his word. Alternately looking at the book and flashing its meaning at each of us with the eyes of a commander, Mehrabani reviewed the troops under our makeshift tent, the Arabic poetry barked out in measured military cadences regardless of meaning or context, all the harsh consonants accentuated, sharpened, an iron rhythm ordering submission, awe of the mighty. Of the three chanters, only Mehrabani ever stopped to correct the pronunciation of a word, emphasizing punctilious adherence to every letter of the law. He was the superior, educated, Tehran deputy of *dulat*. Only Mehrabani told us to weep when we should be moved to weep (being too distracted by his reading to do so). Then on he would goosestep through the Qur'an, lifting aloft, brilliantly ordering, beating every word into its precise form and place.

The villagers had never heard the Qur'an read like this before. There was confusion about what to do. How could Madar-i-Tulaki's spirit find rest? A few thought that since Mehrabani was from Tehran he must know even better than the mullah the proper way to read the Scripture. But others told them just to *listen* to him and judge for themselves. Many said that he was too young to plumb religious meaning. The women explained his rasping voice by his being so far from home and sitting among strangers. Furthermore, his necktie was too tight around his swollen, command-filled throat.

Outside of the White Revolution, Rahmat Abad had other contacts with *dulat,* such as the 2 percent tax that the State collected for village improvements (and of which the State bank had no record when the community wanted to use these accumulated funds to replace broken windows in the schoolhouse). Rahmat Abad took the initiative to approach *dulat* on several matters. Once the villagers wanted to build a bridge over the new canal so they could take their tractors, animals, and carts to the fields on the other side (a bridge they constructed, after *dulat* denied them permission). Another time they tried to settle the former landlord's claim to a disputed area of the village's land, a case they simply abandoned after months of futile trips to the provincial capital and elsewhere. The longer I lived in Rahmat Abad, the more practical the villagers' policy of just not talking to *dulat* seemed, because doing so only entangled you in issues you could never win. I did not record a single instance of villagers fulfilling their objectives in approaching *dulat,* except through expensive bribery.

Dulat's Character

Although the villagers inherited a millennia-long political heritage of dealing with and reflecting upon *dulat* (a word encrusted with hoary lore to them), they could say what they thought necessary about the Persian State in a few words. *Dulat* was crucial to keep order in the cities and hence filled a need for Rahmat Abad, since urban anarchy terrified the villagers even more than agricultural disaster. But while indispensable to the city, *dulat* could be the curse of the countryside. All townsmen (even the urban clergy) were cheats, and *dulat* was quintessentially the urban world. When the technocrats tried to persuade Rahmat Abad to grow more wheat and the villagers called their offer a fraud, one of the engineers present delivered an impassioned speech saying that all Iran's villages *belonged* to its cities; the villagers' work was only for the townsmen's livelihood. "Don't you care if you let Dezful die?" he demanded, revealing a profound reason for townsmen's hatred and fear of the villages. "It is your duty to keep it alive!" he pleaded.

Not only a place, to the villagers *dulat* had a distinct political personality. Several behavioral laws described it. *Dulat* lived free off everyone: It traveled free, ate free when it visited anyplace, could take from stores or tap urban services free. Villagers often said that society was *dulat*'s orchard for the picking (referring to a religious law that allows anyone walking through an orchard to eat his fill without being considered a thief—but only what he or she can eat in passing). If *dulat* needed food for its city people, it just took it from farmers. Another pattern villagers had observed in the State's behavior was that *dulat* usually claimed to act altruistically whereas it always in fact acted out of self-interest. If *dulat* praised its own generosity in giving peasants the land or in making the village a road or in sending the children a teacher, you could be sure self-interest lay behind all these "gifts." Since *dulat* was a freeloader, villagers assumed that everything *dulat* did not only derived from self-interest but would also exploit the beneficiary, even in ways he or she might not know. Pragmatic above all, villagers did not feel oppressed by this parasitism, certainly not outraged. Who could expect otherwise? It simply called for circumspection.

Dulat was hardly a moral entity like Throne City or any neighboring village to which good and evil, right and wrong pertained. In turn, peasants felt no moral responsibility to cooperate with *dulat*'s programs—to tell the truth on a census, to refrain from destroying *dulat*'s property, to teach children respect for the State. One day when Muhammad was loading his donkey next to a pile of grain, the animal defecated on the grain. Muhammad told me that was just the kind of thing *dulat* would do.

A third behavioral law affirmed that *dulat* could in fact be dodged, an increasingly difficult thing to do, but still possible: mainly by looking stupid, being passive, or disappearing. Villagers succeeded in keeping *dulat* at bay by frequently sharpening their strategies, plotting out and pioneering alternative paths of avoidance. "Khanom Grace," Yusuf used to joke with me, "write anything you want about us but God forbid, don't tell anyone Rahmat Abad is here."

The villagers' most important law about *dulat* pointed to its unresponsiveness. *Dulat* comprised a world unto itself. It could impinge on others but others could not affect it. The incidents we have related illustrate how the villagers concluded this. *Dulat* was like Allah, independent of the world of men.

Although *dulat* seemed a monolithic force, almost like a heavy cloud, villagers understood that it comprised many ministries, that one ministry never knew what the other was doing, that ministries in fact tried to murder each other, that all ministries fed from *dulat*'s hand in Tehran, only a dribble of *dulat*'s wealth reaching Dezful, and that throughout it all Rahmat Abad was but a pawn among opportunistic courtiers. At the end of the line, the most minor of *dulat*'s servants—vaccinators, corpsmen, lowest ranking gendarmes, miniskirted teachers, the two men who drilled the well—made their entrance and exit in Rahmat Abad reflecting relations within the court in Tehran. The villagers knew that neither the King nor *dulat* cared substantively about rural contraception or education or irrigation or the likes. Indeed, villagers felt superior to bureaucrats in Dezful who resembled janitors and floor sweepers within *dulat*'s great mansion.

The villagers rarely discussed the King, although they told stories now and again about legendary Kings of bygone days. The King lived within *dulat* rather as one's heart lived inside one's body, but he was in no way responsible for *dulat* or a source of its energy or direction. To the contrary, they perceived the Shah as weak, somewhat vulnerable; one could hardly flesh him out as a person as one could *dulat*'s minions, through the idiosyncracies of certain bureaucrats one had met: This one I once told I was born the year my uncle actually was, this one thinks I am treasurer of the cooperative, remember that this one likes water buffalo yoghurt, this one will be angered to receive withered cucumbers. Each bureaucrat had his distinctive pockmark.

Dulat had more brains that the King, who couldn't build a dam or fly an airplane or be everywhere at once. *Dulat* worked harder than the King and, although remote and freeloading, possessed a slightly better grasp of the hardships of life than one could ever expect of a King of Kings.

When I moved to Rahmat Abad, a technocrat gave me a small plaster bust of the Shah painted gold. One night as we sat around the hearth telling stories and jokes after dinner, Esau, a very clever teenager in the compound, asked me if he could borrow the bust, which I had tried to hide in a niche in my room. That began one of our favorite evening pastimes, which continued off and on throughout the year, Esau presiding over our holding court with the Shah. When dissatisfied with His Majesty's reply, the boy tickled his chin, twisted his ear, occasionally dunked his head in hot water if he seemed especially slow in granting favors. Although the villagers would not have said so, in these hilarious dramas that in time involved everyone sitting around together, the Shah they and he created together seemed little more than a slightly pathetic village headman.

There was no doubt that in Rahmat Abad's political science *dulat* dominated the Persian universe, an urban universe. No need to keep an eye on the Shah, he simply was not the issue. *Dulat* outlasted all the townsmen's kings and dynasties, the palpable air they breathed: hard, greedy, corrupt. Rahmat Abad's hope was to lie low.

We can add to the peasants' understanding of *dulat* our own observations as we have begun to become acquainted with the State from Rahmat Abad's perspective. Often those who have some experience with a social phenomenon but remain peripheral to it still are able to see it with a pristine clarity that everyone loses once enveloped in it. (By the time we meet men and women—even children—in the new model town, who a short five years earlier had been peasants like the villagers of Rahmat Abad, they will have already evolved a political lore about *dulat* that would have been unrecognizable to the latter.) Thus, before we move into the model town, let us conclude our view of *dulat* from the *biyaban,* the waterless wasteland beyond its concentrated rule.

Rahmat Abad's law, as we have seen, transcended the immediate, the temporary, certainly the political. Precedent, common sense, and the community's moral fabric constituted the foundation of its law, with the villagers' almost fanatical insistence on the proximate congruence between law and actual events and behavior. The State, however, detested precedent, even its own. The way everything had been done before now was precisely what *dulat*'s modernization aggressively had to destroy. Furthermore, for its own all-inclusive purposes, *dulat*'s law considered social life superfluous, except for the most obvious symptoms of economics and technology. The State found preposterous the notion that what people actually did on a day-to-day basis might reflect an ongoing, positive, and valuable process of accumulation, adding up to society's constitution.

Mehrabani's generation within *dulat*, lacking the secular vision their fathers had held after or even before World War II, took religion out of the traditional context that they disdained, and linked it with law to forge a political device. Indeed, Mehrabani hardly recognized religion to have any social function *except* political. Still, far more important than this difference between him and the Shah over the use of Islam was Mehrabani's fundamental agreement with the Shah and the Shah's secular technocrats that law was nothing more than a political tool of the powerful for their purposes of the moment. Concerning the basic questions of law, precedent, tradition, consensus, and the community's moral fabric, Mehrabani, who was religious, concurred with the Shah, who was not, on the purely manipulative nature of law. Neither recognized as having a preexisting or transcendent life of its own anything as rooted as Rahmat Abad's law, especially anything as rooted in traditional society, which both reformers despised.

Some villagers could discern this rootlessness of *dulat*'s law. Maham, for instance, a crusty old man who was proud of his Lur accent and mountain vocabulary because he claimed the Lurs had been the last tribe to capitulate to Reza Shah—and had certainly never given the King a woman of theirs to be his queen, as the Bakhtiaris had done!—Maham told me that nothing that was done by the King in the morning could not be undone by the King at noon; nothing that was said was intended, nothing proclaimed would endure. Concerning land reform he concluded, "a decree states only what will happen until the next decree."

Integral to *dulat*'s understanding of law as a political tool and its rejection of the possibility that law might *reflect* people's actual behavior was the State's compulsive preoccupation with image (a preoccupation mirrored in the personality of townsmen like Mehrabani). This overriding anxiety about its image, at least partly the result of the no man's land *dulat* fostered between it and its social base, occupied so much of its time and demanded so heavy an investment from it that what actually happened in society faded in import. Rahmat Abad judged correctly that *dulat* had no serious interest in its rural projects, but the villagers were unaware of the State's need of Rahmat Abad for the sake of its image. Lilienthal shared *dulat*'s values when he wrote, "I prophesy and promise that the Dez area will be watched throughout the world" (1971:265). When the State's regional inspector for education asked the adult villagers attending Mr. Bandari's evening literacy class to send fifth-grade children in their places for the nation-wide final exam, he justified this charade by assuring the villagers that "the world will see how the White Revolution is even teaching the peasants of Iran to read." (It did, too; UNESCO adult literacy figures proved to many observers that the Shah was rapidly modernizing his people.)

Image comprised perhaps the single most dominant need of the Iranian State. After all, it has been from the external that Persia traditionally derived its wealth and symbolic persona. Nadir Shah dramatized this dependence on symbols that had first been legitimated by others when he brought the Peacock Throne from Delhi to be his seat of authority, as though the country had none within itself. Probably Cyrus appropriated Ahura-mazda from the Assyrians in a similar manner. American factories, jets, and universities served the same symbolic purpose in the Pahlavi regime. In time these images, invested with truth and power, took on a life of their own among *dulat*'s technocrats and its foreign advisors and funders. They *were* the new Iran. Perhaps at a deep psychological level and not just out of opportunism, the State ignored Rahmat Abad's initiatives toward it and complied with the villagers' standoff against it, because by doing so it could live uninterruptedly in the world of its image, which simply had no Rahmat Abads.

One often wondered why, given its reputation for ruthlessness enforcement, *dulat* did not in fact enforce its laws more systematically—make sure every adult had learned to read, make sure all peasants got up in the middle of the night to have their cows vaccinated, make sure that women practiced birth control and the men applied fertilizers and pesticide, and so forth. But even securing obedience requires a connection between law and reality, between the top of society and the bottom, which became unimportant as *dulat* lived more and more in its image of itself, imbuing that with reality. No check on its dreamworld existed. When villages were removed from the roadside where the Shah was going to pass, rural poverty was erased from Iran. After the villagers in the adult literacy class sent fifth-graders to take their exams for them as the regional supervisor had ordered, each adult received a certificate for having passed the fifth-grade reading level. Reza—who, like everyone else, really wanted to learn to read, but had only reached a second-grade level so far—asked the regional inspector when the classes would resume so the villagers could finish really learning to read. The inspector was perplexed. He thought that since the fifth-graders had done the exam well and each adult had a certificate in hand, the literacy class had fulfilled its purpose. Presumably, he thought more Iranians could then read. "The program has to move on to new villages," he told Reza unflinchingly.

Thus the gap between *dulat* and Rahmat Abad was not just one of values; rather, the State and the village comprised two separate social worlds deliberately avoiding communication or exchange across the no man's land between them. They played this out for weeks in the incident of the holes. At best each tolerated the other's presence when necessary, the less frequent the better.

Each side of this gap feared the other; but whereas villagers feared being victims of deceit at the hand of *dulat,* bureaucrats and technocrats feared actual physical violence if they entered Rahmat Abad. When I went to the village to live, they tried to insist I take a dagger with me. They would never accept tea (boiling right as poured) from villagers when they were out inspecting the new canal or road construction, conducting a census, or even supervising village elections, because they were afraid of either being poisoned or beaten to death if they entered the community at all! These were nothing more than fantasies. I never saw any basis for these fears, nor did I ever hear of any townsman being mistreated on a visit to a village. We have learned from Mary Douglas (1966) that *dulat*'s obsession with canonical thoroughness in governing the villagers manifested the bureaucrats' apprehension of not being in control over Rahmat Abad: in short, their fear of the villages. For example, the degree of detail in the Judge's Manual of Justice, the solemnity about the cooperative's bylaws and petty procedures, the necessarily elaborate regulations governing how to apply for a rural identification card or urban burial, the months of permissions I had to wade through just to be able to visit Rahmat Abad. Similarly, *dulat*'s obsession with cleanliness in the village sprang from its compulsion to impose its own order on spontaneity it found threatening: Mehrabani's determination to implant the State through his little white entrance-way stones "just like the Palace," the malaria spray team's hygienic perfection, the University of Tehran School of Public Health's preoccupation with compiling village urine statistics, the school inspectors' phobia against cobwebs in the classroom.

Seeming to contradict but in fact complementing this profound division between the State and the *biyaban* wasteland beyond it was *dulat*'s insistence that the village *belonged to* it, that villagers *serve* the city, that the very land they farmed was the State's, as though grasping for ways to assure itself and Rahmat Abad that the village did not in fact have the autonomy it did. One night when drunk, a Dezful bureaucrat compared land reform to the commonly observed action of an infant who keeps dropping his rattle so that his mother will pick it up and bring it to him, in order to reaffirm that a relationship of support still exists, an example that R. D. Laing (1960:185) also uses to illustrate the same dynamic. "In proclaiming land reform the Shah only wanted to test whether those who raise our wheat are still connected up to us. If we can give them something they take, they are still out there at the end of his line," my friend said.

For its part the village rebuffed *dulat*'s efforts toward it almost as consistently as *dulat* rebuffed Rahmat Abad's initiatives. Each incursion of the State into the village measured the rising dynasty's gradual need for more and more village resources: most primitively, an army, then the villagers' land, then their labor, and so forth. Up until the time I left northern Khuzestan, the villagers had accepted few of *dulat*'s advances or offers it did not want, except urban burial, which had been forced on them. Even in the case of the military draft, through their stratagems of misreporting births, they retained considerable de facto control over whom the army might call. Rahmat Abad refused to celebrate White Revolution Day under Mehrabani and the provincial governor's command, which recognized no exceptions, ostensibly because the celebration fell during the anniversary of mourning for the late headman. The village took land reform itself on its terms, not *dulat*'s.

If *dulat* feared Rahmat Abad, villagers, in turn, were afraid of *dulat,* but not with the visceral anxiety that bureaucrats expressed in their fantasies about being poisoned or beaten to death. The villagers feared being embarrassed, cheated, even at worst being deprived of their homes and access to land. But even before the State's efforts to pacify the countryside, village life had gone on, families had held together and survived. Events determinative for *dulat,* like the constitutional reforms of the 1920s or a change of monarchs, bypassed the village, as the villagers indicated in their indifference to the Shah either as a person or as a political actor. The villagers themselves constituted Rahmat Abad. *Dulat* had not given Rahmat Abad its constitution. *Dulat*'s efforts to authorize the community's economy, polity, and even its social foundations only exposed the State's dispensability. As the bottom line, especially during *dulat*'s drive to "modernize," the State needed Rahmat Abad far more than Rahmat Abad needed the State.

Despite that fact, however, when the State took Rahmat Abad's sister communities for the Dez Project, it did not have to negotiate terms or account for its designs. The domain of accountability, the structured social organization that made accountability possible, Lilienthal and Ebtehaj saw as nothingness. The transformers knew only *dulat*.

> **Verily, Pharoah was lofty in the land and made the people thereof sects; each party of them he weakened. . . . Thus verily he was of the despoilers.**   **—Qur'an, Sura 28**

PART TWO

BIZHAN

Chapter 7

The New Workers' Town:
Blueprint for All of Rural Iran

And so in him they became annihilated; the shadows had lost themselves in the sun!   —Attar, from *Mantiq' Ut-Tair*

At the same time that the villagers of Rahmat Abad were constructing Throne City, *dulat* was building five of its first thirteen new workers' towns—or "labor centers," as the technocrats called them—of which Bizhan was the showcase. While Rahmat Abad's peasants garlanded Throne City with their humor, communal endeavors, and exuberant affirmation of the future, His Imperial Majesty, King of Kings, inaugurated Bizhan with gendarmes and cameras. Royalty rode through the avenues of new cinder block houses lined with bayoneted guards, a great plaque announcing to camera and King that every worker earned over $3 a day (although even by 1974, when the agribusinesses to which it belonged were in full swing, most earned barely half that). During the grand opening, new townsmen crowded behind the wall of guards, hoping to slip through and tell His Majesty what lies all promises had already turned out to be, asking him to restore them to their pinched mud villages. But only one old woman (still a heroine five years later) pushed through, throwing herself on the King's car to plead the workers' case. "Being an old woman, I had nothing to lose!" she exclaimed. Being an old woman, too, she didn't give the Monarch pause.

To tell the King became the townsmen's obsession. While the villagers in Rahmat Abad had practically never mentioned the Shah, the model town's subconscious endlessly circled around this one necessity—to reach the King, to tell the King. I never heard a single dream reported in Rahmat Abad, but in the new workers' town people had the most fantastic ones about Our Father with the Crown, each of which circulated immediately and widely. The dreamer's family often received unexpected blessings the next day. Twice in the dreams Our Father with the Crown showered his "love" on the dreamer and his family. In the evenings, too, the ancient Persian Kings wandering their realms incognito regularly frequented our conversations around the lingering coals. Upon various occasions the model town buzzed with the news that just one day ago someone's friend, a taxi driver in Dezful, had picked up a traveler at the train station and, on orders, had driven him to every bureaucracy in the town making an inspection tour—to the agribusiness and State farms, the *shahrak* of Bizhan as well—not knowing who the mysterious passenger was until given a check at the end of the day, before the man departed on another train: a check that turned out to be of solid gold, signed (the banker said) Muhammad Reza Shah Pahlavi.

No one except the learned could converse with the King. One prominent new townsman who had attended high school for a year claimed to have a permanent "ticket" to talk to the King, who told him he cared more about Bizhan than any other settlement in the realm. Above all, we loved to hear told and retold the elaborately rich events of one worker's visit to the Palace during the peasants' congress in Tehran. Our man, after weeks of royalty's dramatic delays, found himself at last in the distant, shimmering glory of the vast Throne Hall, creeping its length humbly, terrified, finally prostrating himself on the oriental carpet until a slight motion of the Shah's left foot commanded him to kiss the bejeweled hand that rested upon Darius' scimitar! Another man said he got all the way to the Gate of the Palace in Tehran, and through the graces of a distant kinsman held vigil there for days, but was shooed away the day His Majesty was coming outside to walk in his rose garden!

In Bizhan an extensive lore informed one how to send a telegram to the Shahanshah in his counting house where he always busied himself moving around his mountains of coins. Although one could never *speak* to the King, on certain days and according to certain procedures you could entrust your urgent needs to a bureaucrat at the Post Office and then await His Majesty's instantaneous reply through the ethereal beeps of telegraphy. Other than the story about how our local man Agha Qutb got his fabulous land holdings by tricking the King, the only communication with the Shah that I ever heard mentioned in Rahmat Abad or other villages was a simple incident dating from his trip through Khuzestan as a young man, to meet his Egyptian bride. Several old villagers told of having seen the prince and his father stopping for a picnic lunch along the river; beckoned by the King's servants and soldiers, the villagers brought cool water in a goatskin bag, then conversed with the royal party, who wanted to know about the place they were in. The directness of this domestic vignette demystified the King, depicting him as yet a fledgling and in strange surroundings, needing the villagers' help rather than dispensing largesse as in all the *shahrak* stories or conversing in electronic code from his remote center of power. (Indeed, the story about Agha Qutb shows locals gaining the upper hand over the King because of the stupidity of his largesse.)

In both Rahmat Abad and Bizhan, people liked to relate stories from Scripture. Rahmat Abad's favorite by far recounted how Mary, a peasant girl, became Jesus' mother when she fell asleep after many hours of sweeping the mosque floors with her little reed broom, and there the Holy Spirit impregnated her. In contrast, the favorite legend of the workers' town followed the captive boy Joseph through years of labor within every ministry of the Pharaoh's rule until he became Pharaoh himself; the story climaxed when the all-powerful Shah Joseph, having ordered a search in the countryside to rout out his brothers, discovered his humble old father in a village in Khuzestan, summoned him to the Palace Chamber in Tehran, and there took the terrified, obsequious old man into loving embrace. I never heard that story in Rahmat Abad. Thus over and over His Imperial Majesty inspired a wealth of fantasy among the workers and their families, living as he did beyond reality: If ever reached, he would solve all problems, alleviate all distress, restore all hope.

During my year in Bizhan, the King came to visit one of the agribusinesses (although not those departments that were troublesome, like the repair shop or the tractor drivers' pool). In anticipation people wrote scores of petitions to hand to him. Women, not allowed near him, wept profusely because of his kindness—that he would even talk to a worker, that he touched the head of a child. One aged doctor, a saintly man from Dezful who could cure people, perform miracles, and command men militarily (or so the workers said), was the only person seen conversing with His Majesty, because the Shah was semidivine. God loved the King more than any other mortal, "God on earth," likened to the Twelfth Imam. One group of workers wanted to sacrifice a lamb in His Majesty's presence. His Majesty touched the forearm of a Scottish administrator at the agribusiness, who workers said could never again wash the spot that held the sacred touch. Some heard the most powerful and hard-hearted Englishman, director of the company, say he longed to walk behind the King like a slave boy, just to put his bare feet in the King's footsteps. When the Shah left by helicopter, workers gazing up at it compared the event to Elijah's and Jesus' ascent into heaven.

A few did not see godliness in the Shah, but their views, too, reflected a similar psychological preoccupation with him. A tiny group told me they hated the King; maybe many others did. Although like the villagers the new townsmen were never obscene, talking about the Shah sometimes brought out coarseness in these men and women. "If I could get near him I would pull down his pants in front of everyone and focus his cameras and ... " 'Ali, a reserved young foreman, fantasized to me. When some of my neighbors saw my plaster bust of the Shah, they wanted to dunk its head in the filth of a latrine, quite a contrast to the villagers' tête-à-têtes with it. Many people in Bizhan said the King would use the petitions workers had handed him for toilet paper.

In the *shahrak,* the story I had heard from the *villagers* about Reza Shah vanquishing the Lurs in a bitter battle, an open match of skill and strength, became a tale of the worst kind of treachery in Iran, with his inviting thousands of Lurs to a banquet and poisoning them. "The King never prays, he drinks alcohol at international parties, he is a creature from hell," Mohsan summarized his own conclusions. "The Shah knows no end to his greed: first King of Iran, then King of Asia, then King of the World—you'd better watch out!" Hasan's old wife predicted. "At least you can try Nixon before a judge," one of the more prominent *shahrak* residents observed, urging me every time he saw me to "write the truth." According to a common theory among these people, the King and his brother owned the agribusinesses, having conned the English and others into running them in exchange for oil; proof lay in the fact that "capitalist" firms had to treat their workers decently to gain their loyalty, whereas only the Shah and his brother could afford to perpetuate the workers' poverty. "Even under the landlord each *joft*holder fed his own family and at least one landless family," Mahmud calculated; "now with brick houses and electricity we can't feed even ourselves. Clearly no Iranian but the King is benefiting from the agribusinesses or the model towns, and the only profit the Shah has in it all is *fis* (image, showing off). He just wants to make himself a John Deere country for Japanese visitors to photograph." "The Shah would never do anything for others, only for himself—all this is for him, to make him stronger and richer."

To most townsmen, the King knew he was "in an orchard surrounded by the high wall his bureaucrats form to keep out truth." Even more difficult than his subjects' getting through to him from *outside* the wall was the task he faced, being *inside* it: having to devise ways of learning what really was going on in his Kingdom. Persian legends describe many Shahanshahs' solutions to this familiar problem, but I was surprised to find some of these still alive in the townsmen's lore. For example, some believed the Shah used to dress up as a beggar to go among the people and find out "the truth" himself; most townsmen assumed he employed inspectors in disguise, who would report directly to him so no bureaucrat could distort what they found.

It made sense to assume that I was either such a spy or the Shah's twin sister carrying out similar work. If a spy, I would have to be a man, because the Shah would never have a woman perform important work; everything the townsmen associated with the *shahrak* reeked of masculine power. On the other hand, Princess Ashraf could present an exception. Being his twin she would be clever as well as trustworthy. Whichever I was, the model townsmen's paranoia resulting from their traumatic experiences after land reform, and their desperate hope to find a way through to the King, immediately focused on me as a direct link to the Shah. Everyone from the outside who was not a kinsman had to be from *dulat*. Although the villagers from Rahmat Abad had helped me move into the model town and had assured their handful of relatives in Bizhan as well as my neighbors there that I was a student, "pure of heart," and although they often came to visit me, publicly verifying my "village" connections, it took months to convince most of the workers I was not a spy. They would make me leave my windbreaker outside in the yard when I visited their homes, thinking the zipper was a television camera beaming whatever it photographed instantly to the King who sat at home watching it. Frequently I had to leave my glasses at home for the same reason (although they all had seen glasses, and had zippers on their own clothes). Mothers forbade their children to go near me; if the children said as much as "darn it!" the King watching his screen might have them killed. In contrast to this massive fear in Bizhan (as though the slightest irregularity in their environment might once again overturn their world), the villagers in Rahmat Abad had felt so much in control of their world that by the third day Musa had told me *he* was appointed to spy on *me,* making me the dependent.

In the *shahrak* I became very discouraged. Hardly several days would pass without someone pleading with me, "Tell the King this . . . when you talk to him tonight." Some people were extreme in what they wanted me to tell His Imperial Majesty, my twin brother! A woman in whose home I had enjoyed tea upon occasion came up to me one day at the street faucet where I was washing clothes with neighbors. "You've taken our land, then our house, now our sons, our life and our peace, our hopes, our garden and cows, *now* what have you come for? *Now* what more do you want? What have you come to take from us now? Have it! *Take* it! Take it away!" she screamed. "*Chizi nist diger. HICH!* There isn't any-thing more! Nothing!" Almost weeping myself, I fled to a wise old neigh-bor woman. "I'm not a spy!" I pleaded with her, asking her how I could convince people. "But we *want* you to be a spy," she replied.

One afternoon, Rahim, one of the several teenage boys whom I had come to know, walked right up to me in public, reached out at my breasts, looked at me with pained courage and a bewildered sneer, and put his hands on me firmly. "They're foam rubber?" he exclaimed, with a ques-tion. Since he and others had ruled out my being Princess Ashraf, my credibility as a friend and not a spy had come to hinge on my being a woman. By physically acting out the turmoil in their minds, in a manner so crude to their sensibilities, Rahim demonstrated the extent of social and cultural erosion that had taken place between the villagers' world and that of the workers of Bizhan.

It is difficult to know what is hallucination in another culture, but the extravagance of these anxieties about my spying and these assumptions about the King's attentiveness could find nothing but contrast in the down-to-earth village culture that these same people shared but a few years earlier in Rahmat Abad. It was as though their trauma had come to be projected upon me, a single non-Iranian woman, in endless contradic-tory, fabulous, often pathetic ways. That my zipper was a camera, that I was the Shah's sister come to live in a cinder block room in their midst for a year just to check on their children's language, that every night His Majesty cared to hear about Bizhan town on his hot line showed the bizarre distortion of power, politics, technology, and paternalism that had made them at once bitter and worshipfully dependent, like people who idealize the man who has hijacked the plane they are in. Mingled with their fear and rancor that I was a spy was the new townsmen's long-ing that I was.

When in later months we discussed these attacks and demands that I must tell the King their loss, the workers and their wives themselves pointed out the nightmarish jumble of inconsistencies in their suspicions about me. Still, they never really could appreciate the wildness of their fantasies, the frenzy that had led some of them to break all rules of their customarily dignified reserve, and above all the unreasonableness of their visions and anticipations, so opposite the villagers' stolid self-containment and empiricism. From a life and from communities whose direction had been in their hands, from a society so transparently structured by its members' own initiatives, from a world of such accountability, they had been reduced to fragments—impotent, dependent, purposeless—and not in a manner that would, in turn, consolidate them.

The World Bank Development Model Then and Now: Scale, Efficiency, and Central Control

Although in some ways the workers and their families in the model town experienced a more concentrated transformation than most Iranians, what they went through manifested the operations of the same political system that governed the entire society. To understand that type of system is one fundamental purpose of our investigation here. Our attention to the *shahrak*'s details should deepen our comprehension of how a polity under such a highly centralized command functions, and what its systemic consequences are. Despite cultural variations, the political mechanisms and the "development" strategies we watch in Bizhan differ little in their basic sociological and historical premises, their fundamental organizational dynamics, from the social systems most Western "development" programs and theories continue to promote today. Our current development models still insist in practice if no longer in rhetoric that society must be centralized in the hands of autocrats and their technocrats. Our development programs still focus on centralized, large-scale, capital-intensive projects, sectoral overhauls, and sweeping government "delivery" programs for social welfare, still aim for overnight transformation with virtually nothing but economic criteria of production as their goal (even when expressed in terms of "equity" or "social" indicators like health). Our development "assistance" still sets out to destroy local and intermediate-level sociopolitical structures that might rein in arbitrary power (even when it claims to strengthen them through the increased largesse of the centralized State). Thus, by its very drama Bizhan helps us see more plainly the political system that came to permeate Iranian society through *dulat*'s development thrust, and the kind of system our development theories and programs continue to foster.

In examining this underlying political order, we need to bear in mind that everything we observe in it was planned and carried out before the OPEC oil boom. The directions for development in which we will immerse ourselves represent economists' best recommendations not for the wealthy country Iran became under OPEC, but for a nation then considered poor in resources.

In the Dez Project, the economic arguments for large agribusinesses and State farms included those usually offered for such centralized schemes: that land consolidation under single management units would enable higher returns to production by benefiting from economies of scale; that foreign investors could most rapidly introduce modern agricultural technology into the country, at the same time investing foreign capital; that food urgently needed in the growing urban areas could be most efficiently produced and released to the cities by large commercial farms; and that these businesses would gain valuable foreign exchange by their export crops (asparagus, for instance), while providing nonagricultural employment through their spinoff industries and the multiplier effect (such as creating a demand for petrochemicals and farm machinery, and supplying processing plants like the sugar refinery, paper factory, and a cotton gin). Northern Khuzestan *in particular* called for massive foreign agricultural investment and management to utilize most efficiently the exceptionally favorable climatic, land, and irrigation resources there, a potential found nowhere else in the country.

Overall administrative priorities, too, called for agribusinesses and farm corporations to displace small farmers, model towns to displace the mud villages. As we still design development schemes in 1986, a massive scale of expenditure and the most advanced technology set the project's basic parameters. The World Bank can only lend huge sums of money—and these only to centralized agencies. It is assumed and often asserted that a given scale of *benefits* directly follows from *the size of investment* in a project. From these *preestablished* levels of expenditure and technology, which become givens, it is argued that incremental, locally directed production will entail too many risks, considering the enormous investment that has already been targeted deductively. Thus, in developing the Dez, economists concluded that only the most streamlined agricultural management could effectively realize northern Khuzestan's potential and the expensive infrastructure to be built (such as over 600 miles of irrigation and drainage canals, over 250 miles of road). If a country desperately needs food and its agricultural capacity is limited, the argument continued, an investment the size of the DIP—projected to absorb over $100 million initially—was hardly the place for training thousands of illiterate peasants, and could hardly be left in their hands. Such projects never derive the costs and scale by using the local population's manifest capabilities as a baseline.

Given the vast scale of the World Bank's loans and their goal of transforming whole sectors of society, it is always easier for the Bank to "monitor" a single, compact, technocratically oriented agency with a highly paid cadre of economists, accountants, and engineers than to try to fathom what seem to the Bank to be the vagaries and minutiae of backward village ways. The Bank's experts—the best paid in Washington, from the West's finest universities—have neither the training, the time, nor the conceptual models for understanding unsystematic, petty, ad hoc production.

The Dez Project's many linkages with industrial developments planned elsewhere in the region would have to be integrated by professional planners with centralized authority. Experts must be able to direct an investment of such magnitude autocratically, so that problems can be spotted as soon as they arise and nipped in the bud, and so that all the nation's needs can be serviced. Finally, because the government was going to give workers in the large agricultural establishments and their industrial spinoffs the complete range of modern amenities, a single, centralized State agency could more cheaply and efficiently coordinate the delivery of these benefits through consolidated model towns.

Thus in the semiautonomous government agency that the Shah established to administer this scheme, the Khuzestan Water and Power Authority, the Bank found its acceptable complement, Iran's most efficient and centralized technocracy.

While the economic analyses established these numerous benefits to be desirable and forthcoming, the most appealing feature of the consolidation approach—consolidate the existing and new irrigation systems under one management, consolidate all the lands under a few firms, consolidate all the villages into a few model towns, consolidate large segments of all provincial economic activity and welfare under one coordinational agency, consolidate all financing of the immense uplift in one bank, and so forth—the enormous appeal of such consolidation was that it facilitated control. Control remains the key priority in all similarly massive Bank projects today. The Iranian planners and technocrats, in setting out to conquer the challenge that they, Lilienthal, and others perceived as a chaotic wasteland, felt compelled to impose order—the order they could comprehend, *their* order—upon the geography, the economy, the society which lay at their creative command. Given that the State assumed the responsibility for society, it was only natural that in uplifting it, *dulat* should remove any threat to its own order. As for the foreigners, they enjoy power, too. It is thrilling to mold huge parts of society—even though other people's society, not your own.

While the World Bank shared Lilienthal's and the Iranians' impatience, confidence, ambition, and certainly the value they all placed on centralized authority, the contract the Bank signed with the Iranian government for the Dez Scheme in fact gave peasant agriculture a larger share in the project than it actually received. In the project contract, the Bank accepted the State's expropriation of 50,000 acres from the peasants for agribusinesses, and 5,000 for State farms. But because the Bank wanted to retain its intensive involvement and increase its leverage in many other sectors of the Pahlavi State's development Plan, when the

Iranians expropriated for the agribusinesses *three times* more land than the Bank had agreed upon and *six times* the area the contract had stipulated for the State farms, the Bank accepted these (and other) breaches of covenance without demur. As we will see with the agribusiness companies, the Bank enmeshed itself too deeply in *dulat*'s designs even to hold itself accountable. This same guiding principle of its development efforts has not changed from then until now.

By 1973 the Khuzestan Water and Power Authority had purchased back from the peasants 170,000 acres in the Dez Project for the first four private agribusinesses, which had a total initial capitalization of $36.5 million. In addition, by 1974 the Haftepeh government sugarcane plantation just within the project area to the south occupied 60,000 acres, and 15,000 acres had been allocated to the State's first four "farm corporations." The State valued the farm corporations' land, to be paid in "shares" given to the farmers, at $1.14 million, although its real market value and the subsequent government investment in these farms are impossible to ascertain (Salmanzadeh, 1980:232–40). The State experimental farm at Safiabad, conducting research for agribusiness crops, covered another 500 acres taken from the peasants. The model townsmen of Bizhan were to supply the labor needs for only three of these enterprises: the Iran-America Agribusiness whose major shareholder was an emigrant Iranian, Hashem Naraqi, one of the largest almond growers in the United States; the Safiabad trial farm; and, along with another *shahrak* nearby, the Shell-Cott Agribusiness, jointly held by Royal Dutch/Shell, Mitchell Cotts (a British firm managing overseas plantations), and several wealthy Iranians. These two agribusinesses, each with a thirty-year lease, concentrated their production in winter wheat, citrus, alfalfa, asparagus for the European market, cotton and some sugar beets.

The Technocrats' Own Model Town

As with so many aspects of the Dez Project's centralized transformation, model rural communities and consolidated settlements under State control were nothing new to Iran. As early as Alexander, conquerors built special rural towns from scratch to turn their armies into settled colonizers and to introduce improvements through "model" settlements. Professor Lambton describes model agricultural centers founded by Rashid al-Din, the Mongol vazir, in the late thirteenth century along organizational principles basically identical to Bizhan's (1953:96). In the early twentieth century the British created a consolidated workers' town for their oil company in Abadan, row upon row of neat although squeezed little dwellings over which the oil company assured itself ownership of everything. Later, the Iranian army and air force in Khuzestan closed off elite ghettos for their highest ranking officers, even within the bases themselves, providing them with the exclusive amenities of north Tehran, off limits for the troops. By 1973, within but twenty miles of Dezful, the State had already constructed five different luxurious "compounds" for its elites, with their recreational clubs, golf courses and commissaries famous for Dutch cheeses—proclaiming that *local* life was unfit for *dulat*'s transformers to live in.

The technocrats governing Bizhan assumed that society should be rigidly segregated by class and (even beyond that) according to the Ministry or the place where people worked. They had years of experience being confined to model towns themselves, for these were common in all the provinces. They drew upon their own ghetto experience to determine life in the *shahraks* they built for the *lower* class. Frequently when I could not grasp the engineers' sociological principles as I watched them shape society in the *shahrak,* I would realize through my visits to their exclusive compound that they were already living out these principles there, and they took it for granted that *their* social organization was God given. For instance, they kept their compound strictly cut off from all urban communications, excluding shopkeepers, rank-and-file bureaucrats, even Dezful professionals and local elites like bankers or Western-educated businessmen from social mixing and certainly from becoming residents. The very sight of a delivery van or exogenous private car in the compound raised alarm.

Each compound of *dulat*'s elites was run by its own ministry, which covered all services needed. That meant that far from any possibility or requirement of *self-direction,* criticism of its management amounted to criticism of the State. So the technocrats knew no community whatsoever. Their efforts to change school policies for their own children, for example, had to be carried out clandestinely. Since the provincial-level ministry for which one worked administered the compound and all its services, every detail of a family's life was channeled through one tiny, concentrated clutch of bureaucrats—from the most intimate medical consultations, the carpenters who came and went through one's house, the guards who inspected everything entering or leaving the compound, the teachers who taught one's children, and, of course, those with access to one's professional record at work. Living in an elite compound, one could hardly find relief from the single, unified network of official scrutiny.

Each house in the technocrats' compound carried a distinct rank; the technocrats moved from one to another every couple of years upon promotion, making houses and neighborhoods merely temporary, State-owned cubicles for replaceable cadre. This frequent rotation, the intense competition for visible symbols of wealth among Iranian technocrats, and the pervasive fear of the secret police, prevented intimacy between neighbors or families, exacerbating the social isolation that was only alleviated by everyone's anticipation of the day when he or she would leave permanently for Tehran.

How could the technocrats conceive, then, that a local polity amounted to more than well-trimmed rose bushes or the assurance there would be cranberry sauce available in November? This is not to suggest that these technocrats in Dezful designed Bizhan, a possibility unthinkable to The Plan Organization. But it is to point out that technocrats who themselves knew no lasting social forms above the family—certainly not community—and whose most innocuous neighborhood initiatives were suspected of undermining the State's authority, determined *the daily life* of the new townsmen, virtually every decision circumscribing what the people of Bizhan could and could not do.

A Walk Around Bizhan

Let us move, then, into a cinder block house in Bizhan. Bizhan lay some nine miles south of Dezful, a twenty-minute trip by local pickup truck. When I lived there, 450 houses had been completed, or about 75 percent of the projected capacity, accommodating around 2,700 people by my calculation, 2,200 by the Ministry's. To my knowledge no accurate official demographic statistics existed on the *shahrak*s; but, based on the government's stated plans and on the area's average of 250 inhabitants per village, before the end of the *shahrak*s' first decade the State planned to eradicate around 225 communities and move their inhabitants into model towns (cf. Gremliza, 1962; Nederlandsche Heidamaatschappij, 1958). The Plan Organization and the Khuzestan Water and Power Authority had reasons to estimate as low as possible the number of persons per *shahrak* house and the total population to be displaced, since the mechanized agribusinesses were not likely to hire many peasants. The Ministry of Water and Power used various ploys to discourage villagers whose land it had taken from requesting a *shahrak* house; some were kept waiting over five years in their old villages, with no work and no land to farm, surrounded by agribusinesses. But almost no one moved to the city instead, which from the Ministry's perspective would at least have solved *its* problems.

Large-scale commercial agriculture and Safiabad, the State experimental farm, surrounded Bizhan on all sides, for miles in every direction. Turning in to the *shahrak* from the paved road that continued on to the south, one found oneself immediately at Bizhan's center, the apex of a right triangle where the *shahrak*'s two main avenues converged by Haji Safar's house and poured like a funnel into the road to the agribusinesses. The location of Bizhan's center on the very edge of the model town, near the State's projects, contrasted sharply with Rahmat Abad's crossroads at the heart of the community's life and at a distance from *dulat*'s dirt road from the outside. Nor did the rest of the new town's layout reflect community interaction. Its two main streets each extended for over half a mile to the edges of the *shahrak*. With no road linking the two extreme ends of the L they formed, along the *shahrak*'s hypotenuse, people living at those far ends enjoyed little communication with the center and virtually none with each other.

Directly along the hypotenuse that might have linked the two ends of town was Bizhan's traditional orchard, carefully preserved during and after the *shahrak*'s construction. Some forty acres of fruit trees, herbal plants, roses, thickets alive with local and migrating birds, crystal-clear canals, abundant wildflowers, and with meandering avenues between the trees, places to picnic, hiding spots for play, this wildly profuse microworld unto itself had been one of the largest orchards in northern Khuzestan. Overflowing and rather unkempt orchard-gardens like Bizhan's constitute an enduring symbol of peace throughout Iranian culture, as prominent in the poetry as in the carpets of this desert land. The Ministry had not preserved the orchard for its commercial value, nor to give the several thousand laborers of the *shahrak* respite from their cinder block houses and agribusiness labor—nor even for students to study there, old women to collect brushwood, or anyone to picnic. Rather, on special holidays top State officials with their families and friends, often their Tehran visitors, claimed the paradise as theirs, driving through the dusty *shahrak* streets with their car windows sealed tightly, up to the great orchard gates that allowed but a glimpse as they swung open and then closed again: for the workers, a glimpse into the bygone, when they had at least unofficially shared the orchard with the landlord.

Next to the orchard, the school principal, one of only two staff members who lived in the *shahrak,* presided over his primary school. All the others commuted by taxi daily from Dezful, often arriving around noon. In contrast to the abundant amenities of the schools in the elite compounds, this one's only provision was the Shahanshah's widely touted free lunch program: daily three or four dates and a cookie. Beyond the school a visitor from Toronto or Tokyo would be shown the clinic and ambulance center with classrooms for popular instruction, modern medical labs, five or six consultation rooms equipped with clinical tables, shiny new cabinets, sinks, desks, sterilization and storage facilities, even the doctor's implements in drawers—all having been ready for opening for five years.

Elsewhere in the model town visitors would see the mortuary for ritual preparations for burial, a slaughterhouse for butchers, two ample bath houses, and a technical high school to retrain younger peasants for jobs modern agriculture required. Like the clinic, these facilities, although equipped and ready, had never been used, despite the fact that the workers had petitioned the Ministry repeatedly to make them available and other Ministries—Health, Education, Labor—had offered staff. Nor would the Ministry let Dezful entrepreneurs operate any of them, as had been requested. An engineer told me that before the *shahrak* was built, peasants to be moved into it had listed these particular facilities as those they considered the primary needs of their new urban center. Perhaps putting them to use, then, would have comprised too great a concession on the State's part. Never did a week pass without a delegation of foreign visitors to Safiabad, the sugarcane plantation and the agribusinesses nearby, admiring these generous, spic-and-span government services for the workers.

Bizhan also boasted a poorhouse (not on the peasants' original list!), a string of closet-sized one-room accommodations for the poorest of widows and the exceptionally indigent out beyond the edge of town. Notwithstanding the Dez dam's generators, which sent electricity for hundreds of miles, officials could not bring themselves to provide electricity for these twelve to fifteen destitutes "lest they start to think they can have *everything.*"

Finally, toward the end of 1974 a visitor would have been able to see Bizhan's mosque rising on a plot of land reluctantly allowed by the Ministry after several workers had lobbied for five years in Dezful. The townsmen from two of the seven villages constituting Bizhan had begun constructing the mosque with funds they raised for its costs (which we will discuss further in Chapter 13). Although every village being moved to Bizhan wanted to build its own mosque, even a small one, to maintain communal solidarity and its special social ties, the Ministry forbade such "separatism." Everyone in Bizhan is part of one *shahrak,* and will worship in one mosque.

Off the two main streets (which were nameless) ran the model town's twenty-nine "lanes" with their rows of four-house units. The State allowed each household in the *shahrak* one house of two unconnected rooms perpendicular to each other in the shape of an L. The larger room was 12 by 18 feet; the smaller 6 by 9. Each had a window and concrete floor. Four such L-shaped houses back to back constituted a single *shahrak* housing unit, architecturally a cross-shaped building with dividers down the middle of all four transepts, each house sharing contiguous house walls back to back with two neighbors. Every such four-house unit sat in the middle of a large square plot so that each of the four individual homes looked out toward a different quarter of it, which was meant for its garden (600 square yards), a tiny outhouse at one end.

The Ministry charged each family $80 for its house and plot of land in the new model town, about a third the actual construction cost according to officials. What the townsmen said the Ministry paid them for the land that it expropriated, including its evaluation of their homes, varied according to my calculations from $10 to $135 per hectare ($4 to $55 per acre). But since the Ministry made no land surveys, since the peasants did not know the hectarage of their villages, and since the Ministry deliberately paid by *joft*—not hectare—in order to obfuscate what it owed each peasant, no one knew what he had received per unit of land expropriated. Ministry officials said they paid $500 per hectare ($208 per acre). My most reliable *official* informant reported that convenience, plus the amount the Ministry's budget could afford, determined village land appraisals, not accurate measurement and certainly not the market; furthermore, he observed that payments varied considerably according to peasants' sophistication.

All *shahrak* houses were uniform. The formerly landless went into debt buying one, a debt they probably never expected to pay. Certainly few *joft*holders except those with many *joft*s or large herds had made a profit from selling their village lands and moving to the *shahrak,* as the new townsmen had no savings except a little gold jewelry. They rarely owned urban land, few had household amenities. These two signs would have been telltale, had they profited from the move. With the average *joft* amounting to some ten to twelve hectares in the region around Bizhan and the market value for a hectare ranging from $425 (for unirrigated land) to $700 ($177 to $291 per acre) each *joft*holder should have received well over $4,250 for his land alone—which always included some irrigated fields—not $100–$500. One simply had no basis of knowing whom to believe, although scholars have documented egregious discrepancies between actual land values and Ministry payments elsewhere in the Dez Project (Salmanzadeh, 1980:31). Perhaps even more important, the State forbade new townsmen from exchanging, renting, or selling their houses or lots in Bizhan, an issue to which we will return later.

The evidence against believing the Ministry's official claims lies in the workers' poverty. Only fourteen I knew owned any urban property or had shares in any. (It would be impossible to own urban property or a share in it without referring to it from time to time over a year's acquaintance.) Urban land would have comprised by far their most likely investment upon accumulating any surplus. For fear of thieves they kept little gold jewelry. Only a handful had bank accounts. It is unlikely that, having received the unsettling shock they had, the vast population would have wastefully "blown" a windfall, nor did my discussions about this ever uncover a single allusion to such a spree. No household had furniture, except for a refrigerator (in which they kept nothing but a bottle of cold water) and a two-burner gas stove, necessary since there was no other cooking fuel in the *shahrak.* The adobe house additions all the model townsmen had begun to construct did cost something—but not much. Many had secondhand motorcycles that in the summer enabled the men to qualify for field supervisors' positions at the companies. In short, I believe my closest friends in Bizhan and the one Ministry informant I considered reliable in this matter, who concurred that each *joft*holding family had left his village, which was then destroyed, with around $500 for land worth nearly ten times that. Many received far less.

The workers liked the fact that the houses were of cinder block. Ministry officials and men like Lilienthal highly praised the *shahrak*'s electricity, reminiscent of Lenin's eulogizing its use; so did the workers, except that they were usually too tired at night to do anything but sleep. Even after five years in the *shahrak,* only a few very prosperous townsmen had been able to save enough to make a down payment on a television set. Offsetting these two assets—cinder blocks and electricity—everything about the *shahrak* manifested the State's niggardliness: the shoddiest materials, the least resources that could possibly be extended, the poorest construction, utterly thoughtless design. The model town appeared as though it were a settlement eked out of the desert through generations of primitive labor, rather than one built for the rightful tillers of prime farmland that had attracted hundreds of millions of dollars of agricultural investment surrounding the settlement in all directions.

We have already seen that the State had constructed a mortuary, butchery, clinic, bath houses, and a high school, but once these fulfilled its own showy ends it did not allow their use even when others offered to staff and run them. This same penuriousness dominated everything the State did in the model town, as though to *make up for* its lavish waste on the agribusinesses and its own elites. For example, the beams of the *shahrak* houses were so fragile that they could not even support a family of five sleeping on the roof, as Iranians do in good weather throughout the country. (In the village, people carried on a good deal of work on the roof as well as sleeping there.) The toilet pits were so shallow, only several feet deep, that by 1974 they were already overflowing, whereas in Rahmat Abad the peasants had dug theirs ten feet deep or more. The walls of the *shahrak* houses were so thin that normal conversations could be heard through them, exacerbating already tense relations among crowded neighbors. (Even in the old *ghalah* villages, houses often shared no walls with neighbors, and when they did they were always constructed of very thick mud.) Whereas the architecture of traditional rural homes—thick mud walls and roofs, and ingenious designs for the circulation of air—kept them very cool in the hot summers, it was frequently impossible to stay in the *shahrak* houses during the middle of the day, when the *interior* temperature reached 100–105 degrees Fahrenheit. The Ministry had placed only one electricity meter per house unit of four families, causing endless friction that could have been easily avoided.

Water, Water Everywhere

The canals to irrigate the workers' vegetable gardens had been constructed much lower than the level of the land, so the gardens could only be watered at great extra cost. In addition, all *shahrak*s had deliberately been located on land too poor for the companies to cultivate—in some areas not even salt cedars would grow!—requiring all the more capital and labor for the workers to prepare the plot so that it could support any garden at all. The street lights for which the workers were taxed monthly were never replaced, so it was dangerous to visit around at night. The Ministry had located street water faucets so stingily that women had to walk farther to them than in the old villages, making five to ten trips a day with six to eight gallons each time. And unlike the village canal, which enabled everyone to do her wash at once, the scarcity of faucets—one for every twenty families or more—required women to wait for turns: like the scarcity of electricity meters and the thin house walls, adding new conditions that led to quarreling. (Electricity was free of charge in the technocrats' compound; the average *shahrak* family paid $2 per month). One entire section of Bizhan had no electricity at all for over a year, although the Ministry would not allow the workers who were electricians to install the lines.

Consider in closer detail the Ministry's water policy for the *shahrak*. When I inquired why the canals were too low to allow irrigation of the workers' gardens (especially in the summer), the engineer in charge clarified that they were meant primarily to irrigate the decorative trees along the two major streets. The Plan had never allotted sufficient water to support vegetable gardens; this explained why the Ministry never let enough water into the *shahrak* canals at the headgate even to enable those families who had invested in adjustments to irrigate their gardens. As a result, workers with large families to feed desperately needing a garden had to stay up into the night, sometimes all night, waiting turns for the trickle of water available, leading to fights between them over another scarce resource. Finally, toward the end of 1974, five years after the problem had been articulated, the Ministry installed additional faucets for the women's and household needs, one outlet for every four to six families; but it denied workers permission to extend hoses from them to their houses in order to have showers. Yet one of the administrators of the Dez Project left all the evaporation air conditioners in his home in the compound running during his own and his family's two-month absence so that the house would be cool when they returned.

Answering my inquiries about the Ministry's miserliness in an irrigation project handling thousands of cubic feet of water per second, the chief engineer explained that while the elites' compound consumed an average of *250* gallons per person per day (showers, swimming pools, landscaping and golf courses, air conditioning, and so forth), the workers were allowed only *12*, precluding sewage systems in the model towns and even the operation of public bath houses, certainly ruling out bathing facilities in the workers' homes. The *shahrak* water was meant for the decorative trees and *minimal* domestic use, not for serious vegetable gardens or daily bathing. (The workers coveted a job at the State farm cleaning out animal stalls, as they could snitch a daily shower for themselves when they bathed the Holsteins and Jerseys, which knew no water rationing.) Ministry officials could not perceive the proportions of these inequities, or the irony of their frequent accusations that the workers were dirty and lived in conditions that fostered disease. Nor did those model townsmen who did perceive these inequities and ironies express themselves in any way.

The grave shortage of water for all purposes in the *shahrak* raised the problem common to every highly centralized system, that one part of the

Plan works against another part. The Plan had originally given each house in the *shahrak* the size garden it did so that workers could compensate (with *their* time, energies, and savings) for the high unemployment rate and, when they did get jobs, for their low pay. Many World Bank advisors and technical consultants had argued for larger house plots, so each family would have its own "breadbasket of core staples'" at hand, relieving the State of responsibility. Such a scheme, which Lilienthal self-righteously advocated, epitomized the planners' ignorance of agriculture and their inability to identify with the workers as people like themselves: for, the very months when one could make a garden flourish were the same months that it was easy to find desperately needed work (mainly, the summer). And when would a man and his wife employed in manual work from six in the morning until six at night tend a small farm for their "staples?"—and with what bodily energy?

The vegetable gardens added nothing nutritional to the families' diets. The new townsmen, having brought high standards of careful farming with them to the *shahrak,* and painfully aware of neighbors' criticisms, perceived that serious agricultural efforts on the plots would lead to embarrassment, not food. Instead, to the extent that the townsmen could obtain water, the gardens came to provide them some outlet for late afternoon relaxation and for creative expression of skills related to those they had prized for centuries, as though they precariously hung on to their ancient agricultural bent which found no fulfillment working for the companies. Many model townsmen took pride in grafting fruit trees, swapping advice about seeds and plants they managed to steal from the companies or Safiabad to try themselves, relishing the variety and experimental ingenuity for which the plots offered a little scope.

Dulat's Blueprint

Three predominant qualities marked the State's policies toward the *shahrak:* fiat from on high; an obsession with neatness; and a longing, once it had fixed life correctly, to make it stay exactly that way. In all three of these salient traits, the State opposed life that tried to emerge out of the particulars, the grass roots. It abhorred initiative, hence, variety and spontaneity.

Through fiat from on high the State created perfection on its drawing boards and simply recognized no deviation on the part of what it created—certainly no point of view from below! For example, the *shahrak* had no lanes with names or numbers. After five years of settlement, the streets between house rows and the houses themselves remained designated as on the planners' blueprints: Instead of streets each *row of buildings* had a number, alternating on one side and then the other across the two main avenues. So, to give directions to his house, for instance, 'Ali had to say "go between row 19 and row 21." The individual homes were

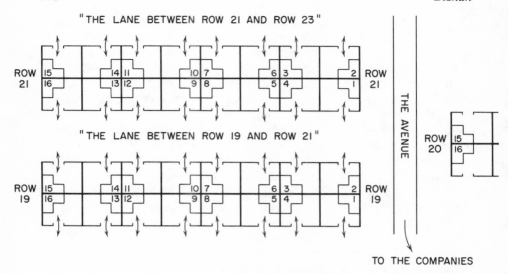

Frozen at the blueprint stage: Diagram showing how the Ministry assigned street and house addresses in the Shahrak.

also still numbered according to the planners' blueprint: Taking each building unit in sequence, the four homes in it were numbered clockwise before going to the adjacent building unit. Houses 1, 2, 3, and 4 made up the first building unit, 5 through 8 the next, and so forth. As a result, when you went down "the lane between rows 19 and 21," for example, on your right hand you passed house numbers 1, then 4, then 5, then 8, then 9, then 12 . . . in no sequence that made sense from the street. To get to houses 2, 3, 6, and 7 of row 21 you had to enter the next lane up. But because there were no cross streets, that meant returning all the way to the beginning of the lane. The constructors' beautiful brick rows had never been allowed to come to life even for people calling on someone they recently met from a different part of the *shahrak,* much less for mailmen, delivery trucks, or visitors from the urban world where streets had names and where house addresses were designated so that people coming and going could locate them.

A different manifestation of fiat arose one day after a few of my neighbors decided to solve a minor problem on their own. Since we had a bakery in our lane, chauffeurs for the technocrats at the companies and State farm came to fetch bread for noontime meals. They always drove fast. This caused many near accidents, and also threw dust onto the gardens and the wash hanging out to dry. The residents' repeated requests that the drivers slow down fell on deaf ears, and one day a child was almost hit. So the following Friday afternoon a few men built a little mound across the road to curb the drivers' speed, a slight sign of collective initiative and self-help. Sunday morning the Ministry grader came all the way out from Dezful to remove their little hump. No exchange of words from either side, reminiscent of Rahmat Abad dealings with *dulat.*

When I asked my friend the engineer in charge, he snorted, "They think they run the place! I suppose they think they're civil engineers!" He understood the *reason* for the hump because he had received many complaints about the drivers' speed, but any such initiative defied the Plan (and, although *he* had not built the road, he took the workers' initiative as a personal insult to him).

Related to fiat was the State's obsession with neatness. The planners with whom I discussed the *shahrak*s, including Lilienthal, considered one of the primary virtues of the model towns to be that the houses were in rows with space between them, in contrast to the villages' meandering, organic layouts. Some technocrats openly lamented that people had to start *living* in the perfect rows of houses, fearing that they would "make it look just like one of those unruly old villages in another few years." One engineer drove me out to a *shahrak* almost completed but not yet inhabited to photograph an "untouched" model town. "How beautiful, how beautiful!" he kept exclaiming, "see how it *was* and *should* be!"

From the outset the Ministry forbade the new townsmen to build walls around their house lots, although brick walls surround virtually all urban Iranian homes. The State wanted to be able to inspect all homes from the street, to make sure the model townsmen kept everything tidy and did not break any rules. At the same time, the workers were told that if they wished to add any additional constructions, even a chicken coop, they had to have the Ministry's permission and they could build *only* in brick: not adobe, wood, or any other material. In response to my protest that adobe homes were far safer than those the Ministry had constructed in the *shahrak,* which already had many large cracks and were too fragile to allow people even to sleep on the roof, the engineer assured me the rule against adobe construction aimed for *neatness* and *modernity,* not safety.

But the workers, like all of us, collected things that might be useful someday. The house lots began to exhibit calves, ducks, old tires, oil drums, handy roofing materials like pieces of sheet metal, ladders and wheelbarrows, broken toys, and families' wash. Having found adobe such a plastic medium for centuries, the model townsmen began to defy the engineers' technology with the elan of self-sufficiency so characteristic of Rahmat Abad, devising for themselves a profusion of outdoor kitchens, wood sheds and storage areas, motorcycle garages, and animal stalls. (The State also forbade animals out of the same concern for neatness, but as many families as possible tried to keep a cow for milk.) If you entered the townsmen's house lots, you would see that the women kept them swept and clean, but from the street the engineers saw only mud constructions for purposes unfamiliar to them (if they bothered to wonder), threatening eyesores for them and their Nikoned visitors. As one perceptively explained to me, these constituted "a breakdown in overall discipline among the labor force."

The Ministry vehemently condemned this increasing "clutter." By 1974 *dulat* had begun threatening to fine people. A Ministry doctor was ordered to launch a health campaign against everything except vegetable gardens on the house lots, because "clutter" fostered schistosomiasis. The *shahrak*'s streets hardly displayed the elite compound's trim lawns with their little rows of marigolds, but what the workers kept in their yards was no less functional (and certainly far more individualized) than the technocrat's plastic play pools, gaudy car ports, and pretentious garden swings. It was the technocrats, after all, and their Western advisors who had departed from ancient Iranian culture by exposing the houses of their compound to the street, in part at least to ape American suburbia. The workers had more pragmatic values.

But the technocrats could not tolerate the *shahrak* "rubble." Although they said it "turned the model town into a garbage dump," at a deeper level it profoundly threatened the Plan's precision and control. So in 1974 the Ministry reversed its policy about walls, now decreeing that all house lots in the *shahrak had to be enclosed* within high brick walls. Ministry employees living there were ordered to set the pattern by enclosing theirs first. "After all, that's the way people in Dezful live, so why don't you people in Bizhan imitate them?" More important than inspection from the street were homogeneity and regularity. Regaining an appearance of everything being in its place, Engineer Tajdar sighed, would "return the *shahrak* to law."

The third hallmark of the State in Bizhan was its craving that it could stop time once it had arranged things, because ongoing change—especially growth—represented initiative upward, hence against the Plan. One could continually see the manifestations of this fear of the State's that—as in the case of the house-lot "clutter"—what the Plan brought forth in pure form might subsequently take on a life of its own, making the Plan only temporarily determinative. Thus the Plan intentionally built the *shahrak* houses to preclude the addition of second stories; its rules in effect prohibited all new construction; it gave the town proper only the land Bizhan occupied in 1974, not an inch for expansion. The Ministry resented having to add more street faucets, not mainly because of the cost but because that meant tampering with the original Plan. The Plan had deliberately made the *shahrak* streets only a little over one lane wide so the flow of automobile traffic would never "spoil the rural atmosphere." The Plan refused to recognize the concept of functional streets, much less street names and addresses. When I asked how delivery vans could find a particular house, the planner replied, "there will never *be* any delivery vans out there." The State forbade stores in the *shahrak*. Indeed, the plan decreed that no *shahrak* in Iran would be allowed to exceed a population of 4,500, because it categorically debarred all of them from becoming towns (which a settlement legally became when it reached 5,000 inhabitants).

The new model town had to be frozen just as it was, within the Plan's bounds. It must not come alive. On many occasions when I would ask the technocrats the reason for their extinguishing a little suggestion or initiative within the *shahrak,* they explained that The Plan Organization hadn't yet decided whether people living in *shahrak*s should be allowed leeway to do that particular thing on their own, and that if the Plan let them they would soon get out of hand.

The Plan did aim to raise the standard of living of the rural people: but only so much, no more. Although professional urban planners had helped conceive and design the *shahrak,* and although the King and his ministers were intoxicated with futurism, the three planners I specially interviewed about Bizhan saw no reason why the *shahrak* in fifty years might necessarily be different from the way it was in 1974. They had girded it all around to make sure that Image Realized would not develop its own momentum, "spilling out and over," as one said. Lanes, yes—but no cars. Brick homes, yes—but not two-storied ones. Gardens, yes—but not horticulture. Running water, yes—but not at home, not for baths. Television, yes—but not cinema houses. Modern, yes—but no expansion.

A poorhouse—but not one with lights; a technical school—but not students and professors; a mosque—but not *two!* Empirically, one could chart the fact that every time the people in the *shahrak* pushed a little bit on their own they immediately met the limit.

A showcase model town, yes—but not Throne City.

Control

In moving from Rahmat Abad to Bizhan, the peasants were meant to become not just better-off workers, but uniformly better-off workers, and workers who knew their place—an incipient caste. Image was not merely (as Westerners thought) a matter of stirring the world's admiration, but also an *internally directed* blueprint of rigid benevolence that prescribed the boundaries of freedom, initiative, and control. The Plan's division of the countryside into three classes of settlement that we described in the Introduction did not simply outline three approaches to the delivery of government services, but rather three socioeconomic categories that the Plan would shape out of rural society.

Taken on its own, the shoddiness of the brand new showcase town— even the State's stinginess—could have been attributed to a concern for form rather than substance, for construction rather than maintenance, which prevailed throughout Iran's drive to modernize: critical for a society wanting profound change, but a widely familiar phenomenon and perhaps remediable. However, the *shahrak*'s pervasive shoddiness became a manifestation of more fundamental societal characteristics when coupled—as it was in Bizhan—with the planners' explanations of what that

shoddiness meant, and when coupled, too, with numerous small incidents by which the State confirmed these explanations behaviorally. For
instance, *dulat* revealed why it gave resources to the *shahrak* so sparingly,
although it could afford to send the grader out from Dezful to level the
new townsmen's hump in the road; why the Ministry prohibited hoses
that might enable showers at home; or why the state rejected Dezful businessmen's offers to open and run the bath houses or the butchery. Other
examples will follow. From such articulations of policy, Bizhan's shoddiness manifested not just chronic mediocrity, but the State's public specifications of limits that defined a social category it was creating.

In this model town of several thousand people, already five years old,
the Ministry had not even a part-time representative, no agency office or
appointed day for consultation or problem solving, and did not acknowledge even a popularly recognized intermediary to synthesize and respond
to residents' communications with whoever administered the settlement.
In short, the Ministry did not find necessary those minimal channels of
interacting with the population that *dulat* did in Rahmat Abad. Model
townsmen could seek out officials in Dezful if they could find them, but
they rarely did; they knew there was no need to ask questions of the Ministry, no need to file requests or complaints. As things turned out, the
workers never had to wait for the State to give *permission* for them to do
something, but rather they learned to wait hoping *the State itself* would
do it. For its part, the Ministry simply never had any need to approach
the workers, no need to call meetings where it would tell people what it
wanted them to carry out or was going to do itself. In contrast to the
various meetings *dulat* arranged in Rahmat Abad (albeit usually for
tokenism), none ever took place during my year in Bizhan, a settlement
over ten times as large, neither with the whole *shahrak* nor with any
subgroup within it. In Bizhan modernization was nonnegotiable. Just as
it could not be altered, neither could it be supplemented. Bizhan was
Rahmat Abad's event of "the holes" blown up town sized—and lasting
not weeks but for good. This, the beginning of *development?*

The technocrats and planners considered the *shahrak* to be evidence
and a symbol of the State's munificence. "Look how much we have done
for these people . . . " officials continually said to me. When *Europe* had
consolidated its farm land, no one provided the peasants sent off to work
in industry with brick homes and electricity. Bizhan was not a punishment for being backward, but a *gift*. We must appreciate the State's paternalistic pride in how its *shahrak* uplifted the peasantry, if we are to
glimpse the control Bizhan embodied, especially as a nation-wide model
for rural development. The Plan would raise up society, but it would
allow each part of society to be raised only as much as the planners determined it should be, and never for a moment giving the key to those it
was uplifting. The former peasants were to become the rural proletariat;
they must not aspire for more or think they could achieve even that on
their own: not even, that in order to protect their children they could

make a little hump in the road. The task of the regionally based techno-crats was—with the Plan's help—to fine tune the uplifting (a control far more subtle than "oppression"), so it should uplift but not spawn expectations, confidence, initiatives. What a contrast to Rahmat Abad, where *everything* was negotiable and no one knew his or her place, where one thing inevitably and exuberantly led to another, because there was no Plan, where expectations, confidence and initiative ran rampant.

Visionaries like Lilienthal thought that "development" meant putting factories and combines on the landscape. But whether consciously or sub-consciously, the Persian State saw "development" in far more sophisti-cated terms. In Bizhan it punctiliously observed what some today call "the process": Development was *its* business. This meant, not the *work-ers'* business! (And maybe not even the business of wealthy, freewheeling Iranians. All the agribusinesses were owned and directed by foreigners, and all the farm corporations, by the State. In the entire Dez Irrigation Project, the model for the entire rural Iran, the only private Iranian with significant decision-making responsibilities was a retired army general firmly ensconced on his American wife's estate in Georgia, who for a short while managed one agribusiness under its owner's tutelage.)

The State's assumption that it could create social reality in Bizhan sim-ply through design and command, its obsession with imposed order there, and its unwillingness to acknowledge the least wiggling in its crea-tion all were traits that reified the Plan's primordial objectification of rural society as its instrument. According to some technocrats, the Plan was intended to be a set of guidelines for *coordinating* development. But if it ever had been this, with the Dez Irrigation Project, The Plan Orga-nization's first massive creation out of "nothing," that political relation-ship shifted. No longer would the State simply orchestrate what the peo-ple themselves thought of doing and did: Now like a sculptor it would take raw clay, make something out of it, and when it was perfect fire it solid. Now the people of northern Khuzestan were to serve the Plan, not it them. And if the Plan judged them unable to serve it, the State would pay them to stand by out of its way. Thus in time local initiatives that the Plan could "coordinate" came to be obstacles it had to suppress.

The fact that the Shah possessed so little charisma was not entirely a function of his personality; his wooden expression accurately depicted the lack of moral integration (hence, *spirit*) between rulers and ruled in Iran—where in Bizhan at least society existed merely for the former's *use*. The Plan could give Bizhan electricity, but Rahmat Abad gave itself a *constitution*. Nothing so vividly symbolized how the Plan severed the bond of social unity than the redolent Bizhan orchard behind its walls in the middle of Iran's model "labor center," waiting there only for the technocrats in their sealed-up cars.

A small core of older townsmen reflected this vertical disjuncture between top and bottom in the Plan's society when they trenchantly insisted, all the time I knew them, that there *was* no Shah; that the man introduced as Shah on television was a paste-up job of the corrupt "engineers" who ran the country from Tehran, and who just traveled this man around as a show (which somehow explained how few words he spoke). Hasan, the crazy boy herding the workers' cows, always broadcast the latest elaborations of this political theory as he sauntered along. Its truth was his "one-uppance" on everyone whose normality made them accomplices in this colossal trick on themselves. Often I met people in the model town who did not believe the Shah existed. Even some who almost worshiped the man that visited the agribusiness later concluded no one ruled the land. There is no contradiction, of course, between on the one hand, longing that someone sanctify a moral unity embracing both the Plan and Bizhan, and on the other hand, concluding that no one did.

We begin to see, then, what we mean by the Iranian State manifesting its own behavioral traits as it elaborated the Dez Project. Although it possessed an institutional identity, its numerous decrees and projects in the region revealing policy intentions of their mother institution, we characterize "the State" not just by inference from its official acts but also from the *culture* of the people who carried them out. Because of their personalistic power (at *every level,* power relative to those not working for the State), and because of their intense interaction among themselves, those within *dulat* evolved their own clearly defined set of assumptions, channels for interaction, and unique patterns of behavior. By no means was this culture unrelated to the overarching Iranian culture, but it did distinctly pertain to the State.

Some planners had in fact *thought out* certain systematic policies observable in the Ministry of Water and Power, such as the importance of imposing neatness on what the Plan created or the necessity of preventing growth in the *shahrak*. But even without *conscious deliberation,* repeated actions like rejecting workers' initiatives or treating the workers with condescension over time became generalized into an inter-Ministerial culture through what was largely an unconscious process, yet especially consistent among the technocrats. The power and aims they shared, the ways their Tehran superiors continually treated them and expected or required them to treat others, the social models presented to them, and, of course, the behavior of everyone they acted *upon*—over time these had synthesized into an ethos with its own premises and its own momentum. At least in northern Khuzestan, this culture of those who implemented *dulat*'s orders corresponded so closely to the State's formal expressions that it reinforced the impression of a political monolith.

The Plan Confirmed

Perhaps attempting to cement together the social disjuncture in the Dez Project and related disjunctures such as that between fiat and reality, the State mounted "theatrical enactments" of what modern Iran must be.

(The concept is Margaret Mead's, which she elaborated in a study of the Soviet Union—1951:44–45). The Shah's theatrical enactment of the Persian Empire's twenty-five-hundred-year anniversary not only sought to impress the world, but also—internal to the realm—actually to secure the crown more firmly on his head (like the grandiose constructions of the British Empire in New Delhi). In the case of the Dez Irrigation Project, the Safiabad experimental farm, symbolically located at the heart of the scheme and right next to Bizhan, constituted just such a staging for the re-creation of rural Iran, a perfect complement to Bizhan itself. Safiabad gave "ritual proof" that the Plan was being realized.

By virtue of its being "scientific," the Safiabad farm was spared the agribusinesses' pragmatic rough-and-tumble, all the better to stage the Plan's ideal. According to most foreign scientists at Safiabad whom I interviewed or came to know, pervasive corruption there prevented serious research. The Iranian technocrats used the farm to sell first-class milk, butter, cream and cheeses, the finest cuts of beef, pork and lamb, and vegetables and fruit hardly available elsewhere in Iran to markets of provincially based foreigners, to Tehran, and even abroad. If so, these incentives and the need to disguise them enabled the farm to serve the purposes of theatrical enactment far more effectively than if it had to experiment in small plots and herds with technology not yet perfected.

Quintessentially clean, exact, efficient, and abundant, Safiabad's weedless fields and orchards, its spotless animals, its white-clad technicians and perfectly calculated statistical findings confirmed to the World Bank, the State itself, the public, and visitors from abroad that the Dez Project was not about peasants and workers but about what modern science could bring forth in Nature under controlled conditions, when directed by experts. As a realization of fiat on public stage, not even the famous Isfahan steel mill could match Safiabad's lush fields of fat Merino sheep which established that *food* was the purpose of uprooting tens of thousands of villagers, the purpose of squalid Bizhan right across the road. The farm's miniature successes plot after plot, stall after stall, each fenced in, marked, and numbered, *proved* that all this was worth it. Without the steel mill's grime of machinery and capitalistic profit, Safiabad affirmed modernization within a traditional Iranian rose garden—all the while surpassing Western agricultural achievements. (Its sugar beets had higher sugar content than America's, its table grapes surpassed Israel's in yield and quality, and so forth.) In scientifically pristine Safiabad a regime of order and intellectual command brought forth plenitude overflowing— the Plan's ritual banquet. Here then, right next to Bizhan, was the State's *moral* content: agrarian harmony and abundance. Here was *dulat*'s theatrical answer to the workers' search for a King who cared about them.

Just as the villagers in Rahmat Abad were told that literacy certificates brought forth literates and clipping cows' ears made them vaccinated, so the Plan affirmed that if streets were not recognized as such, traffic would not appear in them, and that if there was no space to expand into, a town would stay as it was. The point of the Plan was that reality would be accountable to the image. Whereas the image of Throne City had *come out of* and reflected the villagers' actions and interactions, in just the opposite dynamic all actions and interactions in the Dez Scheme were to come out of and truly reflect the image.

> **Gardens beneath which rivers flow ... are the reward only of those who do good.**   **—Qur'an, Sura 5**

Chapter 8

Socioeconomic Organization in Bizhan

The illimitable sea needs nothing from the waves save their breaking.   **—Khuzestan proverb**

The Agricultural Cycle

The singular preoccupation in the model town was finding and keeping a job. Within the workers' narrow range of employment possibilities two factors largely determined success in their search for employment: personal connections and the agricultural season. During the winter the farms grew mainly wheat, requiring almost no unskilled work. A few jobs continued throughout the winter, but for days and sometimes for weeks on end many men in Bizhan dozed until mid-afternoon. Especially during the weeks of rain everyone in the family would crouch over a handful of coals in one dimly lit cinder block room. Rain did not bring the anticipation of a rich harvest as in Rahmat Abad, but only the family having to eat without anyone earning a wage. Few people congregated in others' homes as villagers did during bad weather because they rarely befriended neighbors, and as for kinsmen, each dreaded the possibility that the other might have found a day's work.

By early spring the young men hustled about to find the best job they could. The British company might announce competitions for tractor drivers and other semiskilled positions. A few days before the Persian New Year (March 21) the State farm at Safiabad fired almost all workers and then rehired many the following week—or others in their place, a feared eventuality—so as not to have to give any New Year's bonuses. Before spring was out, all the women and girls who wanted to weed or pick had places on the companies' labor teams, where they could find steady although ill-paid work until the autumn, some of them employed eight months of the year. And by mid- or late spring, too, the companies needed a full force of irrigators and field watchmen, jobs the unskilled men could perform.

Summer, of course, was the busiest time. Night shifts flourished as well as day work. Boys could make what they considered good pay in the arduous sugar beet harvest. Despite the soaring temperatures many had

187

no choice but to take on a twelve-hour work day or more if their supervisors demanded—never a requirement at Safiabad where the State engineers went home early in the afternoon to avoid the heat. In the autumn,
cotton picking brought some good days' pay to the strong, before the rains
began again.

The Family

Predictably, under the severe pressures the *shahrak* placed on social organization, the nuclear family maintained itself intact more firmly than any
other social form, although it too experienced strain. With some concern
for the effects of new housing arrangements on the family, the Ministry
generally allowed male relatives who had lived in the same compound in
the village to apply for *shahrak* houses next to one another, although the
State emphasized that only members of a *nuclear* family had any *claim*
to proximity. Brothers not granted houses nearby could not subsequently
join one another without forfeiting their lots. Four wealthy brothers with
strong connections in the Ministry did secure an entire housing unit for
themselves. Still, for many reasons including the physical layout of the
shahrak homes (back to back, centripetally facing outward rather than all
facing each other as in a compound), few such family arrangements in
Bizhan shared any resources or common space, a sharing that had blurred
the distinction between nuclear and "extended" families and households
in Rahmat Abad. Here, no shared ovens, no shared roofs for drying grain
and beans, no shared latrines, no shared storage areas. Often families next
to each other would not meet for days.

The *shahrak* move severed the women's ties with their families more
acutely than the men's. Other than allowing members of a patriclan to
live near one another, the Ministry deliberately scattered people from
each village all over the new town, often in several *shahrak*s, so women
who had lived close to their relatives in a small village were now likely
to see them rarely. My neighbor Maryam who had visited her mother
daily in the village did not even see her monthly in Bizhan; although they
lived in the same *shahrak,* more than a half an hour's walk separated
their homes.

Many relatives who, before the move, had lived apart in different villages considered their transfer to the *shahrak* as a chance to reunite in
one place, even if their respective villagers were being assigned to different model towns. The Ministry would entertain no such requests, though:
"If you don't like your house assignment, go to Dezful." Before the move,
a widow, Sahra, had three married daughters residing in other villages,
while she lived next to her brother with whose wife she constantly quar-
reled. She asked the Ministry official to relocate her in a *shahrak* where
at least one of her daughters would be living, and near her. He refused.
Not yet used to *dulat*'s ways, she discovered a widower assigned a house
in the new town to which her daughters were going but wanting to move

to the *shahrak* to which she was sent. Delighted, they agreed to exchange house certificates, since all *shahrak* houses in the entire Dez Project were identical, and since the two *shahrak*s in question were being opened at the same time. Their initiative infuriated the bureaucrats, who had suppressed a number of cases like it. Upon inquiring about Sahra's plight, I was told that the secret police had made all house assignments, and their authority could not be undermined by people's own ideas. The particular bureaucrat in charge, a former landlord who had lost his villages in the land reform, seemed to enjoy the sweet revenge of manipulating such details of tens of thousands of peasants' lives, fixing them for generations to come.

If each nuclear family among *joft*holding villagers was able to secure its own separate house in the new town, that was not true of the landless who made up around 30 percent of the population and were more vulnerable to official whims or demands. On my street, two tiny rooms of a single home housed, between them, three formerly landless married brothers plus their wives, their mother, and four children. Typically, the Ministry official appraising houses in the village had counted their small house as a single dwelling, even though every married couple in the village had slept in its own separate room.

Howsoever new townsmen might want to alter their arrangements once they moved into the *shahrak,* such as by buying or selling houses and lots, or renting or exchanging them, all such changes were prohibited. No adjustments in house location could be made to take into account quarrels, marriages, realignments at death, the desire or need to reconstitute an extended family, or other eventualities. In effect *dulat* also ruled out workers' constructing their own new homes on relatives' land. Once the *shahrak* was set, it was frozen—a law villagers from a place like Throne City could hardly imagine.

To be sure, the Ministry did not systematically extend its policy of breaking up villages to the family itself. Still, in many instances it did divide brothers without their consent (those it considered troublemakers), and even from brothers it often required bribes to retain housing proximity. In these, in many cases like Sahra's, and in its treatment of numerous formerly landless families, the Ministry publicized its decisions as symbols to impress the new townsmen that all social organization above the most rudimentary unit, the nuclear family, existed by the bureaucracy's sufferance. In Rahmat Abad, family and household were inviolable.

In addition to the State's policies, the model town's economic organization affected the *shahrak* family profoundly. In the shift from small-scale farming within the corporate village, and from the numerous opportunities for *sharik* partnerships there, to wage labor in an economy dominated by capital-intensive production, brothers or fathers and sons often competed for the same scarce job. Sharing no common interests like village land, irrigation water, *bildar*s, or pooled resources such as a horse or cart—not even sharing the same daily schedules, places of work, statuses, work problems, or associates—kinsmen had minimal reason for interaction at all, even if they lived next door. I saw little exchange of food, resources, or labor between families in Bizhan (such as for construction), even on the villagers' basis of carefully calculated repayment. We will consider the absence of *sharik* partnerships below, but essentially the workers' poverty left them with few complementary resources to share; during good weather even boys in their late teens were frequently too exhausted to visit around in the evenings.

Only those nuclear families consciously striving to retain traditional values withstood the internal strains caused by boys and girls (sometimes wives) earning more than their fathers or husbands. Older men suffered because they could find almost nothing to do either to bring in money or to help, while their technical expertise, command of history, and the recognition and authority they had earned meant nothing. The *shahrak* preempted many family functions, replacing them with the State. The family no longer possessed any means of production. The individual was housed at the hand of the State, educated by the State, guaranteed a job (if at all) by the State; as a last resort, the State provided the poorhouse—at least as a symbol—and a minimum dole. By destroying the villages, the State had created an environment of extraordinary uncertainty that undermined even the primary confidence of many kin ties. When it appeared that my aging neighbor Faridun—one of the poorest men in Bizhan although exceptionally rich in wisdom and wit—lay dying, none of his kinsmen who were summoned came to his side. Since they had occasionally visited his house I knew they were on good terms. Others explained that his relatives were too poor to assume the responsibility of his wife and four children, so they had to stay away. Had it been in Rahmat Abad, the assurance that his wife and at least two of the children could have found work, and that the community would have assisted them out of some sense of responsibility, would have enabled all his kinsmen, howsoever destitute themselves, to respond to that natural urge to be with such a beloved man in his last hours.

In Rahmat Abad the family offered a range of tough structures for support, protection, and organizing resources; and in Mehrabani's world, despite its sharply contrasting amorphous sprawl, the family often served economic purposes. After all, the Monarch's legitimacy and, hence, *dulat* itself rested on the family principle; Mehrabani's network only mirrored the King's, spreading out into society to penetrate it, fuzzing the boundaries between family and smiling friends wherever personal benefits and personal affirmation flowed. In Bizhan, Iran's model town, however, the family struggled to keep its elemental core intact.

Elementary Social Forms Above the Family

As Rahmat Abad demonstrated, the strength and reliability of social forms above or outside the nuclear family constitute requisite building blocks for sustained economic development. In the *shahrak*s, the Iranian State explicitly set out to obliterate these traditional structures, especially the corporate village. It is here—in its demolition or suppression of middle-range organizations and the local initiatives that bring them forth— that we see the most wanton social destruction in this pilot project for all of rural Iran. Members of the same ancient community, even lifetime neighbors, were *systematically* placed far apart from one another in the model town; the Ministry (I was told, the secret police) even dispersed some villages across several different *shahrak*s. The bonds of thousands of friends and neighbors who had lived side by side for half a century or even generations, evolving that communal trust and collaborative strength indispensable for initiative, accountability, and predictability, were now sundered by the whim of some technocrat who himself knew only *dulat*'s vacuous residential "compound." The State spared no links except unknowingly: families previously tied as plowing partners, landless laborers virtually part of a sharecropper's household, friends who merely regarded one another as friends.

"You've forgotten who I am! I never see you, uncle!" two former neighbors protested as they passed each other on the road; after five years one of them could lament, "I'm among foreigners down there still." People from the same original village ("sharers of the same shade," they say in northern Khuzestan) would meet at the bedside of a critically ill friend, the neighbor of all of them since youth; only an extraordinary occasion renewed what was once such an ordinary coming together. Although living in the same town, Batul no longer knew the name of Quli's smallest children. When resolute effort preserved certain ties, the workers' poverty often ruled out hospitality, as not everyone could still afford entertaining a guest, even for tea.

Some people in Bizhan hardly knew their neighbors' names; only people from the same former village could they trust. After years, everyone who surrounded them they called *gharib,* a stranger. Nor could many remember in what house row they could find their former neighbors and friends, even in the same *shahrak,* if they had ever known. While people in Rahmat Abad had come together at the canal or every evening at the crossroads, the new townmen did not socialize by lanes, house clusters, or neighborhoods, nor by groups of workers in the same shift or in the same department at the company or tending the same field area, certainly not by former corporate villages. Talking over the garden fence as you passed by on your way home amounted to the sum of most social relations. In the afternoon, a few young men stood around the rotary circle at the entrance to Bizhan; another handful sometimes gathered near the "hospital," and another beneath the eucalyptus; these twenty people or so comprised the total of public gatherings in the new town of several thousand. Perhaps some specific event in the past discouraged such clusterings; several technocrats told me it was illegal for men to "loiter" in their free time, as they "belonged" at home after work. The women aggregated by the water outlets, but often did their work there in silence. There were so many fights among them that many who had to frequent the same faucet were not on speaking terms. Not even gossip or sensational news would circulate throughout the town. I met people who ten days later had still not heard that in broad daylight brigands had held up the agribusiness manager and his driver, a man from the *shahrak,* robbing them of all the workers' wages and thereby delaying the employees' pay for a week. In Rahmat Abad the school children frequently integrated community news, but not in Bizhan. Apparently they, too, were fragmented.

Such listlessness did not result from spectacles of the State's terror in Bizhan's streets, like public hangings, nor from armed soldiers patrolling the *shahrak,* people disappearing, or stories of torture. To the contrary, the model town embodied *dulat*'s *benevolence:* electricity, brick homes, a guaranteed job for everyone, tree-lined avenues, Safiabad's cornucopia, which would soon flow over into every family meal. Bizhan had become a wasteland because not a single sustaining issue or project—not one ongoing purpose, not one controversy—brought together even a handful of new townsmen; much less could any interest common to *everyone* in the model town come to the fore. In the next chapter we consider several sporadic and highly specialized exceptions, which as such illustrate the State's systematic erosion of political organization in Bizhan by monopolizing all public endeavor.

By its very dynamics the Plan precluded public plans in Bizhan. The *shahrak* comprised no committees (except for the mosque, which we will discuss in the next chapter), no public associations, no religious meetings, no self-help organizations, no factions or interest groups. No one ever took up a collection for anything. The model town allowed not even the most momentary joint efforts, such as building a hump in the road—no civic expressions like mothers participating in the clinic's direction or young people planting flowers in the circle at the *shahrak* entrance. No block organizations took charge of cleaning the canal or repairing the street lights or policing the neighborhood at night. *Dulat* preempted all common objectives around which social units might rally, and those that sought new purposes it undermined. By the time I arrived in Bizhan, only the rare, hesitating initiative like making the hump suggested that under different conditions the new townsmen might have created a structured and energetic communal life in the *shahrak,* rechanneling the momentum we saw in Rahmat Abad. Indeed, without Rahmat Abad's evidence to the contrary—if one had believed Lilienthal's appraisal of the landscape— Bizhan's limp population seemed to *need* the State to assume guardianship over it.

In stepping from the village into *dulat*'s world, the workers had plunged into the State's culture of personalized power we have already described in Part One. Those few villagers with connections had secured the best house locations and jobs in Bizhan; all employment there ultimately depended on personal ties. But even these ties, which one would have expected to flourish in such an environment, found little purpose in the *shahrak* to keep them vibrant. In the mainstream of urban life outside Bizhan, even in the provinces, petty economic activity was sufficiently lively to give personal connections some scope. But in the *shahrak* the paucity of any resources, choices, or variation among such a wide social base restricted the usefulness even of "contacts" (although never the workers' hopes for them). Few new jobs at Safiabad ever opened up, and since most middle-ranking positions in the companies went to men from Dezful, knowing someone could not help one get promoted. As with their technological and economic resources, the workers were simply out-classed in mobilizing social assets. Thus even the main organizational principle—other than family—in Iran's urban culture, the personal net-work, found only restricted scope in Bizhan.

This void of social purpose and social forms in the *shahrak* extended into such an innocuous area of potential social life as public entertain-ment. The Ministry's heavy-handed presence in northern Khuzestan, its obliteration of the villages, and its sponsorship of the agribusinesses and State farm corporations in their place gave the impression—an impres-sion the Ministry perhaps backed up with action—that the outside world could not enter the *shahrak* except as private visitors. (The technocrat had assured me that "there will be no delivery vans. . . .") Hence, in Bizhan, neighbors or those in the same row of houses never even came together around a traveling sideshow, a preaching darvesh, visiting ped-dlers, not even around reformers from some other Ministry in *dulat* lec-turing them how to improve their lives. Although superficial, in Rahmat Abad these events had called forth temporary social gathering. In Bizhan we never watched school athletic games, never attended school programs, never heard about "our" students performing in competitions or on pro-vincial examinations (as we did even in Rahmat Abad!). A businessman in Dezful wanted to establish a small movie house, which would have lent some focus to *shahrak* social life, but the Ministry denied him permission.

The Ministry did organize a soccer team of employees at Safiabad to play other government teams in the region. But since the team was merely a tool of the Ministry—entirely the product of *dulat*—and since it neither required nor requested the new townsmen's support, it never became the focus of *shahrak* "spirit" or identity. It did not even articulate the identity of Safiabad workers as a group. Almost no one attended the games that were played on a back field at the edge of the new town, nor did anyone inquire who won.

Only weddings in Bizhan preserved some of the sociability that gave body to traditional village life. Bizhan weddings drew together kinsmen, neighbors, the groom's co-workers, and former villages, if not explicitly as groups at least in recognition of minimal social categories. This was the one occasion when most members of a patriclan, people who lived in the same row of houses, men who worked the same shift together, or new townsmen from the same former village would meet one another, albeit in a large crowd. Still, weddings in the *shahrak* were already beginning to lose their communal character. Women never dropped in on a *shahrak* wedding as they did whenever they found a little free time in the village, and they rarely danced as the women of Rahmat Abad exuberantly did.

In short, although there were places the new townsmen could gather in public, and although there might have been endeavors the Ministry would have allowed them to undertake, the State had effectively obliterated almost every pulse of social exchange, every vestige of public initiative large or small. As evidence and as consequence, Bizhan society could count on little social pressure to control social deviance. With the knowledge of acquaintances and relatives, many married couples were involved in romantic affairs (although I never heard of any in the villages), and people frequently wrecked the faucets, the Ministry's trees along the two main streets, the street lights, even entering house lots to steal and damage things: actions they never would have done six years before, in the village.

A much more profound summation of the model town's social fragmentation was the disappearance of all traces of social cohesion in mourning. With the villages' transition to Bizhan, a sacramental affirmation of social order itself passed out of the collective experience. Since the communities had been scattered all over the new town, people found it impossible to organize a mourning group, so no corporate delegations presented themselves to give witness to the endurance of human bonds— nor did any group receive the mourners as the bereaved social unit. After all, with a death no community now felt the loss of a part of its whole. Those honored as survivors—"Fatimah and the three children of house number 7 in row 12"—comprised little more than a nuclear family. Mourners could not pay their respects even as family entities but attended the funeral rites individually because a man could go only when he got off work. Only a few people could sit in the tiny *shahrak* rooms so, aware that others were waiting outside to come in, no one could stay long (although, touchingly, neighbors usually congregated in the small side room to leave the former fellow villagers together—even only briefly— with the bereaved in the main one). In its organizational implications, the mourning ceremony resembled an American "open house" more than it resembled Rahmat Abad's collective ritual.

Social Fragmentation and the State: The Culture of the Plan

When we consider the connection between life in the *shahrak* (whether shaped by its material conditions or by sociopolitical dynamics) and the State's creation and management of the *shahrak* world, we cannot help but wonder to what extent the technocrats at any level deliberately intended such social erosion. The question is impossible to answer. The State did articulate *explicitly* many of the basic policies we have described, and it did explicitly set out to atomize the population through some of these policies. It explicitly sought to impose universal regularity, neatness, and homogeneity. Secondly, and most importantly, the State clearly claimed for itself all major responsibility (hence, control) for transforming rural Iran. It emphasized that it and it alone constituted the locus of political power for the job at hand. Finally, while the State never explicitly announced that the rural population had to obey everything the Plan decreed, we can infer that this fundamental aspect of *shahrak* life it also deliberately intended, in effect insisting on it by its show of power, its arbitrariness, and its emphasis on the peasants' poverty, illiteracy, and backwardness: their *generic* incapacity. So unambiguous were these principles throughout the bureaucracy that even agents of the State who were laymen in terms of social science expertise could explain them and apply them accurately in specific situations. They had absorbed well the culture of the Plan. One feature of any culture is that it programs people to carry out certain things automatically, as by habit.

Besides such explicit and consciously deliberated policies, the *culture* of centralized power—the culture within *dulat*—played a determinative role in shaping society in Bizhan. Culture is a living phenomenon that to some extent takes on a life of its own, leading those within it (such as those within the culture of *dulat*'s power) to do many things not specifically spelled out. Planners, especially development economists, usually overlook the great cultural liability inherent in what they call forth: that what they establish in society—any given set of mechanisms they help put in place to achieve *particular* ends—brings with it norms and working institutions that then take on lives of their own. Rulers and planners value this generalizing ability of culture, including its institutional aspects, because it ensures that even the details of distant bureaucrats' most routine decisions will consistently carry out policies the center prescribes.

In northern Khuzestan, *dulat*'s millennia-old culture reaffirmed the technocrats' conviction that "nothing" of worth existed in the landscape, which could be molded into desirable form only through exceptional effort (rare technocratic expertise, huge funds, and political power), and, hence, only through the State. These initial premises logically led, first, to such invasions into local social life as land reform and the expropriation of the villages, which the State justified and achieved without the least resistance. Once such images of the new order that the State promised to bring forth began visibly to fill the landscape (with international "experts'" approval), the cultural foundation for the State's command over society had been laid. By not challenging the Plan's basic propositions publicly, the peasants implicitly ratified them, as did economists and planners all the way up the line to the World Bank, fixing in place the institutional infrastructure of the Plan's culture.

From this beginning, the technocrats—extending from Tehran to Dezful—then just elaborated these fundamentals of power that had been

established, their day-to-day behavior solidifying them in almost an automatic way (certainly unchecked). For instance, the Ministry's leveling the
workers' hump with bitter ridicule shows how the State's planning culture
had set off on its own course and in little time had completely lost touch
with its baseline, where it had begun. Fifteen years earlier, bureaucrats
learning about a hump in a rural road might have concluded that someone had had it constructed for good reason; they might have considered
the hump salutary if they attributed it to a landlord and guessed its purpose; and they probably would have feared leveling it without any inquiry
at all. But as the State had taken possession of the countryside, it came
to assume everything there belonged to it, then every*one* belonged to it,
until finally it had reached the point where it saw the workers' benign
initiative to be in defiance against its authority! Because in its own growth
of power it had one by one extinguished all initiatives emanating from
the base of society, beginning with the larger ones and then smaller and
smaller, gradually the culture of the Plan had become unaccustomed to
anything sprouting forth at all, until now the slightest indication of some
local thought or movement evoked angry retaliation. Fifteen years earlier
dulat's officials had been *afraid* to go into the countryside!

The case of the hump shows that the culture of the Plan (or of *dulat*)
had taken off into full flight. Technocrats from the Central Office of the
Imperial Plan all the way down to Dezful could now intuitively live and
work by it. This culture they constituted would continue to grow incrementally according to its basic directions, one solution leading logically
to the next, albeit a little more extreme each time. Indeed, the culture of
dulat's rule would continue to push its fundamental premises or structures further unless checked, which it certainly was not: for, the process
of establishing it had shaped the rural people, too. The Plan had initially
elicited the peasants' acceptance and submission to the State, by shock,
overwhelming power, and the social fragmentation we have seen. But as
that cultural pattern took root in them, in the *shahrak's* fertile soil, the
model townsmen moved to dependence, the erosion of self-confidence,
then to confusion, possibly even *losing* their organizational skills, and—
many of them—to idolizing the King who would have to care for them.
This progression of theirs, in turn, reified the technocrats' sense of power.
The new townsmen, too, could be acculturated into the Plan. If we do not
know how far their disintegration would have gone, still we can observe
empirically the *fragility* of even such strong organizational forms as those
in Rahmat Abad, and the extent to which these *could* be eroded.

As part of the generalizing process of culture, fundamental cultural
"premises" or structures tend to become systemic, so that the patterns
that emerge and then organize one area of our lives may also shape our
behavior and norms in other seemingly unrelated ones. This systemic
characteristic of culture helps explain the striking *parallels* between *different* areas of behavior that we have already observed, such as the congruence between the technocrats' intolerance for "clutter" in the *shahrak*

house lots and their intolerance for social groupings which would similarly litter the Plan's landscape; the congruence between their perception that detailed blueprints bring forth a dam of exact specifications and their belief that blueprints could make a human town similarly perfect, cast in concrete; or the congruence between the Plan's conviction that peasants who live in mud houses also have backward social forms (and conversely, that men who know civil engineering make good social engineers). This generalizing propensity of culture constituted one of the most critical dangers of the Plan, whose premises established themselves *systemically* not just in the minds of the planners but also in the actual society they were shaping.

What devastated rural society in the Dez Project, and therefore was detrimental to its and Iranian society's sustained development, constituted a positive achievement from the State's point of view. The State had successfully eliminated Bizhan's potential public, driving most social life out of the common arena (where model townsmen would have defined and sought action on issues they shared) into the strictly *private* realm of person-to-person or family-to-family networks—"behind closed doors," as Madar-i-Karim in Rahmat Abad had said of Dezfullis. Any issues that could be construed as of general concern, either to small groups or to the entire *shahrak,* the State had quickly and meticulously preempted. If *dulat* continued long enough to fragment society in Bizhan, suppressing any public field whatsoever for collective expression, the model townsmen's norms, institutions, and skills for structured public life would deteriorate, as these had in Iran's urban culture.

By debilitating interest groups and the former cohesive village structures, the Ministry removed individuals' powerful "little platoons," through which they could organize larger groups and these into larger ones still, notch by notch raising their sights for more ambitious initiatives as they firmed up stronger organizational capacities to underpin them. Contrary to many Western theories, Bizhan and the State's strategies there illustrated that the *individual* was not the *key* to an open and vital public life; rather those *structures* that individuals formed between themselves and the State were. In Rahmat Abad, through these structures' gradation in size as well as their potential combination, they gave individuals leverage (or at least some protection). The relative *scale* of organizational forms in a given social field is essential to initiative, social linking, and social counteraction. If *dulat* removed these intermediate structures, as it did in Bizhan, individuals—although themselves remaining intact as such (especially sheltered by the nuclear family)—would submit to and even *welcome* the Plan.

For example, if the widow Sahra could have resorted to an association of her former fellow villagers from Najafabad, and if that organization could have tapped a confederation of other village self-help organizations, many cases like hers would have come to light, the new townsmen's combined pressure would have enjoyed a greater chance of checking the

State's arbitrary power, and Sahra would probably have been assigned to the *shahrak* she wanted. Similarly, if block associations had been functioning in each lane to clean the canals or even repair the badly rutted road, there would have been some organization ready at hand through which the model townsmen who had made the hump might have sought strength from others—even in exchange for supporting them on their issues. They could probably have stood up to the truck drivers and road grader, curbing the State's arbitrariness in a minuscule incident that nevertheless would have constituted one locally rooted check on its power.

It was these intermediate social structures above the individual, the broadly diffused ability to construct and maintain them, and the assumption that they were natural to social life—this culture made up of specific social skills the workers had brought with them from their corporate villages—that the Plan had to obliterate if it were to rest assured of its centralized control. As we have seen, almost all that remained of the social fabric's tensile strength five years after the villagers were moved into Bizhan was the nuclear family and the bare minimum of interaction outside it, such as attending mourning rites briefly.

On one level or another the workers realized that these final shreds of associational life constituted their last refuge. Not even during my early months in Bizhan, when almost everyone thought I was a spy, were the model townsmen ever protective of their *economic* life; they discussed their wages and the prices they had paid for things far more freely than most people in Western societies. Gradually they even opened up *politically,* telling me their opinions about the Shah. But their ultimate sanctuary, which they guarded vigilantly and to which they only granted me entrance very slowly, much later, comprised simple social interactions like sharing a meal together, joining me on a walk, taking me to visit the sick or someone in the poorhouse, letting me buy a piece of bread or a soft drink for them, or asking me about my family. In contrast, despite the *villagers'* rugged independence, almost from the first hour I arrived in Rahmat Abad they had drawn me into these primary affirmations of our common humanity—eating together, comforting the sick, belonging to a family—which the model townsmen shielded like rare gems.

The lawlessness that according to the peasants and to residents of Dezful had pervaded the northern Khuzestan countryside one or several generations ago—when provinces were isolated; tribes fought tribes, local lords, and the center; when cities could maintain but tenuous contact with each other and with the once-flourishing routes of trade and communication; when factions fought factions within the same bazaar; when quarters fought quarters within the same town—this seeming anarchy that reclaims Iran during weak dynasties apparently did not atomize the society as deeply as did *dulat*'s thrust, which I watched in Bizhan. There the centralized State split even the village and neighbors' bonds, and sometimes, deliberately, those between brothers or parents and children.

Perhaps it is actually in those periods of total "disorder" between *dulat*'s upliftings that rural Iran revives.

Bizhan's Fundamental Structures of Economic Life

The radical contrast between the economic organization of the village and that of Bizhan exacerbated the fragmentation of social life in the *shahrak*. Had the new townsmen been able to count on a more structured social fabric, that might have helped offset the *shahrak* population's profound *economic* insecurity about their basic livelihood, which almost everyone there suffered.

In Rahmat Abad, aside from natural calamities (which few villagers recalled), the peasants' minimal food security under traditional agriculture varied from harvest to harvest, especially when a change among landlords affected the village economy. But since both tenant and landless families stored at harvest for a long period ahead, despite the hunger they may have endured they never faced the tension of *day-to-day* uncertainty about their subsistence base, as they did in the *shahrak*. *Post*–land reform villages which the model town replaced and with which it must be compared enjoyed firm assurance of a permanent basic food supply.

Circumstances ruled out any systematic yet credible study of material living conditions in the *shahrak,* but as far as I could discern food consumption there fell well below Rahmat Abad's standards. In a survey conducted very informally of eight randomly selected house rows (out of fifty-eight) during the month of October, I found that 20 percent of the households had eaten rice—the preferred staple—only three times during the previous week, the norm for but 5 percent in Rahmat Abad. In Bizhan some families did not even stock rice for regular consumption, while everyone did in Throne City. Milk and yoghurt almost disappeared from most adults' diets when they moved to Bizhan, as did meat from their stew of onions and chickpeas. During my two-year acquaintance with Rahmat Abad, no infant there drank powdered milk, and in fact only one mother had ever tried it even as a supplement. In contrast, within the sixteen households on my lane in Bizhan, three infants died from the hazards of powdered milk just during the year I lived there; they had had to depend on it in the first place because their mothers lacked milk. This, in a model town with a well-equipped clinic and Ministry doctor, surrounded by food to be exported.

Nor did Bizhan excel Rahmat Abad in terms of other welfare indicators, except for electricity and brick houses, the advantages of which we have weighed in Chapter 7. As high a proportion of boys continued on to junior high school from the village as from the *shahrak,* since workers' families could not spare them. The villagers bathed daily in the canal, the new townsmen only partially and occasionally at home. The village truck would take a sick person or a woman in labor to Dezful any hour of the night, whereas it was often impossible to persuade those few trucks that stayed overnight in Bizhan (their drivers, not their owners, living there) to do so.

As for entertainment and leisure, in moving to the *shahrak* peasants gave up fishing, hunting, and swimming (even women would refresh themselves in the canal on a hot day in Rahmat Abad—fully clothed but dripping wet). They gave up picnics to local shrines; the agribusinesses had leveled all the rural shrines except one, and who could take off the time anyway? They gave up outings to collect wild greens and herbs, flamboyant darvesh preachers, group trips to nearby village funerals, and the much more informal fun of village weddings lasting for days on end. In exchange, through the five television sets owned in all of Bizhan the workers and their families gained "Star Trek," Iranian singers crooning lamentations that they found silly, and newsreels about patriotic urban parades. (Neighbors could invite themselves to watch television, but such a session hardly provided a social context—people rarely even greeted one another—since everyone crowded so tightly into one small room.) Other than television, Bizhan offered not a single form of entertainment beyond those available in Rahmat Abad; in fact most workers had to go to bed too early to create their own diversions, like Musa's Little Parliament or every village compound's evening gathering.

Finally, proportionally many fewer families in Bizhan traveled to Mash-had on pilgrimage, although if anything the trip meant more to the model townsmen. In a random sample of some fifty workers' families, only two—both among the six most prosperous households in the *shahrak*—reported having made the trip during their five years in the model town.

Economic Opportunities in Agriculture

Besides the dramatic difference between the basic food security offered by the village and the daily worry about food in the *shahrak* (and the former's apparently higher level of food consumption), an extraordinary gap in economic *opportunity* distinguished Rahmat Abad from Bizhan. In Rahmat Abad, because production depended on the *joft*holders' own land, labor, and capital, and because the productive tasks encompassed such a wide range, villagers had considerable leeway in how the family could intensify each factor of production to improve its income. More importantly, by intensifying personal attributes within their control, such as diligence, perseverance, alertness, and care, they could make all three factors more productive. Even the landless could affect their income through industriousness, good management, attention, and collaborative skills, enabling the mobility we have seen some of them enjoy. In Bizhan, though, the average worker could do almost nothing to improve his or her economic situation. A worker had only his or her labor to sell, labor that could hardly be enhanced by diligence and longer hours, intelligence, or even attention, certainly not by good management or perseverence.

In a late summer survey (near the peak period for employment) in Bizhan, I found that 52 percent of all married and 83 percent of the unmarried adults worked when they could find employment—virtually all but a handful as unskilled or semiskilled laborers. Forty-five percent of the heads of household found work on the two agribusinesses, although by no means daily. Almost all other heads of household were on the Ministry's dole, which numbered 600 adult males in 1974. It assured each former household one job at minimal pay if not even one member could find work elsewhere.

While the two agribusinesses "served" by Bizhan workers claimed to offer a combined total of 600 permanent jobs for field laborers and 800 temporary ones (Salmanzadeh, 1980:238) for 2,000 adults seeking work in their *shahrak*s, my survey suggested that many of those positions classed as "permanent" were not, and a third of those that were went to Dezful workers with connections in the companies. Furthermore, in addition to Dezfullis, workers in *three shahrak*s and at least three farm corporations actually competed for all these jobs. According to one estimate given me in the Ministry in Tehran, by 1974 a total of 4,000 adults previously contributing significantly to the family's income as full-time agriculturalists had been displaced by the program, while the project had created approximately a thousand year-round jobs and the same number of temporary ones. None of the promised spinoff industries had been launched. Because of the companies' and the Ministry's conflicting interests in this sensitive matter of the shortage of jobs relative to displaced families, and because of the difficulties of securing accurate information through *shahrak* surveys, no data provide more than gross estimates of the unemployment crisis the workers faced during six months of the year.

Women made up some 30 percent of the temporary workers during the summer; their entrance on the wage market and contributions of cash income to the family economy constituted a major contrast from the traditional village. They earned $1 a day; on the average men earned $2.20. A household spent at least fifty cents a day just for bread. Relatives of villagers and new townsmen I knew in Dezful estimated that an urban family needed an average of $2.30 a day for subsistence; during the summer, with several people working, most households could average $3.75. (The two wealthiest workers in Bizhan reputedly earned $20 and $15 a day, respectively, as supervisors for the Iran-America company.)

Because of the possibility of considerable mobility in the village, to which peasants had become accustomed, and the high expectations the Ministry created in everyone when moving them to the model town, initially the workers entertained high ambitions. The model town's actual conditions had come as a shock. That women could find work somewhat compensated for this disappointment, but the economic cutbacks that the men's long period of idleness required affected even more severely those families that had come to count on the women's earnings as well.

Personal Connections and Employment Strategies

All jobs, wherever the workers found them, depended on personal *parti*. In the peak season the companies did not turn away unskilled laborers, but to get on a crew under a relatively humane foreman or forewoman required contacts. (Some would not let workers pause to relieve themselves or to drink water except at appointed times, and most took cuts from the workers.) The villagers with contacts and those whom the Ministry had moved into the *shahrak* first had staked out the most desirable jobs available. Neither the companies nor the State offered any job training. Because labor remained in such constant flux, with everyone always scrambling for a different position based on contacts rather than skills or experience, the companies had no assurance that those they might train would remain in the position for which they were trained. At any rate, relatives of middle-range supervisors and managers who were not from Bizhan secured almost all positions that might have required a little training; they usually came from Dezful, the other towns of northern Khuzestan, or even from elsewhere in Iran.

As an employee moved up into the pyramid of Iranian supervisors and assistant administrators, personalism turned to plain nepotism the higher one went. One family had four brothers and three brothers-in-law holding positions in seven different departments of one of the companies, right beneath the foreigners! Someone calculated over thirty of their cousins or other kinsmen well placed in the next level beneath these seven men and in other divisions where they awaited promotion, as well as too many personal dependents in the lower ranks to be able to count them. All technical positions—even assistants to mechanics and to drivers of the land-leveling equipment—hence, all significant promotions and all jobs that would give one mobility outward, remained beyond the model townsmen's reach. If a young man could land a job as, for instance, an irrigation "foreman" over several fields he considered himself lucky, even though such positions were seasonal.

Aside from people with effective contacts, a few very bright, well-disciplined young men, especially those who were unmarried or had no dependent children or relatives, could save money; I met four such cases during my year in Bizhan. But even they relied on friends and on corruption, and could look forward to nothing higher than a field supervisor's position if they stayed in the *shahrak*. Of everyone in Bizhan, the ambitious, hard-working young men faced the most discouraging prospects in terms of their plans for life ahead, contrasting sadly with Reza's and those of the other determined young villagers in Rahmat Abad. The former, like Bizhan itself, were blocked on all sides: They could not leave, as there was no work in town and if you did not live in your *shahrak* house you forfeited the right to it; they could not retrain themselves, as outsiders took the jobs that offered such training; they could not attend night school because Bizhan was too isolated from Dezful; and they could not look forward to any advance in the companies.

Facing such an enormous potential labor market of former peasants all accustomed to hard physical labor, the companies had established relatively stringent employment criteria for unskilled work—such as requiring that one be literate or even have finished primary school; that one be under forty years old (almost a universal cutoff point, although it was the older men who had many dependents and whose wives could not work); and that one have a driver's license (which, of course, none of the village tractor drivers had even heard about) or a letter from the Ministry stating that no one else in one's family already had a job. This last requirement referred to an agreement the companies had made with the Ministry to give preference to former *joft*holding households that were jobless, an agreement honored mainly in breach. Some positions even demanded letters of satisfaction from last year's employer.

This flood of requirements provided a booming business for Dezfullis, who (already seasoned by *dulat*'s bureaucratic requirements) faked birth certificates, national identification cards, school diplomas, driver's licenses, marriage licenses, military draft clearances, health certificates, Ministry affidavits, and whatever other papers anyone might need for a job application at any level. As the underground market supplied these, the companies thought up some new ones to require. A fake license for an earth-moving machine operator cost Ebrahim $1,000. Quite often the Iranian engineer determining whom the company planned to hire would dictate for the preferred candidate the exact specifications of the certification he should produce. "I'll give you a permanent job in the machine shop," 'Ali's boss told him, "but you have to get an identification card that proves you're under forty" (he was in his mid-fifties). In sum, the companies' mounting special requirements in actual fact reduced the workers' access to jobs back down to personal connections, after costing them additional outlays.

Like the Dezful counterfeiters, my field work and I benefited from this job involution in the *shahrak*. The pressure it placed on interpersonal manipulation created mistrust at all lower levels in the companies and at Safiabad, especially between workers and their immediate foremen or supervisors. Since under such demand "friends," "cousins," and patrons had to be loyal to a number of heated rivals all at once, the few "gate keepers" to jobs wielded great power. To win them everyone studied diligently the art of personalism; only a handful came out on top. Although the foreign experts who managed almost all departments in the companies had the reputation of being unable to distinguish good field performance from bad, they were also known for relative impartiality if one could get around their frequently despised Iranian assistants. The foreign bosses spoke no Farsi. Workers complained constantly of their political naïveté, that they were too easily swayed by the highly personal Iranians around them.

Thus in the ancient Persian tradition of writing petitions to circumvent bureaucrats and reach the King, the workers made me translator and scribe—via my little field typewriter, never in person—for the many *shahrak* petitioners trying to leap over the Iranian intermediaries and communicate directly with their foreign employers. Spy or not, I now fulfilled a useful role in Bizhan, and by doing so became privy to what went on in the companies' lower ranks. Through the friends I made (especially through our *victories*) I became a part of the model town.

Sometimes several workers at a time would be waiting at my room to help me carefully hone compositions for them, all standing around offering advice to the worker who had been wronged and to me, his barrister. Many of the letters pleaded for reconsideration of an unjust employment decision, or they sought promotions, redress, or payments for job-related expenses incurred (like motorcycle repairs for irrigation foremen). But the essence of all the letters, without exception, was to counter someone else's personalistic advantages with objective facts, a defense or argument based on evidence, which the workers hoped might bear some weight with the foreign administrator at the top. Workers often brought letters for me to write in English to those few high-ranking *Iranians* in the companies, especially in Mr. Naraghi's firm. They knew these administrators to be far more susceptible to personal influences than the Europeans or Americans (which their letters to them reflected), but as though by the power of association they argued that the Iranians might be moved to objective fairness if approached in typewritten English!

The ultimate prayer of most households in Bizhan was somehow to secure employment at Safiabad, safe in the bosom of *dulat*. No one thought the companies would last, but *dulat* would. Furthermore, although *shahrak* workers virtually never received promotions at Safiabad, although personalism pervaded employment relations there even more than in the companies (because cost-benefit inefficiencies hardly affected the farm's principal measure of profitability, the engineers' personal gain), and although the workers at the trial farm sometimes waited weeks to be paid, a tenured job at Safiabad still constituted most workers' utopia. Goals that some theorists attribute to workers, like control over the means of production, the opportunity for self-advancement, just wages, or flexibility, paled beside the new townsmen's singular goal of security—understandable after what they had been through. If one attained a tenured position at Safiabad, then family health insurance and an annual wage bonus followed; but workers generally preferred even a temporary position there to a better-paying one in a company, because the former would give one access to acquaintance with State officials. As Professor Bill has so vividly argued (1973:137), in the past personal proximity to power frequently constituted the road to the highest positions in

Iran; it is not surprising the lowly in Bizhan perceived it the most promising criterion for a job. To illustrate one effect of personalism on the trial farm's management, one foreign counterpart to the farm's director estimated that for every worker the farm needed it employed fourteen.

Because of *dulat*'s largesse at Safiabad, workers there enjoyed another advantage still. The companies made field laborers work arduously, whereas the State in its indifference to economic efficiency barely recorded attendance. In fact, the companies demanded such rigor that during some seasons I was not allowed to join the workers in the fields at all. Despite the companies' higher expectations of the workers, the new townsmen criticized the poor quality of their own work both at Safiabad and in the agribusinesses: They lacked any incentive to maintain farm machinery, irrigation infrastructures like siphons or canal structures, or even the simplest farm tools. They would cut corners, loaf, cheat, and lie without any concern for the crop or the firm. The villagers' intrinsic pride in their work and belief in certain absolute standards about agronomy had totally disappeared, even from among the most conscientious older men with almost a reverence for farming per se. When the women and I picked asparagus, toward the late afternoon we simply stepped on all the tender shoots to destroy them as we walked along row after row; this saved us from having to bend over and cut them. The supervisor required only that he see no fresh green stalks sticking up behind us as we moved along the field. Although I did not blame the workers, this wanton waste right next to the *shahrak* where people could afford no vegetables at all troubled me (the new townsmen had learned quickly how to cook asparagus, and they liked it). I recalled the villagers' pain to see any crop in the field spoil, which only happened for reasons beyond their control; here we were deliberately ruining rows and rows of food as well as income. The women and girls laughed: *"Heif!* What a pity!" How rapidly they had come to see agriculture as the enemy, the burden, not the staff of life.

The companies' administrators blamed the workers harshly for laziness, for deliberate destruction of the companies' property, above all for their inability to learn. One supervisor in a machinery department said that even after two years his drivers could not set the plowing equipment correctly; the American sugar beet expert found workers incapable of changing how they performed the most elementary procedures when shown correctly dozens of times. Clearly the workers were intelligent, but over and over even from sympathetic administrators came the complaint that they would not learn. In their own awareness of their sloppiness at work, many workers might have conceded this criticism to be true.

Most new townsmen had never worked under anyone's supervision in their lives; while they respected the foreigners' technical expertise, they had no regard for their pragmatic comprehension of field problems or procedures, and they considered themselves much more knowledgeable than any Iranian engineer. They were probably correct in at least some of the things they "refused" to learn. Fundamentally, though, they had no reason to make any effort to learn. All the better jobs categorically went to Dezfullis or other outsiders. Stunned by the transition from the village and by the companies' wealth and powerful technology, they (quite understandably) had no sense of proportion about the firms' or Safiabad's costs and returns. For instance, they insisted that young Iranian engineers assisting the foreigners earned $200,000 a year; that leading mechanics or drivers of the most sophisticated equipment earned $100,000. They quoted employees who had evidence or who had asked these men directly. The vast discrepancy between that and their paltry $500–$1,000 embittered them. Many model townsmen said they would work more efficiently if paid a fair wage, whereas the companies argued they would pay more if they could see better work. The two had definitely reached an impasse. The companies moved fast to mechanize all labor-intensive production they could.

Most workers did exert themselves as little as possible on the job. But the initial error lay with the companies and Safiabad, the DIP, and the Plan, which basically shared Lilienthal's view of the social landscape: "nothing, absolutely nothing." When management considered stimulating prodution at the field level, they envisaged machines actually producing yields there, not the workers who drove or maintained them, who irrigated the crop, weeded it, and in many cases harvested it by hand. Carried away by the prospects of technology in Lilienthal's empty moonscape, the farms had no "employment" policies at all. Like the mud villages on the Plan's horizon, the people in the Dez were things that would eventually be removed from the scene when the landscape was modernized. They were hardly the mainspring of modern Iran. Although when they thought about it, most foreign managers at the Shell-Cott agribusiness assumed a moral underpinning beneath their relations with the workers, Iranian administrators and supervisors throughout the Dez considered workers as a burden not an asset to the country's development and to the company's profits. In general, the agribusinesses' and Safiabad's only company mystique was Lilienthal's: technology.

Having experienced the moral context of Rahmat Abad for centuries, how could workers who had been so deliberately fragmented, chopped from this job to the next seasonally, competing against each other for favors, ill paid and considered inferior to the machines—how could they feel any spirit or commitment about belonging to such a form of social organization?

Some model townsmen, as we have mentioned, could find no jobs at all. Life in the *shahrak* burdened older men heavily. On age alone, those above forty were disqualified from permanent jobs and indeed from many temporary ones. The ranks of the Ministry's job corps of makework for the unemployed had proliferated so rapidly that by 1974 officials administering the *shahrak*s had developed a new plan for removing the unemployment crisis entirely: The Ministry owned 24,000 acres of unirrigated land along the remote rims of the project area, at the base of the distant mountains. Why not give each former *joft*holding family that could not find employment five acres of rain-fed land there and encourage them to hire the landless to go farm it for them (a mere *five* acres of *unirrigated* land per family, whereas a family in Rahmat Abad farmed *twenty-four,* a large part of which was irrigated!). The Ministry had never accepted the fact that the *shahrak*s had to be tainted with formerly landless families anyway—they should have gone to the city. This plan would eliminate that social irregularity. Then in the peak season the companies could bring the landless back down to Bizhan as cheap labor, putting up tents for them. What especially pleased my acquaintances in the Ministry about this proposal was that to them it resembled the "Cesar Chavez' migrant workers scheme," which, like so much else in America, they thought Iran should imitate. Hearing this proposal made me wish that there was a way to stop the Plan's ineluctable drive to keep perfecting itself. Even Bizhan was better than the next improvement.

*Sharik*s and the Organization of Local-Level Enterprise

If new townsmen could not all find employment in the companies and Safiabad, why didn't they start their own urban enterprises and services in Bizhan? After all, the town was beginning its local economy from scratch, without markets and stores, artisans, and other services. The *shahrak* was too far from Dezful, and transportation there too infrequent, to rely on Dezful for everything. With alacrity the villagers of Rahmat Abad had combined complementary resources to form *sharik* partnerships of all sorts; why didn't the new townsmen, in the wide open field in which they found themselves in Bizhan do the same?

While on the whole the new townsmen had but a fraction of the villagers' resources, some of the wealthier former peasants had received a small surplus from the State's land settlements, and others had sold their flocks, herds, trucks, and tractors. Why didn't they invest in local enterprises, which, in turn, might have generated local employment? Some of the formerly landless in the *shahrak* had taught themselves an electrician's basic skills; many more could drive than had landed drivers' positions in the companies. Women who could not work in the fields might have done tailoring as a few had begun to do in Rahmat Abad. Many could have developed chicken farms cheaply. In our tour around the *shahrak* we noted that it had no stores. Bizhan needed butchers, bakers, peddlers, bicycle and motorcycle repairmen, grocery stores and general stores selling dry goods, school and medical supplies, and especially transportation services.

Bizhan had no stores that appeared as such from the street, but many people did sell a half a dozen small items like matches and sugar from a back room of the house. Three main reasons explain why after five years none of these tiny efforts had grown into full-fledged stores, and none of the more affluent new townsmen had formed *sharik*s with others (or with Dezful partners) to begin to fill the many local needs. Rahmat Abad had demonstrated that a lack of initiative, thrift, and entrepreneurial skill in the rural population could not account for Bizhan's entrepreneurial vacuum.

First, during the construction of the *shahrak*s and their first year, Dezful entrepreneurs had been able to snatch up those economic openings that the State allowed the private sector to fill. Because they had much more capital on hand, and because they could count on contacts within the Ministry for permissions and licenses, they had been able to jump the gun on the new townsmen, taking advantage of those few opportunities that did exist. For instance, even though some villagers owned trucks, these were not licensed for commercial service on paved roads, for carrying passengers (although all did), nor for running errands in Dezful, which trucks and minibuses servicing the *shahrak* required. Dezfullis obtained those licenses that were available, thus capturing the market early on. Dezful merchants would not grant franchises for anyone in the *shahrak* to sell cooking gas or to represent soft drink, appliance, or motorcycle outlets. The Ministry would not allow a *sharik* partnership of new townsmen to open the bath houses or butchery as businesses or to provide electrician services for the *shahrak*. It gave bakery permits to two Dezful bakers instead of *shahrak* residents and would allow no other bakeries. Dezfullis monopolized the network supplying domestic servants to the elites' compounds, even to the British compound near Bizhan. The workers' inability to rent or sell their *shahrak* homes discouraged their moving out to work with relatives, or to launch an enterprise in town. It also prevented Dezful workers at Safiabad and in the companies, who would have preferred living closer to work and might have brought capital to invest in partnerships in Bizhan, or urban ideas about investment possibilities, from doing so.

The gap between the Dezfullis' political resources and those of the new townsmen repeatedly enabled the former to outclass the latter, excluding them from competition. In Rahmat Abad and its surrounding villages, potential enterprises were scaled to local capabilities, in part because with *dulat* relatively absent its influence did not skew opportunities in favor of the wealthy as it did in the *shahrak* and Dezful. Furthermore, the more gradual pace of development in Rahmat Abad enabled wider participation for people of every economic level.

The second reason few new townsmen were able to earn a living on their own enterprise, despite Bizhan's many needs, was that the State formally forbade all stores and commercial enterprises in the model town— even (according to workers) services like tailoring and carpentry. It allowed only three notable exceptions to this ban, a motorcycle repair shop and two bakeries, all owned and run by Dezfullis. Probably since the field foremen at the companies needed their motorcycles at all hours of the day and night, the agribusinesses had persuaded the Ministry to allow this breach of its rules. As for the bakeries, rejecting applicants from the *shahrak,* the Ministry had financed and set up a Dezfulli in the main bakery. He was allowed as an exception to the ban on stores and commercial enterprises not because the model townsmen needed a bakery (most households had their own ovens) but because engineers at Safiabad liked hot bread for their noon meal. The Ministry permitted the second baker through the baker Mash-hadi Hosein's intercession. In all three cases, local Bizhan residents instead of Dezfullis could easily have opened and run the firms.

Some small, illegal enterprises took the risk against *dulat*'s ban, but these had to remain in back rooms, too. Fear of the Ministry prevented those few families who had been left with a surplus after moving to the *shahrak* from investing it in Bizhan, and also prevented Bizhan's back room stores from growing beyond their minuscule inventories.

A third explanation for Bizhan's entrepreneurial lethargy lay in the fact that two of the main incentives for investment, hard work, and savings—namely, education and improving one's living conditions—had relatively little value in the *shahrak.* As for education, workers quickly perceived that the need for contacts later on when seeking employment limited a young person's ability to make higher schooling pay off. As for upgrading the family's living conditions, the workers did not own their own homes or house lots: The State did. Given what they had already been through, this made them wary of substantial investment in home improvements. Although the State had already taken their *village* homes and although the workers had paid the Ministry for their *shahrak* property, *dulat* frequently reminded Bizhan's residents that, as it retained ownership, it could take back any house or land at any time.

The workers had put up many subsidiary buildings in their house lots, including new rooms. Against the Ministry's regulations most of these they constructed of adobe. (Some faced the adobe on the street side with brick to comply with the law!) But few of these additional structures displayed care or an investment in the future. Thus, while on the one hand the *shahrak* showed Rahmat Abad's same architectural enterprise in the number and variety of new constructions, on the other hand these matched the Ministry's own shoddiness because—perhaps knowing that the Plan had a momentum of its own—the new townsmen felt no permanence even in this latest move.

Why should one be attentive to learn from the company's instructions? For what gains should one hustle to establish one of the numerous enterprises Bizhan needed? With almost all incentives or potential avenues of investment closed—local artisan, trade or service enterprises, returns to investment in children's education, investments in one's home and property, entrepreneurial enterprises that required the State's permissions or licenses, opportunities outside the *shahrak*— the model townsmen were left with few openings they could enter, little motivation, and no protection against risk. All initiative or advancement hinged on personal connections, in which they could not compete with Dezfullis. If in search of better work they left their house in the *shahrak* (where by the Ministry's own definition no economic opportunities could exist), they would lose what little security that provided. The Ministry would not permit the bath houses or other facilities leased out to entrepreneurs, would not permit the technical school opened for workers to learn new skills, would not permit the *shahrak* to develop the orchard. The State allowed no leeway for improving the community, attracting business there; it hardly allowed even enough water to irrigate a tiny garden. Neither the agribusinesses and their compounds nor Safiabad generated opportunities for small spinoff firms that *shahrak* entrepreneurs might have been assisted in starting, such as subcontracting for simple repairs, gardening and maintenance firms for the compounds and company office grounds, or middlemen suppliers of vegetable or dairy needs (which Safiabad, of course, monopolized).

The young people in Bizhan could see very clearly the Plan fulfilled: their stagnation. Mohsan and Muhammad and 'Abdu Sayyed and Kazem used to talk frequently about what they would have made of their lives on the base of a good village income and with the freedom of the intervillage region that had existed around their villages as it did around Rahmat Abad. Instead, they dreamed of even a lowly position in *dulat*'s bureaucracy.

Economic Development: Resource Mobility and Allocational Efficiency

In disembedding all productive assets in the traditional economy of rural northern Khuzestan for a more efficient recombination, the Dez Scheme had closely approximated the goal of the modernizers. It liberated the region's rich land from the stifling bonds of subsistence farming, from the village *joft* system, and from the slow pace and microlevel management of illiterate farmers; it released labor from the confines of the *joft*, the *bonku*, and old patron ties, from its tight corporate communities, from its regional allegiances and even its little *shariks*. It unburdened the State's capital from years of plodding extension programs and credit cooperatives, so that it could invest instead in the huge irrigation system, in "modernized" State farms, and above all in administering the regional Plan. Finally, the project put the land and labor of the Dez at the disposal of the investors' vast resources of new capital and technology. The agribusiness companies tapped years of experience in large-scale, capital-intensive irrigated agriculture, and were widely familiar with economic and managerial conditions in the Third World. In order for the potentially rich resources of the Dez to be assured much greater mobility and allocational efficiency, economists' conventional wisdom called for replacing the traditional organizational forms in which these resources were embedded with modern organizational forms under the supervision of the State. To appraise the increased efficiencies that did result, let us look briefly at a few indicators of the actual gains achieved under the old and the new organizational systems.

The first major gain anticipated from the new organizational forms that the Plan brought to the Dez—the State farms and agribusinesses—lay in wheat production, which can benefit more than many other crops from land consolidation and capital intensification. After five years of experience, the new, large farms in the Dez were harvesting no more wheat per acre (one ton) than local landlords who had retained medium-sized holdings that they worked with local capital and without the advice of expensive Western experts. Indeed, the former produced only *25 percent* more wheat per acre than traditional peasant agriculture had achieved under the experimental extension program in 1958! Furthermore, with wheat comprising the country's major staple import, the 108,000 acres that had been sown to wheat under traditional agriculture had fallen to but 45,000 acres under the new farms (in 1976, a peak year), a shift hardly compensated for by 12,000 acres of sugar beets which, enjoying few economies of scale, could have been cultivated equally efficiently on small farms.

The second major expectation for greater efficiencies lay in the utilization of the Dez Scheme's expensive irrigation system during Khuzestan's precious summer months. We have already seen that, despite its cost, the new canal network increased irrigable land by a mere 30 percent over that serviced by the landlords' and peasants' traditional investments. But even given this modest increase in irrigable land, complemented by much greater capital, technical, and managerial know-how, the modern operations left *50 percent* more of the net irrigable land *fallow* during the summer than had traditional agriculture when managing the very same land: 81,000 acres of irrigable land fallow in 1976, 38,000 acres in 1958. (A Plan Organization study found that nation-wide the State farms left uncultivated—in any season—30 percent of the land that they had expropriated.) As for the exceptional agricultural potential of the *summer months* that the capital- and management-intensive farms were meant to realize to their full extent once they were assured irrigation, the modern farms virtually eliminated the traditional system's principal summer crop, irrigated rice, which was Iran's second staple import. International experts unable to cite any technical or economic explanations for this—certainly not the lack of labor or water—suggested that the foreigners were simply unfamiliar with this crop, the one best suited for Khuzestan's agricultural conditions. The crop had been dropped despite the fact that the modern farms had found no substitute use of the land. Acreage planted to rice in 1958 was 26,400 acres, and in 1976 barely 2,000.

The third major gain anticipated from redeploying the resources of the Dez to highly capitalized modern management was an increase in the value of agricultural production. Taking into account the profitable cash crops (cotton, alfalfa, asparagus, sugar beets, and so forth) that the modern farms substituted for the staples considered above, the large farms did show an increase over the traditional system in the value of their output, but the difference between the two was surprisingly small. If we exclude the value of the animals kept under the traditional system, the gross value* of production on the same land under the two systems in constant prices was:

	Millions of Rials (70 rials = $1)
traditional agriculture (1958)	1,101
modernized agriculture (1976)	1,540

The increase in production from the traditional system (1958) to the modern (1976) that the project realized was at an annual growth rate of 1.9 percent, which is close to the average increase in agricultural output for all less developed countries under normal conditions—hardly justifying the great price paid by the Dez.

Thus after these extraordinay costs of redirecting the Dez's rich resources from their traditional matrix, the new organizational forms did not offer markedly greater efficiencies. Indeed, as we have already seen in Chapter 1, the agribusinesses (and probably the State farms, had they been subject to public appraisal) failed even in their own terms—that is, failed to make a profit for themselves, or to repay Iranian government loans—even found themselves unable to pay the Ministry's notoriously low irrigation fee ($4/acre/year; see Salmanzadeh, 1980:47 discussing Rabbani's report).

The Dez Project had ensured *maximum* mobility of land, labor, and capital, liquidating any traditional structures that might have prevented their efficient recombination. The Project provided optimal agronomic conditions as well for the new organizational forms that emerged. It is beyond the scope of this book to analyze why, given these extremely favorable terms, the new economic configurations that replaced Rahmat Abad's failed so dramatically. Suffice it to point out that if it is to raise production, an increase in factor mobility requires an environment of accountability. In the Dez, as in so many sectors of Iran's thrust to "modernize," the new economic configurations remained beyond accountability.

First, the agribusinesses were too large even to hold *themselves* accountable agriculturally; when operating on such a scale, management found it impossible to control field-level performance in critical areas like land leveling, irrigation efficiency, or pest and disease surveillance, three areas of eventual failure. The final financial blow to the Shell-Cott agribusiness was the loss of virtually its entire cotton crop to cotton boll weevil in a matter of weeks—a pest against which local farmers had repeat-

*I am grateful to Dr. Arthur Peterson for many of these data. See Goodell, 1977: 597ff.

edly warned the agronomists. Secondly, politically the Ministry was unable to hold them accountable. When out of dozens of potential investors Lilienthal had brought to the Dez through a *Fortune* magazine promotional effort in the project's early planning stage, only a handful showed serious interest, it became clear that, given the Plan's command that the Dez be given over to agribusinesses, the Ministry's *dependence* upon those who did invest exceeded its *leverage* over them. Such a relationship made *dulat* a poor watchdog over their annual reports, which showed ominous signs from the outset, over their demands for further concessions (cheaper water rates, petrochemicals, import duties, further loans, and so forth), or over intercompany collusion against competition and government regulations.

Thirdly, the agribusinesses had little accountability to the market itself, for making profits, because in most cases individuals or firms had invested in them—Bank of America, John Deere, Mitsubishi, Hawaiian Agronomics, Atlantic Richfield—only in order to gain completely unrelated privileges in other sectors of the economy, which the Shah offered those who helped launch agribusinesses: exclusive banking licenses, import monopolies, choice factory sites near Tehran, development contracts, and other concessions (in the case of British Shell, oil concessions). These rewards justified any agribusiness losses, which simply became the price investors were willing to pay for special advantages elsewhere in the economy (see Goodell 1977:601ff., and Housego, 1976:31 for elaboration). We have already seen that even the World Bank, the major external agency helping to design, finance, and monitor the project, allowed its own accountability to be compromised by conflicting interests it, too, had in quite unrelated sectors of the Iranian economy, to which it also gave higher priority.

The Dez Project seemed deliberately to defy agriculture's requirement, especially in a semiarid zone, that management be able to respond quickly to minor environmental changes, above all when new cropping patterns and their infrastructural complements are being worked out on a large scale. It seemed deliberately to defy the flexibility necessary for any successful economic enterprise in an arbitrarily governed society. The planners had concentrated virtually all the productive capacity of the DIP in the hands of but four immense, unaccountable agribusinesses and the equally unaccountable State farms (that *dulat* managed for many purposes as a single unit). As though to centralize control over this experiment even more remotely, a special agency in distant Tehran, tied directly to His Imperial Majesty, oversaw these unstable giants, an agency thus itself invulnerable and insulated. Fatimah, my neighbor in Byzun, considered the way old man Qutb had been given some land for his mare to have portended the way the Shah would give away the rest of these lands. Thus the vast resources of the Dez—set free to be recombined "efficiently"—were now embedded in structures incomparably more cumbersome, and in political determinations far more obstructive to rational allocation, than were Rahmat Abad's fine-tuned decisions, "embedded" as they were in traditional society.

The new economic configurations imposed on the *micro*level, in the *shahrak* economy, mirrored the rigidity, inefficiency, and centralized control the Plan imposed on the region at the macrolevel. In the model town's severe restrictions on employment, residence, economic initiative, and the sale of house lots, we have seen how the State prevented the mobility of local factors of production from seeking entrepreneurial opportunities. In contrast to Rahmat Abad's flexible microlevel economy, Iran's new model towns had virtually no economy at all.

Finally, besides greatly reducing factor mobility and efficiency in both large- and small-scale economic allocations, the new order also enervated the *middle-range* economy in Dezful town and in the northern part of the province. Since Iran's oil fields lay in southern Khuzestan, the province had a well-established base of technicians and entrepreneurs. Rather than encourage local initiatives within the project area and nearby, the Dez Scheme gouged out many of those middle-range productive enterprises that existed, absorbed others into the gigantic enterprises, and thwarted the development of new ones in northern Khuzestan. For example, government contracts for the construction needs of the DIP depended upon political connections at the national level rather than on objective qualifications in which provincial firms might have been competitive. The agribusinesses, in order to avoid dependence upon provincial entrepreneurs who were meant to complement their investments, or in order to circumvent government regulations, organized many services among themselves that pre-empted already existing ones. Rather than recruit or train locals, they imported from Tehran personnel as diverse as secretaries and spray-plane pilots. By 1975, while on the one hand, the Ministry employed nearly 1,000 adult men in low-paid unnecessary work either on the *shahrak* dole or in its various DIP offices and in Safiabad, and while it had blocked every effort even of the Ministry of Education to open the technical school in Bizhan for training and retraining programs, companies in the project and on its periphery had recruited thousands of semiskilled foreign workers from Asia for farming and construction, in part to avoid labor regulations. Continuing this process of displacing rather than strengthening local initiatives, the Ministry ran the best local restaurants and a small hotel, not to mention its own hospital, schools, repair centers, even employing its own carpenters and electricians for day-to-day work in the *shahrak*. All of these subsidiary enterprises of the companies or the Ministry siphoned off locally- or provincially based entrepreneurs, managers, and technical personnel into the great concentrations of size and political influence.

To bypass Iranian suppliers entirely, the agribusinesses had begun to pool resources for ordering spare parts, new machinery, and a wide variety of materials (office equipment, household needs, vehicle parts, even food) directly from a central office in Tehran or from London or California. Thus instead of spinoff firms flourishing in Dezful to serve the large farms, the town saw a decline in such enterprises as machinery shops, foundries, and the manufacturing sector of the bazaar. In their place, shops less likely to produce economic development proliferated, like dry cleaners and beauty salons as well as, of course, the servant class and the bureaucracy. Just as centralized development within the State's domain (even in the private sector within that domain) increased the importance of personal connections and subjective criteria in determining economic arrangements, so, too—as the villagers and *shahrak* workers saw clearly—the relative utility of educational achievement and training, of acquired skills, and efficient management decreased at the microlevel, unless these also brought contacts with them.

The greatest loss to society which the Dez Scheme wrought in northern Khuzestan lay in its replacing the *traditional* rural order's two crucial organizational principles of contract and incorporation (and the environment of open give-and-take that they require) with personalistic politics—often enshrined in size itself—that governed the companies, State farms, and *dulat*. The State, now holding the reins in the Dez, could not tolerate impersonal, public contract and incorporation. The *shahrak* workers as well as the villagers accurately predicted that without contract and incorporation the new order had no institutional permanence or economic continuity outside the State itself. Momentarily "freeing" the factors of production from their traditional bonds for more efficient allocation could not suffice, since the Plan had loosened them not in order to let them search out their own efficient recombinations, but rather to control them itself. The cost of destroying contract and incorporation as organizational principles, both of which require public accountability, was the cost of predictability, hence long-term productive investment and the sustainability of any "recombined" economic order. Not even the State could hold the agribusinesses and State farms accountable until they had gone too far to be rectified. So unpredictable had the regional and local economic environment become that the main investment opportunity the Plan left open to the broad base of society in Khuzestan was urban land speculation, in contrast to those that Throne City's *sharik*s and the DIP extension program had begun to discover when they could still operate outside the Plan.

It is ironic that in seeking to pry loose the productive assets of the Dez, the development economists destroyed the underpinnings that an efficient reallocation of the factors of production requires, especially individual and corporate autonomy. They destroyed, too, the context for such autonomy: the public arena of discourse, free information flow, locally shared purposes and locally rooted regulatory mechanisms, and accountability to the base of society through its public arena and middle-range checks against arbitrariness. Traditional village society that the Plan necessarily opposed had fostered these requirements for factor mobility and allocational efficiency.

Rural Fragmentation, and the Transition from Agrarian to Industrial Society

On the surface, the disappearance of cohesive villages and the consolidation of land in northern Khuzestan echo Europe's apparently similar transformation from an agrarian to an industrial base. But by the time the farming enclosure movement in England was underway in the eighteenth century, Parliament and the checks and balances of a public arena had virtually abolished royal monopolies, had gained firm control over finance, trade, the courts, and the army, and had greatly diminished the threat of arbitrary taxation, fines, economic regulations, and the confiscation of property. While economically the changes in the DIP superficially paralleled those of Europe's early industrialization, *politically* northern Khuzestan was moving in *exactly the opposite direction* from its European equivalent. This difference is partly explained by the fact that the process through which the industrial order replaced the rural in Europe was an incremental one, taking place at a slow pace over centuries, thereby allowing provincial, local, and microlevel units within society to readjust and to maintain accountability over the State, just the opposite of the suddenness and enormity of the transformation of the Dez. (In the first *150 years* of the enclosures in England, which was the European country *most radically* subjected to land consolidation and village fragmentation, *less than 10 percent* of the land was enclosed, even in the four most intensively affected counties; see Dobb, 1947:227.)

In dismissing the rural social and economic disintegration we have described in this chapter as inevitable if society is to move toward industrialization, we must not make Lilienthal's mistake, seeing only the technology on the surface: village harvest teams displaced by John Deere combines and *joft* farms displaced by large-scale ones. *Beneath* this change from agrarian to industrial production, the base of European society gained increasingly greater leverage over its own political environment, to assure predictability for sustained development. In contrast, as society in northern Khuzestan passed from Rahmat Abad to Bizhan and the DIP, it (like all of Iran) *lost* hold over its economic and political environment, succumbing to arbitrary power. It is this issue, political structures and accountability within society, to which we must next turn.

> Shall we guide you to a man who will inform you that when ye
> are torn all to pieces, then ye shall be a new creation!
> —Qur'an, Sura 34

Chapter 9

Political Structure in Bizhan

> **O king, apply not the axe to the root of thy tree!**
> —Bahar, from *Khurasan*

Since the villagers and *shahrak* workers returned again and again in our conversations to their abhorrence of cremation, I decided to try to introduce them to Zoroastrianism, to see whether any remnant of their culture's ancient religion would strike a familiar chord. A friend sent me a little introduction to the religion in Farsi, which contained summaries of Zoroastrian stories. Having lent the book to a college student visiting some neighbors in Bizhan, one rainy day when I called on them I found him paraphrasing parts of it to the family and a few others as they all hovered around the little tray of coals. The young man's narration of Zoroaster's conversation with Ahura-mazda sparked a lively discussion from which we never returned to the book (although perhaps in their eagerness to expound on this central passage of the Avesta my friends did in a way fulfill the experiment). The passage was brief:

> Zoroaster, God's dutiful prophet and leader of the earthly kingdom, carried out everything The Lord God commanded, tirelessly, with dedication and perfection. One day Zoroaster asked Ahura-mazda to grant him immortality in exchange for his service, his only request. The Lord replied that *if he made Zoroaster immortal it would not be possible also to restore the living.*

Perhaps because of their religious hero Hosein's tragic death and the strong theme of martyrdom in Shi'ism, my friends found something familiar in this story's paradox, posed by God Himself. I protested that to me it made no sense: Why couldn't Ahura-mazda grant the prophet immortality and still have enough grace left over to save the living as well? But Nur's grandmother, impatient at my having missed Ahura-mazda's point, insisted that it was not a question of how much total grace the two miracles would require. God is beyond measure. Rather, she saw some sort of an intrinsic contradiction between strengthening all common people and uplifting them on the one hand, and giving their leader immortality on the other. 'Ali Akbar quoted a Qur'anic passage that said that a leader had to humble himself below the level of his people in order to enlighten them, but although she could not quite articulate what was

217

wrong with that interpretation, Nur's grandmother rejected it as well. Content that she knew her own mind, she left to finish her work.

A little later the old woman came back in the room snapping at our dullness. "Look," she demanded; "why are you all sitting here miserable and jobless and hungry, our village destroyed? Weren't we happy there and fed? This happened to *us* so *the Shah* can be immortal. Don't you see? It's between his being immortal and us." (Was she almost implying Zoroastrian polar opposites, light and darkness?) She continued, "If *we* do it, then *we*'re strong but no one will ever remember *him,* and if he does it they will but we're helpless and out like this!"

Perhaps Nur's grandmother was right. The two questions she raised, who was going to "do it" and why, comprised the essentials of politics, for it is clear that she had in mind the formulation of policy and directions, not just carrying it out. Perhaps, too, in the Iranian context she was correct to suggest that there could be no compromise: Either the Shah would "do it" or "we" the villagers and workers, but not all together. In these next two chapters we consider political relations in Bizhan and within the State—the scope for expressive initiative, for autonomy, and for purposive association and group life. Based on this we may concur with Nur's grandmother and with Ahura-mazda. If the prophet-king were to gain immortality for himself by uplifting Iran during his short liftetime as he set out to do, necessarily through the central Plan and its commanders, there could be no room for renewing in the people of Bizhan the common purposes and vital interaction they had known as villagers, the polity of the living.

Before turning to those several collective initiatives that during my year in the *shahrak* still remained as faint traces of the former village's political organization and vigor, we need to consider briefly how disputes were settled in Bizhan. Among themselves, new townsmen seemed irritable and frequently on edge, quarreling much more frequently than villagers did in Rahmat Abad. The workers never sought former village leaders or neutral third parties like the school principal to resolve disputes, which often in fact they never did resolve. Rather, they would break off social relations entirely, violating the village's primary rule that everyone should at least speak to one another.

Sometimes one party would bring in the gendarmerie (again, in contrast to Rahmat Abad). On those occasions the State served as a vortex into which new townsmen apart in their separate cement rooms hurled declamations of fury. Bizhan recognized no elders, no communal repository of events, precedents, or values. It did not matter that members of "the public" had in fact witnessed what happened, since people living in proximity to one another barely knew one another and carried no weight with each other. Witnesses could hardly judge right or wrong among half strangers. Who would want the responsibility of civil order, and why? Who cared? Quite logically, disputants screamed their versions and their wounds at the State, which then went away.

One night an antagonism of earlier origins culminated in several new townsmen claiming they caught a man and woman in the act of adultery in house row 16. Officials held no investigation in the *shahrak*—no witnesses or neighbors questioned, no character statements gathered. No open hearing took place in Dezful, although the accused pair claimed they had been forced into the room together and locked there. The man received a jail sentence, whence in a few weeks' time he entered the army to fulfill his military service. *Dulat* returned the woman to her father's family for a divorce, leaving her four children with their father, the plaintiff. He gave one of them, less than a year old, up for adoption rather than allow the infant's mother to have her. Thus *dulat* handled the most notorious scandal of the *shahrak*'s first five years in a matter of days, with a dispatch admirably suited for keeping these identical little brick houses neatly in line, row upon row.

If in Rahmat Abad *dulat* gave priority to judicial powers above even legislative ones, as we saw in Mehrabani's assignment, in creating Bizhan it never let the possibility of locally directed policies or rules emerge in the first place. Yet few challenges offer better opportunities for collective deliberation and endeavor than when people are forming a new settlement, having to define and shape it themselves, facing innumerable needs that could catch the imagination of various groups and involve them in bringing forth *their* town—(in this case, a town *they* could call Iran's model). In Bizhan such needs and challenges for common endeavor abounded, still on a scale and level of complexity that the new citizens themselves could undertake: regulating traffic on a few streets, establishing a workable system of irrigation rotation, curbing petty juvenile delinquency, forming town juries to articulate commonly shared norms through helping to settle disputes, supervising the maintenance of facilities like the water faucets and street lights, expanding the communal uses of the school, seeing that the high school, bath houses, a butchery, a mortuary, and a bazaar were opened. A confederation of the former villages through their leaders, or of lane representatives and interest groups like parents, could have begun to forge a political arena for Bizhan, a town council, holding the Ministry accountable for the responsibilities it assumed as well as taking civic initiatives on its own. Then new townsmen might identify the *shahrak* as theirs. Not that such political life might have come forth smoothly; after all, Rahmat Abad at least had yet to solve its internal problem of authority and hierarchy at its scale, so merging into a larger active political field would have met with difficulties. Yet, as with pioneers everywhere, ample purposes for effective organizational forms and public life faced the new townsmen, making the *shahrak*'s fragmentation and inertia all the more a waste.

In the *shahrak*'s second year, scores of townsmen signed a petition urging the Ministry of Water and Power and the Ministry of Education to open the high school (as such, not as a trade school to keep their young people "in their places"). Later a directorate of the primary school was formed and began to take initiative on its own. In both cases, when the Ministry saw incipient local organization prepared to assume civic responsibilities, it moved firmly to clarify its monopoly over Bizhan's affairs.

Several issues, though, did pierce through the Ministry's resistance during my year in Bizhan, in which the new townsmen focused at least minimal organization upon what they perceived to be needs of theirs. We turn to these now.

The Mosque

The fact that the Plan, in its attention to such details as the poorhouse, did not designate a plot of land on the *shahrak* blueprint where a mosque might be built signaled the centrality of a mosque for Bizhan, as it was for every lower-class urban settlement in Iran. The new model town for all Iran would have to have its mosque; the Dezful clergy would have to, too. (Rahmat Abad had no need for its mosque, but Bizhan was now in Iran's *urban* world.) Did *dulat* determine that the Plan would change *that* as well? In its characteristically tight-lipped manner, the Ministry pretended to assume that when designing the new model town technocratic planning had not missed a single urban need.

The issue had arisen early in the *shahrak's* settlement when the Ministry forbade the individual villages to build small, decentralized mosques, which would have given shared purpose to each as a group undertaking, a symbol of the separate former village identities, and a meeting place to keep alive their ancient bonds. The new townsmen had no interest in a mosque for all of Bizhan, in which their separate local identities would be lost. Having come so recently from village culture, they suspected urban mosques. Unlike Throne City, which had built the darveshes a mosque for no other reason than civic pride, the *shahrak* workers had stopped caring about anything in or for Bizhan, even practical needs like the high school or irrigation water for their gardens. Why should they care about something they had never missed, the clergy's mosque? No wonder after five years nothing concrete had been done about a mosque for Bizhan; it would take the Dezful clergy and some *shahrak* leader to build one, not popular endeavor. Still, even on those grounds a mosque was a necessity from the outset.

With no possibility of political life in Bizhan, spearheading construction of the mosque offered the only legitimate outlet and purpose for a leader in Bizhan. Two former political rivals in the largest village who had been transferred to Bizhan perceived this, although since community no longer existed to make honor meaningful neither man any longer sought *civic* responsibility or *civic* prestige. (The Ministry despised their lack of commitment!)

The two former leaders respectively embodied the old and the new, as did their contrasting proposals for getting the mosque built. Haji Safar, a handsome, extremely congenial gentleman, epitomized traditional village leadership by among other things having kept much of his wealth in sheep (in the grasslands) even after the village had been destroyed. Sultan 'Ali, a younger and much better-educated man, aspired to the modern identification of prosperity with urban property and pretensions to mechanized, scientific agriculture. The move to Bizhan had consolidated both men's large, formerly loose networks of family and clients, although in the process Sultan 'Ali did everything possible to *accentuate* his class superiority (and power) over his followers, whereas in direct contrast Haji Safar—a much more sophisticated politician despite his modest bearing—remained firmly rooted in the workers' society and culture.

Sultan 'Ali, the wealthiest man in Bizhan, hated the Pahlavis, what he considered their State, and the *shahrak*. A representative to Arsanjani's peasant congress in Tehran, a self-styled socialist, a partisan of Mossadegh, and a Muslim genuinely curious about Islamic issues the clergy acknowledged as legitimate, Sultan 'Ali spurned any association with *dulat*. In the early years of the DIP he had exhorted the villagers to resist the expropriation of their lands. But his having declared himself almost an open enemy of *dulat* left him to carve out for himself in Bizhan a position of extraordinary ideological contortion, telltale of an antiregime Shi'ite in the throes of provincial "development." In the *shahrak*'s early years Sultan 'Ali had sponsored the major Moharram public events; even in 1974 he gave alms annually to the poorhouse in well-publicized piety, and hosted expensive Moharram ritual meals centering on minor clerical luminaries from Dezful. At the same time, as the army general's top lieutenant he wielded the most powerful *shahrak* position in Mr. Naraghi's egregiously capitalist and "exploitative" agribusiness. Virtually all employment available to new townsmen in the agribusiness remained at Sultan 'Ali's disposal. With no experience or training in modern agriculture—having grown up in Abadan, not the village—he and his brother were clever and merciless enough to master the general's draconian management demands, for which the company's administrators, predominantly Iranian, praised Sultan 'Ali's "Western" management skills. Now and then "to groom him" the general invited Sultan 'Ali to a meal in the technocrats' compound where the former lived.

Since Sultan 'Ali and his brother could penetrate the *shahrak* population by living there, they assured the company quick, obedient, and cheap human resources. Every evening, foremen from the far-flung corners of Sultan 'Ali's empire would appear in the large, carpeted room he had added to his home, to report lists and lists of neatly tabulated figures. In vivid imitation of the ruthless old landlord class (his being the only household in Bizhan with servants), Sultan 'Ali thought nothing of demanding on immediate call several chickens from some poor household indebted to him (which he would never repay), or of delaying a worker's pay for weeks in punishment, or cutting off an entire family from access to jobs in the company "forever"—dictates of his personal power. Many of his dependents served as spies in the laborers' ranks, pointing a finger at loafers or thieves. Both Sultan 'Ali and his brother were wont to hold court on the spot in the field—or the former, at night on the immense carpet—into whatever irregularity might be raised about a worker.

Sultan 'Ali ruled his little world through fear. Still, he himself has possessed the courage to oppose *dulat* publicly. I was free to drop in on him and sometimes did, but in addition he occasionally summoned me to discuss his worries about Islam's power over those it ruled, and potentially over the world. For instance, Sultan 'Ali considered it a weakness in Islam that John Kennedy had figured out, from Qur'anic instructions, how to assemble a rocket to the moon before any Muslim had (an issue and interpretation direct from the Dezful clergy). He also sought my counsel in more mundane matters, such as how to open a can of Del Monte peaches the general's wife had given him, and what to do with what he found inside. As a further complication to his personality, many of Sultan 'Ali's hangers-on vowed he conversed intimately with the Shah, a reputation he did not disclaim. Intelligent and conscientious, this contradictory personality embodied the political, intellectual, even moral involution of an energetic individual who, like the *shahrak* itself, could find in his social milieu neither the scope for constructive public initiative nor the restraint that public accountability imposes.

Haji Safar, in contrast, served *dulat* and the Ministry well. *Dulat* had given him the prime house location in Bizhan, right on the circle as one entered the *shahrak*. In exchange he would show official guests around the model town and entertain them in his little *shahrak* home. He had no technocratic potential at all, lacking the conceit and the savoir faire to wheel and deal at an agribusiness. In Bizhan's initial years he and Sultan 'Ali had jockeyed to preside over the largest tent for religious sessions during Moharram, but by 1974 Haji Safar had won out. Not that this meant anything in practical or political terms for Haji Safar, as there was no way by which leadership could achieve anything in Bizhan. Nor did his sponsoring the largest tent mean much for the Dezful *clergy* who preached in it, since consistent with the traditional culture he still embodied, Haji Safar tapped them only for ceremonial needs. Doubtlessly they would have preferred Sultan 'Ali's predominance.

After the Ministry had silenced the model townsmen's talk about separate community mosques, that opened the issue of a *shahrak* mosque. No one particularly wanted a *shahrak* mosque, as we have seen, but from the leaders' point of view, bringing about its construction remained the only opportunity for public initiative and the only test of leadership that *dulat* might begrudgingly permit. Then, too, ingratiating oneself with the religious establishment in Dezful offered the only "little platoon" an ambitious model townsman might step upward into (commercial circles, civic and provincial life, and all types of purposeful associations virtually closed to him). Sultan 'Ali announced that through his intercession Mr. Naraghi from California would build a mosque for Bizhan. Such public display of religiosity and largesse from an Iranian who was also an American would have reflected lustrously on Sultan 'Ali, both in the *shahrak* and in the religious establishment of Dezful. However, on his next visit to the agribusiness Mr. Naraghi ordered a cotton gin built instead of a mosque. So Haji Safar proposed to raise the funds among relatives and friends from his former village and a sister village. All the other former communities, determined to preserve their separate identities, still refused to join; when I left Bizhan, they remained adamant.

The approach each leader proposed for getting the mosque built reflected the nature of what little political base he had. Given the gap between the individual on the one hand and wealth and power on the other in the modern Iranian world in which Bizhan had been born, Sultan 'Ali's proposal logically fit the Shah's way of mobilizing resources, of which he himself was a part: having rich outsiders build Iranian agribusinesses in one stroke, whole hog. In contrast, shadows of Rahmat Abad's collective organization and local responsibility influenced the way Haji Safar had thought of getting the mosque built. But despite the workers' apathy and his more conservative ways, Haji Safar proved more influential over a few new townsmen than Sultan 'Ali over his fabulously wealthy employer, as by 1974 the former pushed through with enough money at least to begin constructing Bizhan's mosque. At least in the short run *dulat,* having to allow a mosque, got one *its* man sponsored, not Mossadegh's.

Sultan 'Ali's bid for a collaborative following had been waning for some time, as was evident in his declining public role during Moharram. So, in place of public leadership he would pursue his Islamic identity and commitment and find his little platoon among a more withdrawn fellowship, founding a small Qur'anic study group in Bizhan that, instructed as it was by urban clergymen, I always thought mixed radical political perspectives with genuine religious concerns. *Dulat*'s *shahrak* engineers congratulated themselves that Sultan 'Ali was "off the streets." But in the absence of any political arena in the "streets" of Bizhan, Sultan 'Ali had actually just moved behind the house lot walls that the Ministry thought restored the *shahrak*'s order.

Although both of these gifted leaders had come only a few years earlier from villages as economically and politically open as Rahmat Abad, with its participatory and productive challenges for people to realize their own local plans, they finally sought leadership positions and the creativity of political expression through formal Islam, in Bizhan the only thing left. In Rahmat Abad, formal Islam had attracted no one, least of all the darveshes. In the model town, *dulat* had closed off absolutely all other channels of initiative and group action, of civic contribution or the attainment of individual prestige, of "mobilizing" followers; it had also closed off all other channels whereby *city* people could extend their initiatives into rural society, Iran's base. Islam provided the only remaining frontier. In neither Sultan 'Ali's nor Haji Safar's project, though, did a structured organization emerge. The Qur'anic group met irregularly, with a changing membership; the mosque builders saw a frequent shifting of attendance. The core of each aggregate was the leader, not the purpose.

Since many model townsmen had been employed by the Ministry in building Bizhan, once Haji started to collect a few funds they expressed plenty of ideas about the proposed mosque's location, design, and construction materials. However, when at last Haji convinced the Ministry it had to allow this addition to the Plan, the State suddenly handed him a finished blueprint of the mosque they could build, with sliding specifications for all necessary materials, and sliding costs, according to the funds they could raise. "Go raise the money." No further discussion was called for, certainly no planning or decisions on the new townsmen's part.

The State could not refuse the workers land for a mosque but it could at least completely deflate the project. Imagine the corporate spirit and organization generated out of constructing a new community church in the West. In a single pronouncement the State left the new townsmen with no contribution they could make of their own to the project except donating money, an impersonal contribution reducing participation to a matter of rank according to wealth, and depriving those with special construction expertise or other individual resources of any parity with those who gave money. Above all, the Ministry's blueprint with its completed details removed from the project the many concrete purposes for *interaction* that would have brought together the workers as they designed their own mosque; it made Haji Safar and his partner Sardar mere collectors of dues, not leaders.

Only about forty men and boys of the hundreds in the two villages helped on the construction during the first few days when unskilled labor could be used, although that degree of collaboration still represented an achievement. When they had poured the foundation, Haji Safar held a dedication to spur interest for further contributions. Although in each detail of the Dez Irrigation Project's elaboration, since its inception, the Ministry of Water and Power had asserted sole jurisdiction over all that happened within the project area (above all, *socially*); although it nervously insisted on approving everything down to such customary events as weddings (even the hump in the road!) that took place in the public domain; and although this constituted the only *shahrak*-wide meeting organized by the workers themselves in Bizhan's five-year history, no one from *dulat* attended the dedication. Nor did many women. Nevertheless, one caught a glimpse that afternoon of an enthusiasm and common purpose that might have underpinned the new workers' town had other such endeavors been allowed.

A Muslim divine came from Dezful in his chauffeured Mercedes for the dedication. None of the workers knew who he was except that he had a personal pedigree. He urged everyone to support the mosque: "You are no longer a village, but now a *shahrak,* and every town needs a mosque," he exhorted them, driving home the crucial distinction that, whereas before they might have gotten along in the village without one, now they had graduated, as it were, into the culture of the urban mosque.

Quite the opposite of Rahmat Abad's unitary construction of its mosque (even those who were not darveshes contributing to it, and the whole edifice being raised at once), the construction of Bizhan's mosque reflected both sociologically and architecturally the *shahrak*'s lack of integration. Since the new townsmen had no public arena and no organizational forms to hold accountable the men who were spearheading the project, and since no preliminary planning had welded together a core representative group, few people trusted the organizers. Only about 15 percent of the households from the two villages building the mosque donated money at the outset. Haji Safar had to start building before his group had even a fraction of the mosque's estimated total cost. (If they didn't, that would *prove* their dishonesty.) Evidence then that the building might actually emerge brought a few more contributions for a little further work. As with so many organizational forms in urban Iran, the mosque organizers could not count on members' sustained commitment established at the beginning, not even on individual pledges. Another cause might come along that interested people more.

The mosque comprised a small mihrab chamber facing Mecca and then a large, open yard typical of urban mosques in Iran. Since, unlike Rahmat Abad's, it had no roof, the workers would define the yard that would embrace the gathered congregation piecemeal, as funds came in. Thus architecturally, too, the mosque had a focal point of power, the mihrab, but no overall unity, accommodating itself to the congregation's tentative size and reflecting its social form. The workers had an expression for such an open-ended chain, *teke-teke,* bit by bit, whose meaning combined inching forward temporally, halfhearted commitment, and an additive organization: the absence of boundaries. Sultan 'Ali's original proposal for the mosque construction, to have one rich donor build it, reflected another viable solution to the same absence of corporate social endeavor in the *shahrak.*

"But don't you want to make sure from the outset that you'll end up at least with a mosque building?" I asked Hasan Kuchek. "A mosque isn't like planting another row of eggplants; it's a symbol." "That's how we do things in Bizhan," he explained. "We always want to make sure that if we only get it half done we can still use it. How do we know how many people we can count on tomorrow?"

The Protest for Flour

The soaring price of flour in 1974 brought forth Bizhan's second manifestation of some remaining political initiative and cohesion during my year in the *shahrak.* Most model townsmen bought their supply of flour from the principal baker, Mash-hadi Hosein. In the beginning of the flour shortage he closed the bakery repeatedly to search for the flour in Dezful, both to sell to the workers and for his own bakery. The Safiabad workers complained to the engineers at the farm, since, having set Mash-hadi Hosein up in business, the State was to blame for the crisis. The engineers did nothing. Next some forty townsmen signed a petition authorizing Mash-hadi Hosein as their agent and the entire *shahrak's* representative for buying flour. They hoped this would pressure the State warehouse by reminding it that many families and not just the baker's business depended on his supply. They worked out carefully with him what his commission would be.

Mash-hadi Hosein was known as an earnest man. But *dulat's* authorities, who had no idea of the *shahrak's* consumption needs, suspected the baker was taking advantage of the market's shortfall and of his precarious right to any flour at all from the State warehouse. (Since Bizhan was not an officially recognized town, he could not belong to the urban bakers' "cooperative," which had sole claim to the warehouse in time of emergency.) So the State warehouse sent the baker back to the *shahrak* empty-handed; he simply did not have strong enough connections.

In vain Mash-hadi Hosein and the workers tried other avenues, including the provincial governor in Ahwaz. As flour became impossible to buy at any price, one day a group of angry workers took the problem in their own hands, going directly to what they perceived to be the source of all grain in Iran: which did not turn out to be the Ministry of Agriculture (as I predicted), not the city's wheat warehouse, not the bakers' "cooperative" center, not the Ministry of Water and Power, which managed the entire Dez Irrigation Project, not their own Ministry of Labor, not the Ministry of Health, not the Ministry of Rural Welfare, not even the Holder of His Majesty's Imperial Command in Dezful—but the secret police, SAVAK. 'Ali Reza joked later that since demanding flour implied a criticism of *dulat,* and a criticism of *dulat* is treason, they had decided to put themselves directly in the hands of their punishers.

As the workers gathered outside the door of SAVAK's obscure little private house on a Dezful side street, the doorman said the Ministry therein—vague about its identity—had nothing to do with flour. He listed eight or ten other State offices where they should go. They would not budge. Finally, after a succession of officers appeared, one informed them he would do what he could if the group would disperse immediately. Under no conditions would the State deal with a crowd, nor with a representative of a group. They should go back to Bizhan but not even do that in a group—rather, one by one—*teke-teke.* In a few days, Mash-hadi Hosein did receive enough flour to tide the *shahrak* over until the crisis passed. I asked people for an explanation of their success. "You have to read *dulat* through a mirror," Almas confided (that is, read it in reverse). "If it says that it will only meet us *teke-teke,* that means it only understands a crowd."

As the workers' mobilization for flour had accelerated from asking the Safiabad engineers' assistance to providing Mash-hadi Hosein with a petition and finally to taking public action themselves, each stage of having to step up their pressure made some of them more conscious of the *shahrak*'s population as a social aggregation in itself. This awareness grew partly from the issue's accentuation of their status as victims: formerly, farmers who could feed themselves and others (howsoever poorly, but on their own) and now hungry beggars utterly dependent on *dulat*. They had not yet evolved the concept of bread or food being an innate *right* of everyone in society. But, whereas in the early stages of their concern for flour each worker had spoken for his family, by the end they saw themselves speaking for Bizhan—the first time I heard any new townsman articulate a distinct identity of the *shahrak* residents, embracing everyone living there.

Ironically, then, although in the mosque case the State claimed wanting to foster a sense of *community* in the model town by making everyone join in one *shahrak* mosque, it had instead strengthened workers' resolve to recover their separate communal identities; whereas in the flour crisis the workers for the first time glimpsed Bizhan's unity that the State said it sought, and this came to them as they rose against the State.

Bizhan's Political Foundations in the Mosque and the Mob

It is not coincidental that in Bizhan's brief time as an urban settlement its minimal political life already had come to focus on Iranian urban culture's two classical loci for popular political expression, the mosque and the mob in the street, both here in still rudimentary form. In Iranian urban history the mosque and the mob work in tandem to compensate together for the absence of a structured public and of viable vehicles for political action out of which such a public might emerge (although, as we have seen, Rahmat Abad at the *village* level enjoyed a vigorous, open, and structured political arena). Lacking easily directed, clearly bounded "platoons" between the family and the State for political expression— except for specialized guilds and brotherhoods—the urban society periodically has joined the mosque and the street mob together in a complementary dynamic, the mob taking to the streets with its demands and then seeking refuge by binding itself inside the mosque courtyard: Iran's traditional urban institution of mass political sanctuary, called *bast*. There the mosque walls and the Qur'anic divines defend the mob. This partnership of mosque and mob, while effectively registering protest against the autocrat, protecting protesters, and thus providing some channel for "feedback" from the urban base, time and time again ultimately has reinforced centralized power. It has sheltered individuals within the walls and legitimacy of the mosque from having to form firm, impersonal, public groups, each with its discrete and specific purposes, its members committed corporately to objectively defined demands. Without a combination of these corporate organizational factors, those who periodically compose the mob in desperation cannot over the long run sustain confrontation and negotiation with the State.

Just as the State has to stay *outside* the mosque in *bast,* so the dissenters taking religious sanctuary have to stay *inside* (literally *and* symbolically—as some secular revolutionaries in 1979 discovered about this tradition), giving both sides in the last resort a way out. That has been its grave flaw. Imprisoning the individual within the impersonal collective and the collective within the mosque requires neither party to distill out of inchoate and generalized political expression responsive or focused political organization, and, hence, creates nothing that can require the State to do the same. Both *dulat* and the urban populace, saved from confrontation and negotiation by this traditional union of mob and mosque, are shielded as well from accountability and compromise.

For its part, Bizhan's mosque construction did affirm a certain communal spirit that might have infused the *shahrak;* it certainly promised a moral dimension neither the State nor the companies nor the fragmented workers had given the new settlement. But without specific purpose and corporate form, that enthusiasm would prove ephemeral if not self-destructive. Like all mosque "congregations" in urban Iran, Bizhan's, too, would defy structuration. As we review the requirements for such structuration, hence, for stable and enduring political process, we realize that the mosque was no better able than *dulat* to instill in urban society Rahmat Abad's sound principles.

Following the organizational pattern of Iranian urban mosques, Bizhan's mosque, when built, would not comprise a self-governing congregation of the faithful, corporately representative personnel, nor even determinate boundaries of its domain. Urban mosques have no objectively designated hierarchies and responsibilities (no priesthood) forming a larger institution. There are no parishes, dioceses, and archdioceses or their equivalent, which constitute the building blocks of a church. As for internal regulation, urban Iranian mosques recognize only subjective consensus as the means of establishing leadership and hierarchy, neither with any clear temporal duration (that is, their organization rests on personal reputations ever subject to flux). With no specialized roles or formal assignment of authority, Bizhan's mosque would embody no specific line of accountability. Although in Iran the mosque monopolizes access to any transcendent source of law (since *dulat* knows only arbitrary fiat), it requires no public manifestations of its members' commitment to law. For example, Shi'ites are exempted from their own moral law when among the unfaithful—it is not a sin to deny you are a Shi'ite when placed under stress by non-Muslims.

One could expect that the *shahrak* mosque community might hold man together over an enduring period, but like the mob would never define itself apart from all-inclusive membership, ideals, or purposes. It would never foster corporate "platoons" at any level. The Dezful divine explained that the mosque would govern all aspects of human life. He did not conceive of Bizhan's mosque as being *in* the *shahrak* nor the *shahrak* congregation as being a local component of a larger structure; but rather, the *opposite:* The universal Islamic community *emanated downward* to bring forth this mosque. In short, the mosque's social organization itself articulated a culture that precluded autonomous constituent units, in fact that recognized no outlines except for the distinction between believers and nonbelievers. Reminiscent of *dulat,* this culture gave life to believers and demanded their surrender; all others it outlawed.

Like the mob, without structure Bizhan's mosque "congregation" would not in time establish accountability inside or outside itself, thus could not negotiate or compromise. Without a charter of limited purposes it would relinquish nothing to civil government—just like the mob. Consistent with these principles, the mosque had never come to recognize the State's existence apart from itself, so it was only fitting that the State, which claimed governance over Bizhan, had sent no one to the mosque's inauguration. Just as *dulat* had drilled its holes without explanation and the villagers had silently salted *dulat's* rice, just as the workers had made a hump in the road that *dulat* had leveled unspeakingly, just as the King had to dress as a beggar to learn about his kingdom, just as to tell him the truth people cherished a spy, so, too, the mosque—providing *bast* even in day-to-day life—institutionalized the irreconcilable standoff between society and the State.

Not coincidentally but again according to ancient urban political culture, the construction of the mosque had caused Sultan 'Ali, the "intellectual" of Bizhan's two leaders, to hive off from the halfhearted popular endeavor. Leaving that to Bizhan's traditional politician Haji Safar, Sultan 'Ali had convened the *shahrak's* Qur'anic study group. Between the two, they divided the labor. According to the dynamics of *bast,* without those who study the Qur'an the mosque's walls alone cannot protect the mob from *dulat's* destruction. When Sultan 'Ali moved "off the streets," *dulat,* thinking like Lilienthal that it mastered tradition and history, naïvely concluded that Mossadegh's man had left the mosque project entirely. No, he was in fact establishing the necessary mortar of ideas and explanations needed to make the walls strong.

The workers' angry street crowd constituted the bare minimal form for political action. As the mosque's partner in urban politics, the street crowd could turn commitment into concrete initiative swiftly, indeed into public defiance, because in contrast to the mosque it claimed an immediate, specific objective and was not encumbered by divines. But this nascent mob (which in future crises would be able to storm back to its mosque in Bizhan) had none of the mosque's endurance through time, and made even fewer demands on its members than the mosque did. In effect, neither the mosque (generalized and timeless) nor the street crowd (specific and momentary) promised corporate political development, lasting but at the same time clearly bounded. The mosque has rarely sustained coherent governance in Iran. To the extent that Sultan 'Ali's handful of *shahrak* intelligencia would need to ally itself with an *organization* in order to sustain political engagement, it, too, had nothing to rely on in the mob.

But the instability of this molecular fusion of the mosque and the mob did not let *dulat* rest assured. Although the State seemed driven to put all villages in Iran into urban centers or "poles," at the same time a paranoia about urban settlements obsessed it—and with justification. Unlike Europe, villages in Iran have virtually never threatened the State, whereas townsmen often do. Thus the Plan's determination to urbanize the villages contained a foolhardy element. Thirteen *shahrak*s each with one single mosque hardly constituted a sounder political foundation for rural northern Khuzestan than 200 autonomous villages with none. It was no accident, then, that the Plan had omitted a mosque in its model town for all rural Iran.

Workers' Strikes in the Agribusiness

Besides these two traditional urban political forms, an alternative, potentially corporate form of political organization had begun to emerge in Bizhan, important to our theoretical understanding if not (as we will explain) to the workers' long-term political development: groups of workers striking for better employment conditions. Strikes had taken place in the agribusinesses before I arrived in the *shahrak,* but during my year in Bizhan I observed marked development in three groups of workers, and the beginning of a fourth association. For instance, starting two years earlier as a tentative cluster of men who hardly knew each other, the tractor drivers had grown into a clearly defined, cohesive organization with specific demands, a responsive and confident leader, and members who could rely on each other to carry out the group's decisions and support one another within its charter of collective action.

Before we look more closely at these groups and how they emerged, several points provide necessary background. None of these rudimentary groups could be compared—at their stage in 1974—to a labor union. All, however, did include workers from different villages of origin and from different *shahrak*s: that is, a *common purpose* in each case held the members together, rather than personal ties. None was organized by someone outside the group of workers voicing their demands, nor by a former village leader; all these initiatives came from the workers themselves. All the groups we consider here undertook several protests, going beyond one-time mobilization like the demonstration for flour.

Aside from problems specific to one agribusiness or to one department within a company, Bizhan's new townsmen faced many overall difficulties in trying to organize for repeated strikes. As peasants they had never belonged to occupationally based unions and had never participated in strikes. Indeed, in just the opposite dynamic of a strike, when discontented with the landlord they had abandoned the village. Work in the companies demanded so much that in off hours they had little time or energy to spare for groundwork organizational efforts. (Some of the leaders attended an evening literacy class!) Workers in most departments— especially those paying the least—could build very little on previous years' organizational foundations because so many of them changed jobs from season to season. Nor could they tap organizations or even loose networks along former village lines, since these had virtually disappeared in the *shahrak*s. Finally, because of the workers' vulnerability, because the foreign experts enjoyed years of experience managing plantations in the Third World, and because the Iranian administrators possessed such skill in personalized conflict, management could easily play workers off against each other and foster jealousies between them. Nevertheless, several workers' organizations began to articulate themselves.

All these groups started by focusing on wages, but after gaining that, a few had taken on issues such as annual bonus payments, holidays, improved working conditions (including maintenance allowances for motorcycles used on the job), and finally very difficult negotiations about the transferability of workers from one job to another, job permanence, and specific refinements in ranking. By the end of the autumn harvesting season of 1974, three groups of workers had moved to these more complex negotiations, and were stable enough probably to sustain their organizational momentum during the coming year with the same core members and leaders. They had consolidated sufficiently to start accumulating a common fund of expertise, a steady reputation, and even a backlog of ongoing relations with other nascent groups. In one, core members visited potential dissenters the night before a strike to apply personal pressure, and volunteers kept "members" informed on a weekly basis.

The most mature group comprised the Shell-Cott tractor drivers, who struck successfully four times in 1974, reaching the point of demanding that when the farm had insufficient tractor work they would not be required to accept "coolie" positions in order to remain on the payroll. Shell-Cott's managerial procedures significantly facilitated the drivers' organizing. Unlike Safiabad or Mr. Naraghi's company, the British announced a test each spring for new drivers; the applicants had to demonstrate their skills in front of all other competitors as each waited his turn. Each driver hired received a classification (one of six ranks) according to his test score and other standard qualifications. In a rationally structured hierarchy characteristic of the entire firm, each classification had its uniform contract and rules. From the first day, then, as the men stood around trying out for the job, they became acquainted with other drivers according to their levels and learned the standard criteria for each category. So, from the outset the drivers thought of themselves as categories, making it easier to negotiate collectively. Once on the job, all drivers met every day to review that day's instructions and to set out for work at the same time. Thus to some extent management itself unified them, bringing them together repeatedly as a group with logically designated subgroups whose membership was public knowledge.

In just the opposite sociological patterning, tractor drivers at Mr. Naraghi's Iran-America agribusiness under that firm's *Iranian* middle-level managers had each been hired individually through a well-placed friend, usually as a personal favor. Not offering objective qualifications or skills, many had been trained on the job, so they had no impersonal measure of whether they could market themselves elsewhere and no standard of general performance. Each driver held an individually tailored employment agreement that he was loath to discuss with anyone else lest it reveal his special concessions, his lack of expertise, and his dependence. These arrangements privatized his employment, indebted him to his supervisor, and hence increased his sense of inadequacy and risk, precluding participation in a strike. Furthermore, workers at the Iranian company rarely arrived at the same hour, shifts being highly irregular. Even tractor-driving jobs could hardly be compared with each other as daily assignments often altered according to personal preference and convenience, special fields needing intense work, mid-day schedule changes, and so forth. The company's management style discouraged workers from seeing themselves as groups.

Isma'il, a prominent worker, told me that many men struck for improved terms in Mr. Naraghi's firm: individually! each by pleading with his supervisor or someone above him, in personal terms. One Iranian administrator dispelled an attempted strike by going down the line of workers who had made their demands, addressing each one personally: "But Hasan, after I got you that medicine from Andimeshk, you'd do this to me? And 'Abdu, knowing that your son is in the army, how can you afford to quit? Murtaza, get the hell out anyway, you ungrateful man!— This was the third time I found you a job—now I've helped you too much as it is! And Rajab, why, you saw that young chap, sent by Agha Samadi, hanging around the other day looking for a job as a welder...." Each apologized and "repented." Personalized and individualized employment obstructed worker organization as much as standardized management facilitated it.

A second group of very aggressive workers comprised those with expertise in the Shell-Cott repair shop. One afternoon they attacked the British head of the department physically, on another occasion they threatened the life of the personnel manager. Probably many of them had belonged to unions in the oil company or in Tehran. Such skilled positions went only to city people, which made them consider themselves superior to "peasants." Since none of them lived in the *shahrak*s and since few *shah-rak* residents worked alongside them, workers in Bizhan learned little from them about labor organizing—and I, little about their organization.

The field irrigators constituted a third group within the British company that had begun to articulate collective demands, although this group lacked the militancy of the first two. Geographically dispersed in their work, never convened as a group for meetings, having no objectively defined skills that would give them leverage, subject to seasonal changes in employment, and frequently including older men who favored conservative relations with management, the irrigators faced by far the most difficult organizational challenge of the groups we consider here. Consequently, by 1974 the irrigators were still tackling quite elementary issues like pay (initially "beseeching" management for a thirty cents a day raise in a wage that had not changed in three years). The letters I translated and typed for them supplicated obsequiously: adorned with prayers, compliments about the administrator's kindness and humanity, apologies for the letter's inconvenience, personal wishes for the Englishman's family, a litany of evidence of the workers' "faithfulness" to Shell-Cott, enumeration of their hungry dependents, and at the end, signed "your servants"! But by the end of the summer the company had repeatedly tested the irrigators' resolve to strike, and the latter had won their first concession.

The last group of workers to organize themselves by the time I left were the lowest of all employees, the women pickers at Shell-Cott. Despite their status, the women enjoyed the assistance of several organizational advantages: first, that an announced *decrease* in daily wage sparked their initial organization (a much more provocative incentive than the possibility of an *increase*); secondly, that they were recruited and paid through team foremen (which meant that the pickers were already well organized into cohesive constituent units often based on a core of relatives and neighbors); thirdly, that many were women of Arab ethnic background, far less intimidated by management than those of Iranian stock—indeed, often ready for a fight!

Factors Favoring These Nascent Organizations

The cases we have reviewed here have several features in common. First, in each case a mini*public* or *shared arena* had previously emerged from individual workers' frequent interaction with one another, easily seen among the tractor drivers, the mechanics, and the women pickers who already belonged to their familiar "little platoons" at work and only needed to merge these in a common effort. The irrigators faced an exceptional challenge in having to bring forth a minipublic of their members without ready-made, face-to-face groupings. But over several years the irrigators' supervisor, a somewhat idealistic young English agronomist (who knew them individually and respected many of them, yet dealt with them in objective not subjective terms), had encouraged a moral rapport of shared responsibility among the men and between the corps and himself. Mr. Mullin had consistently rewarded collaboration rather than competition among the foremen, which was imperative for the efficient distribution of water down the gravity system and out over the company's vast hectarage; in fact, the foremen stressed with the field men this concept of integrating their work. Complementing this collaborative ethic, the flow of water itself imposed onto the irrigators a hierarchy of specific, empirical operations with standard categories referring to area irrigated or overseen, and so forth, and with frequent vertical reporting from station to station. Thus the irrigators' work more than that of any other department relied on effective channels of communication and on pyramidal representation, which could then be mobilized for the laborers' own purposes. Under Mr. Mullin they saw hierarchy as a unifying and productive form of organization, not an exploitative one.

Each of the workers' organizational efforts that coalesced, then, sprang from a little public that their work relations generated, a palpable, even measurable coming together of individuals, or their linking in a single-purpose social chain with regularity and frequency. Actual give-and-take had created these social arenas; they were not just theoretical unities (see Arensberg, 1972). Furthermore, the public arenas of the pickers and irrigators comprised small *building blocks between the overall strikers' organization and the individual.* In the case of the irrigators' field units and the pickers' teams, individuals could mobilize the microunits to which they belonged, and easily link with other ready-made units like theirs. The tractor drivers, too, had these constituent microunits, at least conceptually, through their six company-imposed standardized categories; when it came to advancing *their* interests, these formed natural "committees." The workers had been able to sustain effective organization over a period of a year or more and through setbacks, because in all these cases individuals were already part of *responsive, socially alive ministructures,* which conserved organizational resources and gave them as individuals small, familiar "platoons." Since these ministructures had clearcut identities and frequently repeated behavioral links, it was difficult to divide and rule them. Finally, they could sustain their new little organizations under adverse conditions because each shared a specific, clearly defined common enterprise.

The advantages of the organizations that these minipublics developed into, enabling the workers to overcome the obstacles any strike attempt faced in the agribusinesses, dramatically illustrate why the State systematically suppressed any general public arena from emerging in Bizhan, howsoever small—any coming together in public for any purpose, especially regularly (even for commonly shared entertainment). We can now understand why the secret police placed people likely to join together, in house locations *physically far apart;* and why the Ministry so punctiliously removed from the environment any cause for preexisting groups to persist or new ones to form, even any little focus like the hump, that hinted of shared purpose. Any social clotting might become a pattern, as it did among the strikers.

The strengths of the strikers' decentralized structuration even within their overall associations indicate what the *shahrak* lost—both in morale and in organizational economy—each time the State destroyed social building blocks that might have merged into publics, like the former villages, latent *shahrak* neighborhoods, or emergent interest groups. Even *dulat's* preference for one large, necessarily impersonal *shahrak* mosque rather than smaller, cohesive ones was profoundly rooted in its political self-interest, as the new townsmen would take years to complete a mosque for the entire settlement, doing so *teke-teke* not corporately, and when they did finish, its congregation would remain unwieldy, structureless, alienating except when creating mobs. In contrast, the micropublics of smaller communities retaining their integrity might have sparked communal trust and elan, congealing with constituent units for a structured *shahrak* polity and for sustainable social or political initiative, perhaps town-wide.

A second characteristic all these emergent workers' organizations shared was the British company in which they evolved. Although a few workers in Mr. Naraghi's firm and at Safiabad sporadically attempted strikes, in neither did they achieve the level of clearly defined, persistent organization we have seen here, beginning to initiate and sustain definite action that moved from one undertaking to the next.

If worker strikes counted the occasional success in these other farms, they were isolated not systematic, and tied to personal intercession. Some of the British administrators found it ironic that of the three farms, the management that the workers held in the highest regard for its efficiency, reliability, fairness, and organizational clarity would be the one suffering the most frequent and effective strikes. In contrast to workers at Safiabad, where the State's management seemed arbitrary (although usually benign to workers), and in contrast to workers under the Iranian-managed agribusiness run by military officers, workers at Shell-Cott, by applying company policies, precedents, and instructions, could generally comprehend the actions of at least the British administration. Shell-Cott workers received their pay regularly and fully, and the foreign supervisors rarely treated them with the condescension that Iranian superiors did everywhere. Although the new townsmen did not understand the Englishmen's individual psychology, on the whole those who had worked under the British for any length of time could express demands in terms of rules, former agreements, comparable pay scales, and the cost of living, and could cite cases analogous to their own in arguing for similar treatment— objective evidence and principles available to everyone. If Safiabad or Mr. Naraghi's company operated systematically, the workers could not perceive that.

Furthermore, especially with administrators like Mr. Mullin, an expectation of fairness in the British company encouraged workers to demand fairness. Their assumption of a minimal moral coherence, a due recognition on the part of management that workers were honest and had domestic needs, reinforced the predictability of rational management. Management defined themselves and the workers within the same social order, almost as though within the same community. (Fairness—after all, a form of predictability—means shared norms.) Although some Iranian administrators in the other farms felt these moral dimensions perhaps even more deeply toward their workers, it strictly violated their we-they managerial strategies to reveal any shared moral sympathy.

These factors, plus the foreigners themselves appearing more exposed to *dulat,* their not speaking Farsi, and the hopes they raised by offering a higher initial pay, contributed to making Shell-Cott an environment generally propitious for employees' initiatives throughout their work, thus for employee organizations and for bargaining with management. The workers began to overcome the drastic social fragmentation they had suffered at the hands of the State.

In discussing the articulation of the nuclear family out of its social matrix in Rahmat Abad, of the village as a corporate entity within the intervillage region, of *sharik* partnerships freed from their traditional personal bonds, and of the villager's individual, self-directed personality, we saw that for each of those social forms to crystallize with an autonomous integrity it required a *challenge* prompting it to tighten its organizational structure. But in addition, since the incorporated nuclear family, village, and *sharik*s congealed out of their members' *patterned initiatives* in frequent concert, the articulation of these organizational forms also required *predictability* within their respective fields of action. Furthermore, people will not coalesce for common initiatives unless they find themselves in a milieu of at least minimal *acceptance* or with an underpinning of minimal available help. On the one hand, these characteristics of the broader environment accounted for the emergence of corporate and contractual bonds in the nuclear family, the village, and the *sharik,* and between individuals themselves. On the other hand, the absence of these characteristics in *dulat'*s domain made it impossible for the intervillage region to evolve an analogous organizational structure, and impossible for Rahmat Abad to work out a solution over time to the organizational need it had begun to face, of hierarchy consistent with accountable authority. Turning back to Bizhan's nascent workers' organizations, we see, similarly, that the existence or absence of predictability and basic moral assumptions in the three farms in which the new townsmen found themselves— Shell-Cott, Mr. Naraghi's farm, and *dulat'*s Safiabad—significantly affected the initiatives that workers could take and hence the bonds that they could form between one another, their organizational potential. Only the context of Shell-Cott's management was conducive to contractual and corporate initiatives; the two Iranian-managed farms' arbitrariness fostered dependence upon private personalistic links.

In short, these cases of quasicorporate structuration that we have seen beginning to emerge among the Shell-Cott workers developed *outside the domain of the Iranian State* (Safiabad) and *outside the culture of urban Iran* (in as much as that culture pervaded Mr. Naraghi's firm, he himself being Iranian by birth, and the firm being managed by virtually an all-Iranian staff). While the Shell-Cott strikes benefited workers in the *shahr-ak*s, we have no grounds for suggesting that they might in the long term have led to new organizational possibilities for the model town. Professor Bill has shown us in his analysis of Iranian institutions passing from Western to Iranian management after decades how quickly centralized, personalized power can undermine corporate structures (1972:78–87).

Shell-Cott workers had organized their strikes and had gained some political leverage outside their own world, in a political field in which they themselves did not exist. Socially, economically, politically, cultur-ally they lived in that vast archipelago ruled by the Plan in Tehran, where they were still rows of cinder block buildings on an architect's blueprint. In that political field there was no conceivable vertical link of respon-siveness, howsoever remote, between them and those in Shell-Cott who interacted and even compromised with them in their strikes—those who, despite their position, recognized and confirmed the workers' organiza-tional reality. Although, in contrast to the standoff between *dulat* and the villagers or workers, the British management did negotiate with workers making demands on it from below, fundamentally these successful strikes resembled *bast*. The common political arena the two sides seemed to be evolving was illusory. When the chips were down, *Shell-Cott* was a part of the *Plan's* political arena, which Bizhan could never enter. In the last resort the strikers would never have been able to hold management accountable. More importantly, they would never be able to transfer the pattern of vertical negotiation they achieved within the company into the Iranian *civitas*.

Indeed, no link of a common polity existed even between Sultan 'Ali and the workers under him, living in the same *shahrak*. As was evident from his abundant false promises, Sultan 'Ali was beyond the new towns-men's reach. Just as the mosque and mob with which Bizhan had begun to equip itself offered no resolution to Rahmat Abad's challenge of hier-archy and accountable authority, neither did the Shell-Cott strikers' successes.

In Bizhan, in the General's and Mr. Naraghi's Khuzestan world, in *dulat's* realm at Safiabad, only individuals could constitute building blocks, only individuals could slide in and out to negotiate their own advance. Clumps of individuals stood out too conspicuously on the land-scape to be able to operate effectively, just as Agha Keyvan had convinc-ingly argued about Rahmat Abad's venture into the margins of *dulat's* domain when it had wanted to build its canal. Like anachronisms crop-ping back up from former village days, the Shell-Cott strikers' interme-diate-range corporate groups were obsolete in the new model town for all rural Iran, obsolete because they required a *public*. Except for the mob on its way to *bast*, politics within *dulat's* realm, politics in urban Iran, stayed "behind closed doors" (as Madar-i-Karim had observed when she mistakenly thought she could obtain identification papers openly across a bureaucrat's office counter). Politics moved off the streets, as Sultan 'Ali and his unidentifiable band had done, to read the Qur'an in a private home. Those who had successful "strikes" in Safiabad and in Mr. Naraghi's firm did so as individuals, through private arrangements. This is not to suggest a mere difference in political *styles:* public-private, individual-corporate. In dealing one to one, in private, the stronger can always retain the upper hand.

Incremental Expansion and the Political Order

By 1974, Rahmat Abad villagers' initiatives over and over again seemed to be pushing against the outer limit of their domain. The wealthier villagers needed a broader arena in which to launch larger investments; the poorer but very energetic ones looked farther afield for *sharik* opportunities. Collective civic initiatives, like bridges, the aqueduct, and the school, were ready for greater sophistication, hence more complex organization; collective commercial initiatives, too, like agreement with an urban wholesaler to purchase the village's beans, needed wider scope. The "grass roots" had gotten its house in order—increasing the corporate autonomy of clearly articulated units at society's base, the flow of information among them, the freedom of a genuinely public arena, a commitment to moral cohesion, while preserving political accountability and expanding that order out and out beyond each individual village, linking it to others. The next logical stage was the town, whose sociological configurations we see in Bizhan: where former villagers would have expanded from half-day *bildar*s to public supervision of the town's canal system and street lights; from investments in tractors and sheep to building and managing a variety store or a bath house; from a parents' primary school association to a school board for the technical high school; from annual negotiations between harvesters and *joft*holders to nascent labor unions; from bringing the office of headman under village direction, to making the provincial Ministry responsive to the model town.

The foundations for such incremental expansion of local initiative, predictability, and political control had been laid when Rahmat Abad moved from personal networks among kinsmen and personal relations with the landlord to territorially based organization which was corporate and impersonal, and which brought forth a public. Then Rahmat Abad had girded that foundation by retaining its *joft* system until it could work out the means to hold hierarchy and authority accountable in the next stage of expansion, as though the villagers consciously knew that organizational strength lay in keeping their objectively based common purpose. But when taking their next evolutionary steps required immersing themselves in *dulat*'s environment, we see in Bizhan's organizational forms that rather than evolving further, the village's impersonal, corporate, contractual, and public structures collapsed back down to sole dependence on the most rudimentary social bonds of kinship and the personalistic dyad. The State could tolerate no other principle of social organization, because it could tolerate no public arena or the initiatives that create it.

In watching Bizhan emerge as Iran's prototype new town, it is provocative to reflect on the economic and political foundations of Western urban culture that were laid during the late Middle Ages when thousands of towns emerged spontaneously from the agrarian base as it developed, towns alive with their mini-incorporations of all sorts—guilds, partnerships and joint ventures, parishes, ward councils, foundations, long-term business contracts, civic associations—creating by their interaction vigorous public arenas of markets and fairs, cathedrals and local colleges, courts of law, public meetings and town governments themselves incorporated and chartered to regulate these settlements' internal affairs and to deal contractually with other similar corporate entities. The vitality of these small European towns (and what in time they came to sponsor) emerging out of agrarian village society rested on the fact that they developed entirely *outside the State's domain* (diametrically opposite Bizhan), as self-governing polities strictly *protected from* the ministers and plans of *dulat*, and from the King's prerogatives. That was in fact the point of European town charters!

Some day Bizhan, too, would be granted "self-government" according to the Plan. "Some years down the road" (Engineer Ahmadi had thought the matter through), "once these peasants have acquired urban culture." Most engineers whom I interviewed, dealing directly with the model towns and with the Plan's projections for the future of rural Iran, foresaw the day when Bizhan and all settlements patterned after it would need some form of government to carry out the Plan at the local level. But they feared that the model townsmen were "too fresh from the villages" with the spirit of initiative and independence to be reliable yet for "self-governance." "They have too many primitive ideas and don't understand the Plan." Even Western policy advisors like Lilienthal felt the villagers too "immature" for political participation, somehow associating literacy with political "maturity." Many Western development theorists like Lilienthal envisage policy makers switching on local "government" (like a new program) at a certain safe time. They imagine that these skills and institutions acquired so precariously, the norms, and even the interest in structured political life will all be there ready for activation at the ruler's flip of his switch. The fragility of Rahmat Abad's accomplishments when subjected to the modernization thrust of *dulat,* and the difficulty of the village's own political evolution even under optimal conditions hardly encourage such hopes. Nor, above all, does evidence from the top of society, of the Plan's cultural durability through millennia.

The Muslim divine who attended the mosque dedication in Bizhan told this story in his sermon:

> A wealthy man was determined to build a great religious shrine entirely on his own, accepting no help at all. People came wanting to contribute to it but he turned them away: this was *his* monument, only his. The shining edifice began to rise, certain to make him famous; still people begged to be a part of it and still he refused. One day a beggar took a few pennies and bought one new brick in the bazaar. That night secretly he slipped it into the masons' pile of bricks for the shrine.

Although the Dezful clergyman interpreted the story as illustrating everyone's desire to participate in building a mosque, some workers told me later that the beggar's triumph lay in the fact that—although by trickery and under the cover of darkness—he had managed to participate in "the King's" accomplishment, from which "the King" had rejected everyone in the country. Accepting their amendment, I inquired what the story meant: why would a King spurn his own people who wanted to help?

"Because if he made it all himself he could decide exactly how he wanted it and wouldn't have to listen to anyone," Jahangir explained. "And then he'd get all the glory without anyone else getting any, even a little bit!" his son Naser added.

He who is pure is only pure for himself.
—Qur'an, Sura 35

Chapter 10

The State and Bizhan

Saith Darius the King: By the favour of Ahuramazda these are the countries which I seized. . . . I ruled over them; they bore Tribute to me, that they did. My law: that held them firm. . . . My law—of that they feel fear.
—Darius' code inscribed at Susa, quoted in Ghirshman, 1971:41

No one in Iran feels secure because no one in Iran is safeguarded by laws. The appointment of governors is carried out without laws. The dismissal of officers is done without laws. The monopolies are sold without any laws. The State finances are squandered without laws. The stomachs of innocent citizens are cut open without laws. . . . Everyone in India, Paris, Tiflis, Egypt, Istanbul, and even among the Turkman tribes, knows his rights and duties. But no one in Iran knows his rights and duties. . . . Even the brothers and sons of the Shah do not know what tomorrow will bring.
—Malkum Khan (1890), quoted in Abrahamian, 1977:28

An Incorporeal Polity

If the polity of Rahmat Abad—corporate, visible, and contractual—rooted itself in laws that were constant over time, brought forth and reaffirmed in the public arena; and if villagers and others could predict Rahmat Abad's behavior and hold it accountable, the opposite characteristics marked *dulat,* the polity of Bizhan. Fragmented, incorporeal, personalistic, the Iranian State was governed by laws constantly subject to change without public knowledge; it suppressed any public arena. Just the opposite of Rahmat Abad, the people of Bizhan, unable to hold their polity accountable, could not predict what might happen next.

Muhammad Reza, a Safiabad worker from Bizhan, collapsed while helping to load a truck with heavy bags of cement. Directly from Dezful, the Ministry of Water and Power whisked him off to distant Tehran in an ambulance, one relative with him. Upon reaching Tehran he was separated from his kinsman at the hospital to die alone if he had not died en route. No one ever saw him again. For months no one could even find his "case." Relatives from Bizhan made trips to Tehran, wrote letters,

241

tried to talk to doctors and staff at the hospital, telephoned, pleaded with Safiabad to follow up what had happened. Since Muhammad Reza was the only wage earner in the family, his bereft widow, Shahtela, asked for compensation; in response *dulat* angrily insisted the man had died of a congenital disease having nothing to do with his job, and dragged members of the family to Tehran "for tests" to prove this. On one such trip Shahtela spent days before she could even locate a grave in an obscure corner of a Tehran cemetery where the State claimed to have buried her husband.

Whatever the correct medical details, the interactional events were clear enough: With Muhammad Reza's body in hand, *dulat* had fled in a flash into the depths of its labyrinth in Tehran, where it buried the man personally, institutionally, literally, and demanded his family and friends to do the same. The pattern is familiar to us by now, from Rahmat Abad's hole drillers, from the road grader that silently leveled the new townsmen's hump in the road, from *dulat's* conspicuous absence at the mosque dedication: A no man's land separated society and its governing mechanism. How could individuals who congregated or found common purpose within *dulat's* domain even organize themselves in a group, when the only thing with which they could interact in carrying out their initiative was this anomalous, impalpable yet all-consuming power?

Iran's ancient lack of territorial integrity as a polity, and the absence even of enduring corporate fiefdoms or constituent princely States with their circumscribed territories within Iran (as in Europe where these smaller structures were confederated later into kingdoms), is of central importance in understanding its culture. Frequently throughout its long history others have occupied parts of Iran for centuries, and Iran has continually dominated lands outside its cultural domain, non-Iranian peoples forming internal enclaves while the State laid no claim over Iranians next door (as, anciently, in Baluchistan). In other cases the state did lay claim to its people: Under the late Shah the State demanded allegiance from the foreign-born offspring of Iranians naturalized as citizens in other countries. Particularly in times of crisis the State has officially appointed foreigners to its own highest responsibilities of government.

Historically, Persia has rarely sustained self-defense, an indication of a people's corporate integrity. The late Shah's army capitulated immediately and almost unanimously at the outset of the revolution. In times past, localized buffer peoples on the State's perimeter protected themselves against intruders. But even when ruled by an organized government, Iranians did not look upon the Greeks or Romans or Byzantines, the Arabs or Mongols as attackers on the fatherland or an integrated empire. Iranians have sometimes defended themselves in religious wars, but these must be distinguished from the defense of a polity.

One remarkable exception throws light on Iran's political amorphousness with its permeable boundaries. The Sassanians (c. A.D. 226–640), alone among Persian dynasties for their "defensive mentality," built extensive walls to mark their boundaries and protect the State; indicatively, this dynasty above all others fostered the flowering of Zoroastrianism, Iran's native religion, of lawmaking, and of decentralized investment in society's rural base. Sassanian landlords resided in the countryside like European manorial lords, in contrast to the absentee lords predominating in virtually all other periods of Iran's history.* This cluster of contrasts the Sassanians present in Iranian history suggests a relationship between on the one hand, the polity's corporate integrity (its territorial self-definition and measures to ensure self-defense, its concern for systemic law, the flowering of an indigenous moral order) and on the other hand, its vertical economic and political integration. That is, Sassanian society, perhaps exceptional in the history of the Iranian State, suggests a correlation between society's corporate integrity and the willingness of its elites—not just the State—to commit themselves to long-term, local development, which in an agrarian economy meant dispersing themselves into the very fabric of the rural order, accepting decentralization's implicit demand for local give-and-take. We will explore this position further in Chapter 13.

Many historians like Abrahamian conclude that the Iranian State's recurrent problem of tribalism *caused* its indeterminate form (1973); in contrast, our analysis considers the persistence of such political diversity through millennia a *symptom* or *consequence* of the Persian State's lack of corporate integrity, evidence that the State never incorporated its social base into an organic political system.

In this study, when the villagers or new townsmen were successfully eluded by the Pahlavi State in their efforts to find or deal with it, they were encountering not a corporate entity's integral resolve against attackers but rather the State's ancient formlessness. When *dulat* extended its jurisdiction into every detail of life in Bizhan, this reflected its rejection of a charter for itself, with boundaries. When it told the workers demanding flour that a group of citizens could never negotiate with the State face to face, it expressed its inability to appoint an accountable institutional representative as all villages and even families could do. (In these basic ways the social organization of an Iranian mosque mirrored *dulat* itself.) Muhammad Reza's wife learned that no one could hold *dulat* responsible. It is no wonder that the workers' fantasies about the exact, visible setting in which the King lived, about communicating directly to him, and about his singularly directed power (even potential cruelty) focused on their longing that the State possess a corporeal and responsible center that would hold, and the the polity comprise a coherent system of governance.

Nor did *dulat* in its amorphousness manifest consistency through successive events—unity through time. For instance, although legalistic obsession pervaded the Ministry's housing policy for the *shahrak,* allowing no buying, selling, renting, exchanging, or alteration in assigned lots,

*I am grateful to Professor Richard Frye for many of these points and for discussing them with me.

and no resident outsiders, *dulat* gave a house lot with piped water, subsidized electricity, a special building loan, and a bakery license, which new townsmen themselves had wanted, to Mash-hadi Hosein from Dezful—far beyond the simple requests which widows from expropriated villages had made. *Dulat* did this solely out of the engineers' petty self-interest. Personalism and favoritism preclude predictability or systemic internal organization.

While the villagers of Rahmat Abad recognized contradictions between various ministries with which they dealt, their relative remoteness from the State and their collective efforts to stand off against it enabled them to project onto *dulat* the consistency of their own corporate polity. Above all, the villagers could reduce the State and the King each to a unitary simplicity because in their self-confidence they assumed that they could meet both eye to eye. In contrast, the new townsmen, engulfed in *dulat's* power, had no sense of being able to fathom it, and they often attributed their same confusion to the Shah (whose character they therefore found convoluted and fragmentary). Their dependence psychologically confirmed their empirical experience of *dulat's* incoherence. On the one hand, the State gave them whatever they needed, and on the other hand, it physically disappeared in the face of any initiative of theirs—in both cases depriving them of any challenge against which they could extricate their own separate autonomy from the matrix of *dulat's* omnipotence.

Ultimately, both empirically and, to the workers, subjectively, what deprived the State of corporate integrity was its sheer power. In Bizhan the Ministry could (and it reminded new townsmen that it could) "bulldoze down" any home it wanted to, whereas in Rahmat Abad "for fear of the dogs" Musa felt he needed permission even to enter a compound. In Bizhan the very proximity of family members to one another *derived from dulat*, and on a whim Sultan 'Ali could deprive a family of its livelihood. Such raw power over the elementary needs of life had not even a remote equivalent in Rahmat Abad's politics of persuasion and prestige; it even dwarfed what power the landlord had had. Unanswerable, power in the model town had become unbounded, and hence those who wielded it, detached from any social framework.

While it was the heroic figures of 'Ali and Hosein who focused the villagers' religious imagination in Rahmat Abad, before I moved to Bizhan I could learn little about the Shi'ites' belief in the Twelfth Imam. In contrast, many of the workers were eager to tell me about this central figure of Shi'ism, its savior, who unlike the Prophet is still alive as their divinely directed leader—although over a thousand years ago (A.D. 872) he went into hiding and has rarely been seen since. According to the model townsmen, no one knows where or how to reach the Twelfth Imam; but in an uncanny suggestion of *dulat* itself, at any time he will appear and demand extraordinary sacrifices of all, which will transform the world according to the divine plan. He might come to one's house as a passing stranger asking for tea, confirming momentarily that he is alive although normally invisible, unknowable. Shi'ites' guide to the hereafter, he is not subject to a believer's petition. Like his secular counterpart *dulat,* Iranians' spiritual immanence is ultimate everywhere, and at the same time, intangible.

Just as the Twelfth Imam, key to truth and the Shi'ites' conclusive authority, deliberately conceals himself from his followers, similarly the workers' all-powerful King could be reached only through telegraphic code. The angry urban mob could only lock itself inside *bast* to keep its protests beyond its ruler and its ruler walled off from it. The urban society that Iran's model town embraced was divided into two realms, public and private, the streets and behind closed doors, *dulat's* domain and society's, form versus the substance of everyday life. The State in which this culture culminated lacked corporate integrity primarily because it divided rather than integrated the society it sought to govern. A no man's land separated this society's two worlds. Shahtela could not cross it to find her deceased husband, *dulat's* employee and patient. Hamda could not cross it to learn why the holes were drilled at the edge of Rahmat Abad. Lilienthal could not cross it to see villagers in the "wasteland" around him. *Dulat* could not cross it into Sultan 'Ali's Qur'anic study group, at home. To the Ministry, walls built around the house lot "clutter" would restore the *shahrak* to order.

In Bizhan and even in Rahmat Abad, the Iranian State would not recognize officially (and, in time, not even unofficially) society's everyday world, which, whenever *dulat* was present, moved into the privacy behind closed doors. *Dulat* believed that only the street-appearance world existed, which it could control and which came to acquire its symbols that became real in its terms—a world that finally became utterly detached from everyday life of society itself. Thus *dulat* acclaimed Mehrabani's yellow mailbox seen from the roadside as service to an illiterate village. Because of cobwebs in the classroom, it punished the teacher whose students excelled on national exams, while rewarding the one who gave fifty reading certificates to peasants protesting they still couldn't read. Fiat breathed truth into *dulat's* street appearance world: raising Bizhan's health standards by shiny laboratories never allowed to open, paying workers generously by television announcements their actual wages belied, giving new townsmen vegetable gardens with no water for growing vegetables, modernizing the countryside by abolishing mud villages the Shah might pass by. Safiabad showed the present and future Khuzestan how to feed itself from air-conditioned barns where Brown Swiss cows produced butter for hotels in Tehran. As fiat's parade of symbolic enactments took over and became the real world, fiat simultaneously denied the existence of whatever diverged from its form, freezing the *shahrak* on its blueprint with its little toy lanes and unpeopled house rows.

It was not just the State that lived within *dulat's* world of street-appearance truth; in times others became acculturated also. An urban mullah from Qum under whom I was learning about Islam told me I had to call myself by an Islamic name as initial preparation for possible conversion, so from then on my name was Ma'sumeh. Many of the *shahrak* workers were thrilled and switched to calling me Ma'sumeh. When I visited Rahmat Abad I asked villagers there to do the same, explaining why. Most found it funny; some grew angry: "But you're Greeeis!" the children shouted; "changing your name won't do a thing!" The adults scolded me for believing that attaining a pure heart had anything to do with one's name. A pure heart, after all, was what Islam was all about. Apparently they didn't understand fiat and the dominant reality of form.

The State's first step in splitting its domain of power and form from society's everyday world was not to recognize the substance of the workers' life in the *shahrak*. Next, in place of that substantial life, it endowed the Plan's own forms with truth through a sheer act of its will. Finally, it confirmed the no man's land between *dulat*'s public and the life of society it had driven into privacy: between form and the substantive irregular bustle of everyday life, between fiat from above and reality as it continued being lived "on the ground." Rahmat Abad still kept a tenuous flow between the two worlds, because the village retained control over itself, and *dulat* was a visitor. In Bizhan the interface hardened, the worlds drew apart, the channels between them closed. Occasionally in the model town, *dulat* communicated downward through intimidation or command (although even that, much more rarely than it interacted with Rahmat Abad). But never did society communicate upward into its own governance and never did *dulat* enter behind society's walls. To the contrary, the State resented and even feared that everyday reality might impinge on the Plan's form: women needing more water faucets or men dying on the job. By ruling the *shahrak*'s public arena, the State destroyed that public and lost access, too, to the private world into which the model townsmen retreated, taking with them the substance of life.

Whereas Rahmat Abad would rather slow its economic development lest the top and bottom of its corporate polity drift apart from each other, in Bizhan *dulat affirmed* this split, unchallenged and now unfettered. Periodically the State's officials performed their own little *bast* in the *shahrak*'s paradise orchard, happy that the Plan had created harmony and plenty by (as one said to me) pruning overgrowth here and there so that nature herself would bring forth greater luxuriance.

Middle-Range Structures

In considering the radical transformation of the Dez, we continually find ourselves returning to examine the middle range of society between the individual (or between the village) and society at large. On the one hand, these middle-range structures appear of salient importance because their weakness or absence defines the split between everyday life at the bottom of society and formal law at the top; on the other hand, their vitality becomes crucial in the expansion of grass-roots initiatives upward into provincial or national life, and in local efforts to hold political power accountable. Again and again the social fabric—or its absence, the "wasteland"—between the micro- and macrolevels proves determinative to society's vertical integration, compromise, feedback, and accountability, to local expansion and autonomy, in the development of the Dez.

As we saw in the preceding chapter, it was, after all, this middle range of provincial and rural society that the State had to abolish before it could successfully fragment the rural population at the base, whether that population lived in Bizhan or Rahmat Abad.

Before we examine further within Bizhan's relations with *dulat* the radical dichotomy between the State and the new townsmen, let us backtrack to trace how in years preceding the construction of Bizhan the State had already eliminated major potential buffers or intermediate focal points above the village level, and how it planned to maintain that vacuum in the coming years. We attributed some of Rahmat Abad's strength in defending itself against the State to the layers of governance as well as protection above it, such as the tribes that Reza Shah had first to eliminate in order to lay claim to rural Khuzestan, then the former community of landlords in Dezful town that the State next undermined, then the intervillage region around Rahmat Abad that we saw *dulat* beginning to threaten (for instance, in Dubendar). What happened to these and other protections above Bizhan that might have forestalled or at least minimized both the social fragmentation we have been describing, and the splitting of all society into the workers' realm and that of the State?

As we can recall, Lilienthal originally proposed the Tennessee Valley Authority as the Shah's model for the Khuzestan Water and Power Authority (KWPA), which was incorporated as a semiautonomous entity to direct the Dez Scheme under the guise of the then-popular concept of "regional development." In Western terms, establishing an independent agency would assure its responsiveness to local interests, needs, and resources by locating its direction at the subprovincial level. But since the KWPA remained subject to The Plan Organization and to Tehran's Ministry of Water and Power, giving it such power effectively liquidated the leverage of all other ministries working within the Dez region, placing everything in the project area directly under a few individuals in Tehran. Even Mr. Lilienthal's company's operations were directed from Tehran. Thus the very creation of this specially centralized and powerful agency precluded the *shahrak* workers' strategies for holding the Ministry accountable, or even for playing rival government bureaus off against one another to their own advantage, as Rahmat Abad sometimes did. In the diversity of local bureaucracies the local population might have been able to buffer itself from the State's power (*upward* divide-and-rule) and might have put the project to work for local interests. As early as 1965, a team from the University of Tehran protested the disappearance of every vestige of "regional" relevance, participation, or local "authority" (*Tahqiqat-e-Eqtesadi,* 1965:167–73).

Years before the Dez Project had been launched, an association of provincial entrepreneurs had proposed to the Shah that a fraction of the returns from Khuzestan's oil revenues be plowed back into regional development through a participatory, public organization. In my interviews with former Minister Ebtehaj, head of The Plan Organization at the inception of the Dez Scheme, he partly attributed to this provincial initiative the Shah's invitation to Lilienthal, since the articulation of distinct local interests, hence a local group apart from all-embracing *dulat,* alarmed His Imperial Majesty. Indeed, the Minister found it preposterous that after the Shah's father had "given his life" to eradicate all groups standing between the State and the population he set out to rule, a regional center for self-development should be proposed! The King answered the Khuzestani group by creating the KWPA—firmly under the control of the Plan.

When KWPA personnel discussed the *shahraks'* future governance, they outlined how they would push this erosion farther. While the Ministry was willing eventually to concede control over primary education, health care, and maintenance of the *shahrak* public works (after all, it *was* the Ministry of *Water and Power!*), never in the foreseeable future would it give up control over labor, technical or secondary education, the *shahrak's* water supply, the urban institutions allowed in the *shahrak,* the agribusinesses, or its strong supervisory role in Bizhan's judicial affairs: matters it found most "efficiently" managed when "integrated" under its own control. The possibility of subjecting any of these functions to popular review was unthinkable—least of all, subjecting the "regional" agency of KWPA to regional review.

The goverance of Bizhan, then, reported directly to Tehran, bypassing even the civil service, which descended in line of command through the governor. The *shahrak* was allowed no horizontal relationship with other *shahrak*s—such as a confederation—or with other regional towns (as villages near Rahmat Abad were forging around it). Nor did the *shahrak* as an institution have any formal or informal dealings with the agribusinesses whose "labor" it provided, as company towns do elsewhere in the world, which might have led to its articulation at least as a dormitory unit and might even have evolved a public arena of discourse between the companies and model towns. Other lateral associations were discouraged: The *shahrak* baker was forbidden to join the urban bakers' cooperative, and transportation links with Dezful were kept weak. The workers' ties to the wealthy of Dezful through landlords or traders (with whom as villagers—increasingly after land reform—they had developed strong relationships) disintegrated when they moved to Bizhan and had nothing to sell, little enough means even for buying. The Ministry's prohibitions against Dezful entrepreneurs conducting business in the *shahrak* prevented new associations. Because the semiskilled jobs at the agribusinesses went to Dezfullis, there was little social mingling among workers from the *shahrak* and those from Dezful, so the former could not establish new urban links. Even when the companies began forming horizontal ties among themselves for their common interests, they had to do so discreetly.

In short, with no institutional channels among the *shahrak*s, or between them and their agribusinesses, other potentially influential ministries, regional politicians (nominal or real ones, such as former tribal leaders), Dezful elites, former landlords, local or regional businessmen; with initiatives kept at a minimum in Bizhan so that no one would reach out to form such links; with no recognized associations bringing the companies together with each other or with regional politicians or entrepreneurs (whom workers could have then approached); with provincial civic leaders completely pre-empted by Iran's "TVA"; and with all fruits of the Dez Scheme, all products, personnel (the technocrats themselves), income and savings, even innovative ideas flowing straight to Tehran, the State had cleared the provincial social landscape of any potential middle-range structures obstructing its downward command.

And, as we suggested in the introduction to this chapter, the unchecked power of this downward command brought forth two irreconcilably separate domains within the State's polity in Bizhan, the public world *dulat* claimed and the private, customary world of the workers' everyday life. Let us now examine this dualism.

Dulat, Property, and the Middle Class: Haji Safar's Store

One day in July, Haji Safar opened a beautiful store right on Bizhan's main circle at the entrance to *shahrak.* When his son pushed up the corrugated metal doors in the morning, the sun flooded in on two large rooms with concrete floors and the best of roofing—just like Dezful!— displaying a wonderful array of every possible thing one might want to buy: groceries, cookies and candy, medicines and ointment, kerosene, household necessities from buttons to tea kettles, plastic toys, T shirts, and hanging from the ceiling, brightly patterned plastic trays and multi-striped foam-rubber mattresses! Watermelons! What was more, the prices were no higher than those in Dezful. Haji told everyone who came that he was ready to stock whatever the new townsmen suggested and needed. What a social event! No other *shahrak* could claim such a store, so many things available right at hand.

The following day the Ministry of Water and Power entered the store, ordered it closed, and vowed *dulat* would bulldoze it to the ground. The State had not given Haji permission for a store. The *shahrak* belonged to *dulat* and not Haji. The Plan outlawed stores. Where did Haji get the idea that workers could clutter up Bizhan with *stores?*

Haji was stunned. He had expected to have to pay taxes or bribes, but he had never anticipated such an attack. Three years previously he had written the Ministry for permission to build and open his store, but never receiving an answer he had assumed unwritten permission (the common green light from cowardly bureaucrats).

Presumably because he knew the officials personally, he tried to reason with them despite their anger. It was his land, after all, to do with it what he wanted, as he had fully paid for it. Anyway, what was the *harm* to anyone in his opening a store? His prices were reasonable, and Bizhan needed stores: Indeed, even before moving to the *shahrak* villagers had requested that it include a bazaar, which they would need when they no longer had their own fields. The authorities acknowledged Haji's leadership in the *shahrak: all the more* reason he could not be allowed to set a pattern that others might follow. As for the land, it was not his. "Yes, you paid in full for your house and lot, but that doesn't make them *yours*. They belong to the State; you and everyone else have merely paid eternal rent for their use. The State *allows* you to live here, that's all." Finally, the Ministry countered that it was not up to Haji or residents of Bizhan to decide whether stores were harmful to them. It was up to the Plan, which forbade stores.

In the end Haji agreed to remove all his stock except the most basic goods like sugar and tea, to close one room entirely, to conduct business only during conventional store hours, to agree publicly that the Ministry was right, and to do nothing else of the kind: not to expand, not to build more, open more, invest more, or think up any other plans. "*Padar sukhtah!*—may its father burn in hell!" he cursed. "*Dulat padar nadarad,*" a little boy standing by corrected him: "The State has no father."

The incident puzzled me. After five years finally here was a *shahrak* leader taking the initiative to invest in Bizhan rather than in Dezful land speculation: a full-fledged and enterprising public confirmation of his confidence and commitment. In contrast to *dulat*'s exhibitionist welfare buildings, Haji was bringing the place alive, making it the workers' own town; roots were beginning to take hold, a bustle and promise laying some basis for permanence. Maybe someone would give him competition. Maybe *sharik*s would flourish again. Of all people, Haji would set a standard of honesty and service, having been such a highly respected leader region-wide, and so many Bizhan workers having leverage over him (his prestige resting on social approval and not, like Sultan 'Ali's, on power). Like Haji, I couldn't see any *harm* in stores.

I sought out the Ministry officials who had condemned the store. Two of them cursed nervy model townsmen. If the State had explicitly outlawed stores, I asked, why hadn't it answered Haji's request? "Because The Plan Organization in Tehran has to do that," they replied; "but anyway, his request mocked the law. All workers knew stores were forbidden. The *shahrak* must conform to the Plan." When I guessed aloud that maybe Haji and others considered it unreasonable to ban stores, the engineers elaborated.

In the first place, stores *are* harmful. Workers should be saving their money in banks. Haji should become a worker and not a bazaar merchant, the likes of which Iran has a surfeit of already. "It's our responsibility to protect the workers from commercialism and urban exploitation; they should be working for the development of Iranian agriculture," *dulat's* official stated.

In the second place, his assistant added, the case presents a very delicate problem for us. All rural workers' towns in Iran are going to be built on this model, so what we allow will set a precedent. "If we let stores crop up here, they might start appearing throughout the entire countryside," the assistant went on, adding that then *dulat* might not be able to stop them! "Now is the time to decide whether to have them or not, and that is the responsibility of the Plan in Tehran. Workers opening stores could easily get out of hand."

With a bit of caution, I brought up the matter of already existing stores in the *shahrak,* not wanting to implicate anyone. Was it realistic to think that with several thousand people that far from town some stores wouldn't inevitably sprout up? I had in mind the many Mom and Pop back room stores I knew in Bizhan, including a meat shop, small workrooms doing bike repairs, a seamstress, a welder, a furniture maker. These were all illegal, as the after-hours electricians and bricklayers probably were. But life goes on, whether the State accepts it or not. The engineers admitted knowing that Bizhan carried on entrepreneurial and commercial life in secret. Although the Plan prohibited *all* stores, those in the back rooms they found "natural." Commercial life is "inevitable," they agreed, in a settlement the size of Bizhan; "but it shouldn't be seen from the street. What we cannot tolerate is a *public* store," they explained.

Finally, the technocrats clarified that stores belong in cities. The *shahrak*s were not urban and the Plan gave strict orders that they not become urban. They would never even be allowed to qualify for the status of "town." These were the reasons the engineers offered for the ban on stores.

In order to prevent the accumulation of private or tribal wealth, or the strength of intermediate buffer groups, ever since the most ancient times Middle Eastern states (in our own century, the Ottoman State) have claimed ownership over all land, called *miri,* including the right to demolish buildings erected without the State's permission (Baer, 1966:85). The Iranian State had reasserted these claims, initially in land reform and subsequently in laying waste to the homes and farms across the landscape, then leasing out the vast countryside to foreigners completely at its discretion and on its terms. The peasants of Rahmat Abad would not have been surprised by an official telling them that workers had merely given "eternal rent, paid up" for their homes in the *shahrak.*

My wise friend Muhammad once said the two words "the State" and "the land" meant the same thing, unable to grasp how America could have a *dulat* that didn't claim all land. The villagers often predicted that regardless of its agreements, *dulat* would and could throw out the foreign companies whenever it wished, knowing no rules of *sharik*. (Like Allah, it could have no "partner," no equal). In Haji Safar's case, his initiative suggested publicly an alternative to total State control: a local claim. Hence, he challenged the very foundation of *dulat*'s arbitrary power. His conspicuous investment—of a popular leader, and right on the model town's main circle—far more seriously threatened the State's claim on all property than did private exchanges in the workers' back rooms.

A natural tension underlies any relationship between a centralized, authoritarian State and the marketplace, which Haji Safar was publicly introducing into *dulat*'s model town. Understandably, in Persian history the bazaar is frequently hostile to the State, an enmity that is mutual (and was central to the 1979 revolution). The intense give-and-take of the market invariably brings forth a public arena among those engaging in its interaction and exchange, whereas *dulat* systematically *demolished* every public arena in Bizhan. As it showed by its omission of any bazaar area from its plans for the *shahrak* (despite the villagers' explicit request for a bazaar before they moved in), the State hoped to create in Bizhan a town-sized, "consolidated," State-run settlement *without a market,* as its model for all rural Iran of the future.

Like the house-lot "clutter," the institutionalized dickering, bargaining, and risk of the bazaar violated *dulat*'s craving for neatness in pristine rows. Furthermore, any initiative from within society itself, not of *dulat*'s instigation but a spontaneous expression of autonomy at the base of society, the State had come to see as competition to its authority. In this sense Haji's store was my neighbor's hump in the road poured in concrete, and for all to behold. *Dulat*'s engineer on the spot worried that if permitted (and all the more so, if allowed to be *rewarded!*) such initiative taking might catch on and "get out of hand!" Batul told me a Dezful bazaar proverb, "The more the tree bears fruit, the more it will get bent to the ground."

The State also had to suppress Haji's enterprise because into the *shahrak*'s public domain, right at the model town's entrance, he had planted what *dulat* interpreted as a visible symbol of acquisitive wealth. A regime so profoundly reliant on public symbols for its own power (cobwebs, Safiabad's gamboling lambs, the Persepolis coronation, the little "poorhouse" cubicles all lined up, jets on television)—a regime so reliant on *form* as distinct from social processes or the substance of daily life could hardly be expected to consider Haji's store in terms of "development economics" or "individual freedom." To the contrary, the State appraised the store in the coinage it knew. All those material goods and the building itself, not shoddy but substantial, spelled the outcropping of wealth that would produce more wealth that—in *dulat*'s domain—necessarily meant domination. That, on the landscape of the DIP, the State had to nip in the bud.

Dulat did not oppose wealth per se. It opposed publicly visible wealth and the wealth of a middle class, independent of the State. Haji transgressed on both counts.

As for wealth per se, *dulat* never attempted to take the model townsmen's hoarded gold bracelets, or their titles to land in Dezful, just as it never threatened the rich who secluded their beautiful homes in North Tehran. Indeed, it was rather proud of the workers' refrigerators inside their houses until television antennae appeared and Sultan 'Ali's brother bought a secondhand car that he parked on the street. What the State feared was the conversion of wealth into political influence, which could be done only by bringing it into the public arena and making it a visible symbol. Not that any political life at all was possible in Bizhan, but to maintain it that way *dulat* kept up the alert for any public signs of a worker's individual prosperity.

Political ambition did not constitute Haji's principal motivation in opening his store; he told me he had finally sold the last of his sheep and was looking for a simple, convenient way to put his returns to work for him. But by 1974 *dulat* saw everything that took place in public in Bizhan as a ritual enactment of power in its own mode. The location of an enterprise "in the back room" limited the potential scope of its activity. More fundamentally, in *dulat*'s terms a back-room enterprise's lack of visibility deprived it of the symbolic political value available to any enterprise within the public domain. It was this infusion—fiat's infusion—of power and truth into public symbols (a power and truth *dulat* denied to *substantive* processes or structures) that led the State to discount Sultan 'Ali as an opponent once he stopped sponsoring prayer tents in the street during Moharram.

Finally, *dulat*'s suppression of Haji's store derived from its fear—well founded, again, in historical experience—that Bizhan might develop a middle-class "element," precisely what loomed darkly in Haji Safar's bourgeois initiative and bourgeois claim to property. The petty proprietors of urban Iran affirmed *values* unacceptable to the autocratic State; but even more threatening, once let alone to interact they brought forth bazaar associations and crisscross linkings that began to fuse into *a horizontal social plane between the top and bottom of society*. The danger which these aggregations in the intermediate-level social field posed was that although still without effective structure, they needed impersonal law, predictability, and fairness. Through their rudimentary coming-together they affirmed some sense of moral cohesion in the urban setting.

The Plan could not let this complex of social traits, expectations, and intermediate-range associations "crop up" in its model towns, within the no man's land it had so assiduously created between the State and the fragmented population it ruled. It was out of this antipathy to the entrepreneurial middle class that at the same time the State prevented outside workers from moving into Bizhan it urged the companies to hire all skilled labor from outside the *shahrak* (although several wanted to keep promoting *shahrak* boys). Similarly, in those cases of visible enterprise that *dulat* did allow in Bizhan—the bakers and the motorcycle repair shop—it established *outsiders* dependent upon its license rather than permit workers' enterprises to spring up in their own home town, "seen from the street." (Thus, too, *dulat* had sought foreign agribusiness companies rather than encouraging Khuzestani or other Iranian entrepreneurs. The former were far more vulnerable to the State's power, and not interconnected locally. As foreigners, they would minimize the likelihood that local people might want to imitate their example.)

Suspicious—indeed, jealous—of the middle class that Haji might be introducing to the *shahrak,* the Plan had explicitly ordained its model towns to be aggregations of the lower class. None of the three rural settlement models that we reviewed in the introduction and that would comprehend the total rural population of Iran was to be allowed middle-class amenities such as sewage or garbage collection, standard high schools, running water in the homes, street addresses, traffic, or a bazaar. The State had established strict regulations that no *shahrak* expand over 4,500 people: A population of 5,000 defined a town, which had its own government-appointed mayor, whereas eventually the Ministry of the Interior, *not* a mayor, would administer all *shahrak*s. (The Shah had decreed that all mayors had to have college degrees: The technocrats vowed that "no one from a *shahrak* will ever attain that—and if he does, he won't stay in the *shahrak*.") As we saw in Chapter 7, Bizhan was frozen exactly the way the Plan had planned.

Indeed, the official town planners who designed the *shahrak*s emphasized to me that in the future those people in Bizhan who might accumulate some wealth would be required to move to Dezful ("the *bright* workers will be transplanted"), preventing a middle class from "cropping up"; *dulat* would give *their* homes to members of the urban proletariat whom it would select, a process that mirrored the shuffling of houses according to rank in the technocrats' compound. "In that way we will keep Iran's towns for the middle class and the *shahrak*s as rural 'holding stations' for the poor," one planner said. (The technocrats and rich, of course, would live in their own compounds.) This would keep the *shahrak*s at the mercy of the agribusinesses, which, in turn, would assure no middle-class emergence. If the nation-wide program could not limit the size of Iran's middle class, at least it could keep the middle class from "spreading out into the countryside." Above all, it would keep each category in its place.

When I considered the planners' and engineers' hatred toward entrepreneurial "upstarts" like Haji, at first their determination to keep these innovators individually and collectively in their place seemed bitterly hypocritical. All of the technocrats ran businesses from their Ministry offices using *dulat*'s vehicles, separate telephone system, and other official facilities, not to mention the large part of each day's time some spent on making money for themselves. Safiabad was hardly anything but a business. One engineer in charge of Bizhan managed four of his family firms from his Ministry office. Another was said to have a private finance company lending out DIP funds. If this was the pattern in small-time Dezful, one need only imagine what the planners who laid down these rules in Tehran enjoyed, where *dulat* as well as the wealthy concentrated. And these were the men who outlawed Haji's selling Nescafe and plastic toys?! But as I discussed Haji's case with them, I realized that as part of *dulat* they drew distinctions about entrepreneurial initiative that I myself had yet to learn—for instance, the one we have discussed between public and "back room" enterprises.

The engineers confirmed another important distinction that Haji himself had emphasized in his analysis: the difference between on the one hand, State officials with many profitable side businesses, who ultimately depended on *dulat* for their bottom-line economic security (as well as for a politically advantageous base of operation); and on the other hand, "independent" entrepreneurs who did not rely on *dulat's* "cushion." The former, just like the bakers and repair shop owner in Bizhan, posed little threat to the State. Their private flowerings grew out of their official position, "like grafting a fruit-bearing branch onto a tree which no longer bears!" one engineer joked. Furthermore, by the very power that their positions within *dulat* gave them, most of these men remained somewhat isolated from the non*dulat* bourgeoisie, at least in the province. In short, in a crisis the State's men who were *sideline* entrepreneurs might well find themselves with opposite sympathies from the "risk-bearing" or "secular" businessmen.

Whatever I thought of the distinctions the technocrat-businessmen enforced, far from being idiosyncratic, they had solid *political* foundations. Just as one had to distinguish street-appearance from back room wealth, one also had to differentiate entrepreneurs based firmly in the State from the independent urban bazaar that implicitly challenged the State's all-consuming power. The model town could have back room stores and stores dependent on *dulat*. But when Haji, a leader with his roots in the traditional villages and not beholden to *dulat,* could launch a store in public, on his own effort and resources, Muhandis exclaimed, "It could be terrible, if we let such a thing get started!"

The Technocrat Class

These differences the technocrats comprehended instinctively. Entrenching *dulat* was their profession; they were its "engineers." As such they constructed and maintained that crucial no man's land which separated the form from the substance of society in Bizhan, separated the Plan and its blueprint from real life. They guarded that no man's land which preserved the law forbidding stores from all the little stores that flourished. It was the technocrats' job to keep the Plan's public landscape free from local aggregations or clumpings: to keep its roads clear of worker-made humps, to keep investors in their back rooms not overflowing outside, to make sure anyone complaining did so *teke-teke,* one by one. Standing on the edge between fiat's increasingly imaginary world and real life in Bizhan, the technocrats perceived that to hold the line they were appointed to hold, they had to suppress bourgeois "outcroppings" like Haji's.

Antipathy for *dulat*'s "engineers" (a category that in the popular mind included Iranian technocrats in the agribusinesses) was something that almost everyone I knew in northern Khuzestan shared, except the engineers themselves: The agribusiness owners, foreign experts and managers, virtually all workers, the villagers still with their land, the Dezful bazaar, the clergy during Moharram, even ordinary bureaucrats disliked *dulat*'s "engineers." Everyone in the *shahrak* world including the engineers agreed that the latter constituted the only real "class" in local society (although the term itself is mine).

From society's perspective, the engineers defined themselves by their wealth, power, and unredeemable corruption. Most people dated the rise of the engineer class from land reform, which ended the traditional order. Many *shahrak* workers believed that after land reform, the King had to give Iran's land over to foreigners in order to protect Iran and its people from the country's own engineers who moved in to take it over. Despite this hatred of the technocrats, all ambitious fathers wanted their sons to become *dulat*'s engineers.

The engineers, too, saw themselves as a class. When younger and more idealistic (not so long before), some of the most prominent among them had run the DIP village extension program, and in that work had determined to prove that the small farmer could feed Iran. In those years they had found themselves on the *solicitous* end of the relationship with the peasants, a dependence they did not forget later. They recounted how they had given totally of themselves for the thankless, lazy villagers who had failed to meet the challenge; if the peasants had obeyed them, they could have achieved more than even the agribusinesses. (These engineers could not perceive that the State had betrayed them and the peasants, jointly.) To them, the luxuries of *dulat*'s compound, hardly a substitute for life in Tehran, constituted stark compensation for the personal sacrifice they continued to make for the undeserving masses. Those engineers who were religious identified with Hosein's martyrdom, just as the workers in Bizhan did!

The engineers, too, had concluded that the agribusinesses had been the only answer. After all, the companies increased the engineers' power immensely while freeing them from any objectively defined responsibility. Even though the technocrats now had the peasants where they wanted them, utterly under their control, they still despised and feared the peasantry. Their stories about the villagers' filth and dishonesty and murderous bent they now transposed to the vacuous rows of little brick "units" in Bizhan—perhaps as part of their task, maintaining the no man's land.

Like Roman sentries, then, the Dez technocrats glared at the Picts over the wall they held firmly. But unlike the planners who commanded their legion from Tehran, they could dimly peer beyond the no man's land they defended, into the *shahrak's* back rooms. There they perceived—at times, at least—that the Ministry's $3 per day advertisement to the King did not make it a fact, that Muhammad Reza had no congenital disease but died on the job lifting cement for *dulat,* that there really were stores out there where the State forbade them. These men would not have called fiat a sham, but unlike Tehran they knew the blueprint was inhabited, and that the Plan's new world had yet to come to pass in Bizhan.

The State's Polity in Bizhan: Two Irreconcilable Domains

The centralized, authoritarian system that the Dez Scheme reified sundered social fact from political or legal fact, splitting the *shahrak*'s would-be polity into two worlds that we mentioned earlier and to which we now return. For example, although it was natural for people in a town to have stores, and although it was inevitable for them to have their mosque (social facts—what people really did in society), the Plan planned neither, allowed neither, forbade Haji's store, and refused to attend—hence officially to recognize—the mosque's dedication, denying political and legal reality to both the store and the mosque. Whatever the State did not see or recognize did not exist in its realm of reality. Within the State's reality were the public baths it showed to foreign visitors weekly, the absence of donkeys in the *shahrak* streets, an abundance of flour during the national wheat shortage, and so forth. Along with Haji's store and the mosque, outlawed from Bizhan's legal and political reality were showers rigged up from the nearby faucets for people's homes, widows arranging to live near their children, death on the job, adobe constructions, and so forth. To the State, these social facts simply did not exist.

From our perspective in Bizhan, institutionalizing such a split could in the last resort buffer social reality from fiat. Although the Pahlavi State laid claim to all life, lacking corporate organization, it could not carry out that claim. In contrast, in penetrating Western "reforms" like the Inquisition or Hitler's Germany, the legal order took the base of society seriously, seeking to ascertain social fact empirically (often by "scientific" extremes) and to make sure it conformed to the State's law. In Bizhan the driven will of the State was satisfied to divide society with a no man's land between the street-appearance world it ruled—form—and the workers' back rooms where life went on as it would.

Since the State endowed the former with truth, this split created of the entire world of events which *dulat* refused to recognize, an underground that in time came to comprise *most* life: all those people or events that gave lie to the Plan or that *dulat* denied. *Dulat*'s pride in its clinic, for instance, made the workers' lack of health services a fact only in the underground; since the Plan provided no growth for the *shahrak,* the town's actual growth also took place only in the underground. When I pushed them, the engineers admitted that having walls built around the house lots would not really get rid of the "litter"—but then again, it would. All that concerned them was restoring the street-appearance world, *dulat*'s law in the *shahrak,* back to what the Plan had ordained. The walls would protect the Plan from ongoing life in the underground.

This split between on the one hand, the institutions, events, and norms accepted by Bizhan society in its everyday interactions, "customary law," and on the other hand, institutions, events, and norms as the Plan proclaimed them to be, the State's law—this split initially derived from *dulat*'s extraordinary confidence that through its will it could *make* the everyday comings and goings of thousands of people the way it said they had to be. In drawing up the Plan, a public symbol of the State's power, and then in destroying the village's traditional order of life on a vast scale to force that order into the Plan's model, the State proved to itself that it could *in fact* and *deed* make society according to its dictates. Its next step, then, was to expunge the dangers and evils it anticipated "cropping up" in its creation, *in advance of their appearing:* that, after all, is the nature of "planning."

In Rahmat Abad, customary law assumed the villagers' basic freedom to do anything each considered reasonable; law became formal or proclaimed only after someone objected to a very specific event that happened. At that time the villagers would deliberate to find out the community's judgment of the case at hand, given its context and the real-life tradeoffs of new restrictions. Perhaps a new, highly specific rule might be born, but it would be narrowly defined to keep the law flexible. For example, the village asked 'Abdul not to play his radio loudly during Moharram, but it did not go so far as to outlaw radios (which some would have liked to do) or to forbid his enjoying it quietly during the holy days, which also met with disapproval. By placing high priority on fundamental freedom and shared values, and by not freezing shared norms into "legal" expression except for specific problems, Rahmat Abad's customary law gave the public arena over to initiative, individual discretion, responsibility, and trust, leaving all rules—when they *were* needed—up to members of the community themselves to articulate. This accounted for the sense of confidence and open space we saw in the village, as well as for its moral cohesion. The specificity of those judgments that were proclaimed usually fine-tuned political and legal fact (the community's official prohibitions) to match social fact—that is, to match what went on in society and what everyone thought was reasonable.

In contrast, in Bizhan, since *dulat*'s unlimited claim to power generalized all people and events into its universal empire (especially as the *shahrak* was meant to fix the entire rural population of Iran); and since everything that existed within its domain became a public symbol of *dulat*'s authority, there could be no trust, no open-ended norms, and no fine-tuning. The State's law had to fill the entire social space. Because with the Plan the State now assumed responsibility not only for everything that actually happened in the *shahrak,* down to my neighbors' little hump, but also for everything that would in the future, *dulat* was haunted by the possibility that anything malevolent which appeared on the landscape might catch on like a disease, spreading throughout the uniform new order that it was leveling society to bring forth. Rahmat Abad's affirmation of freedom and reasonableness, supported by an incremental legal process, was disastrously risky for such all-encompassing political claims. Those very things that everyone was *likely* to do, those activities, norms, and institutions that came most naturally since they solved recurrent problems or filled common needs and therefore seemed reasonable, *these* the Plan feared the most. These would most likely spread—like making stores, or building on one's house lot, or having a mosque, or stealing water for home showers and for vegetable gardens denied to one although being part of the nation's largest irrigation system. It was especially these most natural behaviors, then, that the State had to anticipate and ban in order to keep its domain pure and safe.

Thus whatever the Plan's original mandate had been, in Bizhan it had to write from scratch (as it were) an entire Napoleonic code of law in advance of any wrong being committed—and to do this for a new town experiment in remote rural Khuzestan! Nothing could be allowed to happen until controls against everything that might go wrong were firmly in place. That was why only The Plan Organization in Tehran could approve Haji's store. On the other hand, life does go on and does not wait around for the Plan. And so, two separate worlds emerged.

The process whereby *dulat,* reifying itself in its domain, drove the new townsmen more deeply into theirs, was circular, because as society retreated from the street-appearance world it abdicated responsibility for keeping the State on any predictable course, and left the public arena entirely to *dulat*'s will. Not even the challenge of constructing the *shahrak* mosque could recover a public temporarily in Bizhan. Yet only in a shared public could the two domains have met.

Fiat and the Word

Bolstered by the power of its decree to bring forth what Lilienthal and others considered "real"—erecting the great high dam, removing eyesore poverty from the landscape, bringing thousands of hectares into sugar cane cultivation, and so forth—and perhaps unconsciously aware that *social* reality in the Dez project contradicted its law, the centralized State attempted to enforce its "facts" by giving the formally proclaimed word

a magical significance. Mead called this the power of "a ritual proof."
Villages whose land was expropriated for State farms had to vote in public assembly that they wanted the State to take their land. All bureaucrats
in Dezful and employees at Safiabad had to express in writing their desire
to join the Shah's one political party, which made their support more real
as a political and legal fact. The Shah had a distinguished professor at
Cambridge University write a history of agrarian reform omitting the
name of the minister who implemented it, which made him never to have
existed. According to *dulat,* if a person confessed to something (albeit
under torture), his word made his having done it a fact—all the more
certain a fact if his word was heard in public, on television.

The absolute truth of the officially proclaimed word pervaded that part
of Iranian culture which lay within the State's domain. To the urban
clergy and many new townsmen, my changing my name to Ma'sumeh
made me more of a Muslim. To my friends in the *shahrak* the fact that
the Christian gospels had not been written down as God dictated them
on the spot (which the Qur'an was, like a State proclamation) disproved
Christianity: How absurd to think The Almighty would have entrusted
truth to informal social processes! Tragically, the boy Ahmad's suicide in
Rahmat Abad was caused by some Dezfullis insisting that, by writing
scandal about a kinsman on a piece of paper, he had turned it into truth
(although his uncle in the village pooh-poohed writing on paper as constituting nothing but "mere scribble"). Similarly, urban Muslims often
wore written prayers around their necks as cures; this infuriated a villager
in Rahmat Abad once, who burned one of those fetishes angrily, in front
of everyone. Although Iranian religious art forbids representations of
human figures, the only decoration on the façade of many great shrines
is the written word, emblazoned over every inch of the mosque's street-
front surface. As Rodinson points out (1973:109), townsmen used the
expression "it is written" to mean "God decreed it."

In short, urban culture frequently gave its consent to the underlying
premise of fiat, that the word—the epitome of form—was power. Bearing
in mind Durkheim's insight that when people affirm God they affirm
their community, we can recall here the model townsmen's definition of
Godlessness: using words falsely, lying.

Just as there was no check on the State's perception or definition of
reality, so, too, the threat that fiat might make a word true left the individual model townsman with little ground for confidence about his or her
own cognition. What appeared to be true was often "illegal." The fragmentation of society in Bizhan made the social confirmation of knowledge much more difficult. Maybe in fact Muhammad Reza wasn't lifting
a bag of cement . . . maybe in fact the baker had plenty of flour and was
hoarding it . . . maybe lettuce does poison people (as Safiabad told its
workers to prevent them from stealing it). As this split between the two
separate domains of "fact" penetrated their psychological perceptions of
reality, we can understand how the workers came to believe such preposterous "facts" about me, or their extraordinary estimates of the relative

productivity and costs of the companies' technology, or their political visions.

Since the Plan had no place for individual cases, for the judgment of particular events in their specific contexts, nor for any qualifying circumstances or details—as the widow Sahra learned, as the villages that wanted their own small mosques learned, as the couple "caught" in adultery learned—it necessarily reduced all individuals and events to stereotypes and categories. Not gaining predictability through its arbitrary command, it sought to impose predictability through cognitive uniformity: Living people it saw as interchangeable labor units kept in cubicles to be mass-produced nation-wide. Variety and individuation that ruggedly maintained the stronghold of customary law, to which the State no longer had access. *Dulat*'s homogenizing further threatened the individual's internal bearings. The only solution was to withdraw as much of one's personality as possible from *dulat*'s public domain, even giving the street-appearance world around one's house only the minimum of one's self.

> The structure of a society in which only one person rules while the great mass lets itself be ruled, makes normative sense only by virtue of a specific circumstance: that the mass, the ruled element, injects only *parts* of all the personalities which compose it into the mutual relationship, whereas the ruler contributes *all* of *his* personality. . . . What each [ruled] personality really is does not enter the "mass"; it does not enter that which is actually ruled by the one individual. . . .
>
> More precisely, a group can be dominated by one individual the more easily and radically, the smaller the portion of the total personality [each] member contributes to that mass which is the object of subordination (Simmel, 1950:202–03).

The process Simmel describes precludes moral cohesion between the ruler and the ruled; the latter no longer belong to society.

The Origin of Law in the Particulars

Although the domination of power and command raining down from the ruler onto the ruled essentially accounts for the dualism in Bizhan's society—for the severe split between the public and private worlds, between the State and the workers, between symbolic form and the everyday substance of life, between customary law and official governance—two concomitant aspects of political relations in the model town elaborate this split: first, the failure of *upward* flows of initiative and information, upward from the base of society in Bizhan, to penetrate its "governor"; and second, the absence of confrontation between the top and bottom of society that would lead to the resolution of their frequently recurring differences. Let us look briefly at both.

In his *Elementary Forms of Religious Life,* Durkheim explains the process by which abstraction emerges out of particular and specific details and, similarly, the process by which social cohesion develops out of interaction among society's members (1915: Chapter 7, 481–85). In the same way, law and governance attain generality, predictability, and permanence by fusing at the level of generality the experiences and perceptions of individuals in particular events. Systems theory describes how in organic systems (if not cybernetic ones) the information-processing regulator receives feedback initiated by the lower subsystems, often the production line. It pools this information, abstracting generalities from it, but generalities closely corresponding to the particulars themselves, and then distributes back downward to them common normative statements, "control values": just as we have seen governance in Rahmat Abad do. At a more complex stage the early medieval circuit-riding kings of Europe did just this, *tied to* the local particulars whom they governed because they literally depended on them for their subsistence.

Professor Arensberg (1972) has shown us how in systemic social groups that take on a life of their own the political and legal "governor" who performs the coordinating function is *given forth* in this same dynamic *from among* the linesmen, "work force," or constituent members of the group to synthesize their behavior and the values it reflects by abstracting from them into law. If he is to perform this coordinational function, such a governor must be *subject to* initiative and feedback from society's social base, which often has to correct the center's generalizing or commanding tendencies, bringing their coordinator back into congruence with themselves, the "linesmen." The interactive tension between the particulars and the "governor," and the interdependence of the two for directing society by generalizing from its mainspring of local initiatives, generates law and in the process unifies governor and work force into one society, as we have seen in the community of Rahmat Abad.

In contrast to this dynamic, Bizhan's rule was the product of a single will and its chosen agents, initiated not in the action of the particulars or "linesmen" but at *the top* of society. Since its "governor" was subject to no initiatives or feedback from the particulars, nor to any of their checks on its generalizing command, it could not orchestrate them and itself into a system. Thus it could not give them or allow them to give it stability and predictability. We have seen this in Bizhan's highly arbitrary governance both through time and internally within itself. Nor could its official directives penetrate into the actual workings of the social system they meant to govern.

Even after years of such domination, during my year in Bizhan the social base of the model town was still initiating some action upward that could have been translated into information and feedback into the *shahrak*'s governance: The hump conveyed the experience of traffic problems; the flour demands, of food problems; the many infants' deaths, of the new townsmen's overall health; Muhammad Reza's fate, of general working conditions; the private hoses on street faucets, of new expectations and daring among *shahrak* residents; the mosque construction, of Bizhan's social structure, self-image, and external relations, perhaps even of its spiritual needs; the constant fights among neighbors, of unusual tensions; the many illegal adobe constructions, of the new townsmen's requirements and enterprise. Haji's request for permission to open a store conveyed various "signals" about the *shahrak*'s needs, norms, and "investment climate." Finally, the way the new town celebrated Moharram conveyed clear signs of social disintegration. None of these events fed into the *shahrak*'s coordinating mechanism. Here we mention only "street-appearance" initiatives that still sprang forth from the workers' "back-room" domain for systemic integration, updating, and orchestration, as well as for curbing the overweening central power; had the workers also been able to *speak* into the public arena, their initiatives would have sounded much louder, as they did to me.

Little Rahmat Abad generated far more initiatives upward into its public arena and polity than did all of Bizhan, the village synthesizing these events and changes—sometimes through its judiciary and its Little Parliaments but often just through public interaction. It weighed those that were problematic, crystallizing them in community decisions and sending the system's ongoing customary law back out to the population as a whole.

What was in jeopardy in Iranian urban society when these upward flows of initiatives were blocked from the State's domain was not simply the regime itself (whose overthrow may only have reified the systemic split we have examined), but, more profoundly, the emergence of law. The ruled and rulers of this society were blocked from evolving into a single polity able to benefit from the Rahmat Abads and Bizhans at its base, the latter from an overarching polity, and society's governing mechanism from indispensable initiatives and checks on its arbitrariness.

The difference, then, between Rahmat Abad and Bizhan was that Rahmat Abad was governed by law. Neither fiat nor the Plan is law. In Bizhan the State discounted the ultimate source of law entirely, the particular participants "on the line" at society's foundation: the details, the context, the daily nitty-gritty that society's constituent members define as essential for their action and interaction—*their* reality. Without these particulars law cannot generalize predictable rules and policies. Consequently, according to popular legend, the coordinator would have to disguise himself as the lowest of all the particulars at the base of society, to enter among them and, temporarily at least, see what they were doing and thinking in order to restore its governance.

Dulat's Core Paradigm: Conflict Unresolved

If the failure of upward flows of initiative to penetrate society's governor constituted one aspect of the State's domination in Bizhan, a second elaboration of this domination was the absence of any confrontation between the two domains the *shahrak* comprised. Both sides had institutionalized the no man's land between them; neither possessed the mechanisms, the skills, or even the expectations that might have resolved these profound differences.

Other than the dedication of the mosque, the largest meeting in Bizhan during my year there took place for the Lions Club to distribute new clothes to the poorer children in the school the day before the Persian New Year. The school's board, a purely titular body said to consist of the teachers themselves and four parents, had made up a list of the "poor" children to receive the clothes, even though it had never exercised any function officially and no one knew who the parents on the board were. Of course, those children not receiving new clothes were going to nag their parents until they bought some for them, so the affair created considerable tension throughout the *shahrak*. No one could find out how the list had been drawn up. Many mothers stormed the principal's office demanding to be classified as "poor," and charging that those on the list were in fact just the rich and their relatives (which was not true, on the whole). I had never seen such acerbic expression of mistrust of the State. Most model townsmen believed Our Father with the Crown had sent plenty of gifts for every child—as any father who loved all his children equally—but the engineers had robbed the best clothes to sell to the rich in Dezful, which explained why only a handful was left. Many also believed the Ministry was giving out the new clothes simply because on the Persian New Year it always brought high officials to picnic in Bizhan's orchard, when it wanted them to see well-dressed children at play in the streets.

Due to the controversy and many parents' determination to get new clothes for their children, the ceremony for distributing them was unusually crowded. A representative from the Ministry of Water and Power presided, with officials attending from the Ministry of Education, the office of the King's Imperial civil service, and the Lions Club (which everyone on all sides—the Lions, too—appeared to consider a part of *dulat*).

After the distribution began, a few mothers politely approached those officials standing on the side, offering a list of very poor families who were not on the list. They intended to suggest that if the shirts-and-shorts sets were split, most children could receive one or the other, which they thought would be better for everyone. No sooner had they expressed their thanks to the men and begun to mention their ideas than in three minutes all the officials disappeared—ZAP! Into their cars and away! Everyone! Ministry of Education, King's Imperial Command, Lions, Water and Power—the lot. No explanation (although clearly sparked by the ladies' initiative), no conclusion—the stage was empty and the cars all gone! "Suddenly there was no one there to complain to!" Madar-i-Muhammad recalled. "*Gorukhtand!*—they fled! We ended up with each other!" The parents' angry letter delivered to the Ministry of Education in Dezful never received a reply.

The event recalled a long pattern: Rahmat Abad's hole drillers, its silent protest against the teachers, Haji's attempt to discuss his store plans with *dulat,* the hump, SAVAK's refusal to talk about the flour shortage with the group of workers, the difficulty Muhammad Reza's widow had in even getting the State to acknowledge that it had taken her deceased husband off to Tehran in its ambulance. *Bast,* both sides walled off. The Lions Club incident dramatized the core paradigm underlying all these episodes: avoidance rather than negotiation—consequently, the absence of a joining mechanism between the bottom and top, the work force and governor, within *dulat*'s realm of Iranian society. What Professor Arensberg calls the "minimal sequence" of this paradigm may antedate Islam and *bast:* Rahmat Abad's ability to flee the landlord when differences became extreme, and his willingness to let the villagers walk out—that is, the inability of the base of rural society to bring its governing authority to negotiation.

There was nothing unique to Pahlavi society or to Bizhan about the latent conflict between rulers and ruled, between hierarchical extremes. What *was* notable was the absence of any interdependence between top and bottom, whereby each could confront and make its demands on the other with the assumption that conflict *had* somehow to be resolved through compromise. The law that Durkheim and Professor Arensberg describe emerging out of initiatives from the base of society, its "work force," and then, in turn, governing them by returning coordinational directives back down to them does not preclude sustained and vigorous conflict. To the contrary, such law and the institutions, skills, and norms that constitute it, accessible throughout the social system, provide adversaries (even stratified ones) the channels for conflict *with the expectation that it can be resolved,* a higher order of synthesis emerging out of differences. It is through such "confrontation" that law functions as information processor, coordinator, and as the necessary mechanism for the base of society to check the arbitrary tendencies of society's governor.

The "minimal sequence" of fleeing from conflict—which we have seen in the State's relations to both the villagers of Rahmat Abad and the workers of Bizhan, as well as in Rahmat Abad's relations to its landlord—carries out just the opposite dynamic from that which constitutes the fundamental pattern of Western law. We see this contrasting paradigm reflected perhaps most plainly in the cornerstone of the Western legal tradition, Gratian's *Concordance of Discordant Canons.** In Gratian's volume, the West's first law book, as early as the twelfth century European culture and its institutions even at the social base had raised to the level of conscious awareness the resolution of contradictory laws, which Gratian systematized. In case after case they are juxtaposed and their contradiction openly analyzed. Characteristically, in no case of "discord" that

*For this and much of my understanding about law and Western history, I am deeply indebted to Professor Harold Berman of Emory University.

Gratian reviews does either of the conflicting authorities cancel out the opposite (as fiat and *bast* do). Rather, over and over, each pair of discordant canons combines in a new truth, but that law, in turn, awaits future modification through the open-ended process of new initiatives inevitably arising out of the particulars: a systemic creativity and flexibility rooted in predictability.

This necessary tension between the particulars and their generalizing governor—between the base of society and its coordinational mechanism—continually resolves in the re-creation of law. (In contrast, Islam—ratifying the foundational paradigm of Bizhan's "law"—admits of no possible further revelations, no accretions. The Book, complete, is closed.) The process at work in the concordance of discordant canons brings forth society's single *public* to unite and displace Bizhan's three mutually exclusive realms: *dulat*'s domain, the workers' back rooms, and the no-man's-land between them. It is this public arena, law itself—or the fusion of customary and enacted law—that enables the emergence of Rahmat Abad's corporate and contractual structures. These structures require a public arena because they require social space for organizing and launching their initiatives: each with autonomy and its exclusive body of common affairs. Because their existence depends on their initiating their own projects and programs into a relatively stable public arena, and on exercising their autonomy, such structures could not develop and maintain themselves in the back room domain of Bizhan, nor in its no man's land—certainly not in *dulat*'s street-appearance world. Moreover, without an overarching order, local "platoons" at the base cannot unite with other separate microunits as they seek complementary resources or undertake broader challenges. Hence they also cannot affect a wider part of society beyond themselves. Rahmat Abad discovered this when it attempted to go beyond the intervillage region, and we can imagine the Shell-Cott workers' groups might have found the same if they had tried to confederate into larger unions.

Thwarting the development of cohesive organizations at the base of society in Bizhan rebounded on the State, for without these organizations and the public arena they would have sustained, official law could not find and incorporate the upward feedback that was essential for coordination; without them, too, *dulat* could not possibly keep itself on a steady track for assuring predictability to the local, the regional, or even the national social system.

Dulat's Ideology in Bizhan

Preventing a concordance of discordant canons, a confrontation and merging of customary law with its own official decrees, the Pahlavi State was left without community—indeed, hardly with society—in Bizhan. The ideology *dulat* proclaimed in the Dez Scheme and in Bizhan reflected this void. But more decisively, it reflected the emptiness of its trumpeter, as the State's vision for the Dez Development Scheme profaned the deep moral order it aimed to displace in Rahmat Abad.

A society's past, its accumulated riches that even the poor and the villages can possess, binds it in common experience. In a society with such a profound sense of history as Iran has, the State's ideology in creating Bizhan sprang from rejection of the past. In contrast to Marxist ideology, which confirms and studies the past as a necessary foundation for the future, *dulat* despoiled Iran's past of its communality and transcendence. It came to lay waste the rural order's shared past, the past Rahmat Abad rejuvenated during Moharram, the past that brought villagers like those from Tajeh back to their forefathers' home, the timeless continuities of corporate mourning, the villagers' sense that they were living still in the stories from scripture. The State said explicitly that it had come to destroy the irregularity and variety of communities literally grown close as they aged, clustering through time around a common focal place, their traditional independence in production and governance. (The State had to raze those decrepit old villages of the Dez physically because workers began moving back into them from the *shahrak*s.) In Bizhan's school, *dulat*'s ideology ridiculed tribal clothes and language. When the State recognized the past at all, it did so merely to manipulate it in opportunistic show, as in the Persepolis coronation.

Thus, when *dulat* had to justify *its* moment in history by portraying what it came to vanquish and by promising its future good, it offered the former Throne Cities of the model town its tinny and crass "modernization" as reward for their sacrifice. "Modernization" embodied no moral triumph. The State was saving Iran from its traditional mud alleyways not in order to trample down bad *men* as in Marxism—not even to be saved from *evil*—but to install electricity and cement canals. The State would construct a new Iran not with even a pretense of moral promise but merely to ape the West, pushing machines through the wheat of the Dez. Far from drawing the workers into an identity with this transformation as being theirs or their children's, the State's paean to the behemoth revealed to them the bald truth: They were being used for the Shah's and the capitalists' greed. Cold and bloodless was this World Bank ideology of a "white" revolution. Finally, for its own technocrats *dulat* meshed together a similar pastiche of economics and machismo, a pastiche of symbols extolling scale and expertise.

The State's escatology, revealed periodically in a new Plan, celebrated matter. Society had no depth, no social forces, no struggle. Lilienthal used to ask me again and again whether electric light bulbs didn't redeem the *shahrak*. For instance, *dulat* left land reform for the peasants to see through as nothing but a political strategem; not even in this, its most plausibly "moral" gesture, could it feign concern for the moral order.

It is true that the State urged the workers to put their faith not just in superior foreigners, but also in the King who was good. But since it jealously refused to attribute moral virtue to any other national figure or to any governmental authorities, this reverence for Our Father with the Crown encouraged the workers' deep-seated mistrust of all the country's leaders except him, especially the technocrats into whose hands they had fallen and who transparently reciprocated their detestation. Thus *dulat* never separated itself spiritually from the political intrigue and the seemingly godless drive for money and power the workers knew in the specific. My neighbor in Bizhan, from an Iranian Arab village, often contrasted *dulat* with their *shaykh* of the region—their intervillage political coordinator, their lawmaker and leader, their judge. Their *shaykh* would never accept a single rial for his governance, she said. "How—*whom*—can we follow here?" she would ask; "the State has no great man, living or dead ... but *dulat is* its men."

The State made no place, not even in its rhetoric, for the workers to participate in bringing about their own and their society's radical change. After they had experienced the village polity's self-determination, the model townsmen saw no way they could throw themselves into the modernizers' movement—no party (not in the *shahrak,* at least), no council of model townsmen, no unions or company teams, no women's clubs or youth brigades, no juries or other contributions from the social base into the process of law. The *shahrak* workers had no awareness that they, Bizhan, were setting the pattern of life for half the nation. Unlike Marxism, which proclaims that it is "the people" who fulfill history, the Pahlavi–World Bank development ethos proclaimed the people of Bizhan the State's albatross: It was they who had *set back* Iran. The source of rebirth lay not in Iran's people but in economics and engineering. In money. In foreigners. In power. Far from being the subjects of change as Lenin had said they were, the people of Bizhan were told they were its object—so superfluous that *dulat* had no need even for occasional appointments with them. *Dulat* had no serious interest in shaping men's minds through educational campaigns; such efforts would attribute to the populace a more important role than they merited, and add a moral dimension to the State's development drive. Although Marxism subordinates the individual to the State, at least it recognizes each person's need to think he or she has a place in the social scheme. For its part, *dulat*'s ideology could not so much as acknowledge one's innermost question, "But where am I in all this?"

The modernizers' theory proved false in Bizhan, namely, that by destroying the village groups that encapsulated you, the State would release and gain your allegiance to it. Stripped of their villages, their regions, their *sharik*s, their ethnic identifications, and their other traditional ties, the new townsmen did not commit themselves to the State, nor—despite their dreams of the King—to him. After the clearing away, there was nothing left for them to attach themselves to. Indeed, *dulat*'s ideology for the model townsmen opposed attachment per se. It explicitly opposed links between people who might recognize mutual obligation. By denying Bizhan any initiative or even an administrative category, by denying it inevitable demographic growth, the State made clear that the "labor center" had no end or direction of its own (much less a *life* of its own) apart from the Plan. Nor did any associational group. No communal destiny—local or sweepingly grand—might spur the imagination or fire the spirit of those who lived within Bizhan's house rows to go forth and create their "little platoons." If nothing else, Lenin had called upon class hatred to bind people together. *Dulat* could never admit any collective purpose to bind the people of its model town.

Nor did the State's ideology conceive of any expression of common life that stood above the *shahrak* to which workers could belong, having lost all other public ties. Iran was no *patrie,* no Mother Russia. The Shah and the Plan were constructing the nation; like the "king" who built the holy shrine all by himself, they left no room for others, each to add but his or her single brick. Even Iran's religion, guardian of society's moral principles and moral cohesion, *dulat* constantly insinuated was an obsolete burden of the past. In this the State expressed, as throughout its vision, its own materialist values. The law itself that governed the model town never so much as claimed to derive from God or custom, from precedent, constitution, or even human wisdom, but only from the pragmatic and momentary, from the Plan's *calculation.* Incomprehensible to society, such fields as economics, technology, and banking offer no ideals to live by. *Dulat* repudiated the transcendent. *Dulat's* ideology mirrored that of the World Bank's and the Plan's Dez visionaries and shaped Iran's model town according to their ideals: men—all foreigners to this place and people—who could draw upon no moral imagination within themselves as they transformed the moon. Unlike Shiraz and Isfahan, Herat and Konya and Baghdad, Bizhan would never beget poets or saints. It would be kept from ever recovering Rahmat Abad's *corpus mysticum,* which the State so triumphantly desecrated.

In the most bitter fight I witnessed in Bizhan—between two women, mothers—I heard the chilling curse of the Lurs I had never heard uttered aloud in Rahmat Abad: "May your only son have to die for *dulat!*"

He it is who has created the heavens and the earth in truth; and on the day when He says, "BE," then it is. His word is truth. There is none to change the words of God.

—Qur'an, Sura 6

Chapter 11

The Individual and Bizhan

I am dying of grief in the very midst of redressers of grief, like a ship burning at sea.
—Abu Talib Kalim, from *Shah-Jahan-Nama*

Reversing the sequence in which we discussed the individual in Rahmat Abad, in Bizhan it has been necessary to examine the State before the individual, as, unlike the villager, the model townsman cannot be considered except in the context of *dulat*'s presence. Having ties to no other social unit outside the family, the model townsman could define and understand himself only in terms of the State.

Responsibility and Self-Esteem

In almost every respect, individuals' relationships to their work, their future, and their proximate social order in the model town—hence, to others we depend on to establish our selves—differed from their counterparts' relationships in Rahmat Abad. While Rahmat Abad expected villagers even at a very young age to make a substantial contribution to family life, by their teens considered them fully accountable as adults, and offered adults little safety net should they fail to meet their responsibilities, the State treated new townsmen as children. Taking all responsibility unto itself (after all, it and not the workers destroyed their village economy), *dulat* promised everyone a livelihood, including in fact most of the former landless. But it provided a guarantee of work so demeaning in the unnecessary tasks it assigned, in the condescension of its technocrat managers, and in its alms-like remuneration, that this public dole simply advertised the new townsmen's helplessness, dependence, and infantile incompetence, as though they lived in a nursery. Even at Safiabad, *dulat* never insisted on reliable work from any worker, never fired a worker howsoever careless or lazy he might be; it saw the model townsmen as children not yet come of age. Women were harshly punished for public offenses, but not even the law really held men accountable, suggesting that the State did not grant them full maturity. We see the discrepancy between local standards of responsibility and the standards the

270

State held for the local population, in their contrasting judgments of a murder in a village that was soon to be moved into the *shahrak,* where a young woman was the victim of deliberate and horrifying violence. The State gave the murderer a three-year sentence, while the villagers—who rarely had a murder in their midst even over several consecutive generations—judged what he did so evil, him so culpable, and public morality so inviolable that they demanded he face the firing squad! Workers in Bizhan called the State's treatment of the shocking event "a joke on us."

In Rahmat Abad, too, each individual villager bore *civic* responsibility for the life and conditions of Throne City, whereas in Bizhan *dulat* would not even allow an individual to select his own house location, or build a simple mosque yard with his friends, or make a hump in the road. When the workers came to ask *dulat* for flour, they were told not to stand there in the street and demand it as though they had any right to bread, but first to accept the vulnerability and humility of children and return one by one to their homes without further murmur, then to trust their father to do as he thought best for them. Rarely did the State deign to explain its behavior to any individual (recall Rahmat Abad's holes, Haji's store, or the Ministry's appropriation of the *shahrak* orchard to itself): A child should accept his or her subordinate place without question. The entire land consolidation program in Iran rested on villagers' purported incompetence. Thus while Rahmat Abad's social environment took the individual seriously, and, in turn, he or she gained a deep sense of self-respect and accomplishment, State domination in Bizhan barely acknowledged that the model townsmen were able to assume adult responsibility.

Far from the constant challenge to ingenuity and self-discipline inherent in the *work* each individual had known in the village, which continually tested and proved one's self, most of the model townsmen performed the same rote labor month after month, requiring no intelligence, no initiative, and little alertness, virtually no decisions: loading bundles, picking cotton or beets, watching a shed at night, being a coolie. Irrigation comprised the most demanding job they could get. Safiabad's and the agribusinesses' specialization of labor left most engaging tasks—even those that might call for a couple of weeks of training, and therefore represented some degree of individual accomplishment—to outsiders. The interchangeability of workers, as seen in the fact that most of them moved from one job to another and between companies each season, testified to the repetitiveness of their employment and its lack of any distinguishing requirements, in radical contrast to the complexity and individuality of work that men, women, and children faced in Rahmat Abad. These jobs' impermanence and lack of selectivity also reduced the supervisors' interest in holding accountable those who performed them. Thus, whereas the village economy required people constantly to savor each individual's character and skills, the State expressed the economic fungibility of individuals by the uniformity and anonymity it tried to impose on its labor center.

In many complementary ways the workers' model town and their
employment drove home to individuals that in contrast to life in the village, they no longer had control over their lives. The modern technology
of the farms understandably overwhelmed them, but this was primarily
due to the fact that they were considered incapable of learning to operate
it. When the villagers of Rahmat Abad took a trip to the Dez dam where
they stood at the base of the immense structure, visited the rooms of
complicated machinery, and learned about the electricity it generated for
factories as far away as Abadan, what impressed them the most was the
size of the fish they could see in the lake! I chided them later for not
appreciating the technological accomplishments, but Akbar replied that
if their sons went to school they, too, could build dams. In contrast to
this self-assurance, the model townsmen attributed superhuman intelligence to the technocrats and foreigners, always in terms of their own self-
depreciation. Their daily lives no longer gave them any objective measure of their competence. A neighbor woman in the *shahrak* wanted to
raise chickens; her husband, sons, and male relatives insisted on hiring
an expensive "expert" carpenter to build the coop, which villagers in
Rahmat Abad would readily have put together themselves.

Not only did the workers' relationship to the technology all around
them emphasize their weakness, their lack of qualifications, and, hence,
their superfluousness, but more importantly, so did the fundamental con-
striction of their lives, which removed from their direction almost everything except their children, their little gardens, and sex. While it is true
that the head male of each household still had to make a living for his
family—a responsibility that gave him some dignity—whether he could
fulfill this responsibility hardly tested his character or skills, as there was
little he could do to affect his situation. This everyone in the *shahrak*
knew. Cynically they neither held each other accountable for their work
nor *credited* each other for status and accomplishment: again, depriving
the individual of any social standard for taking stock of himself. One had
little leeway at best, and within that which did exist contacts largely
replaced an individual's attributes or skills as a primary measure of a person, reminiscent of Mehrabani. The impermanence of any position a
worker might get, the seeming unpredictability of his employer, the scarcity of alternatives, and his confinement (in effect) to the *shahrak* where
competition was so intense and arbitrary even among kinsmen contributed to the insoluble insecurity that pervaded the model town. If it is
through difficult choices that individuals define themselves, the *shahrak*
offered difficult circumstances, but few choices.

So little else of interest existed in Bizhan that all conversations, all
news, all animosities and friendships eventually centered on finding
employment, which itself always reduced to personal connections—a
resource workers neither understood nor could draw upon confidently, a
resource that placed one's density in *others'* hands, utterly discounting
one's particular strengths or resolve. In addition to *parti* (pull), the com-

panies and Safiabad also regulated labor through spies and rampant bribery, making contacts all the more indispensable, and individuals themselves pawns. Many workers told me that if as a Christian I converted to
Islam, I would be able to get at least eight generations of my offspring
into heaven "free"!—a belief that Rahmat Abad villagers vehemently
rejected. (To the latter, each individual has to make it on his or her own.)
Whereas one rarely heard an adult in Rahmat Abad complain of the personality complication *kam ruh* (literally, short of spirit), this was
endemic—almost as a physical disease—in Bizhan: an often-unconquer-
able embarrassment, timidity, or self-consciousness especially in the face
of challenge or social superiors, symptomatic of the workers' desperate
dependence on artificial interpersonal relationships.

One of the most degrading dimensions of life subject to the State's arrogance was its unrelenting reminder of its power in making you wait without explanation, without apology, for whatever you anticipated or
wanted—to wait mainly because the State did not recognize your presence there. Workers in one part of the *shahrak* had to wait a year for
electricity because the State did not feel itself disposed to install a few
wires that required but a half-day's work to connect; workers passed the
public baths day after day for years waiting for their services and other
ones to open, without any reason offered for the delays. Above all, you
invariably were made to wait for hours to conduct the most trivial (but
indispensable) business with the State, often while bureaucrats sat in
front of you drinking tea and chattering. Then they made you come back
to them again and again with childish additional assignments—bring this
next time, bring that, return in two weeks, no, next Tuesday come back
again—only to discover in the end that all such waiting was in vain. It
reminded me of nursery school where children come to show the teacher
their finger painting but are taught not to interrupt her if she is talking
with some adult. The State, like the planets or God Himself, had its own
system of essential principles that was not connected in even the remotest
way with you, a mortal individual on earth.

Learned Helplessness

Although not accustomed to self-pity or self-doubt in the *village*, almost
a third of the households I knew in Bizhan had at least one adult member
whom I found chronically depressed by a sense of worthlessness and
dependence—often a belief that they were permanently unfit for work so
the State would have to support them for life. Four teenage boys who
often visited me itemized specifically what each had done to befriend the
teacher, and whom each had "known," to get himself a good grade in high
school math, which none claimed to understand. These same four—all
bright—insisted on *dulat*'s guardian-like nurturance as a necessity and
their right! "How can we take care of ourselves?" Isma'il asked. In many

studies Langer has demonstrated that when individuals are deprived of choice or responsibility, when others do things for them that they previously did for themselves and could continue to do, when they are not allowed to master new tasks and are treated as inferiors, they acquire an illusion of their own incompetence, what she calls "learned helplessness" or "self-induced dependence" (Langer, 1979; Langer and Benevento, 1978). In the *shahrak* the individual was subjected to all of these. Indeed, one of the State's planners elaborated to me that the Ministry expected those workers who "progressed" beyond the state of menial labor to move out of Bizhan so that the *shahrak* could remain an exclusive ward for "incompetents," people capable of only the most inferior tasks!

It is no wonder that, surrendering individuality and responsibility, individual workers lived more and more in the present, again like children, from day to day. Assured of the basic needs of life if they only submitted to *dulat*'s plan for them, prevented from aspiring to anything more than this, their direction of personal development represented just the opposite trend from that of Throne City villagers who on their own were realizing capacities and an increasingly higher personal status they had never thought within their reach. In Chapter 7 we have already seen how many individuals in Bizhan turned dependency—this inability to make their own decisions or take their own initiatives, and this consequent short timeframe appropriate only for trivial matters—into adulation of those in power. They needed to believe that the men to whom they had to surrender their lives somehow *were* extraordinarily competent and that the King at least was loving, just, and powerful. Then the workers could partake of some of that power and glory vicariously. At the same time, the model townsmen irrationally exaggerated the State's severity in treating its children, when in fact, in Bizhan at least, the State made them docile by inducement not force. It was as though the workers needed to fear *dulat* in order to explain their subjection to themselves and in order to maintain their self-restraint in the face of it. This magnified fear further reduced their self-respect.

Emotional Maturity

While major cultural or personality changes could hardly have become rooted throughout the *shahrak* population during the few years the workers lived in Bizhan, their situation there did curtail two critical dimensions of emotional integrity that mature individuals need in order to support self-esteem: the stimulation for self-involvement and for emotional intensity or sensitivity. Both are contingent upon one's being able to form purposive ties with others and to take initiative, thereby expressing oneself.

Part Two has examined the many ways by which the State dulled the emotional environment of Bizhan by depersonalizing life and work there, even trying to depersonalize interpersonal relations. Just as individuality should not be confused with social fragmentation or "atomization," nor moral cohesion with the dole, so respect for the individual person must be distinguished from personalism, which adopts social manipulation and subjective feelings as the bases of social organization. *Dulat* spurned all appeals to genuine personal needs—the widow Sahra's request to be near a daughter, or the individual core villages' urge to build their own mosques. Instead, uniformity comprised a central dictate of the State, not even giving the *shahrak* street names, and originally prohibiting (then ordering) walls around house lots to enforce homogeneity. On television *dulat* defined the nation not as Rahmat Abad did its polity, in stories about its notable as well as everyday characters, but in pictures of mobs, parades, and crowds of workers streaming in and out of factories. The State categorically forbade all local occasions for the individual's self-involvement, such as Haji's store or the ladies' Lions Club suggestions; it even ran the *shahrak* soccer team entirely by itself. The workers belonged only to the masses beneath the King—hardly a focus for an individual's sustained commitment.

To give of their selves with sustained concern to a part of society, individuals need to belong to some "little platoon" that provides them acceptance and moral assurance but also a vehicle and scope (including a measure of optimism) for involving themselves in purposive projects, for taking initiative. The *shahrak* family remained a strong supportive (moral) unit, and the move to Bizhan did not substantially alter adult *women's* indispensable role within it, although often teenage boys earned a steadier and higher wage than their fathers. But the family no longer required the integral collaborative labor that knit it together in Rahmat Abad; from its active thrust it became a passive, defensive retrenchment. Furthermore, outside of it the individual had lost all other possibilities for sparking and channeling his or her interest (or even, one could say, for "caring"), such as the *sharik* partnerships that so readily enabled involvement and commitment in Rahmat Abad, or the village community itself (a firm moral "platoon"). Nothing had taken their places. Compare, for instance, poor Muhammad Reza's lonely death and his widow's confused search for help afterward, with Ahmad's community that was immediately available when he committed suicide, and the villagers' willingness to sacrifice of themselves for him.

In moving to Bizhan, individuals had also lost those long-term relationships with urban patrons, including landlords, with whom as villagers they had formed harvest agreements year after year—especially after land reform. Even landless laborers had contracted with urban patrons to sell milk, yoghurt, straw, firewood, or to manage a Dezfulli's investment in cows and sheep: ties that rested on *reciprocity,* which no relationship with *dulat* ever knew (since *dulat* needed nothing from individuals—it was independent of their world).

However, besides *dulat*'s systematic prohibitions against any "little platoons" that might draw individuals out of themselves and elicit a feeling of attachment, it was the *polarization of society* as the workers knew

it in the *shahrak*—between the extreme wealth of Safiabad and the agribusinesses on the one hand, and their own helplessness on the other—
that enervated them of all positive emotional responsiveness. *The gap
itself thoroughly gutted any middle-range* places where one could belong,
larger than self but small enough to allow one to make a difference, which
might give one some hope of voice, upward movement, or the viability
of collective purpose. In the State's insistence on homogeneity there were
no social gradations within the worker's reach or view, no rungs on the
social ladder slightly above him or her but still attainable, which might
inspire an individual's projection of self into anything outside of self.

Curiously, many of the younger workers who attended night school or
entered the army to complete military service counted on immediate—
and to me, astounding—success in Safiabad or one of the companies as
soon as they entered the labor market. For instance, many of these young
men at nineteen or twenty, with virtually no experience, envisaged being
given their own new pickup truck or an air-conditioned office in charge
of an entire company operation, like the cotton farm! Others leapt to similarly unrealistic hopes with their boss's slightest word of praise or
encouragement. Apparently when the workers moved to Bizhan a large
proportion of them cherished such confident illusions and continued to
do so for some time (almost suggestive of cargo cults). Coming from relatively egalitarian communities where they readily identified with the
wealthiest person they knew and could plausibly expect to attain his level
over time, these young people just stepping into the future that lay ahead
of them could not grasp, cognitively, the unbridgeable gap that separated
them from the affluent engineers, now part of *their* society. The extreme
and rigid social stratification that actually existed was beyond anything
they could comprehend.

These extraordinarily unrealistic expectations—their equivalent of
other model townsmen's fantasies about the good-fairy King—derived
not from ideology but from the workers' fundamental social experience
in the *shahrak*. In the absence of any social or economic hierarchy at all
between them and the engineers, experts, or top managers, or even
between them and the skilled workers (who were just as remote, coming
from the outside and never mingling with the new townsmen)—in the
absence of any objectively embodied rungs on a social ladder—they
expected the slightest qualification to distinguish them from "the masses"
in this world of only two levels. My friend Jahangir (handsome, charm-
ing, and a close relative of Sultan 'Ali), who at nineteen planned to
replace one Ph.D. expert and one seasoned expatriate agronomist in managing the entire sugar beet operation, actually believed that status in Iranian society amounted to *nothing more* than personalism. He simply
knew no sociological gradations between himself and the sky!—and so
thought that with a third-rate high school diploma he had put himself on
the other side of the great divide.

In contrast to Bizhan, consider the rich socioeconomic and political
texture of gradually intermeshed steps that spanned the elaborate hier-

archies of European and Japanese manors or estates, that developed as villages grew, becoming more complex and stratified. Those minutely gradated rural hierarchies enabled the individual to become familiar with levels near his or her own as well as with the considerable vertical span of rural society. By isolating the *shahrak* from the urban middle class and preventing an emergent middle class within it, the State telescoped society in Bizhan. My friends were being logical in taking literally the implications of the State's social leveling that, removing all variety and class differentiation, left only themselves and the top!

When they failed, then, to become promoted to engineer overnight—indeed, when they were treated as peasants!—they became very bitter and joined the ranks not of aspirants to the middle class but of the despairing: those many middle-aged workers and men who had entered the permanent labor force as children, who had already perceived the unbridgeable gap, those who saw no rungs on the ladder. In some workers the impossibility of inching ahead deadened their feelings, concerns, their involvement; in others it involuted positive emotions into self-pity, dependence, and petty quarreling. This absence of attachment came not from individuals' material poverty, but from the fact that they had little choice of employment opportunities, no mobility outside of the *shahrak* and no promotions within it, from the fact that everyone like them held identical and usually meaningless jobs. It came from the paralyzing disproportions they saw themselves caught in, without any steps or stages that might link their positions to those of prosperity and self-respect. Their *relative* impoverishment was far more severe and destructive than their *absolute* condition.

The company managers were correct in observing the workers' inability to sustain interest or attention in what they were doing, certainly their lack of persistence and discipline, which the managers who thought about such things attributed to television. The workers' slapdash constructions in their house lots and back room stores similarly reflected a lack of pride. But it was not exposure to the media that caused the *shahrak*'s ennui. Rather, this rootlessness of individuals was due to, on the one hand, their loss of *horizontal* associational identity, a "little platoon"; and on the other, to the overwhelming *vertical* gap that left them no rungs upward—indeed, no ladder—to the only other members they could see in their same society, the (to them) exorbitantly affluent and powerful.

Friendship

While social fragmentation in Bizhan led to more fighting among the model townsmen than one ever found in Rahmat Abad (where the rule of having to remain on speaking terms with everyone prepared villagers psychologically for minimizing another individual's faults), at the same time some workers in Bizhan did alleviate their loneliness by forming at least casual friendships with other low-level workers living in the *shahrak.* The older people tried to keep up with a few former village friends by a visit several times a year, and the young men sometimes became friends on the job (occasionally with a foreigner but never with an Iranian above them in rank). For instance, they might make excuses for a friend arriving late to work or leaving early, try to cover up for their friend's mistakes, and help one or two particular friends find jobs. The foremen supervising those workers of the lowest rank, the field labor, sometimes took compassion on them (although they maintained strict separation when riding to the field or eating meals there).

Tension and antagonisms isolated the individual from his co-workers at Safiabad far more frequently and intensely than in either of the agribusinesses (even more than in the work environment under the General). This seems counterintuitive on first glance, but perhaps is explained by the fact that model townsmen valued a position at Safiabad above all others, that personal connections had even more weight at Safiabad and a worker's objectively established skill or performance even less than in the companies, and that Safiabad employed a large proportion of workers who had nothing to do, which was rare in the agribusinesses.

Unlike Rahmat Abad's women, those in the *shahrak* formed virtually no friendships.

Jafar's Lesson

As we have already indicated, religion as a symbol system that expresses a society's underlying perceptions and relationships crystallizes these sometimes almost as a map indicates relationships, for outsiders and those within society to place themselves. One day during Moharram, Jafar, a worker who held a position above various foremen and perhaps the most deeply religious man I knew in Iran, explained to me his version of the battle of Karbala (which we have already explained as constituting the core event of Shi'ite Islam). Perhaps Jafar's religious explanation summarized the state of his individual soul.

I had found Jafar chanting all alone in his empty cinder block room—rare in itself; usually men chanted at an occasion, with others present. The words he chanted reverberated off the cement and plaster and seemed to cause the iron-encased glass of his little room's windowpanes to rattle. "I am with you; I am with you; Hosein you are not alone, I am here with you!" he cried out to the saint over and over in his desolation. I waited outside. When Jafar had finished chanting, he volunteered to interpret Moharram and the chant to me.

According to my friend, when we look at the life and circumstance of each individual who fought for Hosein (some were initially prevented from doing so by Hosein's comrades, as they were considered unworthy), we see that those who stood witness for the truth, those who loved the saint, were orphaned children, widows, servants taken from their families, strangers to the land, even a few pagans. Hosein, slain early in battle, sent his ghost who wandered the gory plain asking, "Is there no one who will fight for me?", and these were the only ones ready to give their lives in response. No one with "a place" left in life or a community defended God's cause. One by one Jafar related the manner in which each had given his life for Imam Hosein. None had a relationship left in life—kinsmen or countrymen or friend—nor did any of those who did have "a place" stay by Hosein's side. It had been an army of the homeless.

Nor was the social fragmentation of the holy ones all that Jafar commented on. None of those who did fight for Hosein had been buried physically intact, of enormous significance to him (reminiscent of Mary Douglas's study, *Natural Symbols*). Again Jafar named them one by one and related how each had been dismembered, arms or intestines or heart itself torn from the body and strewn over the battlefield. Imam Hosein himself had been beheaded, his slain corpse never found in order to piece together his body even in the grave. That had frightening implications for the afterlife, on which Jafar would not elaborate. "After death the *whole* of your prophet Jesus was taken up to heaven, and all of your apostles gathered together in one room," Jafar mused about the Christian story, almost enviously. "But Imam Hosein and the saints of our Prophet were strewn bit by bit in the battle, *teke-teke,* their pieces never reunited to make each person whole even in death. *Ya* Allah! that is the cruelest thing about our Karbala!"

> They said, "What! when we have become earth and bones, are we *then* going to be raised? We have been promised this, and our fathers too, before us! It is naught but old folks' tales!"
> —Qur'an, Sura 23

Chapter 12

Moharram and Ramazan in Bizhan

Their task is to say "For Hasan alas, for Husayn alas"—alas for our country, alas!
—Ashraf-u-Din, from *Nasim-i-Shimal*

The discrepancy between on the one hand, the Iranian civil calendar rooted in seasonal change (the Persian New Year occurring on the first day of spring), and on the other, the Islamic religious calendar completely independent of the seasons, affected Rahmat Abad's culture little, since the agricultural cycle so unequivocally dominated village life. But in the *shahrak,* drawn well into urban Iranian culture, the implications of the clash between the two calendars accentuated the orthodox clerical establishment's claim to an authority even above the causes of winter, the wind and the rain, and early nightfall. According to the workers, only professional holy men in their apparently arcane calculations could compute the Islamic calendar, which, unlike Rahmat Abad's way of measuring the passing of time, was completely beyond the layman's prediction or any objective observations that everyone in society can make. (The same is partly true of Easter, but it always comes in the spring and varies only over a month's span, whereas the Muslim feasts can occur at any time of the year.) Thus society's ritual cycle, in the hands of these priestly experts not even accountable to the ordinary experience of time, unpredictably interrupts the secular rhythm of days and months, symbolically demanding the obeisance of mortals' empirical perceptions and of those very powers of the universe to which civil society has affixed its bearings.

The competition between the calendar of everyday life and that of the clerics reminded one of *dulat*'s separate pace of movement independent of ordinary mortals' needs, perceptions, or values. For example, in moving villages to Bizhan, the Ministry had ruthlessly taken many communities from their lands and plowed under their fields of rich grain but a few weeks before harvest, because experts deemed that that was their hour. Just as one had to drop everything to obey *dulat* without ever anticipating its command, so too, one had to be ready to submit to orthodox Islam at any hour of call. The calendrical opposition between orthodoxy's definitive time and laymen's everyday time sprang from orthodoxy's own first principles, which determined all ritual life within its governance. The supremacy of power from on high, unaccountable professionalism, and (hence) the conceptualization of society's ideals in absolute theoretical constructs constituted orthodoxy's first principles and mirrored *dulat*'s.

Since one of the purposes of ritual is to synthesize the nature and depth of a people's social bonds, in order to understand Bizhan's primary forms of social organization fully we must examine how the model townsmen observed the two great Shi'ite celebrations of Moharram and Ramazan. In the case of Moharram, we will contrast Bizhan's and the villagers' celebration of the same feast.

During Moharram—the Shi'ites' ten-day mourning for Imam Hosein and his followers killed in the battle of Karbala—the orthodox clergy of Dezful launched a systematic religious incursion upon rural society. Like once-a-year missionaries, some clerics had to leave the fastnesses of their urban mosques and move out to the semipagan countryside, renewing the city's precarious hold over rural doctrine and ceremony. In Bizhan, orthodoxy sealed this link through the Ramazan fast. As for Rahmat Abad, the village refused to submit to the Ramazan fast or even to the correct ritual procedures during Moharram, which, as we have seen, the community culminated in its own way with its exuberant march to Dubendar. Thus Bizhan marked the frontier of orthodoxy's penetration into the domain of corporately structured, autonomous villages. In the Dez, wherever the countryside remained beyond *dulat*'s control, it remained beyond orthodoxy's as well.

Despite Islam's claim to rule every aspect of life, and despite Dezful's notorious religiosity, in neither the village nor the workers' town did the clergy aspire to establish itself through a pastoral ministry. To the contrary, the orthodox clergy kept a much greater distance from the rural people than even *dulat*'s agents did. If we recall the relationship between clergy and villagers in agrarian Europe, a relationship that profoundly affects the role of the clergy to this day in the West, nothing could have been more foreign to the pious Shi'ite clerics of Dezful than the Irish monks who settled among the Germanic tribes in their destitute wasteland, each monastery providing security and sustenance to the needy, a spiritual model of community, and economic as well as intellectual advancement to the rural population. Similarly dramatizing the contrast between the clergy's place in rural society in the Christian West and Shi'ite Iran, it would have been unthinkable to find among Dezful's devout any religious figures like Graham Greene's priest gone "native" among the villagers, a type familiar to Latin American Catholicism and its medieval precedents. In Khuzestan neither the clergy nor the religious foundations ventured across the *biyaban,* which separated the village from the city, to bring instruction to village children, to aid the poor, to set up clinics, rural hospices, religious "development" programs, and so forth. When the mullahs did come to Rahmat Abad or Bizhan, they remained too aloof ever to visit the sick or the dying, console the bereaved personally, or seek out the poor (as in the *shahrak*'s poorhouse). Indeed, they barely spoke in a language the locals could comprehend.

Just as they played no role in questioning the State's social and moral devastation of the countryside (which some academics did, proving that opposition *could* be expressed), the clerical establishment of Dezful made no attempt to alleviate the pain of rural "modernization." They never tried to compensate constructively for the fragmentation that the Plan was causing everywhere around Dezful. They could have pressured *dulat* to open the *shahrak* clinic, bath houses, and high school. They could have promoted separate mosques or Friday services for the former villages in Bizhan to find consolidation in their smaller communities; they could have sponsored religious associations, or authorized traditional and local structures in order to defend them and the individual from the State (as has often been a role of religion elsewhere). Islam did not dignify rural culture as such, with its own integrity, as Catholicism did in Europe and continues to do in Latin America.

It is true that the clergy did decide to stake out a claim in Bizhan, thereby defining the *shahrak* as urban, within its realm. But its concerns there were ideological, hardly pastoral: sponsoring a fiery revival meeting, pushing for a centralized mosque under its directive which no one wanted, and promoting exclusive "Qur'anic" sessions. While the clerics constantly criticized the State in sweeping moral terms, their empirically observable behavior, the social and political structures they promoted, their individual relationships with people in Rahmat Abad and Bizhan— and, above all, their unerring refinement of the cultural symbols of domination and submission—proved them to be so entirely within *dulat*'s urban culture (or *dulat,* within theirs) that they only reified the State's radical subordination, atomization, and the subjectivity in which it mired the individual.

Unlike Christianity, orthodox Islam constituted a formal, highly centralized State power—indeed, a conquering empire—almost from its birth, subordinating the political, social, economic, and intellectual orders beneath the clerical. It is not surprising, then, that even though not ruling Iran in 1974, the culture of orthodox Islam that we come to meet in Bizhan—and that Rahmat Abad resisted—accurately represented and in fact reinforced that of the Persian State itself. We will see this as we turn to Bizhan's ritual life.

Mullah Aziz and Mullah Isma'il

Before entering into the Moharram celebration, we should first make the acquaintance of Mullah Aziz, whom Rahmat Abad hired for its high feast days, and Mullah Isma'il, who officiated in a prominent but not the leading tent that, as we saw in Chapter 9, the townsmen constructed in the *shahrak* streets during Moharram in order to hold their rituals inside. Since the villagers and the *shahrak* workers had some choice in selecting a mullah for Moharram, and since each clergyman had officiated for his same group the preceding year, we can assume that these two mullahs fulfilled the religious needs of the congregations that hired them: Mullah Aziz serving the villagers of Rahmat Abad, and Mullah Isma'il, one group of *shahrak* workers in Bizhan. I had no opportunity to compare Mullah Aziz with other clergymen visiting *villages,* but there is no reason to consider him atypical; the villagers did not. In all fundamentals Mullah Isma'il did typify the other clerics whom I observed during Moharram in Bizhan.

The workers in the *shahrak* set up the street tents *(tekiyeh)* themselves in five different areas to accommodate the evening Moharram prayer sessions that, as we recall, the young men of Rahmat Abad had held in a special room in one villager's house. Some of the former villages in Bizhan organized these tents, each hiring its own mullah. However, these tents, although open on several sides, were too small to hold all the men and boys of each sponsoring former village; hence, the more prominent model townsmen invariably monopolized the space inside each one. In the course of a single evening, many workers would shop around from one to another to see what was going on—as I did, at a distance—and a large number of men had nothing to do with *any* of the prayer sessions. So although the tents and the separate arrangements for hiring mullahs represented a certain leadership and social organization still intact from the former communities, the social cohesion they articulated was but a pale shadow of what the workers had known before.

While those who organized each tent in Bizhan found a mullah through the orthodox clerical network in Dezful to bring for the holy days, this was not the case in villages like Rahmat Abad. Rahmat Abad's mullah for Moharram, Mullah Aziz, was not officially attached to any mosque and was hardly recognized by the orthodox clergy; coming from a very poor family and being blind from childhood, he had received little formal education. His worldly sophistication barely surpassed that of the peasants themselves, which Mullah Aziz made no pretense of hiding.

For decades Mullah Aziz had come to Rahmat Abad during Moharram. An unassuming man, he had a "pure heart," the villagers' sole requirement of a Muslim. He always brought along his son 'Aidi—eight years old when I knew him—ostensibly as a guide, who romped about with the village children even in and out of the elegiac laments for Imam Hosein, making his father thoroughly a part of the community. During the rest of the year villagers sometimes stopped by Mullah Aziz's home in Ahwaz to take him gifts of food and learn his wife's gossip. Once while Mullah Aziz was chanting, something happened to make the young boys begin to giggle, which angered him—primarily because, since he was blind, it put him on the defensive. Leaping to his feet, he picked up his cane and thrashed out with it until an adult explained what had happened, at which point the old man sat down and started to laugh and laugh at himself, prompting all of us to join him and the children. Such was Mullah Aziz's natural simplicity and his readiness to relinquish his moment of authority in exchange for one of shared spontaneity.

During Moharram, Mullah Aziz placed himself completely at the villagers' disposal, never leaving the village; even the women would drop in to chat with him during the day. To my knowledge he never objected to my attending any of the sessions, even the young men's breast-beating sessions in which they stripped themselves to the waist. When I sought him out, he treated me as a daughter. Mehrabani criticized Mullah Aziz's rusticity, arguing that the village should invest more money (he came relatively cheaply!) for a cleric who could "teach" them something, but Mehrabani made no headway with Rahmat Abad in this.

Quite in contrast to Mullah Aziz, Mullah Isma'il came from the holy city of Qum, the erudite center of Shi'ite theology. In his conceit about his own virtues and his condescension toward the model townsmen's lack of any, he excelled *dulat*'s technocrats. Although still a theology student (in his thirties), Mullah Isma'il considered himself an expert not only on all religious issues, but also on health and hygiene, politics, the cultivation of sugar beets, international affairs, space technology, modern and medieval history East and West, war, law, petroleum economics, and America. Far from appearing to be a family man, he maintained a strict distance for the same reason *dulat*'s teachers said they did in Rahmat Abad: so that the workers would fear him. No one I knew was ever granted a glimpse into his private life, or a view of him smiling or angry. During his days in the *shahrak,* one could talk to Mullah Isma'il only at special times because he spent long periods "in study" or "in prayer"—again impressing us with his superiority.

Still, while three of the other mullahs visiting the *shahrak* treated me as the devil herself, Mullah Isma'il's curiosity about my work and about the United States made him affect a slightly more open mind—well fortified to be sure (once he allowed me into his presence) by ritual taboos governing our conversation and by continual reminders about my outlaw status. One afternoon I did lure Mullah Isma'il into a visit to my cinderblock room in Bizhan, where although he would not sit down he did momentarily entertain my invitation to follow up *that* venture with even a more courageous step into America itself! (I thought we had the ticket sold when, after he vowed to starve before eating food cooked by infidels, I promised him Black Muslim cuisine.) Touchingly, when I offered Mullah Isma'il tea, he turned it down, saying he had not been feeling too well—not wanting to offend me by standing on legalistic injunction.

The role that Mullah Isma'il played in the *shahrak*'s Moharram celebration contrasted sharply with Mullah Aziz's role in Rahmat Abad, as did the relationship each had with both the men and the women believers. The proportion of time in Bizhan during which the clergy imperiously dominated the ritual itself radically exceeded the brief periods during which Mullah Aziz held the spotlight; hence it greatly diminished the workers' chance to play any role at all. Second, Mullah Aziz's sole function of chanting well-known stories in Rahmat Abad's ritual (which kept clerical superimpositions in check), the orthodox urban clergy altered fundamentally: In the *shahrak* they mainly *preached* and chanted only as a supplement to that. Third, the women's peripheral integration into the communal celebration in the village—serving the communal meals and tea, holding their own evening sessions outside the men's breast-beating room and their own oven blessing, then participating fully in the Dubendar march—disappeared entirely in the model town. There they were strictly excluded from the ceremonial tents where the men did all the serving (although at night the women listened at a distance under the cover of darkness), and from the Tenth Day processions of Ashura. Thus in Bizhan women had *no* part in the rituals; instead, they were rounded up (often involuntarily) to attend special "lessons" the mullahs gave them during the day, like children. The shift to more direct clerical regulation and more preaching in the men's ceremonies reflected the orthodox, urban clergy's elevation of their professional expertise, and their claim to a monopoly over religious authority. Of course, this in turn *depreciated* the workers' own standing, increasing the gulf between them and those who knew the truth better than they could: a direct parallel with what the model townsmen were experiencing vis-à-vis *dulat*'s technocrats. The shift also removed access to collective spiritual experience from the capacities of laymen.

I asked both mullahs to instruct me in Islam. From inquiring among the villagers about my character, Mullah Aziz concluded that I had a "pure heart" because I loved the village children as they were and didn't tell them to go wash their faces (that is, I was not a public health nurse from *dulat*), and because my family in America did not like television. He urged me not to tell lies and taught me to say Muslims' formal *Namaz* prayer (in Arabic) that I should repeat five times daily. When I inquired whether the Lord's Prayer would do instead, he had me translate it. Although finding it beautiful in asking for daily bread and for forgiveness, he said I also should pray the *Namaz*. That completed my instruction! Quite in contrast, Mullah Isma'il categorically ruled out the Lord's Prayer and was not even interested in knowing its content because only the correct form—the memorized Arabic—would do (reminding me of *dulat!*). Mullah Isma'il considered the obligatory *Namaz* not a prayer directed to God but a pledge of submission to a list of beliefs, efficacious if performed correctly: just like the State's many injunctions and bureaucratic forms.

Mullah Isma'il's private instructions for me (always in others' presence), all the *shahrak* mullahs' public preachings, and Mullah Isma'il's lessons to the women, presented Islam as a vast codification of intricate regulations, a grandiose version of Mehrabani's rule book, the Supreme Plan realized! For example, Mullah Isma'il delivered a series of three lessons on menstruation for the *shahrak* women, in which he illuminated the distinctions between a woman's blood appearing during childbirth and her menstrual blood, then the esoteric differences between menstrual blood at each of its "seven" stages, its color and weight and consistency at each stage, all the necessary technical Arabic terms, its divine purposes, and exactly which prayers and ablutions (they varied!) a woman must perform during each stage: when the first drop passes onto the first layer of protective cloth, when the flow increases and penetrates the fourth layer, when it thickens in her "womb," when she feels it "drying," and so forth. Only older women could be found available for these lectures, partly because Mullah Isma'il would not tolerate the distraction of babies or small children, and partly because women still menstruating found this topic embarrassing. These older ladies, squatting on the floor, lighting up cigarettes, reaching into their dresses to scratch their breasts, and murmuring critically among themselves like ruggedly independent older village women, often vehemently challenged the mullah's expertise. They complained that the way he described it wasn't how it "happened," that their ancestors never knew all those prayers so why should they have to learn them, that they were too busy cooking for the men to do all that praying, and anyway, too stupid! The *Namaz* was more than enough. One woman dismissed his threat of eternal punishment flippantly: "Who *cares* if we go to hell!"

Apparently, the men also didn't accept everything the mullahs insisted upon even in their evening sermons. The morning after Mullah Isma'il preached fire and brimstone to anyone who would so much as shake my hand or accept a cup of tea from me, a group of young men appeared at my door, demanding I fix them tea so they could test whether they would die on the spot upon drinking it!

Not only would Mullah Aziz never have considered himself an expert on menstrual blood, nor it a religious topic, but most importantly he would have been embarrassed to discuss it with women. Mullah Isma'il chose this and other questions he raised to show off his legalistic learning, but also to drive home the point—exactly as *dulat* did—that there was nothing so personal over which Islam did not claim dominion, penetrating as it did even the most intimate parts of our lives. Finally, by making menstruation a key "lesson" during Moharram, Mullah Isma'il singled out women to implant urban orthodoxy's elaborate controls over their defilement. The ladies who sassed him back owed their chutzpah to their village origins.

Neither the villagers' nor the workers' Islam simply comprised a system of ideas expressed through ceremonies. Rather, through the religious symbols that they brought into play during their great Moharram rituals, the villagers and the new townsmen elevated the profound realization of society itself, shaping their celebrations of its sacredness according to the only models they knew, those primary social forms and relationships they experienced at the foundation of their lives. It was more than coincidence that the community of Rahmat Abad chose a blind man to lead it into this deep solemnity of its overarching social order (in Iranian villages chanting during Moharram had always been a traditional occupation for the blind), whereas the workers in Bizhan found themselves calling upon a theologian, a learned man of The Book, to take them into the depth of theirs.

Moharram

The most basic change in Rahmat Abad's Moharram rituals that we see in Bizhan lay in their elementary organization. We recall that the communal meal at which the Qur'an was recited *(ruzah khanah)* constituted the core of the great feast's first nine days in Rahmat Abad, a sacramental testimony to the community's corporate integrity. Each family hosted a ceremonial feast (the poorer families sometimes sponsoring tea gatherings), with representatives from every household in the village sharing in each occasion. The ritual rotated house to house throughout the community, as though knitting it together for its corporate march to Dubendar on the tenth day. Since this communal meal also lay at the foundation of the funeral ritual, and in that context we have already reviewed its fragmentation under the many pressures of the model town (see Chapter 8), we have no need to describe again the disintegration of this sacred coming together in Bizhan. Rahmat Abad's most pervasive symbol of social cohesion, the communal meal, was the first aspect of Bizhan's Moharram celebration to be undermined, because the workers were too poor, their houses too small, and above all their social circles too atomized to allow celebration of any associational groups whatsoever. In the *shahrak* many workers would make quick appearances at several small meals in one evening, moving right on from one to the next. The model townsmen no longer maintained their old communal ties—in many cases not even knowing where their former neighbors lived—nor had new ones replaced them.

To dramatize this lack of continuity and solidarity in Bizhan, no longer did one *communal celebrant* embody the meaning of this feast for the entire group of people repeatedly gathered together. In the *shahrak* those workers hosting small Moharram meals had to compete against each other for the services of a mullah who, unlike Mullah Aziz, never stayed through a ceremonial meal but raced frantically from one to the next collecting a fee at each. (One mullah preached and chanted at eighteen different *ruzah khanahs* in a single day in Bizhan. This competition for a cleric reached a peak in Sultan 'Ali's and Haji Safar's open rivalry for a particularly prestigious mullah to officiate at the two men's separate but simultaneous ceremonial meals!) Thus the workers lost the intensified constants of Rahmat Abad's Moharram, the graduated and rhythmical, slowly absorbed rituals of feast and prayer and drinking tea together over a sustained period—the celebration of genuine community under a religious figurehead. All that they had left was the ritualistic form for its own sake. It was perhaps appropriate that just as *dulat* tried to force neat little molds of order onto the society it had ground down, so, too, the clergymen attempted to give some superficial structure to the *shahrak*'s ritual life by emphasizing legalistic rules.

The second change in Rahmat Abad's Moharram rituals when they were transposed to the *shahrak* lay in the style and content of the mullahs' prayer sessions that accompanied these meals, and that in Bizhan reached their peak in the evening tent meetings. After each communal meal in Rahmat Abad and during the evenings, Mullah Aziz would chant a tragic episode from the battle of Karbala in a dramatic style one could describe only as Homeric. Although his narrations were rich in details and suspense, once he approached the climax and the village men (and frequently women, in the background) were all weeping, Mullah Aziz would terminate the story right away, bringing his listeners abruptly back to conversation and tea. With remarkable command over his audience but even more remarkable restraint over himself, the blind chanter resisted using his power to separate each person from being in control of himself or herself. He disapproved of trancelike responses to the Karbala tragedies, sometimes scolding young men who kept moaning within themselves in a stupor.

Furthermore, Mullah Aziz never used these occasions to preach. He had come for the purpose of serving Imam Hosein through this concentrated ritual, which he kept sacred, untainted by the profane. Humbly, Mullah Aziz let the character of the villagers themselves and the ancient stories about the battle of Karbala, the central event of Shi'ite Islam, move the community to tears, tautly preventing them from wallowing in their feelings as some would have liked. Other than exercising this overall restraint, Mullah Aziz served as but a transparent conduit for what ages before had handed down to them.

Mullah Isma'il's style in chanting the tragic battle stories of Karbala differed profoundly from Mullah Aziz's. Before leading into the battle scenes, Mullah Isma'il would first preach to the men, his all-encompassing secular, legalistic, political, and religious orders matching his subsequent all-encompassing command over the workers' passions. Then when he began to chant, the clever theologian would quickly move his narration to the maudlin, pulling his listeners deeper and deeper into emotional indulgence where he held them sometimes for ten minutes or more, gash by gash intensifying the pain, the searing thirst, the abandonment. With his skillful oratorical techniques, Mullah Isma'il gained the workers' mindless subjugation. Emphasizing fear and terror, his sessions pulverized the spirit and then demanded total conversion—obedience—instead of encouraging each individual in his own brave search, instead of affirming what the group together could bring forth.

Although referring to the same historical figures, the heroes of the two mullahs' stories revealed what each man thought of the villagers or workers for whom he was performing the sacred ritual—and, indeed, what he thought of each individual facing the struggle of life itself. Because Mullah Aziz's battle heroes, although vivid, were generalized, the listener could project himself into each role being portrayed. Focusing not on the hero's or heroine's subjective feelings but rather on classical virtues etched by his or her performance of actual deeds—such as endurance, faithfulness, self-discipline, and resolve—Mullah Aziz's episodes often accentuated the social service of virtue, its objective measurement and outward responsibility. Sternly muting the passions, his battles unfolded through the shaping and testing of character. Provocative details familiar to all the villagers conveyed the listener directly into the passage, but Mullah Aziz avoided Hollywood coloratura and sometimes actually left the events hanging as though he was portraying righteous conduct in and for itself. Transcending the agony of life, his saints were noble figures indeed. Through the inflection of his voice and through our familiarity with him, he reminded us that their challenge was ours as well, and that as they triumphed in inner strength and public virtue, so could we.

Again in consistent contrast to the village's blind chanter, Mullah Isma'il drenched these same scenes and legendary figures in excruciating gore, painting characters of such immense proportions that one could not reflect on principles or purpose but only succumb to awe and fear; certainly one could not identify with such grandiose figures or measure oneself by their conduct. He moved on the scale of the State's overpowering monuments—the ziggurat or the huge Pahlavi obelisk in Tehran—or the Shah's vast Persepolis staging. Contrary to Mullah Aziz's religious humanism, Mullah Isma'il's stories intensified to a crescendo of utter loss. Shockingly, many men were not weeping at all. Like the theologian himself, these stories were too far above the familiar to engage these men—or perhaps they cynically determined to keep their souls in their own hands.

From the same Moharram material and tradition, then, these opposite types of battles with heroes serving quite distinct religious ends emerged, each holy man depicting a different purpose of heroism, conflict, and the sufferings of life itself. The pragmatic republican village of Rahmat Abad celebrated the challenge of integrity and social virtue; the atomized and personalized culture within the State's orbit extolled the individual's annihilation in martyrdom. When I asked him to define his and the villagers' concept of Islam, a "pure heart," Mullah Aziz compared it to someone who helps his field-neighbor finish the weeding or consoles a crying child—in short, who projects himself into another individual, recognizing their common bond. Mullah Isma'il, rarely dwelling on mercy or generosity but rather on taboo and punishment, considered the individual always subordinate to Islamic law. He frequently preached about cutting off the hand of a thief for punishment, even if the thief had stolen something small. When I protested that this seemed cruel and disproportionate to the crime, he said that, if so, the value of using the thief as a public lesson compensated for those liabilities to justice. The State is all.

In his interpretation resounded *dulat's* persistent worry that granting individuals an inch, even of what was rightfully theirs, might threaten the entire Plan: Better, then, to turn them inward on themselves to find deliverance there.

The third dimension of the *shahrak's* Moharram rituals that contrasted sharply with Rahmat Abad's celebration of the same feast comprised the young men's evening sessions. In Rahmat Abad the villagers, stripped to the waist, performed their rhythmic athletic exercise—stretching up above their heads, then down to thump their chests in unison, up and down again—as they chanted together and leaped enthusiastically in the circle they formed around whoever offered to lead. (Everyone knew most of the chants by heart.) In the Bizhan workers' equivalent evening sessions, in the place of the villagers' athletic breast-beating, the young men (again in unison) flailed their backs symbolically with hand scourges made of chains. Each worker wore a long black robe with button-up windows on the back, at his shoulder blades, that he would open like shutters to expose two small squares of his bare skin when he would beat himself. In the *shahrak* the young men never flagellated themselves to draw blood, although in Dezful, which they were imitating, many penitents did, using sharp weapons. Still, the intimacy of the villagers' ceremony in Rahmat Abad, where the young men filled the entire room with their vigor, their hurrahs and shining bodies, could never be recaptured in the brightly lit stage setting of the *shahrak* tent opening on one side to the public, where (when not in their frequent street processions) the young workers lined up to perform more for others than for their own little band.

What did this ceremonial change of the young men's ritual, from the breast-beating to scourging, entail?—both settlements looking upon their young men as the bearers and protectors of society's future. To the extent that an obvious symbol of ourselves as persons and as a society is our body (see Mary Douglas's *Natural Symbols*), the young men's ritual in Rahmat Abad asserted the community's individual and collective strength and the maintenance of those strengths through corporate exertion. Physically, the village ceremony celebrated our natural selves; stripping to the waist, the young men created their ritual—their ingenuous thud-thud rhythms—with nothing but their freeborn bodies, ready, presented, without artifice. The workers, on the other hand, reminiscent of Adam after his fall, had been ordered by the orthodoxy (or so Mullah Isma'il claimed) to cover themselves from neck to toe in heavy black, the very lines of their robes insisting on the ritual's ponderousness. That same body whose glistening energy the villagers celebrated exuberantly, Bizhan covered and scourged, the little windows in each flagellant's robe concentrating all attention on the ceremony's driving pathos: chastisement.

The uniformed sameness of all the robed workers honored *dulat's* insistence upon social and economic homogeneity in the *shahrak*. And in place of the simple physical thud-thud of the young men's fists on their perspiring chests, the workers now employed mechanical paraphernalia, the jingle-jangle of their chains almost reverberating *dulat's* admiration of metallic technology. (In requiring the specialized robes and flails, Bizhan's ritual substituted marketplace wares for the participants' natural endowment, shifting the attention of many to the competitive subtleties that inevitably distinguished different qualities, styles, and prices of both of these ceremonial contrivances.)

The workers no longer drew themselves together in an egalitarian circle of community; now they needed a "professional" coach to put them in a long line, single file, ranked according to physical height—entirely beyond one's control to alter. In the spirit of their self-flagellations, the coach on whom they depended for order bellowed out cadences through his bullhorn, to which it was their role but to respond. In the village the young men needed no practice whatsoever, as anyone could instantly pick up the pattern of movement, plainly an agricultural one; the group achieved its synchrony with the same untutored simplicity that characterized these familiar motions of their bare arms. The workers followed orders, while in the opposite dynamic the villagers *initiated their own collective action and coordination.* Each group solemnized its social experiences in the sacred.

The villagers' ritual defined an age set of the community's mature and able-bodied men; children did not participate, nor did those few old men who attended. The *shahrak* ritual aimed to draft every male from the tiniest little boys to the elderly—characteristically obliterating corporate boundaries or behavioral qualifications for membership, hence, any suggestion of responsibility, such a prominent theme in the Rahmat Abad boys' collective expression.

Thus, coming together in their circle, Rahmat Abad's robust believers celebrated their own social force, their community, confidently, ready, bare-skinned, and outward-looking: their deliverance in nothing but their bare selves, their exultant strength in unison. Such almost jubilant confirmation was necessarily a *collective* emotion. Here were the living counterparts of Mullah Aziz's Homeric epic, fortified in their resolve but this time triumphant. The *shahrak* workers, ranked, self-abased, hidden under heavy robes, and then sternly disciplined by their barking Dezful trainer, beat themselves. Immersed in the plodding rhythm of humiliation and defeat, their ceremony's highly personal mourning isolated each mechanically rhythmed integer into his own aloneness, off against the uniformed mass, reproducing the *shahrak* itself. Rahmat Abad's ritual affirmed the objective and social; Bizhan's the withdrawn, the subjective, the fragmentary. In the *shahrak* the chain scourges fell limply, tingling; and when in procession, the workers' steps fell slowly—taking the dirge of Bizhan's vital youth into Bizhan's streets each evening, the only occasion when the model townsmen could fill this public arena collectively. In the flagellants' midst, some workers bore on their bent shoulders a heavy, draped representation of the coffin of Imam Hosein (entirely absent from Rahmat Abad's celebration). People from the other tents or people just not participating in any ceremony looked on. Here, too, then, were the living inheritors of Mullah Isma'il's decapitated, gore-strewn saints, in their ritual death march of sin, withdrawal, defeat, and parcellation: the same ritual, the same feast, the same historic events and saints as those the workers of Bizhan had celebrated in Rahmat Abad's spirit but a few years before.

Finally, Bizhan departed radically from Rahmat Abad in its *climax* of the great Shi'ite feast on the Tenth Day, Ashura, which commemorates the actual battle day of Karbala and thus the essence of the Shi'ites' sacred "paradigm" (as Professor Fischer calls it) of society itself (Fischer, 1980:21). As we recall, after nine days of rotating communal meals in Rahmat Abad, in which the village households articulated themselves as society's primary units and the community honored the corporate cohesion that emerged out of them, on the Tenth Day the village took itself under its great banner in triumphal march across the countryside to Dubendar; there, community by community, the *regional* order in turn ratified its structured cohesion out of the constituent villages that came together by ancient agreement in that holy place. Although the workers had lived in Bizhan five years by the time I went to the *shahrak,* on Ashura ceremonial chaos broke loose there, sharply delineating the model town's social disintegration, in tragic contrast to Rahmat Abad's liturgical consummation of its enduring order. In Bizhan nobody agreed on how to bring the Moharram ritual to its final meaning, not even how a single tent or chain-flailing group or former village might, within itself. It was as though orthodoxy had been precariously holding together a semblance of ritual during the first nine days that the pressure to bring the celebration to its climax simply split asunder.

The individual mullahs, of course, each wanted to continue to preach in his separate tent; however, not many workers cared to attend. A clique associated with one tent insisted that all men should sit together and pray (implying division among them until then), but those who had not entered the tent during the preceding days now begrudged doing so. Thus the mullah there announced he would preach to them *in the street,* if that was what it would take to save them! So that tent, rather than being filled, was emptied for the final ceremonies, and he preached to no bounded group at all. Another devout group trekked back to the ruins of their former community, now razed to the ground, where they wept for Hosein on the grave of a local saint they could still find in the rubble, the search for which had given them their concrete purpose in returning to the site of their origins on this holy day. Some model townsmen did assemble in tents and formed straggling chain-flailing processions around Bizhan's circle, then had their mullahs preach and chant their final harangues to them. Several hastily assembled parties dashed off—without banner, without chant leader, without any formation at all—to the nearby village of Shamsabad, which had not yet been destroyed since it belonged to a

State farm. There the local people had organized a dramatization of the Karbala battle (a *shabih*) with real horses and mock fighting, in the tradition of religious theater indigenous to rural Iran.

Shamsabad, still at least a mud village and thus retaining a legitimacy as part of the old order, lay halfway to Dezful. Perhaps because of its proximity to town, its *shabih* had become completely secular, with cars decorated as floats tooting around, and a commercial air pervading the soft-drink vendors and others. Mullah Isma'il left behind his tent in Bizhan to go to the *shabih*, where he angrily grabbed the microphone to rail against popular religious theater and condemn all assembled, including the clergy from Dezful who apparently authorized the event. Those who had brought him to Bizhan had to disclaim him among their friends and relatives.

Other *shahrak* workers, having no moorings within Hosein's great catharsis in Bizhan, took themselves off to Dezful for the Ashura processions there. A chain-flailing group in Dezful wanted to show off its strength in the public procession, so had recruited *shahrak* boys as members, although they barely knew them; visiting one of the tents in minibuses during the preceding week, they persuaded some of the young men to reciprocate on the Tenth Day. Dezful attracted many people for the showiness of its processions and the drama of its bloody flagellations. *Shahrak* boys too poor to buy robes could not join the parades, but like many others they stood on the side, keeping their eyes peeled for bell-bottom trousers under the flagellants' deliberately short robes.

Wherever the *shahrak* workers celebrated Moharram, they could not avoid confusion about the former villages' great banners, which they still kept. The young men did not want to carry the banners anywhere on Ashura, complaining that they were too heavy (whereas in Rahmat Abad the young men had *bragged* of their banner's weight! After all, the taller it was, the more clearly it could announce our identity to be seen from every direction). Since the young men no longer carried the responsibility of the community, why should they want to carry its banner? In recent years some people in Bizhan had made their own banners, so these no longer symbolized the unity of particular tents or former villages, their totems. But the old men tried to insist that all the original tall banners had to be carried somewhere in procession—around the *shahrak,* to Shamsabad, to Dezful, *somewhere,* they just *had* to. Mash-hadi Noruz told me all the *heavy* things, including the saint's coffin, had to be carried about; that was why they were heavy.

Many men and boys in Bizhan went to a friend's home to watch urban processions on television or stayed home to listen to them on the radio, like Americans listening to the New Year's game. National media defined this culmination of Iranian society's religious expression of itself—for it was Ashura that set Shi'ites apart from the rest of the Islamic world—national media defined this consecration of Iran's unique social bond as an endless urban mass that in the tens of thousands flowed before the cameras, scourging themselves ceremoniously in advertisement of the Shah's power: "Here is the procession of Abadan, center of Iran's inexhaustible oil fields. . . . Now we turn to the deeply religious Tabriz where eight new factories have just opened their doors. . . . Here are the crowds of believers in Isfahan, many of them workers in the country's new steel mill. . . ." There they went across the screen, in mobs and mobs and mobs of the same black robes marching in the same street files beating themselves with the same chain flails, universally indistinguishable one from another in their uniform national piety: tribeless, villageless, without tent or mosque, but orderly, pious, and seemingly infinite. Many Bizhan workers sat passively drinking tea and watching Iran's flagellants flow by.

As for the women, orthodoxy's Ashura celebrations had no place for them, nor did any of the workers' spontaneously assembled groups (except for the one that returned to the former village ruins). Some women—more or less on their own—ran home to get their chadors and go to Shamsabad, but most did housework. Although most had adobe ovens, they held no oven blessing.

No one proposed that the workers' town unite itself in one central celebration of its own on the last day, the separate tents bringing their banners as of old to the ceremonial tent of the largest former village—Haji Safar's and Sultan 'Ali's—which in fact for generations had been the Bizhan region's intervillage ritual center for congregating on the Tenth Day, like Dubendar. How could the workers transpose and carry on that ancient tradition right in the State's brick and straight-laned model town?—so easy and so impossible.

Ramazan

Besides Moharram, the second Shi'ite feast that the *shahrak* celebrated was the month of fasting, Ramazan. Ramazan meant nothing to Rahmat Abad; in the village at the most a few girls and women fasted for a week, and a handful of men for a day or two. Despite the intense physical demands of the jobs most workers held in Bizhan, nearly all of them fasted the entire month, neither eating *nor drinking* anything from dawn until after the sundown prayer. The entire population had taken on this extraordinary discipline only since moving into the model town, perhaps because the Ramazan fast gave the workers and their families a sacred drama in which they themselves could act out, with exacting and accurate detail, in a highly compressed form—tangibly, as a sacrament—the meaning of their new life in the *shahrak* and of themselves there. Even more than Bizhan's Moharram celebrations, the Ramazan fast concentrated this religious expression of the nature of their experience, of urban Iranian society, and of the individual within it, in the symbol of the human body (and in this case, of food, its nourishment).

The Bizhan workers' explanations of why they fasted differed radically from Christianity's traditional explanations for fasting. The latter articulate a culture based on contract and social solidarity, on stern individual responsibility, hence essential freedom. Following from these, Christian fasting expresses organic, "processual" change (as we have seen in Gratian's *Concordance of Discordant Canons*) as distinct either from mechanical, manipulated change or from total transformation. In Christianity the Church instituted fasting out of men's own perception of the self-discipline they needed in order to achieve salvation. Unlike keeping the Sabbath, fasting was never a commandment direct from God but a self-shaping the Christian community took on of its own accord. As a type of in-service training for combat in a world of temptations, its first purpose was building moral character, strengthening individuals' abilities to govern themselves. By recurring periodically, it recognized individuals' needs, year after year, to gird themselves anew for their *ongoing* personal growth. Secondly, through self-mortification, Christians rectified their contract with the Almighty, shouldering their guilt and making due restitution as fully responsible parties to their relationship. Finally, through fasting, Christians signified community with others who suffered, becoming more mindful of them.

In contrast, the *shahrak* workers understood that God commanded man to fast, and that the purpose of fasting was total purification of *the body,* which had nothing whatsoever to do with spiritual cleansing, moral strengthening, or social bonding. Although fasting was difficult, Christians who fast attempt to change their personal attributes or spiritual state, which are mutable; but the workers of Bizhan aimed to stop or reverse the ineluctable decline of the physical itself. They dwelt at length on the biological details of burning out the body's internal impurities, scouring all the organs, flushing out the intestines. In describing this they continually employed the image of racing a motorcycle fast and very far without gasoline, to cleanse its system (a metaphor they found all the more apt for the actual impossibility of running a motorcycle without gas). The difference between these two concepts of fasting is fundamental: The workers sought a physiological rather than a social or relational change—to purge matter itself, not man. And indeed, during the month of Ramazan their ritual was visibly actualized: Everyone became thin and weak, the older people skeletal. We rushed my neighbor Faridun to a Dezful hospital almost dead.

Perhaps deriving as it did out of the longing to conquer matter, or to defy the hand of time (to restore the Blueprint at all cost), the Ramazan fast sanctified violence and absoluteness, forcing the believer within what seemed a hair's breadth of death in order to reestablish physical purity. Driven by the same compulsion that enforced the Plan or the despot's command, the workers scorned vegetarians, or those who fast from food for a few days, or Westerners who see some merit in "giving up" sweets during Lent. To them any partial obedience achieved nothing because the gain could only come from total burnout . . . just as only drastic overhaul could affect the body politic, and incremental change could add nothing. God ordered Muslims to fast; they didn't devise it themselves for their needs. In Bizhan, by choosing the physical rather than spiritual end of fasting, the workers sought to realize within their very bodies the fact that men and women cannot create but can only submit their clay selves to fiat, can only thirst and starve throughout its thirty-day Plan, at the end of which nature would be reconstituted (a vision far beyond any spiritual hopes of the Christian penitent). If the command is to purify, it must level totally.

Fasting in Bizhan, neither expressing a relationship to oneself nor to others, did not pertain to the self, the community, or even the other. Not punishment, not prayer, not even a test of one's faithfulness or endurance, it was simply a submission to the power of nature reclaiming its ground (in which mankind was the most overgrown thicket of the physical world). Far from forming a more responsible, moral being through hourly, daily resolution, Ramazan offered the believer no challenge to conquer his or her own shortcomings or passions. Indeed, it recognized nothing his or her will could do. The violence that was necessary for the fast's purification came *from the outside;* no human initiative—not even a longing from within the believer—could have any effect. You were but the vessel in which the supreme purging seared off all heterogeneous or superfluous accretions (like the old mud villages on the landscape, like the house-lot "clutter" in Bizhan), reducing not the personal or social but the physical down to the minimal "given" of flesh and bone. By evening when Radio Ahwaz would announce the end of each day's fast, my neighbor Khuda Rah, as all the *shahrak,* would arise from his mat limply, perform his ritual ablution, pray before the fading sun, and then quench his thirst. "It is done." Denied participation in what was done, he was observing something outside himself.

One worker told me that all one had to do was endure this solid month of thirst. "I am the earth through which the cement canal has been laid," he said; "to clean the canal a month of drought and the scorching sun will kill off all life, even a blade of grass in a little crack. It is hot out there. It will be done in eleven more days." Personally, he would benefit in no way. *Dulat* had so often told him and Sahra and Murtaza, and all the workers, this. It had to be done. "It isn't the driver of the motorcycle who would be restored," my friends kept insisting, "but the machine's pipes and electrical wires—my veins and my bowels, even my brain, but not my *self.*" Ramazan solemnized the irreconcilable separateness between form, the body, *its* sacred project, and the substance of reality in the little back rooms that it denied: the soul.

Time was suspended during the fast, much as the State recognized only the finished dam, Safiabad's printout statistics, Bizhan's brick houses, not how they got there. (With just the opposite concern, in the Christian fast the *process* is formative, the goal never reached). The more deeply believers had impressed on them the *immutability* of their raw matter, their bodies—immutability measured by the pain of scouring—the more profoundly they would know that power, entirely independent of us, which *can* transform matter.

In the workers' bowing to the command of light at daybreak, in their noonday prostration to the command, in their unjoyful, minimally granted breaking of the fast after the evening prayer—in one little cement room after the other, up and down the lanes and across the entire land, men and women waiting on a frayed rug on the ground, physically withered into humility, parched clean—in the Ramazan fast there is a profound sense of a force that transcends us all. Simultaneously, in one great heave of their nothingness, their dependence, the believers take up water and then bread. In Bizhan, this breaking of the fast, as well as every summons to prayer throughout the day and year, all worship of God, was contingent upon the exact location of the sun. Wherever your momentary spot on earth, your precise meteorological relationship to the sun—to its rising, its zenith, and its setting—determined your religious utterance. Over and over again throughout Ramazan the hungry and thirsty, the wrung out, each one *teke-teke* is reminded as he or she waits for the sun, that it is this dependence on the burning cosmic center overhead that binds us all. No wonder there is nothing that human will or initiative can do; no wonder no horizontal comes forth, no collective.

Given Muslims' ritual dependence upon the sun's central control, which Ramazan accentuates, and given the precision of the sun's demands upon its waiting believers, sunrise and sundown constitute highly technical matters requiring the specialized instruments and knowledge of religious experts in the urban centers, much as the Plan required the technocrats' esoteric determinations. One cannot trust the native eye to know what the sun does "in his chamber." In the *shahrak* we depended on Radio Ahwaz because we had neither high priest nor any means of announcing the correct hour throughout the settlement, but generally every mosque has access to a trained cosmologist. It is these divines who transmit to the fasting world (and daily, to all who pray) the *exact* minute of the sun's command. Thus especially during Ramazan, the sun that unites all Muslims as the elemental source of their ritual regulation demands global homogeneity of all who "surrender." Beneath Ramazan's unrelenting sun there are no variations, no local sociopolitical, cultural, or geographical differences, no petitions or ceremonial vestments, meals or chants or local banners, no saints' shrines, certainly no subtle degrees of individual piety, no spontaneous, self-styled religiosity. Universally, nothing varies in the fast except the *precise* hour of its timing at each distinct spot, that the learned men in each ceremonial center give forth: the one variation that in itself establishes the believers' fragmentation and the singularity of cosmic command.

Imagine the contrast between on the one hand, being called to prayer by the center of the planetary system, the source of light and heat and energy, and on the other hand, by the local church bell of the Christian West, made by man and rung by man for those just within hearing—each valley its own bell, each neighborhood, indeed each chapel within the same church its separate call to veneration, completely local and particular in time and space. Through the cosmic severity of its mortification and obedience, the Muslim fast did imbue a oneness into those it purified. But the power and scale of this vertical accord that joined each to the transcendent precluded an intimate, workaday community among them, precluded the corporate unity of Rahmat Abad, precluded autonomy. Because Rahmat Abad celebrated so fondly its communal meals and its self-acclaiming hurrahs for Imam Hosein, it had to reject the command of Ramazan.

What Rahmat Abad kept intact at the center of all its rituals, as though sacrosanct—when it buried its dead and summoned its neighbors to mourn with it, when it remembered its anniversaries, when it married its young, when it welcomed a cherished guest, when it honored its epic hero Imam Hosein and explained to itself the meaning of life—was sharing a communal meal. Not unlike the Christian Communion in which the community of believers partakes of God, unto themselves, and are nourished thereby, deep within Rahmat Abad's culture lay this ceremonial habit of its communal meal, the renewal of personal and communal strength, the affirmation of organic growth. Ramazan, in reversing this expression of the sacred, shut *outside* into night, into darkness, into shame what in Rahmat Abad was holy. Ramazan sanctified hunger and solitude. The ongoing, incremental process of life itself, the give-and-take of society, it found defiled, elevating static perfection in its place. Rather than strengthening the will as the Christian fast sought to do, Bizhan's fast aimed to break the will. It solemnized *matter*—not to create but to annihilate, not to conjoin but to reduce to *teke-teke* isolation. Directly opposite Rahmat Abad's ceremony, Ramazan sanctified the *denial* of nourishment.

Once all were bowed down in one by one submission, who would keep the sun on its course?

One was struck by the consistency—the harmony, as it were—of the *shahrak's* ritual culture, Ramazan completing the work of Moharram's mullahs and chain flails after these had exited from the streets and left Bizhan once again in its own silence. One admired, too, how consistently and independently Rahmat Abad fused together its ceremonial life, now and then picking something from what for millennia it has seen orthodoxy offer urban society nearby. Like the long agonies Mullah Isma'il drew the men through, Bizhan's ritual life was far more exhausting than that of the village, and in a sense more profound—as Solzhenitsyn's Russia. But the burden Mullah Aziz laid on his listeners when he would not let them weep for themselves was more solemn—the burden Throne City had taken on itself—than the weight *dulat* laid upon Bizhan.

Once Lilienthal and Ebtehaj, the World Bank, and the Shah had restored their landscape to the "nothing" they dreamed of here, the mud villages rubbed out, the peasantries cleansed, the schoolroom cobwebs scoured, the humps removed—the peddlers and gypsies, darveshes and snake charmers and blind old mullah chanters, the landlords and bazaar middlemen, the tribal leaders, village headmen, the peasants' *sharik* partnerships and the regional shrines—once these many accretions of time and process and social interaction were purged, and the Dez had been pared down to a straight-line skeleton of cinder block "units," then who would find Ramazan foreign to the spirit anymore? Who would then bare and beat their breasts for the *victorious* Imam Hosein, and shout "'Ali!" together to catch the night thief, to give blood for Ahmad, or to carry forth the "little platoon's" heavy banner out across the plain? Who would shudder to hear the flagellants' wail?

When I returned to my own cinder block cubicle in Bizhan late in the evening of the Tenth Day of Moharram, I found my dear friend Nabi sitting by the door waiting for me. From the *shahrak,* Nabi studied in high school in Dezful. He had not participated in any of the ceremonies that year.

"I *hate* God," he said grimly before we could even get in the door. "This is His sin."

I felt a little shiver of fear within me. "How can you hate God?" I asked my friend. "That's an impossibility. Maybe you mean He doesn't exist?"

"Of course He exists; He's everywhere, damn Him!" Nabi cursed. "But one can only hate Him, and I do."

Immediately he was deep into explaining God's sin, perhaps as much for himself as for me . . . that the old villages that moved to Bizhan, that he knew as a boy, were ghosts that refused to die. But a *shahrak* town had to be born and couldn't be because of the pieces. Here families clutching each other kept new friends and neighbors from ceremonial meals. The women resented the men. Participants with aluminum chain flails condemned those with cheap iron ones: It had been better when no one had chains. Night-shift workers had to pray in the afternoon and day-shift workers at night. The people with Dezful connections used ceremonial exchanges to impress those who had no connections. Little boys had to stay at the end of the grownups' line, whereas when he was little he had always sat by his father's knee. Now the important men wore sunglasses to imitate Hollywood stars, and who could pray in sunglasses? They surrounded the mullah inside the tents so the lesser men had to sit outside, "just like the Shah." Before, everyone had fit inside together.

Now in Moharram the "stupid" mullahs all harped on John Kennedy's sending his rocket to the moon before any Muslim could. So no wonder (Nabi pointed out) young men like him smoked and giggled and raced off to look for girls at the *shabih* on the Tenth Day! No wonder I didn't see older men in the ceremonial tents or any women or girls even outside them or the poor or students or the kids or neighboring villages visiting—

they were all out of the ritual. There was no more Moharram. That was God's sin.

Somehow connected to his hatred for God, Nabi started talking about how they ought to burn the old village banner that stood in his uncle's house getting dusty. "But it's not God's banner, why would God care?" I kept asking myself. Only gradually did I perceive Nabi's hunch, that he might avenge God's sin by destroying their ancient community's totem that he and his friends—the *shahrak*'s young men—no longer would carry on the Tenth Day in Bizhan, Iran's new model town.

The Builders

One day in spring I went with the children and young teenagers of Rahmat Abad to a nearby folk shrine where only two of us even paid our respects inside, by walking in and once around quickly, but everyone gleefully set right to work performing the essence of the pilgrimage.

Each found stones and twigs and clods of earth to bring to a sunny spot alongside the doorway of the shrine, where we proceeded to build little houses clustered together in a village, each individualized by a leaf or odd-shaped pebble that marked its personality, in a little clay community. We set out little streets and such places as the threshing floor, and the school (at the center of the village), laughing about the details we thought up.

"This is Rahmat Abad in Paradise!" my friends cried; "and here is where Safar will live, and here Musa, and here Reza, Mash-hadi Hamda, and Shiri, Sakineh, and baby Akbar. . . ." One house had to be added onto for a son that was getting married that summer, another given its goat shed, another its outdoor oven, the fanciest in the village. The embellishments expanded as everyone talked at once about Throne City in Heaven, which we crowned with some wildflowers, then prayed over and left there, our celestial community, basking in the sun by the door of the holy shrine.

The following spring I went with a similar party of *shahrak* children and teenagers to a familiar shrine not far from Bizhan that Shell-Cott had left standing. When no one proposed our making a model of Heaven, I did. The young people all laughed with embarrassment for me, inquiring how I knew about such a custom; did we have it in America?

"We *used to* come here to do that!" they shouted, "but now we know better." A mullah from Dezful put a stop to it: "*People* can't create Heaven! It's a place you go to only if God lets you in at the Last Judgment! Heaven is *His* place, He makes it for us. We can't make it ourselves!"

So, taking off our sandals and we girls covering our heads, silently and reverently our little pilgrimage took us all inside. As I had not learned from our Rahmat Abad outing, they had to teach me to circle the tomb three times, kissing its grille continually all the way around, and muttering humbly an Arabic prayer. You must turn then toward Mecca in veneration, kneel, bow all the way down to the earth, and leave the interior by shuffling out backwards, so as not to turn your back upon the Sacredness.

Once outside again, I pushed them further about Rahmat Abad's folk custom. "But the young people in Rahmat Abad know the village they make of stones isn't *really* Heaven; they just pretend because they like to dream about it and pray to God to make it that way. What's wrong with that?" I asked.

"No, no," my *shahrak* friends continued, "there *aren't* any houses and villages in Heaven! It's like Mecca there, Khanom Grace," two of the eldest explained. "See, there won't be any Najafabad or Bizhan or Farrash or Rahmat Abad! There won't be families and villages! In Heaven everyone dresses in white, you and me and Esau and Hosein and Fattie, all just exactly the same as everyone else in the world. You can't even wear your wristwatch or braid your funny red hair. You must be *pure. That's* what Heaven is like, Khanom Grace! It's a sin to make villages and houses with their different twigs at the shrine door! God won't like that!"

I tried to imagine the children of Rahmat Abad in the hereafter, including Mullah Aziz's naughty son: as a reward for leading good lives, not allowed to make another Throne City in Heaven, but instead all issued white robes in which to prostrate themselves before the Ka'ba stone. Not even Heaven could pull off that plan. *Ya* Hosein! *Ya* Allah!

By the scatterers who scatter ... And by the distributors of men's affairs!   **—Qur'an, Sura 51**

Chapter 13

Rahmat Abad's Challenge
Revisited

It happened once that a personage of high rank ... noble character and high intelligence came to be interested in primeval days.... Accordingly, he assembled from their various provinces the aged priests ... and he put questions to them concerning the kings who had once possessed the world.... "How did they," he inquired, "hold the world in the beginning and why is it that it has been left to us in such a sorry state? And how was it that they were able to live free of care during the days of their heroic labors?"

Little by little these revered men unfolded to him the histories of the kings and told how the world's vicissitudes had come about.... "Who was it first," that gifted Dehqan had inquired, "who invented the crown of royalty and placed a diadem on his head?"
— Ferdowsi, from *The Shahnamah*

Economic Expansion and Vertical Accountability

Now that we have contrasted the internal coherence and accountability of Rahmat Abad's government with the lack of coherence and the irresponsibility of *dulat,* we need to step back and see these two polities under the pressures and opportunities of "economic development"—that is, in motion.

The challenge to which Rahmat Abad had come, in fact, constituted the central problem of Iranian society itself as we observed in Bizhan. In the village the increasing differentiation that naturally accompanies economic expansion, and the stronger governing authority that such increasing complexity requires, brought to the fore the imperative that hierarchy must remain responsive to society's base, and governance must be rooted in that base: both, accountable to it. If not, what then will hold society's governance on course?—certainly not that governing system itself.

Herein lay the issue: how to let necessary hierarchy and authority emerge while at the same time ensuring that they were answerable to the base of society. Why to the base? Hierarchy and authority cannot provide their own anchor. The Plan has shown us that anchoring hierarchy and authority in visionaries equipped with their logical formulas and quantitative proofs—visionaries with their abstract principles—makes governance *less* rather than more predictable and accountable. Nor are hierarchy and authority stable, responsive, when anchored in bureaucracies supervised by well-meaning experts. Despite the many shortcomings of the social base, when hierarchy and authority are bound to it, society or any subfield within society retains greater predictability to the members themselves—if only because in fundamental matters the base of society is slow to absorb new cultural values and institutions, and does so gradually. Ultimately, it is the broad base of any society with its many levels that must generate its wealth; but to do this over a sustained period of time, those who can labor, save, invest, create, and produce must "plow" themselves back into society, over and over, which requires their assurance of relative fairness and predictability.

In Rahmat Abad's case the polity was reluctant to dismantle its traditional order until it evolved new institutions that conserved its ancient, fundamental values of participatory control and local autonomy. It remained cautious about adopting new organizational forms that jeopardized these values, even though its caution slowed the pace of its elites' expansion (hence, potentially everyone's) and delayed the establishment of formal communal authority, which the villagers needed. In contrast to Rahmat Abad's insistence upon an order predictable to its own members, in that part of Iranian society that lay *within the State's domain* hierarchy and authority had gone completely amok. Apparently the population at large no longer possessed the institutions and skills to hold governance accountable; perhaps it had even lost the expectation that a population should be able to. In Bizhan's world the disparity of power between *dulat* and the model townsmen, even the disparity in their political skills and available institutions for mutual give-and-take, had become so skewed that there appeared to be no way for the base of society (including the middle class) to regain its former position of balance and leverage. Furthermore, this same precocious power of the State had begun to thwart even *Rahmat Abad's* chance of resolving its challenge of self-governance, although the village lay on the fringe of *dulat's* realm. Thus the balance between governance and accountability is profoundly a matter of proportions.

For the base of society to perform its indispensable job as ballast, it must be *structured.* If they are to hold their immediate political and economic environment on a steady course, autonomous units or subfields throughout society must consolidate locally, then gradually regionally, nationally if need be, each constituent unit first of all becoming cohesive and internally manageable, internally accountable itself. As "development" or expansion proceeds, as we saw in Rahmat Abad's case, these local units must be able to hold their own governance in rein while also linking politically into larger incorporations with other units like themselves. This internal and external consolidation must take place at a sufficiently rapid pace to maintain leverage over whatever hierarchy and authority emerge to govern the overall environment into which the local units are expanding. That overall environment or field may itself be expanding in scope and complexity, as the Iranian State certainly was in northern Khuzestan through the Dez Project's elaboration. But if the overall governance grows in power much faster than its constituent units increase their skills and institutions for checking the excesses of that power, then that power at the center is likely to go berserk.

Once the balance of tension is lost between the base of society and its governing mechanism, the latter can divide and rule different parts that constitute the base of society by playing them off against each other; it can co-opt their leaders and preempt all initiatives that would enable local units to retain their political cohesion; or it can simply overwhelm them by force. In these and other ways it will dismantle their organizational strength. As locals fall into purposeless and factional squabbles, passive contentment and inertia, even into despair, aware that they no longer have the requisite institutions for holding arbitrary power accountable, and isolated from other units whose joint strength they need for doing so, how then will they ever recoup their leverage? The critical turning point is not to let such disproportions between governor and governed become extreme in the first place.

To keep the overall governing mechanism accountable to the base steadily over a prolonged period (which economic accumulation requires) and especially to keep governance accountable during periods of rapid development, the microlevel and middle-range political units within the base of society must maintain their own integrity so that they cannot be divided internally. Likewise, they must maintain their ability to link with cohesive other units like themselves horizontally so as to mount sufficiently strong countervailing leverage when need be. It is the governing mechanism's dependence on the base that gives the latter leverage to hold authority accountable; but if the governing mechanism is dependent on the base only *as an aggregate,* that does not enable individuals and groups within the base to mobilize its strength persistently, deliberately, quickly, and relatively cheaply—over and over again, if necessary. For such flexibility and endurance the base must be structured, not just an aggregate.

Even if the base of society is given the vote periodically, individuals and groups within society remain powerless both between elections and even during election campaigns unless they can make an impact on society quickly and at any given time through structures ready at hand in the base. During the decade of the 1970s, it was the base of American society, *not* its governing mechanism, that in precisely this incremental and structured way changed the nation's policies on civil rights, the Vietnam war, and environmental pollution. Individuals and small groups could mobilize society-wide changes by persuading local, regional, and national organizations and then joining them together for action. While achieving these changes cost participants considerable energy and expense, requiring certain skills (far more than affecting policies in Rahmat Abad ever did), the overall governing mechanism did respond.

Professor Olson correctly emphasizes the costs of initial organizational effort (1965), but those decline radically when existing organizations are kept ready at hand. Without perduring and behaviorally reified organization throughout society, the fact that the base of society or any particular field of interaction elects its governor simply makes it reactive at election time. It can hardly initiate. Nor can it watchdog for its own interests year in and year out. Correctly described as "the masses," it cannot defend itself against divide-and-rule, co-optation of its leaders, its own entropy, the debilitation caused by paternalism, and eventually the loss of its political norms, skills, and institutions through sheer disuse. Even when the base of society overthrows its government in a revolution, the same problems that it faced in the old regime return to challenge it vis-à-vis any new one: how to build and maintain viable "little platoons" locally and extend them upward and outward into effective middle-range vehicles to check arbitrary power.

In sum, to ensure the balance of leverage over the governing mechanism that any field of interaction—or society at large—requires in order to remain predictable, political structure growing upward within the base must remain a match for the governing mechanism coordinating that field (Goodell, 1985).

Iranian society's intrinsic inability locally or society-wide to hold its governing mechanism accountable and on course antedated by generations—probably by millennia—the immense pressure of concentrated power that the Dez project brought to bear upon rural society in northern Khuzestan. Nevertheless, again and again in the Third World the enormous and sudden infusions of economic power and control like those we have seen in the Dez, instead of resolving this latent imbalance between governor and governed, centralize power more rapidly, enlarging the gap between the two into an irreconcilable chasm. This danger is even more acute during periods of rapid technological change, when local people find it especially difficult to hold their own against experts and managers of huge financial resources, all virtually serving the State's command. After all, it is not necessary for centralized power to uproot large parts of society in order to fragment and then dominate them. Nor is it necessary for centralized power to reject the capitalist model of development (as the agribusinesses of the Dez illustrate).

If hierarchy and authority quickly gain a disproportionately powerful upper hand just as society is moving into the complex demands of the industrial era, then it becomes all the more unlikely that the base of society will be able to reverse the imbalance and gain its necessary leverage later on. Centralized power will firmly establish itself. The culture of the Plan takes on a life of its own. More importantly, it will set out to erode the norms, skills, and institutions that might check its own arbitrariness. Once these have been weakened or even "forgotten," after a generation or even less, who will be able to imagine a different way of doing things? Bizhan lies limp after the Ramazan fast. How can those who might imagine a more stable course give society the tools it has lost? These tools are fragile, and take a long time to evolve. The skills and institutions necessary to check arbitrary power cannot be turned on with a flip of the switch when development experts decide society is ready for them.

Although a gap separated the reality of everyday life in the Dez from the State's governance and "Law" long before Lilienthal and Ebtehaj arrived there, *after* the Dez Project that no-man's-land between governor and governed became unbridgeable. The dissolution of society in Bizhan and the extraordinary differential in power between the model townsmen and the State precluded their restoring a sustainable balance as we saw in Rahmat Abad, least of all through a public display of society's fragmentation in street-mob revolution.

If the base cannot hold its governor accountable, although they occupy at times the same territory and even at times overlap in their economic, social, and cultural interactions, both governed and governor remain— as Rahmat Abad's and Bizhan's little back rooms, vis-à-vis *dulat*—basically unconnected domains. The public arena now a vacuum, defense of it becomes unlikely. Over time society cannot keep its governance on course; investment, invention, accumulation, even social interaction and social bonds involute further and further, the State elaborating its domain and the rest of society retreating into personal ties, into privacy.

Despite Iran's resources, prosperity, and enormous opportunity, and despite the fact that it enjoyed an educated and flourishing middle class (expressed as early as the constitutional reforms half a century earlier), by the mid-1970s the *State* still had to account for two-thirds of all industrial investment—just as at the base of society peasants told Professor Lambton that land reform had simply made the State their new master (Housego, 1976:35; Lambton, 1969:145, 230; *Tahqiqat-e-Eqtesadi,* 1965:220). Notwithstanding the abundance of the Dez, the powerful and self-aggrandizing State—unchecked—left virtually no arena of predictability into which individuals or groups could initiate their own projects (except enormous foreign companies. And even they launched their agribusinesses in order to protect unrelated initiatives of theirs elsewhere in the economy—a vivid example of involution).

Rahmat Abad's Challenge Revisited

How had Rahmat Abad held its governing mechanism accountable? Although the autonomous corporate village, with its moral cohesion and clearly delineated charter of purposes, spanned a great range of economic levels, the community enjoyed a relatively egalitarian social and economic ethic, and a ruggedly participatory political arena. The absence of monopolies and of economic or political privileges for elites ensured the village marked social mobility. Rahmat Abad constantly made that hierarchy and authority that it did comprise answerable to the polity at large. Tapping custom, precedent, and a strong tradition of democratic decision making, even during the landlord period the village largely managed its own affairs, doing so with a high degree of internal predictability. As the village's environment had become more stable, it had moved spontaneously away from a personalistic basis for economic dealings toward the greater freedom and reliability of contract that, combined with its corporate character and the free flow of information it assured members, promoted economic rationality as well as political checks and balances. Increasingly it appeared to be extending this predictable public arena into the surrounding region of similar communities. (This difference between the personalistic-based bonding for which there is no alternative in periods or environments of low predictability, and the objectively based, economically rational contract preferred when predictability permits, in part explains the argument between Scott (1976) and Popkin (1979) about the nature of peasant decision making. Both scholars could be correct for the same population under different conditions.)

By the 1970s it was apparent that although these institutions, expectations, and cultural traits were firmly established in the rural population, if the village were to raise its economic and technological level further while also retaining its democratic foundation and corporate autonomy, it would have to encourage *and hold accountable* new hierarchical levels that the regional society was ready to bring forth. In its exuberant recent growth it had stretched to its limit the potentials of its and the intervillage region's informal, relatively egalitarian political mechanisms. The flourishing local and regional economy, as well as the encroaching arbitrariness of *dulat* on the periphery, called for a formal, institutionalized authority in the community (and region), an authority evolved out of the base itself and hence answerable to it—not superimposed by the State and thus accountable to *it*. Unless it could take this next evolutionary step and evolve a higher level of political complexity to keep it abreast of its expanding economic and political field of action, in the coming years Rahmat Abad could not have maintained optimal predictability within its own domain (beginning to appear, for instance, in the Ramazan incident) or in areas into which it would want to undertake new endeavors (building its canal through the disputed land). But if the village were to evolve a formal yet firmly accountable authority and thus let hierarchy emerge, it could open onto a much wider sphere of economic and technological complexity. And if other villages and local groups did the same, the region—perhaps even the province—could have enjoyed the advantages of hierarchy and authority without losing rein on them.

In short, the community's long-term autonomy and the stability and rationality of its environment, into which the villagers wanted to venture more vigorously if they could make it predictable, both depended on the elaboration of hierarchy and authority *downwardly accountable* to the base of society. It was at this point that the World Bank visionaries in their hurry to get on with development stepped in, destroying the region's potential for evolving along such lines. By, on the one hand, giving overwhelming power to the centralized State and, on the other hand, laying waste the evolving middle-range institutions that might have held the State accountable, the project replaced a multitiered society, predictable and expanding on its own initiatives, with its own rigid dichotomy of elites and the masses behind closed doors.

The Dez and Development Projects in 1986

Surely bankers and planners, economists and politicians have learned by now that such a highly centralized development thrust as we have seen in the Dez will fail. Haven't "human resource development," "free enterprise," and "institution building" replaced big dams and slum transformations in the World Bank's portfolio? And don't these current development aims strengthen local structures? Certainly Bizhan was the creation of *yesterday's* visionaries.

Not so. The two most penetrating changes in the social foundations of Iranian society which we have watched taking place in the Dez were the broadly sweeping monopoly of an unresponsive, technocratic, and extremely powerful State over a large population that was previously free from centralized political control; and the destruction of middle-range social, economic, and political institutions and groupings of all sorts that buffered local people from centralized control and that enabled them to mobilize their own initiatives into the wider society—indeed, that in time might have enabled them to hold the arbitrary State accountable. In short, *the two crucial changes the Dez Project wrought were the vast increase in centralized power and the destruction of middle-range groups off against it.* If we were to look inside the projects launched by the World Bank *this year* in the way we have looked inside this one, details would differ but we would find most current projects hastening if not explicitly requiring the same political shift that we have watched in northern Khuzestan, from local, regional, or decentralized control to inaccessible State power. (Projects designed and funded by the World Bank differ little in substance from those of the Inter-American, Asian, and African Development Banks, so our review here comprises only a slice of what continues to take place overall. For our purposes, the following discussion combines the IBRD and IDA loans in referring to the two together as the World Bank.)

For example:

• Projects that make small farmers, fishermen, or herders dependent upon the State, with no alternative recourse, for resources crucial to their livelihood, or to marketing their produce and negotiating its sale price, without *at the same time* strengthening their ability to affect the State's policies that govern them or to rein in its excesses. This type of project includes most "flood control" and large irrigation schemes, in which control over irrigation water gives the State unmitigated power over farmers' crucial decisions; integrated rural development schemes and related programs that usually force farmers wanting government agricultural credit to buy inputs designated by the bureaucracy (from the State itself or companies owned by the elites), to plant only those crops the technocrats deem desirable, to adopt specified agricultural practices, and then to sell to the State (see Goodell, 1983); and programs extending the monopoly of State seed banks, agricultural marketing boards, storage facilities, processing plants, and State-run "cooperatives" at the expense of local- or provincial-level systems that in many cases offer farmers greater leverage. Virtually never do agricultural projects of this type ascertain that small- and medium-sized farmers' substantive political participation keep abreast of the State's arbitrary control over them. The United States voted against a $220 million project that the World Bank nevertheless funded in 1984 for "cooperatives" in India that embody essentially the same principles of State control which governed *dulat's* consolidated "shareholder" farms in the Dez Scheme. Reminiscent also of the Dez Scheme is a World Bank irrigation project in India which is currently forcing over 100,000 farmers and their families to move from their villages and lands: far more people than most earthquake disasters dislocate. There is no evidence that either of these two projects will ensure "beneficiaries" political leverage to counter the social and political erosion such "benefits" bring them, and to offset this escalation of arbitrary power in their society.

Don't projects with such consequences (whether intended or not), affect the social base and hierarchical accountability of a Third World society in ways fundamentally the same as the Dez Project did in northern Khuzestan? In 1984 the World Bank funded 34 projects along these lines, totaling over $2 billion.

• Most programs for upgrading export agriculture in poor countries through measures similar to those we have described above; or by requiring farmers to sell their produce to export agencies controlled by the State (as with cotton, sugar, coconuts, rubber, palm oil); or by in effect promoting large plantations' expropriation of small- and medium-sized farmers' land, plantations invariably linked to the State's technocrats. Rarely does a program improving farmers' production for export also strengthen their ability to contribute to the State's policies whose hold over them the project establishes more firmly, or to serve as watchdogs over these policies' implementation.

Don't projects that tie local economies to exports while at the same time tying exports to unaccountable State controls (often through consolidated management units) share the Dez Scheme's shift away from self-directed farms and local communities to disproportionately powerful international agribusinesses currying government favors, along with their complement, the government dole? How many such projects foster effective producers' associations? In 1984 World Bank projects of this category totaled around $450 million.

- Telecommunications and education projects, especially at the primary and secondary levels, through which the central government frequently gains more systematic control over all textbooks used in the country; monopolizes prime television time nation-wide and standardizes its programs to homogenize cultural differences and obliterate regional identifications; supplants independent teachers' organizations with those it controls; displaces private educational alternatives, especially religious schools; and limits what students can choose to study in order to make each person serve the needs of the Plan. (In fact, one 1984 telecommunications project promising to bring telephone lines to remote Guatemalan villages has been accused of establishing a military monopoly over the nation's rural communications network.) It would be difficult to find any of these education and telecommunications projects administered by State officials who are subject to local elections or effectively monitored by parents' associations or village councils to ensure that the public authorizes the values which such projects inculcate in society's young. Doesn't this type of project undermine local and intermediate-level structures even more penetratingly than the Dez Scheme's relocation of people in new physical surroundings? In 1984 the World Bank loaned $150 million for projects of this type.

- Structural adjustment projects that encourage large loans to one or a combination of whole sectors of a country's economy (such as the agricultural, industrial, or financial sector), through which central Ministries strengthen firms that conform to the State's vision, at the expense of those that do not. Essentially, structural adjustment projects give central planners the financial resources to see that entire sectors of society carry out the Plan. When these projects do not actually require the reduction of market diversity, since the World Bank makes no effort to ensure that their loans are administered in an environment of free competition and public debate, they *in effect* often lead to consolidating many enterprises in the hands of a few elites. For example, the structural adjustment loan in the Philippines explicitly called for the consolidation of all the nation's banks into several (in effect, into the control of several Manila families). That structural adjustment loan caused the liquidation of over 600 provincial family banks (see Broad, 1983; Goodell, 1983). Structural adjustment projects invariably tie beneficiaries more tightly to financial, industrial, and export policies drawn up and controlled by technocrats (often foreign technocrats utterly beyond political reach) without at the same time strengthening beneficiaries' institutions for protecting themselves against the State's excesses. The purpose of structural adjustment loans is to revitalize major sectors of the economy *by bringing them under much closer purview of State economists and planners.* But if producers do not at the same time evolve checks against the State's increased arbi-

trary power over them, can the outcome of these projects differ fundamentally from the inordinate centralization we have seen in the Dez? In
1984 World Bank projects of this type totaled $2 billion.

• Loans to State development finance companies (DFCs) that compete
against and sometimes replace national and provincial-level financial
entrepreneurs with centralized banking bureaucracies. World Bank loans
to DFCs rigidly specify lending criteria to give State technocrats extraordinary leverage for reshaping national institutions. Typically, only enterprises "playing a critical and crucial role" in carrying out "national economic priorities" qualify. Who establishes these priorities and applies
them in concrete cases? Entrepreneurs who are not found fit to carry out
"national priorities" have no access to public debate, nor any role in for-
mulating the policies that define them as such. If priming free market
forces in a centralized, secretive, and personalistic environment merely
enables the rich and powerful to become more arbitrary, how can these
loans foster genuine free enterprise without an open political arena to
ensure competition? Some DFC loans complement structural adjustment
projects as two coordinated arms of the central planning apparatus.
Expanding select technocrats' domain over the diversity of financial alternatives, DFC loans frequently leave the World Bank as the only institution capable of monitoring State lending institutions. Can we distinguish
this chain of accountability and process of centralization from those the
World Bank established in the Dez? In 1984 the World Bank loaned $900
million to DFCs.

• Urban public housing and slum clearance projects, forced resettlement schemes, and urban "management" projects, which fragment large
populations of the poor in the name of "upgrading" them to serve the
State's needs, overpowering their neighborhood organizations. As we saw
in the Dez, it is hardly probable that people who have been forced to
abandon their homes are allowed to develop countervailing measures for
limiting and steadying the technocrats' augmented power over them. In
1984 the World Bank initiated $150 million worth of loans to projects
that appear to involve this kind of social engineering, although this does
not include some of its most massive forced resettlement projects of
recent years.

The six categories of projects we have just reviewed comprised over
one-third of the World Bank's funding in 1984. All these projects are
designed to bring *economic* benefit to their beneficiaries, and many will.
But few diverge from the underlying patterns we have seen in the Dez
Scheme: that unchecked centralized power takes on a life of its own
beyond the grasp of economists' calculations, especially when potentially
countervailing structures are eroded throughout society's base. Can the
seeming benefits from short-term economic gains—rises in GNP or per
capita income, for instance—be offset if society loses the ability to keep
its governing mechanism responsive? Despite the World Bank's insis-

tence that only market efficiency determines which firms or regions a Bank project will benefit, in a society that does not separate economic hierarchy from political power, projects said to be based on efficiency will invariably strengthen the governing elites' hold over society at large. Why is it that educated Western economists, bankers, and planners cannot grasp what Rahmat Abad saw so clearly as it watched the economic efficiency it valued highly being drawn into *dulat*'s domain?

The speed, scale, and technocratic sophistication of investment in most World Bank projects, even those for "social welfare," preclude citizens having a voice in them, as villagers did in every step of Rahmat Abad's development. The *average* World Bank loan in 1984 exceeded $60 million. Economists tell us that speed, scale, and technocratic sophistication are required to justify the millions that must be spent, to respond to the hurry they say is necessary, and to control where societies are headed. No large development projects even experiment with allowing beneficiaries a voice in the future being engineered for them, which would foster for them and their societies Rahmat Abad's predictability. To the contrary, these projects consider the rich organizational potential of local and provincial levels, which we even find in urban slums, to comprise a liability that must be destroyed—not a people's most vital asset, their ship's rudder and ballast.

Few development projects, if any, have brought their great sophistication to bear upon Rahmat Abad's challenge: how to hold the governing mechanism's hierarchy and authority accountable in the process of development, how to keep a hold on the ballooning State.

In short, today's structural adjustment projects and DFC loans, educational or housing blitzes, regional or integrated agricultural development projects read exactly like Lilienthal's dream: Transform a society whole hog—one entire sector of its economy, and then another. Overhaul a region. On outside resources and expertise rev up the motor. Consolidate the messy, irregular, spontaneous, limping-along, those in obscure alley-ways, into a few straight rows easily monitored. Force-feed the strong. Weed out "inefficiencies"—backward villages then, backward firms now. Clear them away so the efficient can command the landscape. The same compulsion of planners and economists to impose *their* order on local, indigenous "chaos"—by establishing the behemoth more firmly.

Although Lilienthal, Ebtehaj, and the Shah are no longer elaborating their vision in the Khuzestan "wasteland," their vision remains intact with new project names.

The Origin of Iran's Problem of Hierarchy: A Hypothesis

We must now return to Rahmat Abad's essential challenge: to let hierarchy and authority emerge while holding them accountable to the base of society. We have said that although the Dez Scheme greatly exacerbated the gap between *dulat* and those it ruled, making the irresponsible State irreversibly so, this split in Iranian society had existed even before Lilienthal, Ebtehaj, and their likes. Let us now try to unravel this perduring anthropological question of Iranian political culture: how the relationship between governor and governed ever might have become so off-balanced in the first place.

The period in any society's development when hierarchical relations first become institutionalized probably plays a strongly formative role in shaping its subsequent political culture. I call this a society's agrarian period. It is during this period of initial hierarchical consolidation throughout what previously were relatively egalitarian communities, that a society first routinizes local-level political institutions, rules, political expectations, and skills for dealing with hierarchy. Especially since the principal conditions affecting local hierarchical relations during the agrarian period may last a very long time without major changes, the way a particular society *initially* institutionalizes these relations may establish a basic paradigm for how it will govern itself throughout many centuries that follow. The argument that underlying behavioral patterns can become "fixed" for such a long time is difficult for some modern people to accept, since they assume that society is very malleable and that all levels of society and culture are continually changing. But the case we have at hand suggests that fundamental cultural configurations such as those pertaining to hierarchy and authority—including a society's actual institutions for regulating these—may be extremely durable.

In order to spell out the hierarchical relations that shaped Iranian society's basic political paradigm during its formative agrarian period, we hypothesize that the salient elements of this paradigm can be analyzed in Rahmat Abad. To understand this Iranian paradigm we propose to compare and contrast it with the similarly formative early hierarchical relations that became institutionalized in northwestern Europe and Japan during those two societies' early Middle Ages. What makes the three comparable? In each of the three the primordial relationship between the village and its lord established the primary terms of hierarchy throughout society's base, where the foundations of any society's political culture are laid (particularly, those that assure accountability.)

Through its long history and recently, after land reform, Rahmat Abad had faced many challenges to its corporate constitution: internal quarrels, thieves, the necessity of constructing and maintaining its canals, deliberation on deals townsmen offered, and the grand realization of Throne City itself. But none of these presented the community with a *sustained* political challenge of internal stratification through which it would have to evolve its own more complex political institutions and skills and hold its immediate political environment on course. Only through the repeated challenge from a stratified (hence hierarchical) superior that was part of the village social structure would the community be spurred to a higher level of internal political complexity, formally articulating any authority it recognized.

Before land reform, one salient weakness that had kept the village from fully solidifying as a corporate group—indeed from *permanence*—was its inability corporately to stand up to its landlord, traditionally the State's agent over it. Although absentee and not necessary for the management of village affairs, the landlord was part of the village polity; he embodied the only stratification within Rahmat Abad's domain that presented the community with repeated challenge from someone it acknowledged as an authority. (The State made but idiosyncratic demands on it directly.) Once this authority was removed from Rahmat Abad's polity—or even if it had not been—how the village would solve the challenge of hierarchy and authority would necessarily be partly determined by the institutions and expectations that had already evolved in its relationship to the land-lord, its traditional, formally designated governor.

Consider the nature of this, the only relationship of hierarchy and authority that the village had institutionalized as part of its political con-stitution. Through the centuries, when the villagers either individually or collectively could not accept the ultimate governance of their landlord, but, in turn, could not hold that governance in check, they had quit the land. And the landlord let them. (So did the State.) Thus in the last resort possibly from time immemorial the village work force and its governor had a way out of confronting one another: avoidance. Although merciful for the villagers (in the short run), this way out ultimately retarded the community's political development and, on a wide scale, Iran's. It insti-tutionalized the pattern we have seen in *bast,* by not requiring the reso-lution of hierarchical conflict—hence, the accountability of recognized authority—within each minipolity of village and lord at the base of Ira-nian society. After land reform, when Rahmat Abad faced the problem of allowing internal hierarchy and authority to evolve out of its own elites, this traditional solution to political conflict—to walk out—was no longer a viable one, but in its place the village had not yet evolved an alternative that was. In working out a way to embrace expansion and accountable authority within its cohesive polity, Rahmat Abad would have to start from scratch.

Rahmat Abad's counterpart communities that later moved to Bizhan, not having developed hierarchical accountability first within themselves and not having extended such accountability into their wider environ-ment, had tragically capitulated to the Dez Project's devastation of the countryside—without, as far as I know, a single case of resistance. The Throne Cities of the Dez found themselves without sufficiently strong, resolute, and broadly based political institutions or skills to impose their corporate, contractual organizational forms, their norms of accountabil-ity and economic rationality, and their open, predictable public upon their wider environment *at a pace sufficiently rapid to keep abreast of dulat's overpowering claims on it.* When faced with ultimate destruction, this time not by foreigners but by a hierarchy and authority they recognized as their own governance (and later when subjected to the technocrats' arbitrary rule in Bizhan), these constituent cells of Iranian society at its base could not rein in the reckless, arbitrary State.

When we ask what characterized Iranian society's primordial relations of hierarchy during its formative agrarian period, we see that the ancient right of the villagers to quit the land—and the fact that the landlords allowed them to do so—is central to the political paradigm both shared, constituting as they did the base of society. Inasmuch as each society's history and cultural forms give it through time its primary behavioral repertoire, and inasmuch as even in the 1970s Iran was still barely emerging from the formative millennia of its agrarian period, this pattern must underpin our understanding of Rahmat Abad and the dichotomous realm of the State off against the workers that *shahrak* society comprised. The right to quit the land constituted virtually the only right Iranian peasants could claim. Throughout Iran (except perhaps Turkish Azerbaijan) throughout history, administrators, court advisors, tax collectors, historians, the landlords themselves complain of peasants exercising this final option of abandoning their villages in the last hour of conflict with the landlord, who at other times more directly personified the State, but who at no time had the right or power to attach them to himself or to the land (see Goodell, 1977:280–84).

Hierarchy and Authority: The Formative Period of the West and Japan

The following discussion attributes the corporate and public accountability of "Western" political culture to hierarchical relations within the isolated communities and early manors of northwestern Europe during the early Middle Ages (ninth to twelfth centuries), where the lord was entirely dependent on his serfs for his livelihood. The persistence of trade throughout these centuries in eastern and southern Europe, as well as the persistence of state-level administration in many areas, freed many eastern and southern lords from the northwestern lords' structural dependence on the peasantry. Hence, this analysis traces contractual and corporate political culture in Europe to the northwestern region, and only to it; only there were the early manors self-contained polities. (The Germanic tribes who became the manorial population were already stratified at the time of the invasions.) While this corporate and contractual political culture is usually attributed to Europe in general, to the extent that eastern and southern Europe have institutionalized some of these traits, they have done so largely by diffusion (see Goodell, 1980:321). The par-

allel formative period in Japan began as early as the eighth century and
continued to the fourteenth.

The core political paradigm of hierarchy and authority that forms the
base of traditional Iranian society embodies a dynamic exactly opposite
its equivalent in northwestern Europe's and Japan's formative agrarian
period. Northwestern European and Japanese societies explicitly denied
the peasant the right to move, tying him (and his family down through
the generations) to one specific place and one specific lord. Thus in direct
contrast to Iran during its agrarian period, medieval northwestern Europe
and Japan (the former through serfdom) bound the village with its members, its hierarchy, and its stratified authority, the lord, in a single perduring polity *without* a way out during political conflict.

Neither in the Iranian case nor in the northwestern European and Japanese is it difficult to explain why the peasants would *try* to leave an
oppressive lord. In Europe and Japan explanations vary as to why they
found this extremely difficult, yet the decisive fact was that the *landlord
consistently acted* to prevent the villagers from quitting the land.
Although European and Japanese peasants constantly tried to leave, as
their Persian counterparts did, both of the former two cultures *institutionalized* ideological, religious, legal, as well as political and military
measures to enforce the bond that joined a peasant and a specific lord—
joined work force and governor (admittedly with frequent breaches).
What remains to be elucidated and constitutes our primary concern here
is why the Iranian lords did *not* take measures to keep the peasants in
their villages.

As a consequence of the European and Japanese peasants' confinement—far more oppressive than Iran's "feudalism"—they had no alternative but to confront their lords with their objections, complaints, and
demands, that is, to "slug it out" with the hierarchical order that governed them. Out of these vertical confrontations, "as natural to the seignorial regime as strikes are to large-scale capitalism" (Bloch, in Hilton,
1973:12), fully corporate communities developed across the base of Japanese and northwestern European societies with vigorous institutions for
resolving hierarchical conflict. This happened very early on when in each
case the political culture of social stratification was just taking shape—
that is, when the nascent polity was beginning to institutionalize its basic
rules and skills of hierarchical governance.

Later, as local society expanded into a broader environment, these primary manorial organizations began to create regional and eventually
society-wide mechanisms which—despite what became full-blown social,
economic, and political *stratification*—held hierarchy accountable on a
wider and wider scale, extending public interaction and predictability.
Therefore, whenever the elites and the State itself gained the advantages
of greater technological complexity and a wider scope for economic
exchange, *their* "economic development" could not take off on its own

for long, unlinked to the base, as happened during the upswing of most Iranian dynasties. Although manifest in diverse cultural forms in the West and Japan, the relationship of accountability between the base of society and its hierarchical authority—structure by structure, one level holding the one above it accountable—which resulted from tying the peasants to the land, is well expressed by Gratian's principle of the *Concordance of Discordant Canons,* just as the contrary principle of *bast* expresses the relationship of avoidance between society's base and its authority in Iran.

The connection between the lords' tying the peasants to the land and the peasants' tying the lords to accountability (and the opposite in Iran— the lords' permissiveness and the absence of a vertical link) leads us to ask why the manorial lords of northwestern Europe and Japan *submitted to* hierarchical accountability? Why didn't they just let the peasants quit the land when the latter raised objections or demands, as the Iranian lords did? The reason Japanese and European lords bound the peasants to themselves and the land in these formative centuries is that in these cases each lord depended completely on the villagers—*his* villagers—for food and defense. The inhospitable geography, the frequent raids of marauding tribes (in Europe), and the weakness of overall governance or infrastructure in both societies during the early agrarian period (the ninth through the twelfth centuries in Europe) compressed the relations of manorial production into small, compact modules. Each lord had to deal with his peasants because he had no alternative source of foot soldiers or of livelihood: In these early centuries there were no towns, almost no trade, and he received no bureaucratic payments from the State.

In both northwestern Europe and Japan, the lords formed alliances among themselves to catch and return runaway cultivators, alliances that encouraged organization among the latter, horizontally. Enforcing the villagers' bond to their lords required expense as well as constant vigilance; the lords' willingness to undertake the necessary costs and organizational efforts—over centuries!—revealed their dependence on their peasants. The peasants, in turn, took full advantage of the leverage the lords' dependence gave to *them,* banding together to insist on demands that escalated from the right to hunt and draw firewood in the lord's forest to charters of self government (numerous, as early as the tenth century in Europe!), control over property, the continual renegotiation of labor and military obligations, eventually the right to appoint their own tax collectors and officers supervising their economic production. Medieval Japanese villages won the right to borrow money, sue and be sued *corporately,* even to administer their own criminal law. In both cultures, when the lord would break his word or impose new conditions the peasants would mobilize once again to check arbitrary power.

Medieval serfs and their counterparts in Japan were extremely poor and remained poor for centuries. Economic gains did follow these political gains, although admittedly more slowly than a paternalistically benevolent autocrat might have granted them. But far more decisive than the short-term economic benefits were these crucial political skills, institutions, and constitutional principles themselves, which gave the peasants and society at large tools for sustained development, tools we see put to use once again (as though still intact) in the early labor movements of the factory age.

These fundamental minipolities of peasants and lord, work force and hierarchical authority, that during the formative centuries of the early Middle Ages constituted virtually *the whole of society* in northwestern Europe and Japan, each hammered out its corporate governance through conflict and the necessity to remain coupled together in the early agrarian period's decentralized, autonomous local modules. (Here we loosely describe these as "manorial" to emphasize the integrity of each as a minipolity congruent with a local production unit. In some cases, though, the lord managed his separate domain land using village labor, which did not change the paradigm. For elaboration see Goodell, 1980:304.) Although pushing these social units to this much more complex organizational form required enormous social energy (which many development economists today would consider a waste), the strata that wanted to split apart from each other but could not had to pay that cost, battling over and over again until they could over and over again reach a mutual accord, because in the last resort the work force and its governance were bound to one another, *unable* to walk out of the manorial unit they shared. In these centuries each society was unknowingly establishing its fundamental patterns of conflict and agreement between opposing hierarchical levels, between governor and governed, laying the foundations of its political culture, of its government.

During this formative agrarian period in northwestern Europe and Japan, when the peasants consolidated for collective demands initially unit by unit (each village against its own lord), each corporately based organization naturally sought to establish links with its neighbors on issues they shared (as, for instance, in the region around Rahmat Abad). As the villages broadened their organizational base, they could make more ambitious demands. Their consolidation elicited an opposing organization from their respective lords. Thus by the tenth century in Europe, villages were raising their own armies that received public oaths of allegiance from all members; in France a confederation of such local and regional grass-roots structures drove the lords out of a province for a period of over five years. Governance would be more cautious thereafter, and village culture would "remember" the checks and balances that had proven so effective. Similarly, Japanese villagers in time liberated whole provinces and governed themselves under the independent rule of cultivators' councils until they, too, won political participation. For political mobilization to be so effective, resisting divide-and-rule from above and able to sustain credible negotiations, it required the corporate cohesion of each constituent unit. Norms and institutions that could successfully demand vertical integration, hierarchy's accountability across extensive regions, became firmly established throughout the base of society. What a contrast to the Dez!

It was out of this process of corporately structured organization spreading horizontally across at the base and also across society's governing hierarchy, it was out of repeated vertical negotiation and renegotiation between the work force and governor compressed into the same minipolity, that the State itself was formed in northwestern European societies and in Japan. Thus the State took shape just as the nature of emergent authority (in Europe, eventually the King's authority) was being brought under full challenge by organized political leverage at the base, just as vertical accountability was being *institutionalized* at society's very roots.

Two remarkable results were that the base could enjoy increasing technological and economic complexity, constantly expanding into new hierarchical levels while in time demanding political and legal equality with its leaders and elites; and that it could accept the emerging State's overarching authority while keeping some hold over that emerging State's arbitrariness (however tenuous at times). The base of society could make these demands because it retained its organizational strength to enforce them over and over again.

A third important accomplishment of this process was to win the individual cultivator's and the corporate village's inalienable right to the land the peasants tilled. Contrary to some Marxist views that the guarantee of private property oppresses the poor, in fact achieving the security of property and then struggling for centuries to protect it against the lord and the emerging State constituted a great victory of the very *base* of society, and only the base could have secured it. To this day Persian villagers, like many in Asia, have never secured what Japanese and European peasants had by the late Middle Ages. In this accomplishment the latter brought full-circle their lords' forbidding them to quit the land: If they could not abandon it, they would *own* it. And they forced the extension of this security of property to every level of society.

In summary, because the northwestern European and Japanese lords had nothing but the peasants to fall back on, the confrontation between hierarchical levels combined with the *requisite* that these levels reach agreement, thereby incorporating both the base of manorial society and the lords at their level into stratified but unified minipolities. This opened the way for the formation of political classes that as such are found only in postmanorial societies. (The work force could congeal as a horizontal class because it found a like opponent; a social class cannot incorporate when it has to contend directly against an amorphous and all-powerful State.) It was during this decisive agrarian period that the institutions, norms, and skills for open vertical conflict between levels of society, and the mechanisms for its resolution forged a genuine public arena. This arena combined the centrifugal force of opposing interests within the prevailing imperative of unity, resolving the no man's land we found in Bizhan and enabling those governed to extend their corporate and contractual predictability further into the environment around them.

Institutionalizing Accountability: Its Pace, Proportions, and Timing

Inasmuch as vertical accountability requires corporate and hierarchical organization in gradated proportions, in early medieval Europe and Japan the relationship between the base of society and its authority, which the base learned to check, also pivoted on the *isolation* and *size* of the elementary political units that were institutionalizing these patterns (the manor and the shōen estate), and the *timing* of their development. During these centuries of the early agrarian period, not only did the lord have no resources to fall back on except the peasants, but with the nascent State still very weak in northwestern Europe and Japan, external forces that might have enabled him to evade the peasants' confrontation were not yet sufficiently powerful, organized, or mobile to come to his aid. At the same time, because of the relatively small scale of his holding and the proximity of laborers to each other in geographically compact and socially interwoven groups, from the outset the politically unformed work force benefited from optimal conditions for consolidation. The lord had little leeway to divide and rule them.

Timing was critical. Had the development of the State been more advanced, even those units that achieved local incorporation would have found it impossible to link with each other horizontally as they extended their organization into *intermediate* ranges of society (just what the Rahmat Abads of the Dez found). But local institutions can only gain power for their members when they are allowed to call together ever larger consolidations if need be. These intermediate-level extensions of grass-roots leverage are indispensable for ensuring hierarchical accountability and predictability. Participatory local associations abound in some socialist societies today (for example, Yugoslavia and the People's Republic of China) which at the same time prohibit active, intermediate-range ones; that gives an illusion of freedom and local self-direction, but in fact leaves the center free to play off local groups against each other or isolate them from one another, thereby overriding them on controversial macropolicy issues. What good is *local* self-direction if people have no leverage over decisions that govern their wider environment? (For an elaboration of this discussion, see Goodell, 1980.)

Iran's Formative Hierarchical Relations Contrasted with Those of the West and Japan

This glimpse into the formation of the West's and Japan's corporate political culture throws light on the elementary political structures and relationships in Rahmat Abad and Bizhan. Although we have referred to Rahmat Abad as "corporate" because of its numerous corporate charac-teristics and because these distinguished it so sharply from urban Iranian society, we must modify this now when Throne City is juxtaposed beside the much more articulated corporate structure and behavior of villages in manorial Europe and Japan during the State's formative period in *those* societies. The intense cohesion of the latter found symbolic mani-festation in each local community having its particular deity (Japan) or saint, each its temple or church as the physical embodiment of communal worship, making sacred one's local "platoon." While Rahmat Abad force-fully expressed its social unity in religious ritual, the fact that this never crystallized concretely in the community's own divine sponsor or inter-cessor with his own temple gave us a clue to the incompleteness of the village's incorporation. (Admittedly, as long as the village remained under the threat not just of individuals having to depart, but more impor-tantly, of their dispersing *in different directions,* the preservation of a local temple would have been jeopardized. But a group that moves cor-porately could enshrine its Holy in a portable temple like the ark of the covenant. The fact that Rahmat Abad did not do this calls attention to the village's *not* having quit the land corporately.)

Grasping now the strength, comprehensiveness, and firm structure of these medieval Japanese and European villages, we can recognize how that structure with the accountability it could demand and its comple-mentary mode of linking through contract came to permeate Western and Japanese cultures. In contrast, we can now appreciate Professor Bill's descriptions (1972; 1973) of the absence of corporate institutions even in the most modern sectors of Iranian society under the Pahlavis, despite those sectors' long exposure to Western education and their technocratic paraphernalia.

As is testified by the manorial society from which modern northwest-ern European and Japanese societies sprang, conflict and even "exploi-tation" may make political groupings into corporate structures (including classes). Indeed, if ultimately opponents cannot walk out, these political dynamics may *integrate* them, leading to closer bonds between them. In the case of *Iran,* the isolation of the traditional village was not the result of its geography, and certainly not of the internal corporate cohesion it did have, but rather of the fact that the village and its governor perceived nothing worth fighting against each other for. (Probably the State was left to claim the land throughout much of Asia, where we frequently find the absence of secure private landed property, because locally *neither* lord *nor* village would insist on claiming the land.) The Iranian lord's domi-nation of the village "alienated" it from urban Iranian society not because of his severity but because of his indifference. But while conflict indicates a common interest, it was the *necessity of resolving their con-flicts* that ultimately bound the opposing strata in each minipolity at the base of northwestern European and Japanese agrarian society; and, conversely, the absence of such necessity that freed governed and governor from one another in rural Khuzestan.

Because they had to resolve their conflict, out of it and out of their continual renegotiation and resolution the Japanese and northwestern European peasants and lords brought forth a public arena between and embracing governed and governor (where in Bizhan we found a no man's land). Even in the early manorial period in Europe and Japan, but all the more so during the High Middle Ages, this busy, richly textured, varied, open, and locally accountable public filled the space between individuals and their families, on the one hand, and the overarching polity, on the other, between the work force and its governing mechanism—as epitomized, for instance, by the multilayered profile of society we have before us in Chartres Cathedral, each layer self-consciously incorporated. This public was able to link governed and governor hierarchically because it depended vitally on contract and incorporation (see, for example, Althusius, 1964). Publicly visible, structured, and enduring—hence, predictable—middle-range groupings provided individuals with many vehicles for lively participation and initiatives in the public arena: virtually every type of association and enterprise in one way or another forbidden from Bizhan!

When instead of these, only personalistic arrangements can buffer against the uncertainties of arbitrary power, as in urban Iranian culture including the *shahrak*—providing networks of friends and kin without objectively defined boundaries of charter and purpose, membership, and duration—these may afford a limited predictability and accountability to their members if not to those outside of them. But in the end a society based primarily on organization through personal networks precludes a public arena. It precludes linking and accountability among strangers (expansion) and precludes objective accountability in all hierarchical relations: Rahmat Abad's obstacle in wanting to extend its activity into the domain ruled by *dulat*.

In addition to the public arena of interaction that these individual initiatives and corporate organizational forms created between the individual or family and the polity in European and Japanese medieval societies, at the same time a formal "governmental" hierarchy also emerged. The process through which it became established resembled that which we have seen beginning in Rahmat Abad but in time extending beyond the village and manor to regional, urban, and society-wide governance, answerable (unlike those of the Pahlavi State) to *local* society that it sought to coordinate. In many cases this hierarchy was appointed or ratified by the peasants themselves—hardly resembling *dulat*'s technocrats, or the obsequious hopes and electronic beeps of the model townsmen's communications with *their* governor.

Hierarchical governance in Europe and Japan, resulting from this flow of commands and checks and balances upward from the base, embodied the dynamics through which the *particulars* give forth Durkheim's *gen-*

eralization and *stability:* in contrast to Bizhan's State apparatus accountable only to those above not below it. Rahmat Abad illustrates why, when the northwestern European and Japanese peasant base insisted that the public arena be responsible to *it,* middle-range structures and vertical links necessarily evolved gradually. It would be impossible to rationalize the wider environment, tying governance or economic expansion to its stable base, except in stages, step by step, a process we watched in Rahmat Abad.

In Iran the scale and speed—and the unanswerable "professionalism" that scale and speed claimed to justify—established the autocrat as immune from accountability, because scale, speed, and expertise necessarily bypassed local and provincial structures and necessarily exceeded the pace with which existing structures could have organized themselves to keep *dulat* in check. Lilienthal's ambitious plans for the Dez constituted only one typical example of this. If accountability is not firmly established level by level, each with leverage over those *above* it, then just as the autocrat may play one group off against another horizontally, so, too, he can play one hierarchical level of society off against the other, as medieval European kings often attempted. In the very speed and scale of development, the World Bank's great scheme, contrasting so dramatically with medieval development, necessarily eroded the true center of society. Authority lost its moorings, the base of society its buffers and leverage, governance its hierarchical foundations downward.

Finally, then, the contrast between on the one hand, Rahmat Abad's predicament and Bizhan's no man's land, and on the other, manorial relations and the modern political cultures that evolved from them, highlights the latter societies' unity which resulted from this step-by-step welding. Their unity was forged during the formative agrarian period not by benevolent pronouncements of the Plan, "development" ideologies, or nationalistic TV extravaganzas, but by real vertical interdependence carried out in everyday local actions, political commitments, local partnerships, upward initiatives, and demands for accountability: the *operative* moral cohesion of economic and political interdependence between social strata. This unity derived from the *indispensable contribution of the base to the support of its own authority:* in contrast to the unity the Plan attempted to impose on society in the Dez, founded as it was on the base of society's uselessness. (Scholars who discuss the superfluousness of "post peasants" in many contemporary Third World societies sometimes write as though it appears only recently, whereas more likely it has characterized some State-level societies for millennia, as we argue it has Iran. What Marxists call "exploitation" must not be confused with the elites' *dependence* on those they "exploit.")

The constitutional principle articulated very early in medieval English society, "the King must be bound by his own law," boldly reduced to the essential this moral cohesion we have examined in early manorial society. Admittedly still an elementary principle of accountability as stated, yet in this radical foundation medieval society asserted that something higher than the King existed, law itself: the overarching community of all hierarchical strata, the authority of society's transcending truth binding all levels. Predictability *in itself* was proclaimed paramount. This accountability of law derived from early Germanic social organization, not from imperial Rome. By the time manorial society had established even this rudimentary center of gravity, it and Iranian society had already diverged from one another in their respective development paths—the former going on through the centuries gradually to elaborate Gratian's *Concordance of Discordant Canons*—not always smoothly, to be sure—while not even by the mid-twentieth century had Iran evolved this minimal requirement for social stability and unity.

Without this moral cohesion that can originate only in mutual interdependence and leverage, the Pahlavi Plan resolved to compartmentalize different parts of society each in its separate and isolated cubbyhole—the elites in their compounds whether in north Tehran or in the Dez project, the bazaar inside its mosque shell, first-class rural workers in their *shahrak*s, second-class rural workers in their State farms, and the third-class countryside in its rural "poles" that could never become anything else. Hence, too, *bast;* the no man's land between *dulat*'s street-appearance domain and the worker's world that *dulat* drove into their little back rooms. Hence, the failure of customary law ever to percolate upward and penetrate formal, enacted law in Iran—or, in the reverse dynamic, *dulat*'s fear it could never penetrate downward into Rahmat Abad except by completely appropriating the village unto itself. Hence, then, the alacrity with which Iranians periodically give over their State to the attacker from East or West or from within—whether the attacker come in phalanx, on horseback, or in robes. Split, partitioned, sealed off under a governance independent of the governed, there is no social whole that can affirm its law above *dulat*'s.

Authority's Independence from the Base

The societies that evolved from these early manorial foundations in Europe and Japan owed their corporate and contractual character to the lord's close dependence on his peasants during those centuries when the minipolities at the base were institutionalizing the accountability of the emerging formal authority, eventually to become the State. In time, increasing trade and alternatives both for livelihood and defense offered by the stronger State freed the lords from this strict dependence. The fact that later on they gained alternatives to their dependence on the manorial work force is reflected in periods when the work force's leverage diminished. But by then a political culture of public accountability, with its norms, skills, and institutions (though rudimentary) had become established. Even when the terms of leverage shifted against local labor and foot soldiers, organized, sustained negotiations for vertical accountability within society repeatedly reappeared. The fundamental values of corporate organization, contract, and public accountability among hierarchical levels were firmly in place in northwestern Europe and Japan by the late Middle Ages.

If the evolution of these corporate and contractual political cultures required the lords' dependence on the serfs during these polities' formative periods, how then do we explain the *absence* of such interdependence between governing hierarchy and work force in *Iranian* society? Does the fact that in Iran each side could evade confrontation derive from the Iranian base having no effective leverage (as northwestern European and Japanese peasants had) over the authority which emerged to govern it during the early agrarian period (when proportions might have enabled such leverage)? Evidence suggests that yes, unlike their European and Japanese counterparts, the Iranian lords did not vitally depend on the peasantry, at least not *in structured proportions* that would enable the latter to gain substantial bargaining leverage.

If the fifty-four major landlords of Dezful town during the 1950s exemplify provincially based elites in Iran and give us—even hypothetically—a clue into the traditional agrarian order (and there is little reason they should not), their economic profiles confirm that although the Iranian landlord collected the agricultural surplus of his villages, he did not rely on any one or several of them in what might have even approximated a one-to-one dependence. In fact, he rarely relied on agriculture at all for his basic livelihood. In the decades before and during World War II, all major Dezful landlords with only several exceptions enjoyed prosperous professional or trading incomes or bureaucratic appointments—frequently *several* incomes at once—which agriculture merely supplemented. Furthermore, the dispersion that characterized their managerial strategies in agriculture substantiated this conclusion, showing that they were basically independent of the returns they received from agriculture.

The Dez landlords hardly invested anything in agriculture, and they diluted every resource: capital, land, labor, even management. Through the generations they offered few technological improvements. We have already discussed the most striking evidence of the lords' indifference to agricultural returns, their allowing the peasants to walk off the land, sometimes leaving it uncultivated for years. In order to tie their cultivators to the land, European and Japanese lords had surmounted far more difficult obstacles than those of northern Khuzestan. Furthermore, by choosing not to live in the countryside, Iranian lords demonstrated that closely supervising production was not a high priority of theirs, although such supervision is critical in semiarid zones, as we saw even in the agribusinesses. They left management entirely to the peasants, investing as little of their own capital as possible. From a landlord's point of view, among traditional agricultural systems' production arrangements, share-cropping, which the Dezful lords accepted, requires the least from the lord and is also the least likely to render him optimal returns.

It could be said that the Dezful lords neglected agriculture because of the same lack of predictability in the countryside that the peasants found in this period. After all, by the 1940s the lords *had* begun to invest in local irrigation (with the peasants' considerable labor), presumably as soon as they found the countryside secure. But they did so only on the margin, to augment their basic income elsewhere, not out of the immediate dependence on agriculture which the medieval lords had experienced. Indeed, their irrigation investments in the 1940s, as soon as order was restored to the rural areas, raises the question as to why they themselves had not taken measures to stablize the countryside—or, more to our point, how they could have afforded *not* to. Contrary to northwestern European and Japanese landlords, those of northern Khuzestan not only provided no supervision or innovational leadership in agricultural production but offered the villagers and crops no protection either. To stabilize the countryside would not have been so difficult in this terrain as it was in northwestern Europe or Japan, made easier here by the landlords' close connection with the State and by locally rooted tribal chiefs whose assistance they could have enlisted (indeed, many of whom were landlords themselves).

Finally, instead of concentrating the *land* for efficient management, the Dezful lords dispersed even it in an extraordinary system of fragmentation and divided ownership far beyond what might be explained as risk control: In the 1950s each of the eighty-seven villages in what was to become the Dez Irrigation Project averaged five owners, one held by as many as twenty-eight lords. And as though this jumble were not inefficient enough, usually the lords minced their separate shares into such hairsplitting fractions as one man owning five shares, each of which was seven-thirteenths of the harvest, or another owning eight shares, each of which was three-sevenths! Poyck (1962) describes similar involution elsewhere in rural Mesopotamia. (For further discussion, see Goodell, 1977:695–711; Goodell, 1980:307–15.) In short, whereas each landlord might have farmed a solid block of 1,000 acres (or 4 of 250, to spread risk), even the very shareholding pattern among them indicated a basic indifference to the investment potentials of the land: again, their fundamental independence from agriculture.

The reason the lords lived in Dezful as urban elites, the reason they neglected their agricultural holdings, allowing these to reflect social and political priorities rather than economic ones, the reason they allowed the peasants to quit the land—the reason society's primordial work force could exert no leverage over its governors—was that at least here and in this century they held their main economic interests in the urban economy as military, bureaucratic, or merchant elites. In this they were carrying out an anciently established pattern: The practice reflected the fundamental law that has governed Iran for millennia—the Iranian State laying claim to all land and from that periodically giving out certain areas to *people who were already elites,* for them to tax farm it. In short, traditionally one was already an elite with another source of livelihood before one became a landlord in Iran. Here the relationship of the village to the lord, which might have bound the hierarchy to the base, did not constitute a minipolity of necessary overarching unity. The *peasants* could walk out of it because the *lord* himself could.

The Iranian Lords: If Not Dependent Upon the Village Then Dependent Upon What?

Although this explanation, well documented by many accounts (see Goodell, 1980:307–15) explains the Iranian peasants' inability to forge a political tie with the authority they recognized as their ultimate governance, and although it also explains the fundamental split between Iran's two primary social strata at least recently, it only pushes the question back and back further to the origin of the lords' independence (if *not* dependent on the village, then dependent on *what?*) and to the pattern's frequency down through the ages. Was there *ever* a time when the lord was dependent on the village? And if so, why didn't the vertical bonding take place then? Let us leave the twentieth century or even "traditional" custom for a moment and flash back to the initial emergence of stratified political relations.

If we imagine, long before the State evolved, the relatively balanced minipolities of egalitarian neolithic villages out of which Iranian society developed—perhaps similar to Rahmat Abad politically and socially—the question we want to ask is, how did some elites suddenly burst forth with the power to dominate everyone else, free from any leverage that those they would rule might exert to hold them accountable (as Rahmat Abad held Musa accountable)? Either those initial elites were able to rely on a source of support outside their villages, so they were not dependent on the base, or they somehow acquired control so quickly over such a wide territory that the local units could not organize fast enough to keep them in check. (In either case the elites would have gained independence from *particular* constituent units even though they might still depend on agriculture *in the aggregate* for their livelihood.) How could an individual family constituting the emerging hierarchy in one or several villages—and another in others, village by village over a given region (the Musas and Karims, for instance)—manage in such a *quantum leap* to free itself from its one-to-one dependence upon the minisociety to which it belonged and on which it relied?—how could it manage to free itself more rapidly and on a larger scale than the work force was able to organize off against it, to check its nascent power? (Once the elites achieved the upper hand, of course, and institutionalized it, they could then divide and rule.) The first stratum to gain power *beyond the structured control* of the work force must have had an economic base outside the villages themselves.

Here anthropological speculation begins. This study leads me to hypothesize that even before stratification developed in the first food-producing villages of the region—that is, while communities were still egalitarian—trade flourished in this area (Kohl and Wright, 1977; Wright, G., 1969; Wright, H., 1977; Goodell, 1977: 684–766). Society's nascent elites, as *traders,* would in time acquire a sufficient supplement to their agricultural livelihood to free each elite from one-to-one dependence on the particular minisociety to which he belonged (a village or cluster of villages). Once he established such independence based on trade, it would have been difficult for the base of society or a part of it, even if it organized itself, to muster the necessary leverage to hold this, its first level of hierarchy, in check. Unlike farmer or manufacturer, *the trader is not tied to anyone territorially* (see Hirschman, 1977). The emergent "lords," securing for themselves this freedom from groups of agriculturists before laying claim to governing authority, would have been able to make a quantum leap in economic and political power beyond any countervailing leverage the villagers might mount in trying to hold them accountable. If these traders, because they eventually required trading stations or collecting and shipping points, invented the first urban aggregations of the region to serve their trading purposes, *they would not have evolved as local and regional leaders part and parcel of the agrarian base.* To the contrary, they would have attracted agriculturalists *to* their trading centers, forging urban settlements whose surrounding villages were *dependent upon them* rather than the reverse.

Before elaborating the evidence and analysis of my argument here, we need to clarify two technical points. First, in this discussion I refer to trade rather than "exchange," the term some archaeologists prefer for the period, because when carried on for social or political ends the latter often denotes a transaction with a highly specific partner, hence an acknowledgment of mutual leverage. In contrast, it is the fact that the trader is prepared to strike a deal with anyone that gives him the political independence which lies at the core of this analysis.

The second technical point we need to clarify is why we carry on the discussion that follows in terms of ancient Mesopotamia, in present-day Iraq, rather than in terms of the proto-Elamites somewhat to the east, which is more precisely the mainspring of Iranian political culture. (Indeed, Susa itself lies but a matter of miles from Rahmat Abad.) For our purposes the social relations in Mesopotamia at this decisive period are far better documented than those of their proto-Elamite sister society not far away, and those factors that are crucial to our analysis here are very similar in both areas. Certainly trade, the key to our paradigm in this study, had taken hold in all proto-Elamite sites of the formative fifth and fourth millennia, precisely the time we see stratified relations of hierarchy and authority emerging in the cradle of Iran's political culture.

With this introductory outline in mind, of how early trade might have affected the political relations that were beginning to crystallize between the emerging elites and the base of society during the culture's formative early period, let us examine the archaeological evidence to test our hypothesis.

According to archaeological data, the most remarkable aspects of how political hierarchy did evolve initially in this region are the phenomenal *speed* and *scale* with which stratification became institutionalized. Urbanism's meteoric rise and the simultaneous burst of a State-level political apparatus onto the sparsely settled and very primitive Mesopotamian landscape during the late Ubaid and early Uruk periods can hardly be explained by the natural (hence, gradual) growth of certain villages into towns, as happened in northwestern Europe, or by a local process of sedentarization (Adams, 1981:69–70). The most plausible although not yet incontrovertibly demonstrated explanation for such an urban explosion—complete with its administrative hierarchies, professions, complicated bureaucratic transactions, and equivalent complexities in the deities' world—recalls Jacobs' proposed reconstruction of Çatal Huyuk's rise in Anatolia: that people with thriving craft manufacturing and trade may have brought immigrants to their settlement to work in these economic activities, and then may have recruited farmers to produce their emerging city's food in the adjacent countryside, overseeing the latter, as archaeologists believe was done in ancient Mesopotamia, through a bureaucracy (Jacobs, 1969:3–48; Adams, 1981:87).

Jacobs' reconstruction explains how, seemingly overnight, the structure of unchecked urban power came greatly to exceed that which individual village landlords might have commanded. As we have said, Mesopotamian archaeologists have shown that, considering its pace and scale, the "hyperurbanization" characteristic of the region could not have evolved out of the local population. Confirming this, Jacobs proposes that it was *not* the villages at the base of society that gave forth the towns, cities, and the State. Instead, each evolving city-State of traders created some villages for itself around it—just enough villages to serve its needs (their size, and so forth, subservient to the city's purposes). As for the vast rural population *beyond* these satellite villages, the State simply left them to go their own way, outside its domain. If the early State was based on an urban trade economy, the great majority of agricultural communities in the *biyaban* wasteland beyond its domain would have had enormous difficulty making the State responsive to their demands. In the entire region around Uruk, for example, we find *no middle-sized population centers.* That means no population centers which through relatively feasible political combinations might have provided a countervailing check on Uruk's power (small settlements being much more easily subjugated

by divide-and-rule). Hence, while the city, with its artificially created satellite villages, took one course of development under the State's
unchecked power, the vast rural population not incorporated into the
State's domain evolved a politically detached society and culture on their
own, just as Rahmat Abad was doing in the early decades of this century.
During certain periods the State might conquer them temporarily, when
they might become attached to landlords, but as appendages, never in
structured mutual dependence; and never able to recapture the proportions necessary for leverage and political balance, which were a matter of
timing. Once the precocious State had emerged without needing them,
the right time for acquiring such leverage had passed.

Whether or not we accept Jacobs' hypothesis, by the end of the *fourth
millennium* B.C. the picture that archaeological data present strikingly
resembles the Dez in the mid-twentieth century A.D.: Urban elites with
their State-level civilization had taken off on their own development
course, drawing into *dulat*'s vortex a portion of the nearby rural population to provide for what urban society needed, the State not tied to this
agricultural aggregate in any structured way and certainly not deriving
from it as its efflorescence. The State kept its satellite rural settlements
the size it wanted them, reminiscent of Bizhan. (Theoretically, an urban
trading center would not have to have *any* agricultural settlements at all
nearby, since traders could exchange goods for nonperishable foodstuffs
whenever they could find them, and once strong enough, could play agriculturalists off against each other for their produce.) The rest of the population in the landscape the State left out there beyond the pale. Contrary
to the process of step-by-step evolution through which the dependent
urban centers and the State in northwestern Europe and Japan remained
integrally joined to the countryside and therefore responsive to it politically, in Mesopotamia during this formative period and those immediately following it little or no administrative continuity even connected
the nearby agricultural settlements to the cities over sustained periods of
time. Nor did the efficiency and intensification of agricultural production
keep up with the density of the urban populations, which according to
Western and Japanese evolution it would have had to feed (Adams,
1981:87–88; Boserup, 1965:38ff).

Absorbing unto its own domain those it periodically took hold of to
use, this State—as seen from the indigenous agrarian base outside its
domain—squatted on the landscape, a separate society. In many other
ways, too, urban-agrarian relations in these early centuries remind us vividly of the Dezful landlords' apathetic management strategies, implying
the cities' loose, *overall* dependence on agriculture but *not individual
elites' dependence on individual agricultural units* for their bottom-line
survival. Some cities appear suddenly without needing the support of
nearby agriculture at all (Adams, 1981:59). The subsidiary communities
that surrounded Uruk, the leading city of the region, clearly did *not* constitute "the core of an attached zone of continuous cultivation," nor did

they elicit long-term agricultural investment from the townsmen or the State (Adams, 1981:88). And the agricultural development that did appear near some cities was managed by elites who resided in town (just as they did throughout virtually all later Iranian history including the modern period). Living far from the fields, such lords apparently were able to choose not to provide the close, sustained supervision that intensified semiarid zone agriculture requires if it is to yield its maximum (Oppenheim, 1964:113; Adams, 1981:87). By definition, too, as absentee landlords they did not depend on their villages to defend them.

Reminiscent of modern urban landlords' economic independence of agriculture, society's political elites in ancient Mesopotamia rarely saw to it that the countryside was secure from brigandage in order to protect agricultural production (Adams, 1981:87, 140).

Finally, during these formative centuries of Iran's political culture, labor relations—which define the emerging hierarchy's dependence on a stable and predictable social base—seem almost identical to those of traditional and modern rural Iran. As though founded upon the peasantry's right to quit the land at will, the agricultural labor force that archaeologists describe for the fourth millennium refused to be forced into sedentary conditions (Oppenheim, 1964:82). The urban centers appeared "helpless" against villagers who frequently fled the land (Moran in Adams, 1974:14). Often a footloose agricultural population not integrated into the urban polity governed itself by completely separate tribal law (Adams, 1981:153), in primordial and perduring independence from the State that had no use for it.

Because ancient Mesopotamian society did not have the intense bonds of mutual dependence between the elites and the agricultural base of society of the type that determined northwestern European and Japanese hierarchical relations as they became institutionalized during these political cultures' formative periods, it is not surprising that the former region is described by so many scholars as having no middle-range institutions whatsoever, being sharply divided between urban and rural, the center of the basically unconnected hinterland, the State off against the agrarian masses. As though in a time-warp fulfillment of the Pahlavi Plan Organization's dream, there were no medium-sized settlements even in the earliest period of Uruk's development, when one would expect to find them. Adams describes the social composition of the population within, versus outside, the State's domain as "polar" extremes separated by radical "power displacements" and lacking intermediate ranges of social and political organization.

Thus at the very outset of formal government in this political culture, we find the no-man's-land between *dulat* and the base of society in place, echoing the drilling episode in Rahmat Abad or *dulat*'s disappearance from the Lions Club presentation in Bizhan. Off against the "excess of centrality" and "extraordinary centralization" of early Uruk's domain lay the unabsorbed rural population (the third- and fourth-rate villages of the

Plan) that had no reason to recognize itself or be recognized as members
of the polity, "far beyond the reach of urban administration" by Assyrian
times (Adams, 1981:72–74, 87, 153). It is no wonder that throughout history, as the fortunes of townsmen prospered during brilliant dynastic
upswings and one level of technological complexity led into the next
within *dulat*'s domain, the broad base of society seems to have continued
using agricultural practices hardly advanced beyond those devised by the
very earliest food-producing communities of southern Mesopotamia. Not
just on the remote fringes or in enclaves but across society's very foundation, the most primitive economic, technological, and social conditions
appear to have persisted *within* one of the world's greatest civilizations—
at its base: recurrently, the most progressive cities of their time surrounded by third-millennium B.C. agriculture. The political advantages
that trade offered even early elites precluded the evolution of a single,
bounded and internally coherent system such as those that emerged in
the West and Japan.

It may be, as some archaeologists argue, that later in these formative
centuries the Mesopotamian State did penetrate the entire countryside
and bring it sporadically under *dulat*'s administrative control. By the
third millennium there appear to be private estates in the countryside
during certain periods (with absentee lords). But by that time the balance
of power had become irreversibly skewed, just as it was when *dulat*
reduced the Dez to its Plan. Although urban society's hierarchy and
authority probably depended on the base for its food, that hierarchy ruled
that base as an aggregate. How then could organized leverage upward
from the base demand and require accountability? Hierarchical relations
had taken the quantum leap to unchecked power.

In this analysis we have hypothesized that through the traders' independence from *particular* territorial ties, emerging hierarchy escaped
beyond the reaches of checks and balances from the base. And we have
shown the social consequences of that independence in two different periods, during the formative centuries of the culture and very recently. From
its birth, the State in Mesopotamia and Elam engaged in trade over
exceedingly long distances. Complementary economic alternatives may
have further ensured the governors' independence from an organized
work force, hence from downward accountability: Both herding and fishing flourished in the region from ancient times. Trade could convert
sheep, fish, and their by-products into subsistence staples without any
reliance on particular agriculturists. Indeed, in time elites could retire
even from trading and enjoy their comfort simply by controlling the trade
routes and customs charges. The State itself could become the master
trading firm. Similar economic, social, and political patterns rooted in the
primacy of trade recur throughout Iranian history. Even the cruelest conquerors, like the Mongols, while laying waste to agriculture have spared
traders and have protected trade routes. In the modern era the Iranian
State relied heavily on customs payments for revenue independent of its
social base. For the State to construct its twentieth-century civilization

on the wealth of petroleum resources similarly frees it from having to establish any connection with the population it rules.

Thus virtually from the outset of village settlement, when the fundamental relationship between political hierarchy and the base of society began to crystallize, two interacting but essentially independent strata emerged on the Iranian landscape. We see these etched sharply when we go to live in Rahmat Abad and Bizhan, but the terms of their relationship are not new—perhaps because once having reached a certain scale in their formative period, and then having become institutionalized, these terms could not be changed.

Rahmat Abad, Bizhan, and Anthropological Theory

Comparing the economic and political dynamics that hypothetically brought forth and then institutionalized social stratification in ancient Mesopotamia, with those that did the same in manorial Europe and Japan, calls for anthropologists to refine their analyses of State-level societies and the emergence of the State in prehistory. Here I can only touch upon a few of these theoretical implications of this study.

In analyzing State-level society, both functionalists and Marxists depict a polity whose levels are vertically interdependent (either by concession or coercion). Is this accurate, though, for the society we examine here? In some degree, at least, the separate Iranian subsystems of governor and "governed" shared the same overall symbolic world (Moharram illustrates how far), and the State with the urban population in its domain depended economically on the overall agricultural work force. But if sustained political interaction—hence, a polity—needs the give-and-take between interrelated structures, how did these aggregates connect with one another in Iran? Such mechanisms as existed for the flow of information upward or downward required *no systematic responsiveness* on the side of society's governor or its governed. Indeed, although the elites extracted surplus from the base, they did so without having systematically to organize, support, or manage it as a work force.

Had the higher strata found it necessary to mobilize the broad base of society's labor (even "exploitively"), thereby together with labor forging a social realm that both shared off against nature, then each level would have entered into the other's terms. But those primary producers who *were* periodically tapped retained their traditional right to walk out of any organized production, while it appears that the elites' main base also lay outside the would-be political arena between governed and governor. Their base lay in trade (leaving the State to "own" the principal means of production, the land, by default). If the governing center of a "system" has more frequent and dependent interaction with external entities than vertically with those it governs, and if to it *adaptation* in the last extreme requires response to external rather than internal pressures, then we would expect the "system" periodically and voluntarily to give up the

integrity of its boundaries to outside governance—as Iran has done regularly through the centuries, conquered and ruled by non-Iranians for
over a thousand years, usually with little resistance. In this light doesn't
Marx's concept of control over the means of production reveal his bias
as an economist? For political analysis isn't control over one's ultimate
means of *livelihood* more useful?

Howsoever harsh at times the Iranian landlords' demands, and howsoever primitive the agriculturalists' welfare, if our criteria are political
rather than economic ones can we refer to the "power" of the State in this
case, or to "exploitation" of the work force?

Even at its strongest, Iran's center did not completely engulf that part
of the base whose resources it selectively sought (as we saw in Bizhan
when the latter retreated behind closed doors and did there what it was
"forbidden" to do). But more telling, the Iranian center seems to have
had *little interest* in absorbing the entire land and people within its borders, and may not have had for millennia. In exchange, and in contrast
to the often feisty European and Japanese peasants, throughout history
the agrarian population of Iranian society has rarely shown inclination to
rebel either for or against any regime (nor did it in the past few years): as
though the State being fought over now and again is someone else's State
but not its own.

When social scientists analyzing stratification in State-level societies
have emphasized the economic conditions of the base or its relationship
as an aggregate to those governing it—the "masses" without internal corporate structuration—they often overlook the difference that *organization* makes in shaping these relationships and, hence, in determining the
nature of State-level society. The solution to Rahmat Abad's problem of
accountable hierarchy ultimately lies not in economic factors—ownership of the means of production or the enjoyment of more comforts,
amenities, and economic opportunities—but in political organization. In
a related oversight, anthropologists studying the processes of social
change have all too often attributed society's shift to a higher level of
productivity to the effects of demographic, ecological, and economic factors on the social aggregate (Boserup, 1965; Spooner, 1972; and many
others). But the connection between demographic pressures and technoeconomic change is necessarily and always mediated by the base of society's political organization, hence, by the intermediate-range structures
the base does (or does not) bring forth. Otherwise, how do we explain the
poverty of India and China? What we may conclude about vertical relations in society when we consider "strata" only as aggregates may contrast sharply with what we will find if, taking a microscope, we look at
how each level does or does not structure itself in hierarchical interaction
with its governors in discrete political modules that give it leverage.

Involution, which splits resources inwardly for want of a secure environment into which to expand and for want of reliable methods for new
forms of bonding, occurs when, as Durkheim indicates, political struc-

turation and coupling—political density—does not keep pace with the volume of demographic and technoeconomic interaction a given social unit is generating (1933:262). Unless organization through accountable political modules progresses along with whatever increase takes place in demographic and technoeconomic intensity, the latter pressure will eventually push a status-based society toward reifying its personalistic, subjective, secretive, and fragmentary forms under more centralized rule (Goodell, 1980:318–19). If the base cannot expand the scope of available linkages beyond those offered by personalistic ties—that is to say, if it cannot expand its range of integration—then while a society may move to a higher technoeconomic level, its political structures and relations may become fixed at a very simple organizational stage. Over time this may lead into a qualitatively different evolutionary line of "development" from that of structured societies which maintain internal integration.

Most scholars accept the assumption that all State-level societies transcend kin-based organization. While I have not proposed here that a vast State-level society like modern Iran is organized strictly on kinship, I do argue that it did not evolve beyond *status-based* political and economic organization at the macrosystem level. Furthermore, I propose that in terms of social evolution, those societies which evolve types of political (and legal) organization based on impersonal contract and corporate structures accountable in a public arena during the formative agrarian period when the terms of authority and hierarchy become institutionalized, may constitute a distinct "line of development" from those societies whose political (and legal) organization remains based on personalistic status even after hierarchy emerges. We should not consider status-based complex societies as merely an earlier stage along the same continuum, because as the two types evolve in technoeconomic complexity and scale, they fork off radically from one another (Goodell, 1980). Despite the fact that Pahlavi Iran resembled contemporary northern European societies in having a State-level administrative apparatus, industrial technology, expanding society-wide literacy, and a growing middle class, in evolutionary terms the two political cultures had substantively diverged from one another by the tenth century A.D. From this it would follow that beneath the superficial *similarities* between all societies that have entered the industrial era, the basic structures and relations of *industrial* Iran will probably carry out the configurations that predominated in its *agrarian* period, not those Western scholars associate with "modern" society in general, like political or legal accountability (the underpinning of Weber's economic rationality).

Just as social change at the level that concerns us here takes place slowly (through centuries in medieval Europe and Japan), students examining it must be willing to consider decades, generations, or centuries as their analytical units. Furthermore, in considering evolutionary stages we must bear in mind that in every evolutionary process there is *an optimum time* for the development of a new structure within the organism, or for a particular shift in crucial relationships between its constituent parts. This timeliness is due to the complexity and delicacy of organic interaction and to the intricate dynamics of scale, even more important in human society than in less complex organisms. The agrarian period out of which many Third World societies are just now emerging is one such decisive time, as it was for northwestern European and Japanese societies—decisive because the terms and the scale of political relations are then optimal for local political organization to learn to match the State's institutions of society-wide governance, which are rapidly consolidating. If the base cannot keep pace at *this* point, making sure that these institutions and the fundamental principles that underpin them serve to *coordinate* rather than to *command,* then it may find it impossible to regain lost ground later on: not only because of the increasing disparity of sheer force and the tendency for involution to become routinized, but because once an absolute center has evolved it will divide and rule, or it will co-opt the base by removing motivational incentives for organization and collective effort. Through long periods of political inactivity the base may lose the norms, habit, and institutions for organizing itself, causing it to crave and depend on autocratic rule out of fear of itself.

To understand this question of timing more clearly, consider the costs people must incur in order to organize themselves in any way, a matter that interests many economists these days particularly with regard to grass-roots participation in developing countries (Olson, 1965; Johnston and Clark, 1982:33–34, 171–73; Johnston and Tomich, 1984:99). Far more important than the fact that there is a price to be paid for moving to a higher organizational level, or for intensifying organization, is the fact that the costs which a fragmented work force incurs in trying to bring forth organization in a *relatively neutral* political space vary enormously from the costs of doing the same in a *highly skewed* political matrix; and that the costs of organizing new structures once old ones have fallen into disuse are far greater than the costs of *maintaining* organization which has already been established. Thus when we speak of there being an "optimal time" for certain organizational developments within an organism, we point to the extraordinary range in organizational costs depending on the relative balance that exists within a system and on the strength of organizational retention.

The governance of any system is essentially a matter of *proportions.* Once a certain balance has been lost between "governor" and "governed," then two rather tenuously related social systems may evolve, not with one being an enclave surrounded by the other, but the two being populous partial societies coexisting in the same or adjacent spaces, one superimposed in and between the other. The possibility grows dimmer and dimmer for these two levels to establish a structured and systematically unified political life or common governance, not because of their disparity in "power" or wealth, but because of their disparity in the relative costs of organization. It is in this eventuality, not revolution, that the greatest danger of our current "economic development" policies lies.

The development of local and intermediate-range organizations and skills probably cannot be postponed until after a complex society reaches a previously designated level of economic prosperity, as many development economists and others hope it can be. Higher levels of technology, standards of living, or education in and of themselves will hardly give a society the ability to hold its governor on course, or give to the lower orders the ability to insist that elites open up room for their expansion. Nor can these abilities be instilled by training the State's bureaucrats or professionals in Western universities. Indeed, they cannot be created *at all* from the top of society, since one of their essential functions is to hold the top accountable, which the top resists.

In our studies of these imbalances in State-level societies and how they evolved, anthropologists have paid far less attention to the positive organization of the base, society's work force, than to the negative considerations of stratification, power, and exploitation. Despite many theorists' vigorous denials, the decades of almost singular preoccupation with these three issues may be explained by scholars' greater interest and indeed *confidence* in the elites and the State, as *the positive forces of society,* than in the determinative potential of the base. In effect anthropology has sought to explain the social base in terms of the State and its hierarchy, rather than explore the opposite dynamic. If as anthropological analysts we shift perspective to focus on a would-be positive, active, and responsible base of society—not one passively being ruled but one customarily impelled to initiate its projects and ready to protect them if need be— then the research and theoretical issues that arise from this focus differ from those raised by a focus on *elites* or bureaucracy as society's often culpable driving force. For example, what conditions favor the base sustaining its creative, long-term initiatives as society's driving force? One of the foremost conditions is not economic at all, but rather a relatively predictable environment (predictable to the bottom of society, not just to the top). Then what role must the base play in ensuring itself predictability? If we accept the fact of social stratification in all complex societies, how does the base mount political leverage to hold hierarchy accountable? (Few anthropologists today write as though they believe this is even possible.) As the base launches its projects and seeks to check arbitrary interference in them, how does it evolve intermediate-range structures that are decisive to all organization and to organized expansion—certainly decisive for holding governance on course? Will networks suffice or must these intermediate-range structures be corporate?

Because the paradigm of political centralization has monopolized so many of our studies of the State (more often implicitly rather than explicitly), anthropologists and other social scientists have virtually ignored the systematic problems of predictability and accountability, issues *foremost* to a creative and dynamic base but, of course, not to the centralized State.

In proportion to the attention we have given to the State's power, we have explored very little how corporate structures sustain resistance to it—again, not a probable research priority for scholars concentrating on political relations from *the State's* perspective, but crucial to the base. We still do not understand very thoroughly the distinction between on the one hand, intermediate-range structures and indeed intermediate strata growing out of the base, to serve *its* interests ("hierarchy" in an organic sense) and on the other hand, those put into the intermediate range by the top, to serve its domination, embodying the opposite political dynamic. Again, because of scholars' underlying hope in the creative potential of a non-exploitative centralized State, we have seen much more extensive theoretical or empirical work on bureaucracy, the *State's* "intermediate-range structures," than on the formation, persistence, and crucial functions of the base's own projections.

Revealing an intellectual bias common among many social scientists and historians who equate political centralization with civilization, development, justice, and equity, or indeed with culture itself in State-level societies, Service (1975:82) adamantly insists that the decentralization of Europe after the Roman Empire's collapse could "certainly not [be considered] a stage in the *development* of a polity." These formative centuries' extreme type of *local control*—society's most salient feature during this period—must account for his sweeping dismissal of their importance to Western development. Service then would reject the notable line of Western political analysts like Althusius (1964) and Gierke (1900) who help us trace not only the evolution of northwestern European polities from this decentralized period, but in specific, the development of these polities' distinguishing characteristics, corporate pluralism and authority's vertical accountability downward. Contrary to Service's conclusion, it was during those very "darkest" centuries that the essentially new culture of northwestern Europe arose.

In his implication that no evolutionary advance could take place when society radically decentralizes, Service reflects the bias of many archaeologists and anthropologists studying the prehistoric State, as well as many historians studying periods and societies within the reach of history, who for understandable professional reasons find the peaks of centralization more significant than relatively decentralized State-level societies or periods—as though political centralization constitutes an evolutionary goal. It is possible that in this bias against political decentralization some scholars are influenced by their opinions about contemporary politics. In this study our examination of the highly decentralized manorial periods of northwestern Europe and Japan points to quite a different interpretation of the political formation that takes place in periods of *local* consolidation and governance, and a weak State-level authority.

It may be difficult for laymen and perhaps even some scholars to entertain the hypothesis basic to this study, that events as long ago as the tenth century (in our culture—or the fifth millennium B.C. in Iran's) could still have as profound an effect upon societies today as I have argued that they do. While Dobb (1947) was correct in pointing to serfdom as the critical attribute of European feudalism, he fell short of pinpointing serfdom's profoundly formative political role, and the formative political role of similar institutions in Japan. In this study we carry an analysis of these effects a step further, showing the lasting social consequences of Iranian political culture's *not* having had this agrarian institution in its "genetic makeup." Indeed, it is possible that the absence in Iran of the decentralized manor's long period of political formation, and the presence instead of a way out for the lords—a way out such as trade—have affected a much wider culture area than we have discussed in this book. That political culture which is rooted in the ability of the work force to quit the land during the agrarian period when hierarchical relations were first becoming institutionalized in society—that political culture was far more widespread than were the rare conditions of early manorial Japan and northwestern Europe. Since large parts of Asia, the Mediterranean region, and even Russia probably sustained uninterrupted trading for millennia throughout the decisive formative agrarian period, perhaps here we are examining the political culture of the entire area Marx had in mind when describing the "Asiatic mode of production." Inasmuch as Mediterranean society manifests the particular cultural traits, or variations of them, that have interested us here, we should include it in the same political culture.

Finally, this study rejects the assertion of Weber and theorists of "modernity" who follow him, that a formalistic legal order and bureaucratic administration constitute the determinative conditions for contract-based capitalism; and it challenges their argument that capitalism's essential underpinnings became established in Europe only *after* the breakdown of the medieval order.

Like Weber, this study locates the foundations of sustained capitalist development in a social environment that is locally predictable, enabling increasingly systematic interaction both in detail and in scope, and facilitating relatively long-term decisions and purposeful exchanges on the basis of instrumental criteria—not hampered by the privileges of status or by the weight of untested subjective assumptions. Like Weber, this study confirms the importance of law, society's continued refinement of conditions and means for calculability that is easily accessible to but transcends the individual. In short, we concur with Weber that information, impersonal contract, and predictability are decisive for sustained capitalist development.

But in contrast to Weber and the theorists of "modernity," this study has found the seeds of these essential social conditions in "backward," illiterate Rahmat Abad, and found them destroyed in the formal legal order, the scientific and professional expertise, and the highly systematized bureaucratic governance of *dulat*—not because formal law, professionalism, and bureaucracy per se are obfuscating, but because they work

against calculability *if they are not kept accountable to society's base.* Formal law, scientific and technological expertise, professional specialization, and the would-be impersonal order of public administration do not
in themselves foster predictability, but only do so in a particular political
context, in which a structured social base holds its governing mechanism
(hence, these instruments for organizing governance) on course.

Many theorists of "modernization" have attributed to these tools per
se, which merely lie *on the surface* of society, the intrinsic function of
social calculability. From that they locate the historic origin of society-
wide predictability and free exchange which requires predictability, in the
rise of the centralized State that collected these mechanisms together as
its coordinating apparatus. On the basis of these two grave errors, theorists as well as agencies like the World Bank then conclude that to put in
place the requisites for sustained capitalist development, a "modernizing" society must perfect the equipment for centrally organized control—
technocrats with their national, provincial, and local-level ministries,
consolidated irrigation systems, factories integrated into a national industrial plan, national telephone and school systems, central banking institutions, public administrators with university training in statistics, health
policy, and so forth. They overlook the fact that long before these manifestations of economic and coordinational activity appeared on the social
landscape in Europe and Japan, society had firmly institutionalized, level
by level, the accountability of governance to those being governed.

In Europe and Japan the State's organizational advantages did indeed
help capitalism to blossom forth, but only due to the checks and balances
on hierarchy that were firmly in place by the late Middle Ages, and that
did not spring then nor will they spring now from formal law, streamlined
formal administration, or greater national wealth (see Goodell, 1985).

This study accepts the likelihood that some forms of capitalism do not
require the conditions of *impersonal* calculability which Weber says capitalism does. Perhaps status-based societies may continue *as such* and
evolve their own distinctive form of status-based capitalism, at least as
far as personalistic ties, interpersonal predictability, and personalistic
networks (rather than corporate organization) may allow. Anthropologists have documented at least small-scale and short-term means by
which those linked personally hold one another accountable. We see personalism supporting considerable economic development at the macrolevel in some Latin American societies, and at the microlevel in overseas
Chinese family firms, for example. Bizhan and Iranian society within
dulat's domain may come to enjoy a similar course of development in
time. Much more research is needed to distinguish these forms of predictability from the impersonal calculability Weber discussed, and to
document the limits of predictability and trust in status-based versus contractual State-level societies.

To the extent that contractual and corporate organization offer complex, industrial society greater flexibility and scope than personalistic

linkages can, along with a genuine *public,* and firmer accountability, this study has documented Throne City's development potential with its after-dinner-teapot parliament out in Lilienthal's wasteland, and how the State hemmed in and then undermined that promise.

Ibn Khaldun Reflects on Rahmat Abad's Challenge

Despite the assistance of so many Western savants, far from resolving the problem of hierarchical accountability that Rahmat Abad and its sister villages had begun to tackle, the self-assured Pahlavi–World Bank thrust to develop Iran exacerbated that problem on a society-wide scale. Many other Third World societies face the challenge we have examined here, based as they also are in small, relatively corporate and autonomous villages with their culture of economic rationality and dynamic local potential, their political accountability, their open public arenas, their frequently contractual linking, and their ancient mechanisms to guard predictability and permanence against arbitrary rule. Now is the time, when the State-level political culture is becoming institutionalized (or reestablished anew) in many of these societies, laying down the fundamental terms of initiative, balance, and accountability, to develop rather than undermine these strengths where they are found. Domestic tranquility may or may not be at stake, but far more important, the basic structure of the polity is.

Mr. Lilienthal "prophesied and promised" that the world would be watching his transformation of the Dez. Would that in *that* prophecy he had been correct! The Dez will not see him or Mr. Ebtehaj again, the founder of one more dynasty's Imperial Plan. But many other northern Khuzestans across the world will, as we continue to send out myriad visionaries like them to transform the "nothingness" wherever they can find it: with the same self-serving vision; the same certainty of engineers, economists, and bankers that the "majesty of man" will "master this behemoth" by building *"things";* the same blindness to the landscape; the same grandiose schemes that we can construct "the everlasting" in it— the same confidence in developing others through the fiat of centralized rule over them from on high.

Six hundred years ago the accomplished historian, social scientist, diplomat, and distinguished civil servant Ibn Khaldun, after traveling widely in these lands and pondering why societies' rise to prosperity under the command of the centralized State led over and over to their rapid decline, wrote this advice for rulers and development visionaries: All society needs government. Under the *optimal* government people are

> guided by the courage or cowardice that they possess in themselves. Self-reliance eventually becomes a quality natural to them. They would not know anything else. If, however, the [State's] domination with its laws is one of brute force or intimidation, it deprives them of their power of resis-

tance as a result of the inertness that develops in the soul of someone who cannot defend himself.... Those who rely on [the ruler's] laws and are dominated by them from the very beginning, in time can scarcely defend themselves at all against hostile acts.... This situation and the fact that it destroys the power of resistance must be understood.... Governmental and educational laws destroy fortitude [when] their restraining influence is something that comes from outside. (Ibn Khaldun, 1967:95–99)

Verily, God is independent of the worlds.
—Qur'an, Sura 29

Epilogue

What has happened to the people in Mr. Lilienthal's dream since the collapse of the agribusinesses and the State farms, since the Iranian revolution and the subsequent war, is impossible to discern from afar in any detail. By 1976 the first five *shahrak*s were fully occupied with peasants whose land had been expropriated. The experimental stage completed, Iran had embarked full force on extending the model towns nationwide. Then, even more suddenly than it had risen, the Dez Project collapsed. Within two years the agribusinesses were declared bankrupt. Royalty and the State took them over. *Dulat* asked the former peasants to return to farm most of the land it had shortly before given them and then taken away.

Northern Khuzestan showed one of the first clear public signs of the impending revolution when as early as 1976 a band of high school boys declared Dezful to be a new Islamic People's Republic. Having drawn up its manifesto, they marched on the nearby air force base—one of the country's largest—to occupy it! One lad was killed in the military's attempt to defend itself. I am told that the peasants of the area, though, played virtually no role in the revolution, either for or against their Father with the Crown. The villagers in Rahmat Abad had warned me, when we listened to the Ayatollah on radio: "He will fill the city streets, Khanom Grace; he will fill the streets with townsmen."

The entire province of Khuzestan has paid dearly for the revolution, battered as it has been by the war with neighboring Iraq that immediately ensued. The cities of Khorramshahr and Abadan have been emptied, resembling the remains of Susa in visitors' descriptions of them; parts of Ahwaz, Dezful, and the elites' compound nearby have also been laid waste by bombing. Wild barley grows in the technocrats' once-plush living rooms, someone said: one of the first crops mankind learned to cultivate here in these very Mesopotamian uplands millennia ago. Doubtlessly, Noshirvan's owls have moved in to claim their newest ruins.

The sharp twists so characteristic of the Dez since the visionaries first caught sight of it continue to reverse history's expectations. The Ayatollah's revolution finally completed the Shah's land reform for him, distributing land even to the landless (although one wonders whether villages like Rahmat Abad have kept the *joft* system, or whether others have perhaps reconstituted it). The revolution also broke up the State farms, surely a confirmation that these had already failed. Since the former irrigation system that local farmers could manage on their own had been destroyed within the DIP, and since the revolution has suffered a grave loss of technical manpower able to manage and maintain the World Bank's new canals, the rich lands of the Dez receive but erratic irrigation and no independent capital investment. Furthermore, fertilizer is expensive; the revolutionary government forbids the cultivation of cash crops in lieu of the less lucrative grains the cities need so badly. Thus some of the formerly prosperous farmers like Sultan 'Ali and Haji Safar have begun to lease the land that the revolution gave back to the landless and smaller farmers; the former then hire the latter to work it, consolidating fields once again in the hands of a nascent postrevolution landlord class.

Many who constituted the traditional landlord class have emigrated to America or France. I have heard no reports of any of the prominent figures having lost their lives at the hands of revolutionaries. Indicatively, most of the leading locally based technocrats of our story have remained in comfortable—some in powerful—positions in Iran, bearing out the wisdom that lay in the *shahrak* mothers' and fathers' advice to their sons: not to aspire for money or land but only for a job with *dulat*. Some of the Dez Project's technocrats have formed a capitalist consulting firm designing new irrigation projects for the Islamic Republic.

Ironically, too, it has taken the sufferings of revolution and war finally to set Bizhan free from the Plan and bring it into the mainstream of provincial life. During our conversation the night of the Tenth Day of Moharram, when the holy days had finally drawn to a close, Nabi had blamed God bitterly for bursting the old social fabric asunder yet not allowing the new model town to be born in its place, with a life of its own. Perhaps in response to Nabi's plea God sent the remedy He did. Endangered by revolutionary chaos and the Iraqi air attacks, the people of Dezful—especially the prosperous bureaucrats—have sought refuge in the villages and *shahrak*s for protection, moving out to the countryside en masse: particularly to the *shahrak*s, where new construction flourishes, the population has grown far beyond the Plan's determinate bounds, shops, schools, and other urban amenities have blossomed. Perhaps even the small mosques have now bloomed, the mosques that the model townsmen had wanted to build themselves from the outset close by their homes, not for the Friday prayer and sermon but in order to guard their ancient ties and traditions safely from the ravages of *dulat*'s changes.

**He who will set the world in flames, put out his lamp of life.
One man on fire is better than to see everyone get branded.
—Sa'di, from *The Bustan***

Bibliography

This bibliography does not attempt to include all the major works in various languages on Iranian land reform, Iranian agricultural development, the model towns, the Khuzestan Development Scheme or Dez Irrigation Project, the many studies on rural Iran during the time period covered, nor modern Iranian and Middle Eastern history and prehistory. Extensive materials exist on the Dez Project and plans related to it, which constituted background for this study. Here I only list materials cited specifically in the text.

Abrahamian, Ervand
  1974 "Oriental Despotism: The Case of Qajar Iran." *International Journal of Middle Eastern Studies,* 5(1):3–31.
  1979 "The Causes of the Constitutional Revolution in Iran." *International Journal of Middle Eastern Studies,* 10(3):381–414.
Abu Talib Kalim
  1972 Selections from *Shah-Jahan-Namah.* In *A Golden Treasury of Persian Poetry.* Edited and translated by M. S. Israeli. New Delhi: Indian Council for Cultural Relations, p. 396.
Adams, Robert McCormick
  1962 "Agriculture and Urban Life in Early Southwestern Iran." *Science,* n.s., 136:3511.
  1966 *The Evolution of Urban Society.* Chicago: Aldine.
  1974 "The Mesopotamian Social Landscape: A View from the Frontier." In *Reconstructing Complex Societies.* Edited by Charlotte Moore. Supplement of the Bulletin of the American Schools of Oriental Research, 20.
  1981 *Heartland of Cities.* Chicago: University of Chicago Press.
Adams, Robert McCormick, and Hans Nissen
  1972 *Uruk Countryside.* Chicago: University of Chicago Press.
Althusius, Johannes
  1964 *The Politics of Johannes Althusius.* Translated by Frederick Carney. Boston: Beacon Press.
Arasteh, A. Reza
  1970 *Man and Society in Iran.* Leiden: Brill.
Arensberg, Conrad M.
  1961 "The Community as Object and as Sample." *American Anthropologist,* 63:241–64.
  1972 "Culture as Behavior: Structure and Emergence." *Annual Review of Anthropology,* 1:1–26.
Asakawa, K.
  1929 *The Documents of Iriki.* New Haven, Conn.: Yale University Press.

Ashraf, Ahmad
  1978 "The Role of Rural Organizations in Rural Development: The Case of
       Iran." In *Rural Organisations and Rural Development: Some Asian Expe-
       riences.* Edited by Inayatullah. Kuala Lumpur, Malaysia: APDAC Pub-
       lications, pp. 115–61.
Ashraf, Ahmad, and A. Banuazizi
  1980 "Policies and Strategies of Land Reform in Iran." In *Land Reform: Some
       Asian Experiences.* Edited by Inayatullah. Kuala Lumpur, Malaysia:
       APDAC Publications, pp. 15–60.
Ashraf-u-Din
  1914 Selections from *Nasim-i-Shimal.* In *The Press and Poetry of Modern Per-
       sia.* Edited and translated by E. G. Browne. Cambridge, Eng.: Cambridge
       University Press, pp. 184–85.
Attar
  1954 *Mantiq' Ut-Tair.* In *Conference of the Birds.* Translated by C. S. Nott.
       London: Routledge and Kegan Paul.
Baer, Gabriel
  1966 "The Evolution of Private Land Ownership in Egypt and the Fertile Cres-
       cent." In *Economic History of the Middle East, 1800–1914.* Edited by
       Charles Issawi. Chicago: University of Chicago Press.
Bahar
  1914 Selected Poems from *Khurasan.* In *The Press and Poetry of Modern Per-
       sia.* Edited and translated by E. G. Browne. Cambridge, Eng.: Cambridge
       University Press, pp. 264–68.
Barth, Frederic
  1965 *Nomads of South Persia.* Oslo: Universitetsforlaget.
Beresford, Morris
  1976 "The English Medieval Village." Lecture delivered at Harvard College,
       Cambridge, Mass., 21 April.
Berman, Harold
  1983 *Law and Revolution: The Formation of the Western Legal Tradition.*
       Cambridge, Mass.: Harvard University Press.
Bill, James
  1972 *The Politics of Iran.* Columbus, Ohio: Charles Merrill.
  1973 "The Plasticity of Informal Politics: The Case of Iran." *Middle East Jour-
       nal,* 27(2):131–51.
  1975 "From Rags to Riches: Iranian Millionaires." Lecture delivered at Har-
       vard College, Cambridge, Mass., 27 March.
Bloch, Marc
  1961 *Feudal Society.* Translated by L. A. Manyon. London: Routledge &
       Kegan Paul.
  1966 "The Rise of Dependent Cultivation and Seignorial Institutions." In
       Cambridge Economic History of Europe, I. Edited by M. M. Postan.
       Cambridge, Eng.: Cambridge University Press.
Boserup, E.
  1965 *Conditions of Agricultural Growth.* Chicago: Aldine.
Broad, Robin
  1983 "Behind Philippine Policy Making: The Role of the World Bank and
       International Monetary Fund." Ph.D. diss., Princeton University.
Buchanan, G.
  1938 *The Tragedy of Mesopotamia.* London: Blackwood.
Coon, C.
  1951 *Caravan.* New York: Henry Holt.
Clapp, Gordon
  1957 "Iran: A T.V.A. for the Khuzestan Region." *Middle East Journal,* 2(1):1–
       26.

Curzon, George N.
1890 "The Karun River and the Commercial Geography of Southwest Persia."
Proceedings of the Royal Geographical Society, 12:9.
Denman, D.
1973 *The King's Vista.* London: Geographical Publications.
Dobb, Maurice
1947 *Studies in the Development of Capitalism.* London: Routledge & Kegan
Paul.
Douglas, Mary
1966 *Purity and Danger.* New York: Praeger.
1973 *Natural Symbols.* New York: Random House.
Durkheim, Emile
1915 *The Elementary Forms of Religious Life.* Translated by Joseph Ward
Swain. London: George Allen and Unwin.
1933 *The Division of Labor in Society.* Translated by George Simpson. New
York: The Free Press.
Ehlers, Eckart
1975 "Traditionelle und moderne Formen der Landwirtschaft in Iran." *Marburger Geographische Schriften,* 64. Edited by C. Schott.
Ferdowsi
1967 *Shahnamah* in *The Epic of Kings.* Translated by Reuben Levy. Chicago:
University of Chicago Press.
Fischer, M.
1980 *Iran: From Religious Dispute to Revolution.* Cambridge, Mass.: Harvard
University Press.
Fried, Morton
1960 "On the Evolution of Social Stratification and the State." In *Culture and
the History.* Edited by Stanley Diamond. New York: Columbia University Press.
1967 *The Evolution of Political Society.* New York: Random House.
Friendly, G.
1969 "Developing Iran's Desert." *The Washington Post,* June 1979, p. 31.
Geertz, Clifford
1963 *Peddlers and Princes.* Chicago: University of Chicago Press.
1970 *Agricultural Involution.* Berkeley: University of California Press.
Ghirshman, Roman
1954 *Iran.* Harmondsworth, Eng.: Penguin.
Ghirshman, Roman; Vladimir Minorsky; and Ramesh Sanghvi
1971 *Persia, the Immortal Kingdom.* Boston: New York Graphic Society.
Gierke, Otto van
1900 *Political Theories of the Middle Ages.* Translated by Frederic William
Maitland. Cambridge, Eng.: Cambridge University Press.
Goodell, G.
1975 "Agricultural Production in a Traditional Village of Northern Khuzestan." *Marburger Geographische Schriften,* 64. Edited by C. Schott.
1977 "The Elementary Structures of Political Life." Ph.D. diss., Columbia
University.
1980 "From Status to Contract: The Significance of Agrarian Relations of Production in the West, Japan, and in 'Asiatic' Persia." *European Journal of
Sociology,* 21:285–325.
1983 "What Life After Land Reform?" *Policy Review,* 24:121–148.
1985 "The Importance of Political Participation for Sustained Capitalist
Development." *European Journal of Sociology,* 26:93–127.
Gremliza, F. G. L.
1967 *Selected Ecological Facts on Health in the Dez Pilot Irrigation Area.* New
York: Development and Resources Corporation.

Gundersen, K.
    1968 "Dynamics of Rural Relationships in Iran—Change and Moderniza-
        tion." Master's thesis, University of Texas at Austin.
Haas, J.
    1982 *The Evolution of the Pre-Historic State.* New York: Columbia University
        Press.
Hafiz
    1893 *Ghazels from the Divan.* Translated by Justin Huntly McCarthy. London:
        David Nutt.
Hilton, Rodney
    1973 *Bond Men Made Free.* London: Temple Smith.
Hirschman, Albert
    1977 *The Passions and the Interests.* Princeton: Princeton University Press.
Hooglund, Eric J.
    1982 *Land and Revolution in Iran, 1960–1980.* Austin, Tex.: University of
        Texas Press.
Housego, David
    1976 "Quiet Thee Now and Rest: A Survey of Iran." *The Economist,* August
        28, pp. 1–44.
Hyden, Goran
    1980 *Beyond Ujamaa in Tanzania.* Berkeley, Calif.: University of California
        Press.
Ibn Khaldun
    1958 *The Muqaddimah, II.* Translated by Franz Rosenthal. New York:
        Pantheon.
    1967 *The Muqaddimah.* Translated by Franz Rosenthal and edited by N. J.
        Dawood. Princeton, N.J.: Princeton University Press.
Issawi, Charles
    1966 *Economic History of the Middle East, 1800–1914.* Chicago: University of
        Chicago Press.
Jacobs, Jane
    1969 *Economy of Cities.* New York: Random House
Johnston, Bruce, and William Clark
    1982 *Redesigning Rural Development.* Baltimore, Md.: Johns Hopkins Uni-
        versity Press.
Johnston, Bruce, and Thomas Tomich
    1984 "Feasibility of Small Farm Development Strategies." Special report for
        Aurora Associates and USAID. Mimeographed.
Khuzestan Development Service
    1961 *Status of the Dez Irrigation Pilot Project.* Ahwaz, Iran: Imperial Govern-
        ment of Iran.
Kohl, P., and Rita Wright
    1977 "Stateless Cities: Differentiation of Society in the Neolithic and Near
        East." *Dialectical Anthropology,* 2(4):275–84.
Laing, R. D.
    1960 *The Divided Self.* Harmondsworth, Eng.: Penguin.
Lambton, Ann
    1953 *Landlord and Peasant in Persia.* London: Oxford University Press.
    1969 *Persian Land Reform.* London: Oxford University Press.
Langer, Ellen
    1979 "The Illusion of Incompetence." In *Choice and Perceived Control.* Edited
        by Lawrence C. Perlmuter and Richard A. Monty. Hillsdale, N.J.: Law-
        rence Erlbaum Associates.
Langer, Ellen, and Anne Benevento
    1978 "Self-Induced Dependence." *Journal of Personality and Social Psychol-
        ogy,* 36(8):886–93.

Layard, A. H.
   1846 "A Description of the Province of Khuzestan." *Journal of the Royal Geographical Society,* 16:1–105.
   1887 *Early Adventures in Persia, Susiana and Babylonia,* Vol. 2. London: John Murray.
Lestrange, Guy
   1930 *Lands of the Eastern Caliphate.* Cambridge, Eng.: Cambridge University Press.
Lilienthal, David
   1971 *The Harvest Years* (vol. 5 of his *Journals).* New York: Harper & Row.
Lorimer, J.
   1915 *Gazetteer of the Persian Gulf.* Edited by R. Birdwood. Calcutta: Superintendent of the G.P.O.
Mair, Lucy
   1962 *Primitive Government.* Baltimore, Md.: Penguin Books.
Mead, Margaret
   1951 *Soviet Attitudes Toward Authority.* New York: McGraw-Hill.
Moore, Barrington
   1966 *Social Origins of Dictatorship and Democracy.* Boston: Beacon Press.
de Morgan, J.
   1914 "Feudalism in Persia." *Annual Report of the Board of Regents, Smithsonian Institution.* Washington, D.C.: G.P.O.
Myrdal, Gunnar
   1968 *Asian Drama,* vols. 1 and 3. New York: Twentieth-Century Fund.
Nederlandsche Heidamaatschappij
   1958 *Report on the Dez Irrigation Project.* Arnhem, Holland: Nederlandsche Heidamaatschappij for the Imperial Plan Organization of Iran.
Nisbet, Robert
   1969 *The Quest for Community.* New York: Oxford University Press.
   1973 *Social Philosophers.* New York: Crowell.
Olson, Mancur
   1965 *The Logic of Collective Action.* Cambridge, Mass.: Harvard University Press.
Oppenheim, A. L.
   1964 *Ancient Mesopotamia.* Chicago: University of Chicago Press.
Osgood, O. T., and M. T. Nassiry
   [1955–56] *Farm Development in the Shushtar Area.* FAO: 57/3/2/2199. Published by the Agricultural Division of FAO and the Independent Irrigation Corporation of Iran.
Polanyi, K.
   1962 *The Great Transformation.* Boston: Beacon Press.
Popkin, S.
   1979 *The Rational Peasant.* Berkeley, Calif.: University of California Press.
Poyck, M.
   1962 *Farm Studies in Iraq.* Wageningen, Netherlands: Laboratory of Agricultural Economics of the Tropical Agriculture University.
Rodinson, Maxime
   1973 *Islam and Capitalism.* Translated by Brian Pearce. New York: Random House.
Rumi
   1961 *Tales from the Masnawi.* Translated by A. J. Arberry. London: George Allen and Unwin.
Sa'di
   1911 *The Bustan.* Translated by A. Hart Edwards. London: John Murray.
   1945 Selections from *The Gulistan.* In *Kings and Beggars.* Translated by A. J. Arberry. London: Luzac and Co.

Salmanzadeh, Cyrus
  1980 *Agricultural Change and Rural Society in Southern Iran.* Cambridge, Eng.: The Middle East and North African Studies Press.
Scott, James
  1976 *The Moral Economy of the Peasant.* New Haven, Conn.: Yale University Press.
Service, Elman
  1975 *Origins of the State and Civilization.* New York: Norton.
Simmel, Georg
  1950 *Sociology of Georg Simmel.* Translated and edited by K. Wolff. Glencoe, Ill.: Free Press.
Smith, M. G.
  1974 *Corporations and Society.* London: Duckworth.
Smith, T. C.
  1959 *The Agrarian Origins of Modern Japan.* Stanford, Calif.: Stanford University Press.
Spooner, B.
  1972 *Population Growth: Anthropological Implications.* Cambridge, Mass.: M.I.T. Press.
Statistical Center of Iran
  1976 *Land and Holding Distributions in Iran.* Tehran: Imperial Government of Iran.
Tahqiqat-e-Eqtesadi Research Team
  1965 "Rural Development in Khuzestan" *Tahqiqat-e-Eqtesadi* (University of Tehran) 3(9–10):153–83.
de Tocqueville, Alexis
  1864 *Democracy in America,* vol. 2. Translated by Henry Reeve and edited by F. Bowen. Cambridge, Mass.: Sever and Francis.
Umar Khayyam
  1975 *The Ruby'iyat.* Translated by Parichechr Kasra. Delmar, N.Y.: Scholars' Facsimiles and Reprints.
Wilson, S. G.
  1895 *Persian Life and Customs.* New York: Fleming Revell.
Wright, G. A.
  1969 "Obsidian Analyses and Prehistoric Near Eastern Trade: 7500–3500 B.C." In *Anthropological Papers,* 37. Ann Arbor, Mich.: University of Michigan Museum of Anthropology.
Wright, Henry
  1977 "Recent Research on the Origin of the State." *Annual Review of Anthropology,* 6:379–97.
Yoffe, N.
  1979 "The Decline and Rise of Mesopotamian Civilization: An Ethnoarchaeological Perspective on the Evolution of Social Complexity." *American Antiquity,* 44:1, 5–35.
Zonis, Marvin
  1971 *The Political Elite of Iran.* Princeton, N.J.: Princeton University Press.

Index